WRITING IN REAL TIME

Modelling Production Processes

Writing Research

Multidisciplinary Inquiries into the Nature of Writing

edited by Marcia Farr, University of Illinois at Chicago

Arthur N. Applebee, *Contexts for Learning to Write: Studies of Secondary School Instruction*
Barbara Couture, *Functional Approaches to Writing*
Carole Edelsky, *Writing in a Bilingual Program: Había Una Vez*
Lester Faigley, Roger Cherry, David Jolliffe, and Anna Skinner, *Assessing Writers' Knowledge and Processes of Composing*
Marcia Farr (ed.), *Advances in Writing Research, Volume One: Children's Early Writing Development*
Sarah W. Freedman (ed.), *The Acquisition of Written Language: Response and Revision*
Judith Langer, *Children Reading and Writing: Structures and Strategies*
William Teale and Elizabeth Sulzby (eds.), *Emergent Literacy: Writing and Reading*

IN PREPARATION
Christine P. Barabas, *Technical Writing in a Corporate Setting: A Study of the Nature of Information*
Robert Gundlach, *Children and Writing in American Education*
David A. Jolliffe (ed.), *Advances in Writing Research, Volume Two*
Martha L. King and Victor Rentel, *The Development of Meaning in Writing: Children 5–10*
Anthony Petrosky (ed.), *Reading and Writing: Theory and Research*
Bennett A., Rafoth and Donald L. Rubin (eds.), *The Social Construction of Written Communication*
Leo Ruth and Sandra Murphy, *Designing Writing Tasks for the Assessment of Writing*
David Smith, *Explorations in the Culture of Literacy*
Jana Staton, Roger Shuy, Joy Kreeft, and Leslie Reed, *Interactive Writing in Dialogue Journals: Practitioner, Linguistic, Social, and Cognitive Views*
Elizabeth Sulzby, *Emergent Writing and Reading in 5–6 Year Olds: A Longitudinal Study*
Stephen Witte, Keith Walters, Mary Trachsel, Roger Cherry, and Paul Meyer, *Literacy and Writing Assessment: Issues, Traditions, Directions*

WRITING IN REAL TIME

Modelling Production Processes

edited by

Ann Matsuhashi

University of Illinois at Chicago

ABLEX PUBLISHING CORPORATION
NORWOOD, NEW JERSEY

Printed in the United States of America

Library of Congress Cataloging in Publication Data

Writing in real time.

  (Writing research)
  Bibliography: p.
  Includes index.
  1. Rhetoric. I. Matsuhashi, Ann. II. Series:
Writing research (Norwood, N.J.)
PS301.W74   1987   808   86-22214
ISBN: 0-89391-400-2
ISBN: 0-89391-417-7 (pbk.)

ABLEX Publishing Corporation
355 Chestnut Street
Norwood, New Jersey 07648

Contents

For my parents,
   Morton and Florence Feldman
For my grandparents,
   Louis and Sally Weingart
And for my husband,
   Kazumasa Matsuhashi

Writing Research

Multidisciplinary Inquiries into the Nature of Writing

Marcia Farr, series editor
University of Illinois at Chicago

PREFACE

This series of volumes presents the results of recent scholarly inquiry into the nature of writing. The research presented comes from a mix of disciplines, those which have emerged as significant within the last decade or so in the burgeoning field of writing research. These primarily include English education, linguistics, psychology, anthropology, and rhetoric. A note here on the distinction between field and discipline might be useful: a field can be a multidisciplinary entity focused on a set of significant questions about a central concern (e.g., American Studies), while a discipline usually shares theoretical and methodological approaches which may have a substantial tradition behind them. Writing research, then, is a field, if not yet a discipline.

The history of this particular field is unique. Much of the recent work in this field, and much that is being reported in this series, has been conceptualized and funded by the National Institute of Education. Following a planning conference in June 1977, a program of basic research on the teaching and learning of writing was developed and funded annually. The initial research funded under this program is now coming to fruition, providing both implications for educational improvement and directions for future research. This series is intended as one important outlet for these results.

Introduction

Ann Matsuhashi

The chapters in this volume reflect the growing research interest, principally within the last twenty years, in writing processes. This interest developed from two sources, initially, during the first half of this century, from educational need, and more recently from an intellectual curiosity about the nature of writing. Educational prerogatives—the need for information about the teaching of writing—led researchers to adopt the questions and methods of experimental studies, largely for the purpose of comparing the success of instructional methods. When the traditional research methods and the instructional questions failed to produce a better understanding of writing, researchers began to ask questions about writers' behaviors and cognitive processes. These new questions reflect the conceptual frameworks provided by cognitive psychology (in particular, the information-processing approach), psycholinguistics, studies of speech production, and studies of reading comprehension. From answers to these questions, researchers hope to develop theory-driven instruction—instruction based on the best current knowledge of how writers write and learn to write.

With the new questions and frameworks, researchers realized it was desirable to observe carefully the behaviors of small numbers of students as they wrote. Thus, they produced a first generation of "generic" studies of the writing process with three characteristics. First, researchers nearly always cast their subjects as either seriously disabled basic writers, moderately competent writers, or practiced writers. Second, these writers were studied in laboratory settings with little concern for the impact that the writing environment (classroom, home, job) might have on their work. Third, most often researchers described what they observed; but even the early process models simply outlined the key components of a seemingly monolithic writing process. This volume moves beyond these generic studies to report on finer, more specified, investigations of real-time processing.

As the title suggests, this volume focuses on how writing is produced both during the moment-to-moment process of inscribing a text and during real time broadly conceived as the context for studying the writing process as writers plan, draft, revise, and confer with others. The chapters in this volume break open these generic categories by studying special populations of writers not studied before, by specifying the writing environment, by developing more detailed models of the writing process, and by offering critical analyses of current research methods and paradigms. In a renewed climate of educational need such as we are now experiencing, research on writing processes can contribute an important piece to the puzzle of effective instruction. Theories of instruction ought to be integrated with theories of learning and both must incorporate knowledge about writers' processes. The chapters in this volume move toward such a view of research on writing.

By urging researchers to attend to the context for research, Chapter 1 advocates that researchers acknowledge that the same processes may be studied from other perspectives (i.e., sociology, anthropology, linguistic) and with a variety of methodologies. Keeping the focus narrowly on the experimental methodologies of psycholinguistics, Chapter 5 offers a critical review of the current state of research design. Relationships between text comprehension and text production provide the conceptual framework for a process analysis which combines an analysis of behaviors with sophisticated discourse analysis (Chapter 10). Reports in this volume move beyond the generic classification of writers to consider special populations—the profoundly deaf (Chapter 7), the child emerging toward literacy (Chapter 6), the second-language learner (Chapter 2), and the accomplished writer learning to use a word processor (Chapter 4). Two reports focus on specific aspects of writing processes—revision (Chapter 8) and idea generation (Chapter 9). Finally, the language of a writing conference is studied as a slice of time during which the teacher-student interaction can inform us about the nature of writing instruction (Chapter 3). Taken together, these chapters all view writing as an important domain for research, a domain driven by powerful intellectual questions as well as by pressing social need.

OVERVIEW OF THE CHAPTERS

1. Writing and Meaning: Contexts of Research

In the volume's opening chapter, "Writing and Meaning: Contexts of Research," Beaugrande argues that the notions of scientific objectivity which informed traditional linguistic studies of the well-structuredness of language have severely limited our study of human language. The notion of scientific objectivity, however, need not be abandoned; instead, it should be integrated into a broader, ongoing project which takes into account the human subjectivity of communicative situations. Typically, researchers have studied only one of several views of meaning, excluding other possible contexts or approaches. Beaugrande recommends that we view theory-building as a mapping process with a central inner domain and an outer domain, which reflects the larger context of the research arena. The researcher, then, can address the question of the relationship between the two domains, establishing priorities, setting up ground rules, and providing for future syntheses of others' research.

Beaugrande proposes a theory of written meaning within the context of a broad theory of action. Communication originates with an intention to be meaningful. Meaning, a mental event which recognizes significances, can be represented as processing actions. Such a broad-based context suggests a variety of questions: How does language provide a means for organizing and managing experience? How is written meaning processed in real time by humans? What are the phases during which intentions are deployed and how do they achieve their intended result?

2. Composing in a Second Language

In Jones and Tetroe's "Composing in a Second Language," the context of the second-language learner—proficient in his or her native language but not yet proficient in a new one—provides a "natural experiment" in studying writing processes. A common approach to second-language learning has been to ask how the first language *interferes* with the learning of the second language. Jones and Tetroe, however, take a facilitative point of view, studying how writing processes, in particular planning and goal-setting processes, *transfer* from the first to the second language.

Using real-time data from think-aloud protocols, Jones and Tetroe compare the planning and goal-setting processes of six adults in their first, proficient language (Spanish) with those in their second, less proficient language (English). The six subjects composed aloud, reporting on their plans and goals, first, as they produced conventional narrative and argumentative compositions in Spanish and in English, and second, as they produced compositions for which an ending sentence had been supplied. (e.g., and that is how Melissa came to be at the wrong laundromat, in a strange city, with a million dollars in her laundry bag, and a trail of angry people behind her.)

The content of the writers' plans, whether in Spanish or English, were classified in a hierarchy of goal-setting activities. In the conventional tasks writers did very little planning, but even with these scant results, Jones and Tetroe found that subjects who planned abstractly in Spanish planned abstractly in English as well. The ending-sentence tasks promoted planning activity by providing specific goals to plan toward and resulted in a marked increase in the sheer quantity of plans. Those writers who planned abstractly in the conventional tasks continued to plan abstractly in the sentence-ending tasks. Furthermore, their papers received higher quality ratings. Even so, success in accounting for all aspects of the ending sentences was poorer in English than in Spanish, suggesting that, for even relatively proficient writers, working in a second language takes up cognitive space.

3. Pedagogical Interaction During the Composing Process: The Writing Conference

Because the writing process involves more than the time during which pen is put to paper, Freedman and Katz study the teacher-student writing conference as part of the full spectrum of writing activities of one writer completing an assignment for school. Writing conferences, long recognized as a highly effective instructional activity, "work" because they foster verbal interaction between teachers and students; but, in fact, little is known about how and why they work. By viewing the writing conference as a structured speech event occurring in real time, these researchers explore the ways that the teacher's and student's roles are played out in the conference setting.

The chapter illustrates how analytic schemes describing two types of speech events—conversational turn-taking and classroom lessons—allow Freedman and Katz to infer from the conference what the teacher intends and what the student understands. In the conference under discussion, for instance, the teacher manages rather than controls and the student initiates topics, making the speech events less like a classroom and more like a conversation. On the other hand, long pauses are much more frequent than conversation would normally allow. Throughout the conference, the student's struggle to articulate the source of her writing difficulties and the teacher's struggle to find the most effective sort of intervention will convince the reader of the importance of the kind of analysis undertaken here.

4. Composing and Computers: Case Studies of Experienced Writers

In "Composing and Computers: Case Studies of Experienced Writers," Bridwell, Johnson, and Brehe observed eight published writing instructors writing with traditional scribal tools—pens or typewriters—and then observed them as they made the transition to word processing on microcomputers. The case studies are based on information from interviews and from observations of the writers' composing activities. To observe the writers' transition to word processing, Bridwell's group used a special computer program which recorded, in real time, all keystrokes and commands used during a writing session, allowing them to document the time and location of pausing, producing text, revising, formatting, and moving or deleting blocks of text.

In vignettes of the eight writers, two 'types' of writers emerge: one type, the "discoverer," writes to find out what he or she has to say, and another, the "executor," plans extensively and then carries out the plan. The "discoverers," unable to engage in their usual prewriting activities, found the transition to word processing more difficult than the "executors," who, having solved their large-scale problems in advance, used the computer for straight-away production. From the keystroke record, Bridwell, Johnson, and Brehe point out how one "discoverer" paused throughout the session, scrolling back and forth continuously, while another writer, an "executor," paused for a long period of time before writing. Throughout the study, these authors observed practiced writers working to adapt successful rituals with pen or typewriter to the new word-processing technology.

5. Writing as Language Behavior: Myths, Models, Methods

Kowal and O'Connell argue for a methodologically sound treatment of writing as a specific mode of language production. For the past one hundred years, the study of writing has been ignored, resulting in psychologically unsound definitions and methodologically naive approaches to its study. Specifically, Kowal and O'Connell adopt a psycholinguistic view of writing as "language behavior unfolding in time, open to direct observation and therefore to systematic empirical investigation" (p. 108). These authors opt for as much external control as possible in the experimental situation in order to identify behavioral characteristics from which internal cognitive processes may be inferred.

A career-long study of speech production provides the context for Kowal and O'Connell's extensive critical review of studies of the temporal aspects of writing. They review studies which examine temporal patterns in the following situations: copying from memory, retelling a story, and composing a story; handwriting, typewriting, and stenotyping; speaking and typewriting in response to the Thematic Apperception Test; oral, dictated, and written interview responses; spoken, dictated, and written letters; and writing produced for differing discourse purposes. The authors identify a wide range of methodological problems such as: not controlling for word length, ill-defined analytic schemes, use of arbitrary cutoff points for pause lengths, use of inexact measurement devices, shifting methods of measurement, conceptually and operationally ill-defined notions such as planning, and inappropriate reliance on subjects' verbal reports. With the latter criticism, Kowal and O'Connell extend the current debate on the use of protocol analysis for writing research. Kowal and O'Connell urge us to rethink "what is process and what is product" (p. 108), paying particular attention to refining the basic methodologies for studying temporal variables and constructs such as planning and revising.

6. Children's Development of Prosodic Distinctions in Telling and Dictating Modes

In Chapter 6, "Children's Development of Prosodic Distinctions in Telling and Dictating Modes," Sulzby illustrates how kindergarteners with emerging literacy skills can distinguish between oral and written features of language. Theoretically, this study makes use of two kinds of oral delivery, telling and dictating stories. Telling stories promotes the face-to-face oral monologue which, for young children, more often resembles adult–child conversational interactions. Dictating, however, often used for activities such as writing letters, reflects an intermediate step between oral and written language. Methodologically, since speed of speaking and length of pausing has been shown to reflect oral and written language styles, and since young children are usually unable to explain differences between oral and written features of language, this study demonstrates the development of these crucial distinctions through real-time observation of children's performances.

The 9 kindergarten children (rated in groups of three as high, moderate, or low in emergent literacy skills) told and dictated stories at three intervals during kindergarten and at a fourth trial during the first grade. Sulzby found that naive judges could distinguish between telling and dictating more easily for the high-rated students than for the low-rated ones. With regard to pauses and speech density, these data present a complex developmental pattern. By the fourth trial all three groups behaved in similar ways: They dictated stories slowly, reflecting the time needed for the integration of ideas required by writing; and, they told stories more rapidly reflecting the ease of spoken conversation. Yet the path to this developmental endpoint differs in interesting ways for each of the three ability groups. For the high-rated groups the distinction between telling and dictating stories appears early and becomes stronger over time. The low-rated students were slow at both telling and dictating until trial 4, whereas the moderate students were fast at both telling and dictating until trial 4. These differences may reflect the low-rated students' dependence on orality and the moderate students' overcompensation for written features of literacy. Results such as these, which apply real-time observations to naturally occurring language activities, can illuminate our understanding of oral and written language relationships.

7. The Influence of Syntactic Anomolies on the Writing Processes of a Deaf College Student

In Chapter 7, "The Influence of Syntactic Anomolies on the Writing Processes of a Deaf College Student," Kelly explores the nature and causes of syntactic errors in the profoundly deaf. Little is known about the persistent errors or anomolies which can appear in even the writing of the highly educated profoundly deaf. Among the several causes posed for these errors are an inability to hear spoken English, lack of practice with writing, and interference from the first-learned signed language. Yet studies of the writing of the deaf (as, until recently, general writing studies) have focused on classifying the surface features of the writing and not on descriptions of the real-time processes of deaf writers, descriptions which might yield clues to the persistent patterns of errors.

Recent studies of the writing processes of basic, underprepared college writers suggest that they are so error conscious that they read and reread each sentence hoping to correct it before moving on. When a writer's attention is focused on error, cognitive resources are not available for the other complex decisions and processes which must go on during writing. Studies of deaf writers, however, are much more ambivalent about the role of attention vis à vis error during writing. If, as some think, the written language of the deaf functions as a second language, then the errors that appear in final prose may have been produced fluently, with little attention, as a native speaker produces conventional English. Kelly explores this possible difference in attentional focus by observing pause times and revisions during the real-time writing process of a single deaf college freshman.

8. Revising the Plan and Altering the Text

In her chapter "Revising the Plan and Altering the Text," Matsuhashi notes that the current interest in revision processes grew in reaction to the traditional view of revision as error correction. Currently, though, studies of revision processes stress the relationships between revision and higher order thinking processes. In cognitive-based studies the pattern of revisions—as they occur in real time—can reflect a writer's shifting focus of attention and pattern of decision making. This emphasis on thinking processes has resulted from work on text comprehension, which, for some years now, has focused on the construction of a mental representation of the text as a meaning-making strategy. Studying revisions as they contribute to meaning-making (rather than solely to error correction) allows Matsuhashi to view revising as shaping at the point of inscription—a strategic, goal-oriented, cognitive activity.

By studying time-monitored videotapes of a single writer drafting a reporting and generalizing essay, Matsuhashi tracks revisions as they occur in real time. By studying the content of the revision, its location, and the point in time the revision occurred, Matsuhashi is able to demonstrate that the writer uses different revision strategies for the two discourse types. In composing the generalizing essay, the writer made revisions which affected the meaning of the essay during time-consuming forays back to completed sentences. In composing the reporting essay, a different pattern emerged.

The writer completed most meaning-related revisions within the current sentence, using much less time. The results of this study confirm the importance of close textual analysis and what it can suggest about writing processes.

9. Idea Generation in Writing

In Chapter 9, "Idea Generation in Writing," Caccamise investigates how models of the writing process, memory representation, and memory retrieval can inform us about the processes of idea generation during writing. These models provide the conceptual framework for exploring how a writer selects and organizes ideas for writing. Specifically, Caccamise adapts a model of memory retrieval used extensively in the study of list-learning tasks which assumes that first, one's ability to retrieve information from long-term memory (LTM) is limited, and second, LTM consists of an associative network. By recasting the retrieval model within the idea-generation process, Caccamise proposed a model of idea generation based on a writer's goals and the task's requirements. For instance, the number and kind of items retrieved from LTM are constrained by the text topic, the text type, and the intended audience.

The two experiments reported in this chapter offer some preliminary evidence for the organization of the idea-generation process. In the first experiment undergraduates generated ideas orally and verbalized their thoughts to prepare for writing essays. The tasks varied topic familiarity (familiar/unfamiliar) and specificity (general/specific). Audience (adult) was held constant. In the second experiment topic familiarity and audience (adult/child) were varied. Both temporally and organizationally, meaningful groups of ideas were clustered together, more so for the familiar topic than for the unfamiliar one. The topic variable had little influence on idea generation. The intended audience variable resulted in no difference in number of ideas; however in the child-audience situation the ideas were not well organized and lacked elaboration. More ideas were repeated for the child audience than for the adult audience. In addition, it took subjects nearly twice as long to generate new ideas for the child audience. This hesitant production was accompanied by verbal comments in the protocols which were concerned predominantly with the appropriateness of the material for a child audience. Even though the subjects in this study did no writing, by exploring the real-time performance of subjects preparing to write, we gain access to an aspect of writing processes which is obscured from study by the completed text.

10. Discourse Analysis of Children's Text Production

In "Discourse Analysis of Children's Text Production," Fredericksen, Frederiksen, and Bracewell present a model of text production that is based on recent research on the cognitive processes and structures involved in text comprehension. This model describes how writing processes operate in an unconscious, routine manner, as well as how plans modify routine processing. The research reported in this chapter aims to link models of text-production processes to the actual texts produced and to study relationships between the processes of text comprehension and production. To this end, the authors devised experimental tasks that would allow constrastive analysis of comprehension and production tasks based on similar conceptual content. The focus in this chapter is on detailed analyses of stories produced by two subjects. Through comparative discourse analysis, the authors discuss the relationships between frame structures and text-level linguistic structures of children's texts as they reflect the cognitive processes employed in constructing and expressing meaning.

CHAPTER 1

Writing and Meaning: Contexts of Research

Robert de Beaugrande
University of Florida, Gainesville

LINGUISTIC THEORIES AND THE PROBLEM OF CONTEXT

Now more than ever before, language research in America presents the appearance of an open and diverse field. In past decades, American linguistics and psychology were dominated by small, inflexible sets of narrowly defined postulates and methods. Today, few such dogmatic restrictions upon admissible research remain. This new openness is due partly to the point of diminishing returns attained by the older paradigms and partly to a rising pressure to define and explore an ever-wider range of language-related concerns in an increasingly complex society.

A significant factor has been the gradual acknowledgement that the human sciences cannot be a neutral, disinterested embodiment of "scientific objectivity" in the same sense as the natural sciences. A human science that disavows its own social context is not disinterested; in effect, it just affirms the prevailing interests of science. Such tactics can promote isolationism and fragmentation. As long as the relationship of a given theory to the realities of society is not explicitly and carefully discussed, the fundamental assumptions incorporated into the theory tend to remain invisible and immune from attack. The theory can then be presented and treated as the only possible one—as an essential presupposition for all research and experimentation that therefore cannot challenge the theory as a whole but only rearrange its details. Finally, the theory *supplants* the reality as the object and goal of scientific inquiry.[1] Thus, a science that ignores or obscures its own context is in danger of becoming circular, stagnant, or irrelevant.

The present state of freedom and diversity in linguistic theory offers a

---

[1] Something of the sort seems to have happened in American linguistics when formal grammars threatened to push natural language completely out of the picture. No one ever demonstrated that these grammars were a particularly insightful model; they were simply more tractable than real language for certain problems.

good opportunity to reflect on the essential principles of scientific inquiry
into language. A science of language might be expected to address questions like these:

What is language?
What is the biological basis for language?
What is the cognitive basis for language?
What endows language with meaning?
How is language understood?
How is language learned?
What are the purposes of language?
What are the relations between language and the achievement of human
    goals?
How does language interact with other forms of human activity?
What language problems confront society and how could they be re-
    solved?
How can a person's language skills be improved?
How should we gather and interpret evidence about language?

The selection of questions actually addressed by linguistics was historically determined by the context wherein linguistics sought to establish its
credentials as a science. As a general rule, the prestige of a science, in
America at least, depends on its success in showing its object domain to
be *well-structured*. In consequence, the main goal of linguistics as an emergent science has been to propound theories that affirm (and methods that
display) the well-structuredness of language. Despite their differences,
nearly all successful linguistic theories concurred about the need to postulate one or more substrates of structure. The Neo-Grammarians sought the
laws governing the historical evolution of sounds, words, and grammatical
paradigms. The Structuralists viewed language as an abstract system of
stringent relationships (especially equivalences and oppositions) on distinctive "levels." The Generativists argued in favor of a set of "rules" that
describe the grammaticality ("well-formedness") of sentences. The seeming diversity of languages and language events was counterbalanced by a
continuing emphasis on uniform, abstract theories concerned with systematic structure.

The search for well-structuredness naturally fostered a predisposition
toward asking certain questions and accepting certain answers. The aspects
of language deemed most conducive to this search were given priority, for
example, the cataloguing of sounds and forms in the compact, orderly
taxonomies of phonology and morphology. In contrast, the aspects that
implied variety, diffuseness, and complexity were postponed, for example,
the relationship of language to meaning. Of course, decisions about what
was or wasn't well-structured were influenced by the nature of the linguis-

tic categories made available by theory. These categories imposed order and unity on some domains while making others seem diverse or chaotic, so that those same decisions tended to be repeated and reinforced by research.

To take full advantage of the recent opening of perspectives, we could set aside the traditional categories for a time and seek to *define the process of linguistic inquiry itself as a human activity*. In normal practice, any statement made by linguists is a direct or indirect consequence of their own experience with *language events*. This experience is the ineluctable precondition for knowing the language and knowing what language is for. However, there are many possible methods for obtaining such experience, and for deriving a theory from it. The linguist enacts a reduction, abstraction, and isolation of language entities in order to determine what is typical, general, and repeatable (Hartmann, 1963). The resulting object necessarily has the empirical status of a *derived effect,* of a *second-order phenomenon* produced via "theorization" from the first-order phenomenom of language experience. The crucial issue is what to remove and what to retain from the totality of available experiences, that is, what aspects of real contexts to consider relevant or irrelevant for analyzing, describing, or modelling language. Although at an extremely fine degree of detail, every context is unique—in respect to time, location, participants, motor actions, exact choice of words and phrases, and so on—most contexts share some features or aspects that identify and define the communicative community. This shared substrate must have a determinable structure in order that people can use language reliably amid the vast variety of circumstances that do or can occur. However, we have no grounds to assume a priori that this structure can best be defined or described in the categories of linguistic theories designed originally to classify sounds, word forms, and phrase structures. On the one hand, those categories can engender a more detailed and abstract (idealized, formalized, etc.) description than a human actually constructs or utilizes. On the other hand, they may circumvent or disguise important factors in human communication. Either way, the theory powerfully forms our perception of the object domain.

In this view, linguistic inquiry based on the formal structures of grammar and syntax is a specialized mode of language activity implying both an overinterpretation and an underinterpretation of the evidence. The linguist can compute an exact and exhaustive structural description of each phrase according to the theoretical apparatus: demarcating constituents, discovering ambiguities, assigning features or markers, postulating underlying structures, and so on. But normal participants in communication are hardly likely to enact such an analysis on every utterance they produce or receive, given that everyday discourse typically seems structurally fuzzy or incomplete when viewed in grammatical terms alone. It seems rather that humans use phrase structures as one organizational sub-system among many, including intonation, world-knowledge, personal roles and goals, gestures, facial expressions, and so on. Discourse processing probably focuses on the *strategic subset* of linguistic features that supply *relevant input or output* for the interaction with these other sub-systems; and the analysis actually performed by the communicative participants on their utterances is no more detailed than is required for the purpose at hand. If so, linguistic inquiry cannot afford to enumerate all features in a single subsystem by itself, because much of what occurs in that system is affected by its operational integration with the other sub-systems of language.

The converse of the ability to use language in context is the ability to imagine a context for a given word, phrase, or utterance. Knowing an item or a rule of language means knowing how and when to use or apply it (cf. Bolinger, 1968; McCawley, 1976). This evident principle has a complex corollary: that the item or rule conclusively establishes its existence and identity in the moment of its realization; thus a removal of context may entail a removal of essence. The loss may go unnoticed precisely because the linguist, like anyone else, can replace the context or imagine another one. Yet it is questionable whether real participants interacting in a context have the same intentions and motives as linguists supplying contexts for specialized purposes of classification and description. The *synthetic* act of everyday language users has a different emphasis than does the *analytic* act of the investigator. Accordingly, considerable effort may be needed to find a theory or method to account for the two acts in a framework clearly relevant to both (and not just to the investigation).

The quandary of context confronts psycholinguistics in a different way. The customary experimental approach calls for the observation and explanation of concrete events situated in real time. The context thus created is specially controlled for factors external to the hypothesis being tested. Yet these same controls can also make the context dissimilar to ordinary language activity. Psychology hopes to attenuate the problem of context by multiplying the number of persons and experimental events and thereby restricting the relative weight of situation-specific factors. But it is still uncertain why a cross-section of artificial contexts should necessarily distill out the same general factors as a cross-section of natural contexts. By itself, statistical generalization is no guarantee against missing or misrepresenting the shared substrate of structure that enables humans to negotiate and manage the communicative events of everyday life. Something may happen very often in an experiment and yet very seldom in ordinary communication.

One solution might be to compare linguistic versus psychological findings and accept the commonalities as having the strongest support. Conclusions in experimental psycholinguistics are explicitly based on a tightly defined corpus of experience (experimental procedures on certain occasions), whereas those in theoretical linguistics are implicitly based on a very loosely defined one (communicative activities on all sorts of real or imagined occasions). It stands to reason that results attained by two such diverse methods of reduction, abstraction, and isolation ought to carry more conviction than results attained by only one. But this solution holds only if the confirmation is truly independent; if psycholinguistics is construed as a derivative enterprise testing theories and hypothesis taken over from linguistics, a convergence of results may be trivial. The linguist's claim that humans process a sentence in such and such a way can readily be translated into the psycholinguist's prerogative to design experimental tasks which elicit that processing. For example, in a setting where the meaning and purpose of a sentence are not relevant, people have more free resources than usual to process syntax; and the role of phrase structures is likely to be exaggerated.

I shall accordingly suggest another solution to the problem of context. A suitable methodology of *discourse analysis* can assist us in identifying and incorporating contextual factors that seem relevant to the selection and utilization of linguistic options in a particular domain of discourse. The condition of *domain relevance* guides and limits the accumulation of linguistic data that, in some more abstract perspective, might all look uniform. Empirical evidence from spontaneous activities would be used not only to test individual hypotheses, but also to define the extent and conditions of various domains of discourse so that new inquiries can be appropriately designed. Thus, the discovery of given structures, dominances, features, and so on, would always be controlled by clearly stated epistemological predispositions regarding relevant modes of evidence within a particular set of communicative contexts (cf. later in this paper, "Toward a Theory of Written Meaning"). The question then is no longer "What is the structure of language?" but rather "What language events or aspects of those events lead people (including linguists) to infer or enact a structure?" We can then inquire how far a given linguistic theory projects an empirically plausible account of the language knowledge gathered and used by people at large.

Linguistics is a typical science to the degree that many of its participants adopted its prevailing categories as inherently valid for language in general. Yet linguistics is unique to the degree that its object domain is simultaneously its most powerful vehicle of discovery: Language study is regulated, expounded, negotiated, and influenced by language itself. Linguistics could well become the prime example (the "paradigm case") for incorporating the scientific activity into the object domain. The results should be highly significant for the human sciences at large. As Papert (1980) observes, the usual state of affairs has been one of passive, naive acceptance:

It seems to be nobody's business to think in a fundamental way about science in relation to the way people think and learn it. Although lip service has been paid to the importance of science and society, the underlying methodology [. . .] is one of delivering elements of ready-made science to a special audience. The concept of a *serious* enterprise of *making* science for the people is quite alien. (p. 188)

The point is not to abandon the whole notion of "scientific objectivity" but to treat it as an *ongoing project*—not a stable situation, but a constant attempt to confront and counterbalance human subjectivity—whose cognitive and communicative conditions are in pressing need of investigation.

WRITING RESEARCH

In accord with the line of argument pursued above, writing can be defined and investigated as a human activity with elaborate social and psychological determinants and consequences (cf. survey in Beaugrande, 1984). Collections of theoretical and empirical research on writing, once hard to find, are now appearing frequently, such as those edited by Frith (1980), Gregg and Steinberg (1980), Hairston and Selfe (1981), Martlew (1983), Mosenthal, Tamor, and Walmsley (1982), Nystrand (1982), and Pellegrini and Yawkey (1984). The diversity of approaches adopted in this literature suggests how many aspects a linguistics of discourse can pursue. Some of those aspects are (cf. also the scheme in Bereiter & Scardamalia, 1983):

Writing
As *a controlled configuration of motor actions* (MacNeilage, 1964; Rumelhart & Norman, 1981; Smith, McCrary, & Smith, 1960; van Bergeijk & David, 1959). Humans appear to command specific, highly skilled patterns of movement that execute the "inscription," that is, the actual production of handwriting, print, or typing. The movements are not absolute, but relative to a set of fairly consistent spatial and temporal parameters. In this respect, writing is quite similar to human actions and controls of all kinds (cf. Norman & Shallice, 1980; Schmidt, 1975). Many errors can occur on this relatively shallow level due to the error potential of the action routines that run without supervision (cf. Norman, 1981).

As *an observed activity with a characteristic rate and rhythm* (Blass & Siegman, 1975; Chafe, 1982; Drieman, 1962; Flower & Hayes, 1981; Gould, 1979; Matsuhashi, 1981, 1982; Scardamalia, Bereiter, & Goelman, 1982). The much slower rate of writing as contrasted with speaking affects the role of memory, attention, feedback, and so on. Matsuhashi's work suggests how an exact record of a writer's pauses and hesitations can help us draw inferences about underlying mental processes.

As *a modality with distinctive proportions of linguistic and grammatical options* (Blankenship, 1962; Chafe, 1982; Danks, 1977; DeVito, 1966; Einhorn, 1978; Fraisse & Breyton, 1959; Gibson, Grunner, Kibler, & Kelly, 1966; Green, 1958; Harris, 1977; Moscovici, 1967; O'Donnell, 1974; O'Donnell, Griffin, & Norris, 1967). This approach has been popular because it can be done with the procedures of categorization and tabulation already established in linguistics. However, the findings are not all consistent, indicating that the entire modality of writing is not uniform, but adaptable to many discourse domains. For example, formal speech, as in a radio broadcast, is much closer in its linguistic proportions to writing than is casual conversation. Hence, we need to go beyond counting and explore why certain proportions obtain in particular domains of discourse. And we should bear in mind that the linguistic categories we are measuring may not be comparable to the operational categories people use in speaking and writing.

As *a language variety influenced by dialect* (Baron, 1975; Hartwell, 1980; Marckwardt, 1966; Stubbs, 1982). The tendency of writing to reflect standardized lexical and grammatical choices signals the balance between social diversity and written communication. But, here also, writing is not a single or uniform social manifestation. We still need to determine where it coincides or interferes with spoken dialects, and why.

As *a tool for organizing and integrating ideas and knowledge* (Bereiter, 1980; Berthoff, 1972; Caccamise, 1981; D'Angelo, 1979; Elbow, 1973; Emig, 1977; Horowitz & Berkowitz, 1967; Horowitz & Newman, 1964; Irmscher, 1979b; Lemke, 1974; Macrorie, 1980; Murray, 1978; Nystrand, 1977; Nystrand & Widerspiel, 1977; Odell, 1980; Scardamalia, Bereiter, & Goelman, 1982; Wason, 1980). The experimental studies, such as those of Caccamise or of Horowitz and colleagues, complement the more rhetorical and pedagogical explorations, such as those of Berthoff, Elbow, D'Angelo, Irmscher, Macrorie, and Odell (who are all expert writing teachers as well). Of special import are studies with a dual outlook, such as those of Emig, Nystrand, or Bereiter/Scardamalia and colleagues, that combine precise observation of learners' writing behavior with the concerns of writing education in the classroom.

As *the modality used in letter recognition during reading.* Recognition of the surface text is undoubtedly related to spelling, for example, in regard to letter familiarity (Richek, 1977-78; Speer & Lamb, 1976), sound-letter correspondences (Guthrie & Seifert, 1977; Mason, 1976; Venezky & Johnson, 1973), and sound segmentation (Fox & Routh, 1976; Liberman, Schankweiler, Liberman, Fowler, & Fischer, 1977). However, researchers disagree about how far the reception of script in reading corresponds to the production of script in writing. Most (but not all) people read better and more easily than they spell; and practice in the one skill does not necessarily improve the other (Frith, 1978, 1980; Marsh, Desberg, & Saterdahl, 1981). So far, the dispute still rages over the respective roles of the *visual* processing for the *graphic* aspect of a text, versus *acoustic* processing for the *phonological* aspect (cf. reviews in Bradshaw, 1975; Perfetti & Lesgold, 1979). Some researchers claim that reading always recodes the graphic version into a phonological one (e.g., Gough 1972; Rubenstein, Lewis, & Rubenstein, 1971). Others say the visual modality is primary (e.g., Baron, 1973; Barron, 1978; Bower, 1970; Goodman, 1970; Green & Shallice, 1976; Smith, 1973). At present, the most plausible view seems to be that the tendency to consult these two modalities varies according to reader habits, difficulty of words, time pressure, and so on. Resolving this debate should clarify the possible relationships between the traditional linguistics of spoken sounds and a future linguistics of written symbols (cf. Vachek, 1973). Marcel (1980) indeed reverses conventional priorities by asserting that "for each learner today, the concept of the phoneme (tacit if not explicit) comes from rather than leads to the particular alphabetic system with which he or she is confronted" (p. 401f).

As *the modality used in reading comprehension.* Here, we are dealing with a deeper level of reading than the recognition of letters. A focus on the processing of extended discourse has become a trend in cognitive psychology only in the last decade (cf. Frederiksen, 1977; Kintsch, 1974, 1977; Kintsch & van Dijk, 1978, 1984; Meyer, 1975; Rumelhart, 1980). Just as a writer organizes ideas, a reader reconstructs them into a coherent unity. Like the graphic versus phonological controversy reviewed above, attempts to determine whether comprehension is fundamentally different for written texts versus spoken texts have had mixed results (DeVito, 1965; Durrell, 1969; Oaken, Wiener, & Cromer, 1971; Sticht, 1972). Though people may be able to remember whether a language sample was presented visually or acoustically, their abilities to recognize or recall are not much affected by the difference (cf. Bray & Batchelder, 1972; Hintzman, Block, & Inskeep, 1972; Kintsch, Kozminsky, Streby, McKoon, & Keenan, 1975). Written presentation gives a slight advantage for remembering surface features (Begg, 1971; Sachs, 1967), but not necessarily main ideas (Horowitz & Berkowitz, 1967). Future research ought to explore how far studies of writing can take advantage of the much-larger corpus of studies of reading (cf. Meyer, 1982; Shanklin, 1982).

As *a vehicle of social interaction* (cf. Britton, Burgess, Martin, McLeod & Rosen, 1975; Heath, 1982; Kantor & Rubin, 1981; Shanklin, 1982; Steinmann, 1982; Tierney & LaZansky, 1980). Modality has implications for the organization of interaction, for example, space and time (Goodman & Goodman, 1979; Rubin, 1980) degree of participants' involvement (Chafe, 1982), formation of personal judgments about social standing (Gere & Smith, 1979), and many more. Readers expect writers to fulfill certain responsibilities, such as supplying background knowledge, eliminating mistakes and ambiguities, upholding coherence, treating topics of general interest and relevance, and supplying good motives for doing the reading in the first place. But all this demands effort: It doesn't happen by itself just because people write instead of speak.

As *an educational process and goal* (Braddock, Lloyd-Jones, & Schoer, 1971; Hairston & Selfe [Eds.], 1981; Humes, Lawler, & Gentry [Eds.], 1981; Irmscher, 1979a; Shaughnessy, 1977). The epistemological benefits of writing as a tool for organizing ideas are as desirable as the social benefits of literacy as a tool for professional success (cf. Faigley, Miller, Meyer, & Witte, 1981). As Shaughnessy's work has shown, mechanical problems in writing, many of which arise in the shallow-level motoric actions of inscriptions are a selective filter against the academic and professional careers of the disadvantaged. Readers may react to "errors" in extreme and diverse ways (Hairston, 1981), though even writing teachers show little consensus about what constitutes a genuine error (Greenbaum & Taylor, 1981). A complex of public attitudes, class biases, educational traditions, and institutional prerogatives are entwined with learning to write and often block efforts to make teaching more effective.

As *a continuation of classical rhetoric* (cf. Corbett, 1971; Kinneavy, 1980). Obviously, an effective writer applies some strategies similar to those of an effective orator, such as the methods of building up or refuting an argument (cf. Perelman & Olbrechts-Tyteca, 1969). Oddly enough, however, rhetorical strategies were for many years not well represented, either in psychological research or in the composition class. A new look at the rich tradition reaching back to Aristotle and beyond can be a major asset in appreciating how to present materials, and how to make audiences respond.

As *the primary vehicle of literature* (cf. Green, 1982; Rader, 1982). The greatest body of analysis done on written texts has been devoted to literary samples. Most of this is oriented toward individual works or authors for purposes of criticism, elucidation, evaluation, and the maintenance of cultural institutions. Few attempts were made to establish a concise, consistent, or explicit theoretical foundation for literary studies until the last few decades, when new impulses come out of linguistics, stylistics, poetics, aesthetics, and phenomenology. Still, this large accumulation of studies might, in principle, be assembled within a unifying theoretical framework after the fact (cf. Beaugrande, 1983; Schmidt, 1982).

As *a special source and manifestation of knowledge about language*. This final approach suggests the main incentive for writing research. By expounding the issues enumerated above, we serve not only the interests of individual projects, but also those of language science as a whole. In line with the argument set down earlier in "Linguistic Theories and the Problem of Context," delimiting domains of discourse is a valuable step toward finding an empirical foundation for linguistics and for deciding what theories and categories can best serve any scientific enterprise. Hence, I have defended with considerable elaboration the view that this extremely broad approach not be postponed, but adopted at the outset of research as a guideline and rationale (Beaugrande, 1984).

Though it may seem optimistic to assert that it can be achieved, we could greatly profit from a framework integrating all these past approaches, along with those developing in the future. Serious obstacles could arise in regard to academic attitudes, research procedures, social policy, and the credentials of science itself, unless we can agree that writing is both a complex, challenging domain for research and a social need whose neglect among language scientists has a serious impact on human development, at least in our own culture. We must negotiate the terminology, methods, underlying assumptions, and scientific ambitions that best serve both aspects. If we succeed, we will then not only have furthered the progress of language science by explicating the status of our methods for obtaining, interpreting, and evaluating evidence, but will also have expanded the potential of the educational system to provide effectual improvement of language skills to all sections of society. If we can reestablish the context of science and its transmission into realistic successful practice, we will have achieved a synthesis long overdue.

TOWARD A THEORY OF WRITTEN MEANING: TRADITIONAL APPROACHES

A classic case of an issue whose investigation has remained fundamentally problematic is the relationship between language and its meaning. Saussure (1916) and his successors emphasized that this relationship is *arbitrary* in the sense that sounds alone are not meaningful by themselves. However, this opinion evidently led linguists to suppose that the relationship is also *poorly structured* and hence not rewarding as an object of inquiry within the dominant theories. Some linguists tried to set the problems of meaning aside by arguing that language structure can be described without consulting meaning (e.g., Chomsky, 1957; Harris, 1951; Trager & Smith, 1951). But most preferred to reduce the problem, as in Charles Carpenter Fries's (1952) project of distinguishing *structural meaning* from *lexical meaning* (definitions of words) and *social meaning* (total contextual significance). Fries's linguistic methodology used "structural meaning" as a way to study grammar: "The grammar of a language consists of the devices that signal structural meanings," these signals "consisting primarily of patterns of arrangement of classes of words" (pp. 56, 71). For example, a "noun" would be any word that could occupy a given slot in an "utterance frame"; structural meaning would remain constant as long we substitute any noun in that slot. By "making certain whether with each substitution, the structural meaning is the same," we need not "define the structural meaning" itself (p. 74). What it "means" to be a noun in a pattern is whatever is shared among all nouns inserted in that pattern; the same is true for any other word class in its appropriate slot. Of course, Fries is careful to stress that this "structural meaning" is only "one type of meaning" and "does not account for all the meanings in our utterances" (p. 294).

Fries's solution was a typical one in American linguistics, carrying over into generative grammar via the notion of "meaning-preserving transformation." But seen in a wider context, some complex postulates are involved here. By implication, the emphasis falls upon language as action to the extent that whatever cognitive categories people really use for "nouns," "verbs," and so on, are tied to procedures for putting words in order. In fact, the only firm empirical basis for grammatical word-classes in a language like English (where many class distinctions are not marked in the word-form itself) is precisely the tendency of ordinary-language users to place words capable of belonging to that class in some utterance positions and not in others. As far as word order influences the meaning of utterances, we could postulate a "structural meaning" or, more precisely, a "syntactic contributor to meaning." But two problems persist. First, it is not clear that such a "meaning" is appropriately described with such labels as "noun" or "verb"; more probably, the human categories in communication are rather defined in terms of "object," "action," "event," and so on—the determining aspect being the organization of experience, rather than the syntax of sentences. Second, an independent, non-circular proof that "structural meaning" stays the same after we make a "substitution" would be very hard to obtain, the more so when we are not given procedures for defining meaning. In real communication, judging the sameness of meaning is a complex action easily influenced by one's opinions about what aspects of meaning are relevant for some context; and, in Fries's approach, the only context admitted for the issue is the "utterance frame" as a pattern of grammatical "slots." Surely some meanings are constituted during processing without being committed to any such patterns.

Thus, Structuralist solution to the issue of meaning raises at least as many problems as it resolves. Whether "structural meaning" is a valid or useful notion still needs to be shown; it cannot be taken for granted as a self-evident corollary of the traditional word-classes, whose empirical status is equally far from secure. The same is true in general for traditional approaches to the study of meaning: They all need to be expounded in their wider contexts, and their underlying assumptions and implications need to be tested.

Perhaps we could start off with a rough classification of the traditional accounts of meaning in terms like these:

Lexical definition: Somewhere in an abstract "lexicon," for example, an ideal dictionary, the meanings of all words are defined (cf. Chomsky, 1965, 1972; Gleason, 1955; Petofi, 1980). Being meaningful would be like finding a word for a definition or looking up a definition for a word. One difficulty here is that, just as a culture assembles a body of knowledge and experience far greater than any one individual is likely to do, the whole lexicon isn't available to the normal language user (probably not to any user). We still need to find out what the average person's lexicon may look like, and how items are actually entered in it or looked up during text processing.

Semantic features: Meaning is a composite of basic minimal entities ("features") like "animate" versus "inanimate," and so on. (cf. Greimas, 1966; Nida, 1975).[2] Using a word meaning would entail activating or recovering its set of features. This position is easy to combine with the foregoing by envisioning a "lexicon" built out of semantic features (cf. Katz & Fodor, 1963). That scheme offers the attraction of compacting the lexicon, provided there are fewer features than lexical entries; but it might turn out that the number of features needed to fully characterize all definitions is as large as, or much larger than, the number of entries. Moreover, many features become relevant to a word's meaning only within a particular context and would hardly be expressly stated in the lexicon (Bolinger, 1965).

Propositions: Meaning involves assigning to a "predicate" one or more "arguments," that is, giving some property to one or more names of something (as in "Socrates is a Greek," with "Greek" as the predicate and "Socrates" as the argument) (cf. van Dijk, 1977; Jarvella, 1977; Miller, 1970). This approach favors a view of language as a device for asserting (i.e., presenting as true) properties of relations (or making judgments) about objects. The difficulty is again that the context, not just the logical structure, of an utterance decides what is being "predicated" versus what is already presupposed; properties may be mentioned for many reasons other than to assert them, for example, to single out one item from similar ones within the current visual field (Krauss & Weinheimer, 1967).

Semantic interpretation: The meaning of every sentence is given one or more representations of its "interpretation" in terms of logical forms and relations (cf. Chomsky, 1972; Jackendoff, 1972; Olson, 1977a, 1977b). Generativists disagreed about where the semantic interpretation should fit into the design of the grammar, for example, how far "surface" or "deep" structure is the determinant. But they did agree that a logical structure of

---

[2] The inspiration was of course the "phonological features" that worked so well to describe sound systems; but those "features" were defined via classes of manifest articulatory events; no such basis was ever agreed upon for "semantic features."

concepts was the basic entity involved. The "structural meaning" sought in conventional linguistics was destined to play a central role here.

Behavioral response: The response of the text receiver equals the meaning of the text; the receiver's behavior reveals and enacts that response (cf. Bloomfield, 1933; Quine, 1960; Skinner, 1957). The attraction of this approach is that it purports to deal solely with observable events. The difficulty is that these events cannot be identified or categorized in terms or external actions alone. Very different meanings can elicit the same outward response and vice versa (cf. Chomsky, 1959). Only by applying elaborate cognitive schemas are people able to interpret external actions as responses or nonresponses.

Reference: Things or states in the "world" are "referred to" by language; if the language denotes an actually existing state of affairs, it is "true" (cf. Frege, 1892; Linsky, 1957; Russell, 1905; Strawson, 1950). This approach seeks a different external correlate than overt behavior, namely, the manifest world with its objects and properties. The consequence is to raise acute problems about the range of objects referred to, for example, their number, their existence, their necessary (defining) properties, and so on. Behind the issue of "logical quantifiers" are complexes of processing activities whose nature is barely understood at this time.

Intention: Meaning is what a text producer intends the receiver to understand (cf. Gardiner, 1932; Grice, 1957; Searle, 1969). The intention might be to make a predication, elicit a response, refer to something, or whatever; but the intention is the ultimate recourse for knowing what is meant. This time, the problem is how the intention is formed and implemented, and how it may fail.

These traditional approaches imply various methods of abstraction, reduction, and isolation. Three main points of focus can be readily distinguished. In the first four approaches (lexical definitions, features, propositions, interpretations), meaning is treated primarily as *a representation cataloguing particular components and categories.* In the next two approaches (behavioral response, reference), meaning is treated primarily as *an external event or state of affairs depending on conditions of the world.* In the last approach (intention), meaning is treated primarily as *the outcome of an act of the human will.* These three broad focuses have not been reconciled so far, and may indeed foster divergences. Investigators can adopt one of the three without making a commitment on issues raised by the other two. If we focus on representations, we must rely on after-the-fact transcriptions of interpretative acts by trained analysts, and these acts differ both as behavior and as intention from the acts of everyday language users. If we focus on external events or states of affairs, we construe the linguistic action as a result, not as an action in its own right, and deemphasize the actions of speakers and hearers deciding what's going on and what to say about it. If we focus on intentions, the ways in which logical conditions and the state of the world constrain the human will may be obscured.

TOWARD A THEORY OF WRITTEN MEANING: A PROCESSING APPROACH

The problems aired above in the previous section are, I think, symptomatic of most attempts to formulate a theory of written meaning directly within a traditional linguistic or philosophic framework. The whole tradition is replete with idealizations, reductions, and limitations that obscure as many empirical issues as they illuminate. I suspect that traditional accounts, though certainly not without value, are typically *inconclusive;* and that to establish their empirical status, we cannot remain inside the inner domain of these accounts. That is, we may be able to validate after the fact certain traditional theories of language and meaning, but *not in their own terms.*

Instead, we need to examine all theories in their wider contexts. It might be argued that the inclusion of context in linguistic science threatens us with an infinite regress, an endless widening of scope that eventually leads to the entirety of human culture and history, into a vast, universal survey of the human situation. Until we agree to ignore some factors, we cannot explore any at all. Though this line of argument carries conviction, it does not dictate *which* limitations we should accept; nor how we should design any specific theory.

It might be helpful to view a linguistic theory as a map with borders: there is an *inner domain* of theoretical exploration surrounded by a much larger *outer domain* of contexts. The question of how the relationship between the two domains should be regulated is something each new theory has to decide. If the outer domain is totally ignored, the theory can be consistent and reliable in its scientific context only to the extent that the linguists themselves participate in a common culture and work with reasonably uniform presuppositions and interpretations. The validity of such a restricted theory might be established after the fact by showing that the outer domain, though excluded from the scope of investigation, is at least stable among the community of scientists. Conversely, the theory might be discredited if no such uniformity emerged. For example, a theory of formal grammar could be supported by finding that this community of grammarians has been performing the abstraction and formalization from language experience according to uniform, reliable procedures. To the extent that those procedures of theorization maintain a continual access to the first-order phenomenon of language experience, the fact that formal "grammaticality" has the empirical status of a derived effect or second-order phenomenon produced by theoretical abstraction would then be of less consequence. The opposite conclusion would be reached if great diversity were found: the theory would not be reliable because the derived effect may be a different object for each individual study or investigator, so that generalizations across the whole theory could be illusory or metaphorical.

The same methods might be applied to traditional theories of meaning. As I pointed out earlier, these theories have had three main emphases for setting up their inner domain: meaning as a representation, as a mode of behaving in the external world, or as an act of will. Usually, each type of theory selected one of these outlooks as its inner domain and left unspecified the relationships to the outer domain (all human meaning) that includes, among others, the remaining two. It might be possible to create a general theory that assigns each of these three outlooks a place within one unifying theoretical framework. But this procedure, I suspect, would have to discount some of the stronger claims each outlook made being the only proper one. And it would still be undetermined how far particular sets of research could be salvaged, precisely to the extent that such claims were too strong, especially in respect to their generality. For instance, Skinner (1957) took his examples of simple utterances, usually commands or direct responses to everyday events, as evidence to assert that he was accounting for all of language; and as many authorities have since noted (e.g. Chomsky, 1959; Osgood, 1963), these simplest cases will not support such a general application.

In future work, we might save ourselves such difficulties by addressing the question of validity in wider contexts before the fact, rather than after. We could try to sketch in some of the more prominent features of the outer domain that influence the structure of the inner domain covered by the linguistic theory at hand. The theory could then be more readily extended to encompass relevant contextual factors when they become tractable at a later stage of research. Provisional exclusions could be overcome if they prove inhibiting to progress. For example, a theory that treats language as one mode of *human action and interaction* could be strategically situated in the outer domain of an overall *theory of action*. General concepts of action would be specified for the linguistic concepts of planning, uttering, asserting, denying, questioning, informing, and so on (cf. Beaugrande, 1979a, 1980a, 1980b). This procedure would allow more powerful explanations wherever discourse is found to be determined by the structure of interaction, for example, the dependency of conversational utterances on the projection of personal roles. If neighboring disciplines such as sociology, anthropology, and developmental education also agree to stipulate their central concepts by specifying the concepts of action theory, hypotheses and findings could be traded from one discipline to the next without elaborate translating. Thus, even though contexts would still be limited and selective, new inclusions should be readily manageable.

This perspective suggests some ground rules for linguistic inquiry, such as:

The investigator defines the basic units as actions, and the domain as a domain of action.

Linguistic items, features, or patterns are interpreted and classified according to their relevance for the performance and success of actions.

Phrases, sentences, texts, or other structured entities are studied in terms of how they are created and used in communicative events.

The investigator openly declares the limitations and selections of the inquiry with respect to the motives of research as an action in its own right. That is, the theory is expressly acknowledged as an inner domain, and its position within the outer domain is clearly stated.

No single set of limitations and selections can be definitive; other needs can establish other sets. Further areas of the outer domain should be steadily incorporated.

Evidence is not invented by the investigator, but gathered from real actions occurring under stated conditions.

Interdisciplinarity is recognized as essential for the wider validity of particular findings.

Such ground rules could help bring out into the open the motivations and interests affecting linguistic inquiry, and the relations between the evidence under consideration versus the totality of available evidence. The inquiry is thereby both more and less than a description of language as an abstract system: more, because "action" is a more general notion than "phoneme," "morpheme," or "sentence"; and less, because not all features of language samples will be equally relevant for any one action domain. The nature of scientific objects would be plainly recognized as a derived effect of the motives and preconditions for scientific inquiry.

We can now pursue some issues of meaning and written meaning in terms of processing actions. We can start from the indisputable fact that people[3] use language as a means of acquiring, storing, using, and conveying knowledge. The outer limits of the domain of meaning are therefore the outer limits of knowing, where "knowing" is defined not as "being certain" (convinced, clear, positive, etc.) as in commonsense parlance, but as "having awareness of real or possible significance." "Significance" is any symbolic relationship, that is, any equivalence created between non-identical objects or events[4]—setting something alongside or inside some-

---

[3] Infants just learning to communicate are not included in this sketch.

[4] In every day usage, "significant" is usually reserved for nontrivial symbolic relations; but that is because routine significances have become automatized enough to seem inherent in the objects and events themselves. In my sketch, nothing is "significant" until people

thing else. A human "knows" about the world, whether or not the world seems to make sense, because experience interacts with innate symbolic capacities for organizing, interpreting, classifying, generalizing, differentiating, and so on. Thus, when we define "knowledge" as a "human system," we are merely saying that a human's knowledge is made up of components that are interrelated at least because they are all known to that one human and are classified and understood in nonrandom ways. The human may have no explicit or distinct awareness of what those interrelations are. But the interrelations have to be systematic enough to enable the person to recognize types of situations and to perform appropriate types of actions. People may misunderstand or perform erroneous or unsuccessful actions; but they always have some hypotheses about what things mean and what should be done.

"To mean" is a subtype of the action "to know": whereas knowing requires only *being aware of significance,* meaning requires *being significant,* that is, *doing* something with significance.[5] Many aspects of experience "have meaning" or "are meaningful" in the sense that humans give them significance and can then process that significance for a relevant purpose. Thus, meaning is always a mental event, not a stable object. The event may at any time alter the significance itself. For example, when people use a known concept to define a new experience, they can easily adapt the concept, at least in its details, in view of that experience. The formation of a concept is never totally definitive or completed, though a relative (rather than absolute) stability may be attained over time through a convergence of processing results for that concept.

To "use language" is a further subtype of the action "to mean," namely, one deploying language as a product and manifestation (sign, signal) of the action of meaning. Language is the most familiar and obvious instrument of this action, though not the only one; a language action is typically in the context of other modalities of behaving in a way that indicates significance (body movements, eye contact, facial expression, etc.). An utterance (text) may be the clearest, or even the only, documentation of the action of meaning, yet is not identical with it: Specialized linguistic processes have been added. Like the action of meaning, the action of using language to mean may not only deploy previously available significances, but may also change them. For all these reasons, it is never strictly justified to claim that an *utterance* (sentence, text, etc.) "means" something, but only that *people* "mean" something which is in part initiated and docu-

---

make it so, and the processes involved are certainly not trivial from the standpoint of language theory.

   [5] Again, "meaningful" is normally reserved in everyday usage for nontrivial cases; but the same line of argument applies here as that stated in Footnote 4.

mented by their utterances (cf. Morgan, 1975; Morgan & Sellner, 1980). What is actually "meant" must still be determined by the people involved, working with a fuzzy range of more or less probable significances, including any changes occurring on that very occasion.

To sum up, "meaning" could be defined as "a configuration of processing actions performed on significances"; "knowing what a word (text) means" could be defined as "having an ordered set of hypotheses about what processing actions to perform on the word (text)." From here, we can try to restate some of the classical notions of meaning as sketched earlier in "Traditional Approaches." *Lexical definition* is a stated (or statable) predisposition toward a certain set of hypotheses and their typical order, where "order" is imposed on both the structure of the action and on its sequence. *Context* is the set of currently prevailing factors that interact with those predispositions, and with each other, to influence what actions really get carried out. *Intention* is the set of decisions that particular processing actions or configurations of actions should be performed with a characterized result; if this outcome is attained, the intention has been "successful." The text producer intends certain nonrandom significances, and the text receiver accepts certain nonrandom significances, partly (but not exclusively) via hypotheses about what the producer intended. The utterance serves as a complex signal to activate processes, but these processes presuppose the intention of the people involved to deploy and share significances. Humans presumably impose a threshold when they consider processing satisfactory for the intention or occasion. Like concept formation, the production and reception of texts are open actions that could in principle be prolonged, restarted, or revised, if appropriate motives were exerted. The intention can thereby control both which processing actions are done, and how intensely or elaborately.

The context includes the external configuration of real or possible causes and effects depending on the text. A fairly simple causality obtains if a real event elicits the production of the text, and the reception in turn elicits a further event. This causality is the paradigm case for the approach to meaning as a *behavioral response*, but is far too simple to cover language communication at large. Objects and events are typically experienced in complex configurations to which humans assign significance; and these configurations are often not directly stimulated by, or prefigured in, the current environment. It is most unlikely that the simplest case can be extended to encompass these more complex assignments of significance. Rather, behavioral responses to (or in) language should be seen as classes of effects whose causes can include the act of meaning. The *temporal* proximity of a "stimulus" and an utterance does not imply a direct or single-natured *causality*. The "stimulus" (if it's not a sharp pain or the like) must first be made meaningful before the response occurs.

If language is in part a means of organizing and managing one's experience, there should be a steady reciprocation between cognition and the experienced world. *Reference* would be the act of using the significances attributed to the experienced world in order to invoke or create additional significances. The possibility of reference is already negotiated by most cultures; yet the act itself can always be further negotiated in context. Whether or not a text producer is committed to a given status of the experienced world is in principle an open question. The reality, existence, and number of world-components is more relevant in some contexts (e.g., a legal transaction) than in others (e.g., a conversation in a bar). Rather than verifying the correctness or scope of reference, people routinely agree to suspend disbelief at least as far as necessary to communicate. Verification is reserved for special cases where the act of asserting (presenting as true and accurate) has decisive human consequences. Philosophers have created unnecessary difficulties by treating quantification and truth-conditions as issues to be resolved a priori, before a theory of meaning is formulated and tested.

The very fact that any one action of "meaning" is situated in a wide-ranging complex of preconditions and results—experience, knowledge, intentions, external events, lexical definitions, behavioral responses, and so on—suggests how fuzzy the borders of the action itself can be. Linguists have proposed a distinction between basic meanings ("denotations") versus accompanying, associated meanings ("connotations") (cf. survey in Molino, 1971). Theoretically, "denotations" would be the definitions assumed in most people's lexicons as the *identifying* or *necessary* stipulations of meaning; "connotations" would be the significances that arise relative to a person's systems of belief, value, and experience. Still, uniformity of culture can create very general connotations that figure in most people's knowledge. An impersonal lexicon of pure denotations (free of personal experiences and values) can be but an artificial construct, a compilation of those significances primarily used by a culture to identify the concepts related to the words or standing phrases of the vocabulary. Such a lexicon could hardly be the basis of normal communication, nor an ideal for the latter to imitate.

Creating *semantic theories* is one mode of generalizing about meaning by reducing, abstracting, and isolating certain acts or outcomes involved in the broader activities sketched above. Conventional semantic theories in linguistics approach meaning as an object already constituted. This tactic is not essentially different from the standard methods in phonology and syntax. The actions of articulating sounds and linearizing words in phrases are fundamentally presupposed in any analysis into features and structures. But the uniformity with which linguists carry out this prior constitution of objects is evidently greater for language sounds than for word sequences, and greater for word sequences than for meanings—hence the relative estimates of "well-structuredness" among these three domains. Therefore, the likelihood that an isolated theory can be validated after the fact in its wider context is stronger for phonology than for syntax, and stronger for syntax than for semantics. Apparently, the routine externalization of sounds and phrases in consistent acoustic sequences and graphic representations during ordinary communication has led to a uniformity of analysis that semantics, lacking a comparable mode of externalization, did not offer.

This lack is no doubt the motive behind the continuing search for a consistent *semantic representation,* that is, for a reliable, uniform externalization of meaning. Because the action of meaning is typically complex and open, researchers could in principle design a large number of possible representations. Any one representation for meanings obliges its designer to incorporate epistemological decisions (Brachman, 1979), for example, when to impose a threshold of processing, how to verify a reference, and so on; and here, too, validity of results hinges on uniformity and consistency in making these decisions. Typically, the semantic representation selected by a group of theorists had a powerful impact on how they perceived and stated the issues. Presumably, the representation, being the most tangible part of the procedure, was readily confused with the object domain; hence, having a representation could be confused with having a semantic theory.

The problems involved became evident during attempts to analyze meaning into *semantic features.* Each investigator followed his or her own predispositions and parameters for deciding how detailed, abstract, exhaustive, universal, and complex such features should be. One major factor is the number of cases to be accounted for. Most investigations have been merely illustrative, listing features for a few concepts like "bachelor" (Katz & Fodor, 1963) or "chair" (Pottier, 1964). The design of a set of features for the entire lexicon can hardly be worked out from a few listings selected because they were intuitively judged well-structured and tractable. We need features that (a) serve in many definitions, (b) can have internal structures, and (c) can participate with other features in more complex structures, and so on (cf. Brachman, 1978; Fahlman, 1979).

A representation in terms of *propositions* poses similar problems, but does not force a specification of details to the same extent. A proposition is a configuration of concepts whose relation to each other helps to limit and define potentially relevant meanings. And, in fact, recent propositional representations, though by no means fully uniform, are fairly similar among various investigators (compare Anderson, 1976; Beaugrande, 1980a; Frederiksen, 1977; Kintsch & van Dijk, 1978; Meyer, 1977)—at least more so than semantic-feature schemes. To take the classic example, "Socrates is a Greek'', the proposition itself indicates that the nationality of "Socrates" is the main concern, as compared to all other things we might know or mean about him; and that "Greek" signifies a person's nationality rather than a language, a life-style, and so on. Hence, many possible features of the concept "Greek" need not enter our analysis. This effect would grow steadily stronger, the larger and more detailed the context, for example, if Socrates' loyalties to the Athenian state were being discussed. As the whole text unfolds, we are better and better able to decide what aspects of meaning are relevant for the current needs.

The *semantic interpretation* envisioned by generative grammarians is also constrained by its purpose. The analysis is again in terms of predications, but with special emphasis on structures that can easily be integrated with the structures in the syntactic representation. As Stockwell (1977) explains, "the semantic representation of the sentence" is "an abstract construct" that "allows us to single out those aspects of the total meaning which are carried by the syntactic structure of sentences, as distinct from those parts that depend on context, on the particular words which a language arbitrarily correlates with actions, events, ideas, things" (p. 32).[6] As such, the representation is a descendant of the "structural meaning" that grammar was thought to signal by its patterns. The "transformational" design of the newer grammar made it important that paraphrases of one sentence be interpreted with the same semantic representation (cf. Mel'čuk & Žolkovskij, 1970; Ungeheuer, 1969). Aspects of meaning that were assumed to remain stable during paraphrasing—and, due to the design of the grammar, this covered most aspects—were not considered the essential issues for the theory.

Finally, *the written text* is itself a graphic representation of meaning. This seemingly trivial fact points to an unacknowledged anomaly in the practices of linguistic inquiry as a discipline. When syntax emerged as a central topic, for example, in immediate constituent analysis and transformational grammar, investigators found it inconvenient to represent sample sentences as streams of sound. It was easier to start off with *already written* samples whose segmentation and structural description were heavily *preconfigured in the graphic representation itself*. The stable identity of constituents in chains or parse trees was greatly enhanced by the visual clarity of the written samples. Moreover, the linguists themselves were mostly literate academics long accustomed to an effortless transition between speech and writing. Their sample sentences were often taken from what Abercrombie (1965) called "spoken prose," that is, written discourse quoted aloud. The samples had the complete structure and the well-marked

---

[6] Note the key word "arbitrarily," which seems to suggest that meaning is not a reliable domain of study.

boundaries most conducive to the procedures of assigning consistent structural descriptions. Hence, the obviousness and universality (even "innateness") of formal grammatical categories was greatly overestimated, at least for theories that purported to address spoken language or all of language. Still, this practice probably favored consistency and uniformity in the practices of different linguists—a key issue for validating their theories.

To appreciate this factor, consider the dual nature of the text. On the one hand, the text is a "surface" entity in being a linear pattern of words or word parts, and may thus appear indeterminate and impoverished. On the other hand, people (including linguists) have much more skill and experience in assigning meaning to texts than in designing features, propositions, or formal interpretations; and the text offers the most elaborated and widely accepted document of the context for determining what is relevant. Therefore, the written text should be the semantic representation that people will treat with the greatest uniformity and consistency, despite its "surface" appearance. If so, the need for another complete or exhaustive representation is not so acute; what we need are (a) clear procedures for analyzing textual meaning; and (b) specialized auxiliary representations to reveal meaning relationships the surface text downplays or conceals, for example, hierarchical rather than linear ones. This way, we are in no danger of confusing one representation with the object domain; but we can still have recourse to the representations and use the advantage they offer. We can hope to bring linguistic analysis more in line with the uses ordinary people make of texts.

A viable theory of *written meaning* should be conceived in terms of how written meaning is processed in real time by humans. Whatever commonalities are found to be the shared guiding principles of human processing should form the empirical center for theories of written meaning. Specializations could be included for appropriate sub-domains, for example, scientific discourse, didactic discourse, story-telling; and presumably, the specific conditions under which the written modality is used are reflected in the ways people process written meaning, as distinct from other modalities, especially speech.

An intention to be meaningful is the normal origin of a communication, that is, the initiating impulse that eventually results in the production and presentation of the surface text. The intervening processes that execute the intention may be quite complex in all but very straightforward situations (e.g., reacting immediately to an external object by saying a word or phrase that names it). Usually, a range of options—meanings, expressions, phrases, and so on—is available to realize a communicative intention within a discourse. There are several phases in text production where options can be confronted (cf. the model in Beaugrande, 1984). An intention may be mapped onto various ideas that act as conceptual control centers for discovering and integrating content. An idea may take various pathways during conceptual development, where concepts are added, detailed, or integrated under the control of ideation. A concept may correlate with several expressions in the language. And a set of expressions can be fit into more than one phrase linearization, that is, a syntactic pattern allowed by the grammar of the language, or by some motivated modification of it.

The text producer need not consider all discoverable options; search can be terminated when such options are found as are considered adequate for the occasion. Indeed, the text producer has to limit the size of the sets of options being considered at the various branching points, lest the total range become unmanageable. (This factor is known as "combinatorial explosion" in computer processing: a geometric progression of possible decision pathways that degrades the operation of the whole system). We can safely assume that a person's knowledge of the world and of the language is elaborately prestructured in memory. When certain content or expressions are required, the memory search causes certain nodes in the "network" of storage (as an electrochemical impulse configuration) to become active by raising their excitation level above a critical threshold (cf. Fahlman, 1979; Morton, 1970). This activation automatically spreads to associated nodes (Collin & Loftus, 1975), so that a range of related options is now available for selection. The nodes actually selected become the new centers of activation, while the nonselected ones fade and become inactive. Probably, the text producer can influence this whole process by manipulating its thresholds and search criteria, even though the structures of knowledge may be extensively prefigured in storage. If the text is important for one's goals, the search may be prolonged and concentrated, and the criteria to be met may be detailed and rigorous. Many options immediately activated would then be rejected as too obvious, too commonplace, too trite, too personal, and so on.

Each decision at any point can affect the "meaning," that is, the assignment of significances. But the producer may have no clear awareness of these effects in every case. It may be necessary to make some provisional choices simply to obtain any version of the text at all, and to then test the results against an intuitive estimation of the meaning one intended to signal. That is, options may be rejected out of hand not because they misrepresent the intended meaning, but merely because a linear modality such as language constrains what can be implemented simultaneously. Further consideration may reveal that the chosen option was not the best candidate after all.

The issue of selection seems to me crucial for a theory of written meaning as compared to spoken meaning. Inscribing is normally much slower than uttering (Blass & Siegman, 1975; Gould, 1979), partly because the motor actions involved are more effortful, and partly because a writer is under less pressure for continuous output than a speaker is. This slower tempo should allow a more focused and deliberate selection process. For one thing, the activation of contiguous options in memory storage would spread to larger sets. Also, more care could be expended on matching options against one's intentions and specifications. Because the written text is preserved, the producer can use it as a configuration of cues to restart the search and selection process at any strategic point. This review should draw a lighter processing load than the original act of production, because one might consider only a subset of choices and take the rest as given (at least for the time being); and because the act of inscription is replaced in the review by the less demanding act of recognition. Hence, more resources are free to focus on specific choices and their relevance to intentions and meanings. Also, having the whole text recorded on paper makes it easier to relate any particular choice to the overall pattern of preserved cues. Each review should further decrease processing load as the number of residual problems is steadily reduced.

In consequence, the written text should ideally be a more exact representation of the intended meaning than a spoken one would be. The remoteness of the audience from the writer could be offset by a text design precisely calculated in advance to fulfill an intention. But this situation is an obvious idealization, because it presupposes an optimal process organization and fails to consider possible obstacles. First, the slower tempo of writing could encourage the decay (loss of activation) of transitory memory stores in which options are being held for review or implementation. In that case, the writer is in peril of forgetting what can or should be done. Second, the chances are greater that attention may be distracted before an intended meaning gets recorded. For example, daydreaming appears to be a release valve: Conceptual search, when left temporarily unguided in order to focus on other phases, may revert to extraneous content accessed via mental associations or preoccupations from the background. Third, processing overload is an imminent danger when the writer tries to consider too many options. If each option in one branching leads on to its own branching, and this multiplication of branching continues on down the line, processing will undergo combinatorial explosion in the sense discussed earlier. Suppose a writer insisted on reviewing every conceivable option with all its implications—what is called "brute force search" in computational theory. The wealth of details would draw such great resources that little would remain to uphold the coherence of the total context. Then, the criteria for selection could be obscured rather than clarified.

It follows that writing offers its benefits only if processing is appropriately reorganized to maximize the advantages and minimize the disadvantages of this particular mode for conveying intended meanings. Special training, whether self-initiated or imposed from outside (e.g., by schooling), is needed to be a skilled writer. The written modality does not by itself compel its users to attain such skills. On the contrary, a large proportion of written texts manifest an imperfect and approximative realization of their potential. As a writing instructor and consultant, I am atypically sensitive to this factor; but I know from interviews that most people are insecure and anxious about their own writing abilities as well as about individual texts they have produced. Apparently, it is common to retain a residual awareness that one's intended meaning has not been faithfully conveyed, though one may lack the strategies to remedy the discrepancies.

Given the complexity of cognitive processes, and the difficulty of reorganizing them once they have become routine and automatic (cf. Norman & Shallice, 1980; Shiffrin & Schneider, 1977), the development of skilled writing processes is certainly not a trivial task. For example, if the slow tempo of writing incurs on-line memory decay, writers need to develop a specialized, enduring memory store for writing; or to supplement available storage with specialized processes for maintaining and reinstating stored materials. Loss of attention via distraction or extraneous association could be offset by imposing tight control on the conceptual associations that search can follow up, or by imposing a relevance threshold to detect and gate out irrelevant intrusions. Combinatorial explosion could be contained by recasting the simultaneous consideration of options into a successive one, so that at no time does the total number of active options become unmanageable. The review process for written drafts demands specialized evaluation procedures for critical elements and configurations. All these developments are certainly complex and poorly understood so far.

Most currently practiced educational methods for writing instruction are conceived and implemented on a much grosser level, namely, the intuitive evaluation of surface texts according to the idiosyncratic, implicit standards of individual teachers. There is no way to tell whether and how the methods may (or may not) encourage the cognitive reorganization needed for an effectual use of the conditions imposed by writing. The present decline in literacy skills suggests that we are largely shooting in the dark and hitting few, if any, important targets.

What is in fact pressingly needed is a substantial and innovative research program. I tried to show above why it not likely that traditional research paradigms can suffice. We should study traditional beliefs, attitudes, and values regarding writing as social determinants, but we should not accept them as a framework for designing new theories. Written meaning is a special case of knowing and being significant. Its peculiar nature arises from the processing conditions of the medium and of the discourse domains where written texts are routinely the main vehicles of commincation. These conditions influence the timing, resources, intentions, and criteria during the act of putting meaning into writing. We shall have to carry out detailed empirical research on activity of meaning under various conditions. Important variables include: writing skill, reading skill, extent and success of revision, readability and memorability of text, text type (essay, poem, story, etc.), text quality (judged by a sampling of experts), and communicative effectiveness (how the text helps achieve the writer's purpose). This research should in turn be used to evaluate instructional methods for their impact on each variable. Only then can we develop theory-driven approaches to the teaching of writing (cf. Beaugrande, 1985).

Multiple modes of evidence will certainly be needed. Some of these are emerging from research already under way (see also the literature reviewed heretofore). We can have writers think out loud about what they're doing (Hayes & Flower, 1980). We can relate the pauses of speech and writing to their location in syntactic or topical groupings (cf. Flower & Hayes, 1981; Matsuhashi, 1981, 1982; Rochester, 1973). We can compare how a person expresses the same topic in speech and in writing (Beaugrande, 1982a, 1982b, 1984). We can gather ratings of different versions of the same written text (Beaugrande, 1979b). We can interview writers after the fact about how they compose (Emig, 1971; Daly, 1983). Despite their diversity, these methods should reveal some consistent factors in how writing is used to record and convey meanings.

The fact that "to mean" is a way to act, as Halliday (1975) was one of the few linguists to emphasize, is both a difficult abstraction and an everyday experience. Humans agree that language *can* communicate meaning; but how this action is done and who means what requires continual negotiation. The effort of meaning should be fairly distributed between writer and reader. As long as we are uninformed about how written meaning is constituted, the trade-off is typically settled at the expense of the reader, who has to struggle with obscurities, inaccuracies, inconsistencies, and irrelevancies. Writers can be given reliable, transferrable strategies for making their texts efficient (easy to process) and at the same time effective (suited to the purpose) only if research can discover how written meaning correlates with textual options. Otherwise, there is no serious alternative to the whims and fumblings of unskilled writers, and little motivation to hope for anything better. Just as a text affects one's beliefs, one's beliefs determine how a text can document one's intention to be meaningful. Thus, a solid theory of what it means to mean can provide the ambience for a more enlightened and effectual practice in being meaningful.

REFERENCES

Abercrombie, D. (1965). Conversation and spoken prose. In Abercrombie et al. (Eds.), *In honour of Daniel Jones.* London: Longman.

Anderson, J.R. (1976). *Language, memory, and thought*. Hillsdale, NJ: Erlbaum.

Baron, D. (1975) Non-standard English, composition, and the academic establishment. *College English, 37*, 176–183.

Baron, J. (1973). Phonetic stage not necessary for reading. *Quarterly Journal of Experimental Psychology, 25*, 241–246

Barron, R. (1978), Reading skill and phenomenological coding. In M. Gruneberg, P. Morris, & R. Sykes (Eds.), *The recognition of words*. London: Academic.

Beaugrande, R. de (1979a). Text and sentence in discourse planning. In J.S. Petöfi (Ed.), *Text vs. sentence* (pp. 467–494). Hamburg: Buske.

Beaugrande, R. de (1979b). Psychology and composition. *College Composition and Communication, 30*, 50–57.

Beaugrande, R. de (1980a). *Text, discourse, and process*. London: Longman.

Beaugrande, R. de (1980b). The pragmatics of discourse planning. *Journal of Pragmatics, 4*, 15–42.

Beaugrande, R. de (1982a) Psychology and composition: Past, present, future. In M. Nystrand (Ed.), *What writers know* (pp. 211–267). New York: Academic.

Beaugrande, R. de (1982b). Cognitive processes and technical writing. *Journal of Technical Writing and Communication, 12*, 121–145.

Beaugrande, R. de (1984). *Text production: Toward a science of composition*. Norwood, NJ: Ablex.

Beaugrande, R. de (1983). Surprised by syncretism. *Poetics, 12*, 83–137.

Beaugrande, R. de (1985). *Writing step by step*. New York: Harcourt Brace Jovanovich.

Begg, I. (1971). Recognition memory for sentence meaning and wording. *Journal of Verbal Learning and Verbal Behavior, 10*, 176–181.

Bereiter, C. (1980). Development in writing. In L. Gregg & E. Steinberg (Eds.), *Cognitive processes in writing*. (pp. 73–93). Hillsdale, NJ: Erlbaum.

Bereiter, C., & Scardamalia, M. (1983). Levels of inquiry in writing research. In P. Mosenthal, L. Tamor, & S. Walmsley (Eds.), *Research in writing: Principles and methods*. New York: Longman.

Bergeijk, W. van, & David, E. (1959). Delayed handwriting. *Perceptual and Motor Skills, 9*, 347–357.

Berthoff, A. (1972). From problem-solving to a theory of imagination. *College English, 33*, 636–649.

Blankenship, J. (1962). A linguistic analysis of oral and written style. *Quarterly Journal of Speech, 48*, 419–422.

Blass, T., & Siegman, A. (1975). A psycholinguistic comparison of speech, dictation, and writing. *Language and Speech, 18*, 20–34.

Bloomfield, L. (1933). *Language*. New York: Holt.

Bolinger, D. (1965). The atomization of meaning. *Language, 41*, 555–73.

Bolinger, D. (1968). Judgements of grammaticality. *Lingua, 21*, 34–40.

Bower, T.G.R. (1970) Reading by eye. In H. Levin & J. Williams (Eds.), *Basic studies in reading* (pp. 134–147). New York: Basic Books.

Brachman, R. (1978). *A structural paradigm for representing knowledge*. (Tech. Rep. No. 3605). Cambridge, MA: Bolt, Beranek, and Newman.

Brachman, R. (1979). On the epistemological status of semantic network In N. Findler (Ed.), *Associative networks* (pp. 3–50). New York: Academic.

Braddock, R., Lloyd-Jones, R., & Schoer, L. (1971). *Research in written composition*. Urbana, IL: National Council of Teachers of English.

Bradshaw, J.L. (1975). Three interrelated problems in reading. *Memory and Cognition, 3*, 123–134.

Bray, N., & Batchelder, W. (1972). Effects of instructions and retention interval on memory of presentation mode. *Journal of Verbal Learning and Verbal Behavior, 11,* 367-374.

Britton, J., Burgess, T., Martin, N., McLeod, A., & Rosen, H. (1975) *The development of writing abilities (Vols. 11-18).* London: Macmillan.

Caccamise, D.J., (1981). *Cognitive processes in writing: Idea generation and integration.* Unpublished doctoral dissertation. Boulder: University of Colorado.

Chafe, W. (1982). Integration and involvement in speaking, writing, and oral literature. In D. Tannen (Ed.), *Spoken and written language: Exploring orality and literacy.* (pp. 35-53). Norwood, NJ: Ablex.

Chomsky, N. (1957). *Syntactic structures.* The Hague: Mouton.

Chomsky, N. (1959). Review of *Verbal Behavior,* by B.F. Skinner. *Language, 35,* 25-58.

Chomsky, N. (1965). *Aspects of the theory of syntax.* Cambridge, MA: MIT Press.

Chomsky, N. (1972). *Studies in semantics in generative grammar.* The Hague: Mouton.

Collins, A., & Loftus, E. (1975). A spreading-activation theory of semantic processing. *Psychological Review, 82,* 407-428.

Corbett, E. (1971). *Classical rhetoric for the modern student.* New York: Oxford.

Daly, J. (1983, April). *Evaluating writing attitudes and beliefs.* Paper presented at the meeting of the American Educational Research Association, Montreal.

D'Angelo, F. (1979). *Process and thought in composition.* Cambridge, MA: Winthrop.

Danks, J. (1977). Producing ideas and sentences. In. S. Rosenberg (Ed.), *Sentence production* (pp. 229-258). Hillsdale, NJ: Erlbaum.

DeVito, J. (1965). Comprehension factors in oral and written discourse of skilled communicators. *Speech Monographs, 32,* 124-128.

DeVito, J. (1966). Psychogrammatical factors in oral and written discourse by skilled communicators. *Speech Monographs, 33,* 73-76.

Dijk, T. van (1977). *Text and context.* London: Longman.

Drieman, G. (1962). Differences between written and spoken language. *Acta Psychologica, 20,* 36-57 & 78-100.

Durrell, D. (1969). Listening comprehension vs. reading comprehension. *Journal of Reading, 12,* 455-460.

Einhorn, L. (1978). Oral and written style. *Southern Speech Communication Journal, 43,* 302-311.

Elbow, P. (1973). *Writing without teachers.* London: Oxford University Press.

Emig, J. (1971). The composing processes of twelfth graders. Urbana, IL: National Council of Teachers of English.

Emig, J. (1977). Writing as a mode of discovery. *College Composition and Communication, 28,* 122-128.

Fahlman, S. (1979). *NETL: A system for representing and using real-world knowledge.* Cambridge, MA: MIT Press.

Faigley, L., Miller, T., Meyer, P., & Witte, S. (1981). *Writing after college: A stratified survey of the writing of college-trained people.* (Tech. Rep. No. GRG 106-A) Austin: University of Texas.

Flower, L., & Hayes, J.R. (1981). The pregnant pause. *Research in the Teaching of English, 15,* 229-243.

Fox, B., & Routh, D. (1976). Phonemic analysis and synthesis as word-attack skills. *Journal of Educational Psychology, 68,* 70-74.

Fraisse, P., & Breyton, M. (1959). Comparaisons entre les langages oral et écrit. *L'Année psychologique, 59,* 61-71.

Frederiksen, C. (1977). Semantic processing units in understanding text. In R. Freedle (Ed.), *Discourse production and comprehension* (pp. 57-88). Norwood, NJ: Ablex.

Frege, G. (1892). Ueber Sinn und Bedeutung. *Zeitschrift fuer Philosophie und philosophische Kritik, 100,* 25–50.

Fries, C.C. (1952) *The structure of English: An introduction to the construction of English sentences.* New York: Harcourt Brace Jovanovich.

Frith, U. (1978). From print to meaning and from print to sound or how to read without knowing how to spell. *Visible Language, 12,* 43–54.

Frith, U. (1980). Unexpected spelling problems. In U. Frith (Ed.), *Cognitive processes in spelling* (pp. 495–515). London: Academic.

Gardiner, A. (1932). *The theory of speech and language.* Oxford: Clarendon.

Gere, A.R., & Smith, E. (1979). *Attitudes, language, and change.* Urbana, IL: National Council of Teachers of English.

Gibson, J., Gruner, C. Kibler, R., & Kelley, F. (1966). A quantitative examination of the differences and similarities in written and spoken messages. *Speech Monographs, 33,* 444–451.

Goodman, K. (1970). Reading, a psycholinguistic guessing game. In H. Singer & B. Ruddell (Eds.), *Theoretical process models of reading.* Newark, NJ: International Reading Association.

Goodman, K., & Goodman, Y. (1979). Learning to read is natural. In L. Resnick & P. Weaver (Eds.), *Theory and practice of early reading* (pp. 137–154). Hillsdale, NJ: Erlbaum.

Gough, P. (1972). One second of reading. In J. Kavanagh & I. Mattingly (Eds.), *Language by ear and by eye* (pp. 331–350). Cambridge, MA: MIT Press.

Gould, J. (1979). *Writing and speaking letters and messages.* (Research Rep. RC-7528). Yorktown Heights, NY: IBM.

Green, D., & Shallice, T. (1976). Direct visual access in reading for meaning. *Memory and Cognition, 4,* 753–758.

Green, G.M. (1982). Colloquial and literary uses of invention. In D. Tannen (Ed.), *Spoken and written language: Exploring orality and literacy* (pp. 119–153). Norwood, NJ: Ablex.

Green, J.R. (1958). *A comparison of oral and written language: A qualitative approach.* Unpublished doctoral dissertation. New York: New York University.

Greenbaum, S., & Taylor, J. (1981) The recognition of usage errors by instructors of freshman composition. *College Composition and Communication, 32,* 169–174.

Gregg, L., & Steinberg, E. (Eds.). (1980). *Cognitive processes in writing.* Hillsdale, NJ: Erlbaum.

Greimas, A. (1966). *Sémantique structurale: Recherches de méthode.* Paris: Larousse.

Guthrie, J., & Seifert, M. (1977). Letter-sound complexity in learning to identify words. *Journal of Educational Psychology, 69,* 686–696.

Grice, P. Meaning. (1957). *Philosophical Review, 66,* 377–388.

Hairston, M. (1981). Not all errors are created equal: Nonacademic readers respond to lapses in usage. *College English, 43,* 794–806.

Hairston, M., & Selfe, C. (Eds.). (1981). *Selected papers from the 1981 Texas Writing Research Conference.* Austin: University of Texas English Department.

Halliday, M.A.K. (1975). *Learning to mean.* London: Arnold.

Harris, M.M. (1977). Oral and written syntax attainment of second graders. *Research in the Teaching of English, 11,* 117–132.

Harris, Z.S. (1951). *Methods in structural linguistics.* Chicago: University of Chicago Press.

Hartmann, P. (1963). *Theorie der Grammatik.* The Hague: Mouton.

Hartwell, P. (1980). Dialect interference in writing: A critical view. *Research in the Teaching of English, 14,* 101–118.

Hayes, J., & Flower, L. (1980). Identifying the organization of writing processes. In L. Gregg

& E. Steinberg (Eds.), *Cognitive processes in writing* (pp. 3-30). Hillsdale, NJ: Erlbaum.

Heath, S.B. (1982). Protean shapes in literacy events. In D. Tannen (Ed.), *Spoken and written language: Exploring orality and literacy* (pp. 91-117). Norwood, NJ: Ablex.

Hintzman, D., Block, R., & Inskeep, N. (1972). Memory for mode of input. *Journal of Verbal Learning and Verbal Behavior, 11,* 741-749.

Horowitz, M., & Berkowitz, A. (1964). Structural advantage of the mechanism of spoken expression as a factor in differences in spoken and written expression. *Perceptual and Motor Skills, 19,* 619-625.

Horowitz, M., & Berkowitz, A. (1967). Listening and reading, speaking and writing: An experimental investigation of differential acquisition and reproduction of memory. *Perceptual and Motor Skills, 24,* 207-215.

Humes, A., Cronnell, B., Lawlor, J., & Gentry, L. (Eds.). (1981). *Moving between practice and research in writing.* Los Alamitos, CA: Southwest Research Laboratory.

Irmscher, W. (1979a). *Teaching expository writing.* New York: Holt, Rinehart, & Winston.

Irmscher, W. (1979b). Writing as a way of learning and developing. *College Composition and Communication, 30,* 240-244.

Jackendoff, R. (1972). *Semantic intrepretation in generative grammar.* Cambridge, MA: MIT Press.

Jarvella, R. (1977). From verbs to sentences: Some experimental studies of predication. In S. Rosenberg, (Ed.), *Sentence production* (pp. 275-306). Hillsdale, NJ: Erlbaum.

Kantor, K., & Rubin, D. (1981). Between speaking and writing: Processes of differentiation. In B. Kroll & R. Vann (Eds.), *Exploring speaking-writing relationships: Connections and contrasts* (pp. 55-81). Urbana, IL: NCTE. National Council of Teachers of English.

Katz, J., & Fodor, J. (1963). The structure of a semantic theory. *Language, 39,* 170-210.

Kinneavy, J. *A theory of discourse.* New York: Norton, 1980. First edition 1970.

Kintsch, W. (1974). *The representation of meaning in memory.* Hillsdale, NJ: Erlbaum.

Kintsch, W. (1977). *Memory and cognition.* New York: Wiley.

Kintsch, W., & Dijk, T. van (1978). Toward a model of text comprehension and production. *Psychological Review, 85,* 363-394.

Kintsch, W., Kozminsky, E., Streby, W., McKoon, G., & Keenan, J. (1975). Comprehension and recall of text as a function of content variables. *Verbal Leaning and Verbal Behavior, 14,* 257-274.

Krauss, R., & Weinheimer, S, (1967). Effects of referent similarity and communication mode on verbal encoding. *Verbal Leaning and Verbal Behavior, 6,* 359-363/

Lemke, A. (1974). Writing as action in living. *College Composition and Communication, 25,* 269-274.

Liberman, I., Shankweiler, D., Liberman, A., Fowler, C., & Fischer, W. (1977). Phonetic segmentation and recoding in the beginning reader. In A.S. Reber & D.L. Scarborough (Eds.), *Toward a psychology of reading* (pp. 207-225). Hillsdale, NJ: Erlbaum.

Linsky, L. (1957). *Referring.* London: Routledge & Kegan Paul.

Lotman, J. (1976). *The analysis of the poetic text.* Ann Arbor: University of Michigan Press.

MacNeilage, P. (1964). Typing errors as clues to serial ordering mechanisms in language behavior. *Language and Speech, 7,* 144-159.

Macrorie, K. (1980). *Searching writing.* New Rochelle Park, NY: Hayden.

Marcel, A. (1980). Phonological awareness and phonological representation. In U. Frith (Ed.), *Cognitive processes in spelling* (pp. 373-403). London: Academic.

Marckwardt, A. (1966). *Linguistics and the teaching of English.* Bloomington: Indiana University Press.

Marsh, G., Desberg, P., & Saterdahl, K. (1981). A comparison of reading and spelling strategies in normal and reading-disabled children. In M. Freedman, J.P. Das, & N. O'Connor (Eds.), *Intelligence and learning* (pp. 363-367). New York: Plenum.

Martlew, M. (Ed.). (1983). *The psychology of writing: A developmental approach.* London: Wiley.

Mason, J. (1976). The roles of orthographic, phonological, and word frequency variables in non-word decisions. *American Educational Research Journal, 13,* 199-206.

Matsuhashi, A. (1981). Pausing and planning: The tempo of written discourse production. *Research in the Teaching of English, 15,* 113-134.

McCawley, J. (1976). Some ideas not to live by. *Die neueren Sprachen, 75,* 151-165.

Mel'čuk, I. & Žolkovskij, A. (1970). Towards a functioning text-meaning model of language. *Linguistics, 57,* 10-47.

Meyer, B.J.F. (1975). *The organization of prose and its effects on memory.* Amsterdam: North-Holland.

Meyer, B.J.F. (1977). What is remembered from prose. In R. Freedle (Ed.), *Discourse production and comprehension* (pp. 307-336). Norwood, NJ: Ablex.

Meyer, B.J.F. (1982). Reading research and the composition teacher. *College Composition and Communication, 33,* 37-49.

Miller, G.A. (1970). Four philosophical problems of psycholinguistics. *Philosophy of Science, 37,* 183-199.

Molino, J. (1971). La connotation. *La linguistique, 7,* 5-30.

Morgan, J. (1975). Some remarks on the nature of sentences. In *Papers from the parasession on functionalism* (pp. 433-449). Chicago: Chicago Linguistic Society.

Morgan, J., & Sellner, M. (1980). Discourse and linguistic theory. In R. Spiro, B. Bruce, & W. Brewer (Eds.), *Theoretical issues in reading comprehension.* (pp. 165-200). Hillsdale, NJ: Erlbaum.

Morton, J. (1970). A functional model for memory. In D. Norman (Ed.), *Models for human memory.* (pp. 203-254). New York: Academic.

Moscovici, S. (1967). Communication processes and the properties of language. In L. Berkowitz (Ed.,). *Advances in experimental psychology (Vol. 3,* pp. 225-270). New York: Academic.

Mosenthal, P., Tamor, L., & Walmsley, S. (Eds.). (1982). *Research in writing: Principles and methods.* New York: Longman.

Murray, D. (1978). Internal revision: A process of discovery. In C. Cooper & L. Odell (Eds.), *Research on composing: Points of departure.* Urbana, IL: National Council of Teachers of English.

Nida, E. (1975). Exploring semantic structures. Munich: Fink.

Norman, D. (1981). Categorization of action slips. *Psychological Review, 88,* 1-15.

Norman, D., & Shallice, T. (1980). *Attention to action: Willed and automatic control of behavior* (CHIP Rep. No. 99). La Jolla, CA: Center for the Study of Human Information Processing.

Nystrand, M. (1977). Language as discovery and exploration. In M. Nystrand (Ed.), *Language as a way of knowing* (pp. 75-105). Toronto: Ontario Institute for Studies in Education.

Nystrand, M. (Ed.). (1982). *What writers know.* New York: Academic Press.

Nystrand, M., & Widerspiel M. (1977). Case study of a personal journal: Notes towards an epistemology of writing. In M. Nystrand (Ed.), *Language as a way of knowing* (pp. 105-121). Toronto: OISE.

Oaken, R., Wiener, M., & Cromer, W. (1971). Identification, organization, and reading comprehension for good and poor readers. *Journal of Educational Psychology, 62,* 71-78.

Odell, L. (1980). Teaching writing by teaching the process of discovery: An interdisciplinary enterprise. In L. Gregg & E. Steinberg (Eds.), *Cognitive processes in writing* (pp. 139–154). Hillsdale, NJ: Erlbaum.

O'Donnell, R. (1974). Syntactic differences between speech and writing. *American Speech, 49*, 102–110.

O'Donnell, R., Griffin, W., & Norris, R. (1967). *Syntax of kindergarten and elementary school children.* Urbana, IL: National Council of Teachers of English.

Olson, D.R. (1977a). From utterance to text: The bias of language in speech and writing. *Harvard Educational Review, 47*, 257–281.

Olson, D.R. (1977b). Oral and written language and the cognitive processes of children. *Journal of Communication, 27*, 10–26.

Osgood, C.E. (1963). On understanding and creating sentences. *American Psychologist, 18*, 735–751.

Papert, S. (1980). *Mindstorms: Computers, children, and powerful ideas.* New York: Basic Books.

Pellegrini, A., & Yawkey, T. (Eds.). (1984). *Development of oral and written language.* Norwood, NJ: Ablex.

Perelman, C., & Olbrechts-Tyteca, L. (1969). *The new rhetoric: A treatise on argumentation.* Notre Dame, In: University of Notre Dame Press.

Perfetti, C., & Lesgold, A. (1979). Coding and comprehension in skilled reading and implications for reading instruction. In L. Resnick & P. Weaver (Eds.), *Theory and practice of early reading* (pp. 57–84). Hillsdale, NJ: Erlbaum.

Petofi, J.S. (1980). Einige Grundfragen der pragmatisch-semantischen Interpretation von Texten. In T.T. Ballmer & W. Kindt (Eds.), *Sprache und Logik* (pp. 146–190). Hamburg, Germany: Buske.

Pottier, B. Vers une sémantique moderne. (1964). *Travaux de linguistique et de littérature, 2*, 107–137.

Quine, W. (1960). *Word and object.* Cambridge: MIT Press.

Rader, R. (1982). Context in written language The case of imaginative fiction. In D. Tannen (Ed.), *Spoken and written language: Exploring orality and literacy* (pp. 185–198). Norwood, NJ: Ablex.

Richek, M. (1977–1978). Readiness skills that predict initial word learning using two different methods of instruction. *Reading Research Quarterly, 13*, 200–222.

Rochester, S. (1973). The significance of pauses in spontaneous speech. *Journal of Psycholinguistic Research, 2*, 51–81.

Rubenstein, H., Lewis, S., & Rubenstein, M. (1971). Evidence for phonemic recoding in visual word recognition. *Journal of Verbal Learning and Verbal Behavior, 10*, 645–657.

Rubin, A.D. (1980). A theoretical taxonomy of the differences between oral and written language. In R. Spiro, B. Bruce, & W. Brewer (Eds.), *Theoretical issues in reading comprehension* (p. 411–438). Hillsdale, NJ: Erlbaum.

Rumelhart, D. (1980). Schemata: The building blocks of cognition. In R. Spiro, B. Bruce, & W. Brewer (Eds.), *Theoretical issues in reading comprehension* (pp. 33–58). Hillsdale, NJ: Erlbaum.

Rumelhart, D., & Norman, D. (1981). *Simulating a skilled typist: A study of skilled cognitive-motor performance.* La Jolla, CA: Center for the Study of Human Information Processing.

Russell, B. (1905). On denoting. *Mind, 14*, 479–493.

Sachs, J. S. (1967). Recognition memory for syntactic and semantic aspects of connected discourse. *Perception and Psychophysics, 2*, 437–442.

Saussure, F. de (1916). *Cours de linguistique générale.* Lausanne, Payot.

Scardamalia, M., Bereiter, C., & Goelman, H. (1982). The role of production factors in writing ability. In M. Nystrand (Ed.), *What writers know* (pp. 173–210). New York: Academic Press.

Schmidt, R. (1975). A schema theory of discrete motor skill learning. *Psychological Review, 82,*. 225–260.

Schmidt, S.J. (1971). *Ästhetizität*. Munich: Bayrischer Schulbuchverag.

Schmidt, S.J. (1982). *Foundations for the empirical study of literature*. Hamburg: Buske.

Searle, J. (1969). *Speech acts*. London: Cambridge University Press.

Shanklin, N. (1982). *Relating reading and writing: Developing a transactional theory of the writing process*. Bloomington: Indiana University Press.

Shaughnessy, M. (1977). *Errors & expectations*. New York: Oxford University Press.

Shiffrin, R., & Schneider, W. (1977). Controlled and automatic human information processing II: Perceptual learning, automatic attending, and a general theory. *Psychological Review, 84,* 127–190.

Skinner, B.F. (1957). *Verbal behavior*. New York: Appleton-Century-Crofts.

Smith, F. (Ed.). (1973). *Psycholinguistics and reading*. New York: Holt, Rinehart, & Winston.

Speer, O., & Lamb, G. (1976). First grade reading ability and fluency in naming verbal symbols. *The Reading Teacher, 29,* 572–576.

Steinmann, M. (1982). Speech-act theory and writing. In M. Nystrand (Ed.), *What writers know* (p. 291–323). New York: Academic Press.

Sticht, T. (1972). Learning by listening. In J.B. Carroll & R. Freedle (Eds.), *Language comprehension and the acquisition of knowledge*. Washington, DC: Winston.

Stockwell, R. (1977). *Foundations of syntactic theory*. Englewood Cliffs, NJ: Prentice-Hall.

Strawson, P. (1950). On referring. *Mind, 59,* 320–344.

Stubbs, M. (1982). *Written language and society*. In M. Nystrand (Ed.), *What writers know* (pp. 31–55). New York: Academic Press.

Tierney, R.J., & LaZansky, J. (1980). *The rights and responsibilities of readers and writers: A contractual agreement* (Reading Education Rep. No. 15). Urbana, IL: Center for the Study of Reading.

Trager, G., & Smith, H. (1951). *An outline of English structure*. Norman, OK: Battenburg.

Ungeheuer, G. (1969). Paraphrase and syntaktische Tiefenstruktur. *Folia Linguistica, 3,* 178–227.

Vachek, J. (1973). *Written language*. The Hague: Mouton.

Venezky, R., & Johnson, D. (1973). Development of two-letter sound patterns in grades one through three. *Journal of Educational Psychology, 64,* 109–115.

Wason, P.C. (1980). Specific thoughts on the writing process. In L. Gregg & E. Steinberg (Eds.), *Cognitive processes in writing* (pp. 129–137). Hillsdale, NJ: Erlbaum.

CHAPTER 2

Composing in a Second Language

Stan Jones
Jacqueline Tetroe

Carleton University and
Carleton Board of Education
Ottawa, Canada

As our descriptive understanding of the normal process of composing in one's native language has increased (as the papers in this volume testify), it has become possible to devise experiments that intervene in the natural process, that disrupt it, in order to test that understanding. Some researchers (e.g., Scardamalia, Bereiter, & Goelman, 1982) have used direct experimental interventions to investigate the nature of the writing process. There are, however, every day situations that might be viewed as natural experiments, as interventions that allow us to look at aspects of the composing process but do not require us to alter that process. Writing in a second language, our particular interest, is such a natural experiment. Second-language writers, unless they are truly bilingual, must deal not only with the usual problems of composing, but also with the problems of doing so in a language in which they are not as competent as they are in their first.

Of particular interest is the interaction between composing skill(s) and second-language competence. Traditionally, instruction in (and theory about) second-language composing has assumed that the most important variable, if not the only important variable, is grammatical accuracy in the second language. As Vivian Zamel (1976) has described it:

> . . . Methodologists have devised particular exercises which while not based on learning grammar *qua* grammar, are in fact based on the grammatical manipulations of models, sentences or passages. For them, writing seems to be synonymous with skill in usage and structure, and the assumption is that these exercises will improve the students' ability to compose. Influenced by audio-

We owe a special debt of gratitude to Lee Rosas-Shapiro who listened to and transcribed every protocol and who prepared all the translations. We also want to thank Aviva Freedman, who read and graciously commented on several drafts of this chapter, and Joan Haire for her assistance in running the experimental sessions. Our research has been supported by the Social Sciences and Humanities Research Council of Canada (Grant 410-81-0800).

lingual methodology, writing is seen as a habit-formed skill, error is to be avoided and correction and revision are to be provided continuously.

With this assumption, texts and courses have focused almost exclusively on the presentation of surface grammatical rules. As such they have followed models of instruction in first-language composing and, with the change of approach in the latter, calls for similar changes in second-language instruction have been made. Thus Taylor (1981), for example, proposed that instruction in second-language composing should focus on the process of writing rather than the product. This call has come, however, with little detailed research on the second-language composing process (but see Zamel, 1983, for a recent case study). We may assume that it is similar in important respects to the first-language process, but we need evidence that such is the case.

This chapter is one of a series of reports we have made on our studies of second-language composing (Tetroe & Jones, 1983, 1984; Jones & Tetroe, 1983; Jones, 1983, 1985). Here we intend to focus, first, on whether the process in the first language is transferred, independent of other factors, to second-language tasks. Our initial finding, in relatively conventional writing situations, was that it did. We also tried a series of experimental manipulations to see if we could create situations that would focus directly on planning. Although these manipulations did have some effect on the process, the effect was the same in both the first and second language, providing further evidence for transfer.

Our second focus, quite parallel to the first, is to report on the way(s) in which the first language is used directly, in planning, while writing in a second language. This, too, pertains to transfer. If, for example, writers consistently set highly abstract goals—trying to take a novel approach to an old topic while writing in the first language but not in the second—one might claim that the difference was simply a result of the lack of vocabulary for such planning in the second. But, if it was discovered that writers typically used the first language when they lacked the vocabulary in the second, then some other explanation would be necessary.

THE TWO ISSUES

The interaction between proficiency in the second language (the degree of knowledge of the second language) and skill in first-language tasks (performance ability) has been little investigated in studies of second-language acquisition.[1] Only recently, in the work of Cummins (1980) has a serious

---

[1] Proficiency has traditionally been used to refer to degree of knowledge of a second language, to what linguists call linguistic or grammatical competence; we will use it in this way. In order to distinguish that from performance ability, we will call the latter skill or ability. The two are closely related, both conceptually and observationally, but it is useful to keep them separate in order to ask questions about their relationship, as we wish to do.

theory of first- and second-language interaction been proposed. Cummins, in research with school-age children, found that a certain minimum of proficiency in the first language is required for successful performance in the second. But his work says little about how that interaction might take place. It also is principally a theory of content, rather than process; Cummins simply identified a level of first-language ability that is necessary for successful acquisition and performance in the second. He has little to say about how the strategies of second-language users are affected by their first-language competence.

It is obvious, we assume, that the level of performance in the second language will be less than that in the first (save for true bilinguals). But, because research on the question has only just begun (Faerch & Kasper, 1983), no one knows whether or not the strategies people have for using their language competence will differ systematically from first to second language or what factors might affect the difference if they are not the same. Raupach (1980) did find that the pattern of pauses in the speech of his subjects was similar in both their first language (L1) and their second language (L2). (The subjects were native speakers of French and of German learning German and French, respectively, as a second language). In particular, he found that individuals who deviated from the norm in L1 deviated in the same way from the norm in the L2. However, he did not report on the second-language proficiency of the subjects, and so, we cannot assess the interaction between strategy and proficiency.

In the case of composing it might be that second-language writers with effective strategies are able to use those strategies to compensate for the limitations imposed by their imperfect knowledge of the language. We would expect to find little difference between the composing process in the first and second language in this case. At the other extreme, those with poor strategies may find that the burden of second-language composing imposes such additional constraints that their second-language processes are markedly different from those in the first. Or composing strategies may interact with second-language fluency such that even good composers cannot overcome low second-language proficiency and poor composers are not helped when their second-language competence improves. Finally, it may be that all second-language composers are affected in the same way regardless of first-language processes. We can summarize these possible outcomes as the following: (1) Good first language strategies are immune to second-language deficiencies, but poor ones are not; (2) good and poor strategies are both affected, negatively, by the second-language problems; and (3) both good and poor strategies carry over, with little change, to the second-language task.

Our data suggest that, within the limited range of skill represented by our subjects, it is the latter that is the most likely of these outcomes. That is not to say that the strategies will be as effective in the second language as in the first, but that they will be the same strategies. Our answer to this first issue will be that the current best bet is that skills do transfer, largely intact.

We cannot be as definitive about the second issue, how writers can directly use the first language, but we did direct our research to the following questions: What strategies do they use to meet the additional challenge of writing in a second language? Do they do most of the cognitive work in their first language, using the second only to translate text generated in the first? Is the first language the language of high-level planning, whereas the second is used for all text generation? Or is the first used at all in second-language composing? We found, as might be expected, that there was considerable variation, both between individuals and within individuals from time to time. Although we would like to be able to point to the factors that determine how, and when, the first language will be used, our data is not extensive enough to support more than informed guesses.

STUDIES OF TRANSFER OF SKILL

The role of first-language knowledge in the acquisition and, more particularly, in the use of a second-language has been one of the central issues in research on second-language learning. Traditionally, however, this transfer of first language (L1) patterns, whether phonological, syntactic (Lado, 1957; Wardhaugh, 1970), or rhetorical (Kaplan, 1972) has been investigated as interference, as a source of errors in second-language performance. Although the standard theory allows for transfer to be facilitative as well, this aspect has seldom been systematically explored (but see Gass, 1979).

Recently, though, researchers interested in the processes of language performance, especially in reading and in writing, have been asking whether language skill (as opposed to language competence) transfers and whether first-language expertise can facilitate L2 performance and acquisition. That is, whether a good reader can overcome low proficiency in the second language simply because his strategies compensate for lack of L2 knowledge. Cziko (1978), for example, found that performance on first-language reading tasks correlates strongly with second-language reading scores for children in French immersion classes.[2] In studies concerned more directly with process, Hosenfeld (1977) found that poor L2 readers employed the

---

[2] Exactly which way the transfer works for these immersion students is an interesting question. Although their first language is English, the first instruction in reading for most of them was in French.

same strategies that characterized poor L1 readers and, conversely, that good L2 readers did the same things as good L1 readers. Unfortunately, she did not compare L1 and L2 reading within the same group of subjects.

Clarke (1979) did compare processes, indirectly, in the first- and second-language reading of his subjects. He found that the best readers in the first language, as measured by scores on a cloze test, were the best readers in the second as well. His evidence for process comes from the type of errors the subjects made in the cloze test. In the first language, the good readers tended to preserve semantic readings at the expense of grammaticality, whereas the poorer ones were more likely to maintain syntactic form but miss on the global meaning. Although the good readers were better at preserving both meaning and syntax in the second language (the poor readers were likely to be wrong on both, the good readers only on one or the other), the difference between the two groups was less than in the first language. Clarke did not interview his subjects about their responses on the cloze test and so we do not know if the poorer readers were attempting to maintain grammaticality in the second language and failing because their knowledge of the language was insufficient, or whether they had adopted some other strategy.

Jones (1982) found that the syntactic and rhetorical factors—T-unit, paragraph boundaries, and abstractness of topic—that affected pause times in Matsuhashi's study (1981) of first-language writers worked the same way in the second-language composing of his L2 subjects. There were individual differences in how these factors affected pause times (one writer simply used much more time than the others) but the patterns discovered by Matsuhashi were also found in this group. No data on first-language composing is available for these subjects, however.

There have been two studies that do compare L1 and L2 composing in the same subjects, but they have reported contradictory results. When Chelala (1981) looked at the first- and the second-language composing process of two subjects, both native speakers of Spanish writing in English, she found that not all the components of the first-language process appeared in the second language. In particular, her subjects did less reviewing and revising while writing in the L2. She also reports that the use of Spanish while composing in English (she used a think-aloud protocol technique) did not facilitate L2 composing. As there were few intersubject differences in L1 composing, Chelala was unable to relate differences in L2 processes to differences in L1 process. It should be noted that when she claimed there were differences, these were differences of quantity, not pattern.

On the other hand, Nancy Lay (1982, 1983) in her studies of native speakers of Chinese writing in English found that use of the first language (again determined from think-aloud protocols) did facilitate L2 writing for her subjects. Specifically, better compositions were produced by subjects who had more L1/L2 switches in the protocol. Unfortunately Lay did not measure the relative amounts of L1 and L2 use nor did she report whether there was any pattern to the switches, making her findings difficult to interpret. She did find that some of her subjects preferred to use Chinese characters when making planning notes while composing in English. These students appeared to have well-developed strategies for employing the structure of the characters to evoke new images that they could utilize for invention (somewhat as in synectics). (This is probably a finding that is relevant only with Chinese as the L1 and not one that is generalizable.)

It is not altogether clear why Lay and Chelala found different effects for the use of L1 in second-language composing. There may have been differences in English proficiency, in first-language composing skill, or even in instructions given to subjects. Because Chelala had only two subjects, who were very similar, she may not have had the variation across subjects necessary to detect what was significantly similar and what was significantly different between L1 and L2. The difference in results may also be due to the subjects' own assumptions about the appropriateness of using the first language while performing second-language tasks; many learners are taught that it is incorrect, even harmful, to do so. Finally, it may be that the difference in the findings is due to the fact that the native language of Chelala's subjects was Spanish whereas that of Lay's was Chinese.

The picture that emerges from these studies comparing L1 and L2 production and comprehension processes is that when there is a range of skills in the first language represented there seems to be evidence for transfer, but none of the studies could be said to have offered strong arguments for this. Further, it appears that studies that count quantity as the principle criterion for similarity find cross-language differences, whereas those who look for patterns, or quality, find similarities.

FOCUS OF THE STUDY

In our research on L1 versus L2 composing processes, we focused on planning strategies because we see planning as a critical high-level composing activity. Although Chelala and Lay both looked at aspects of planning, neither of them systematically investigated in detail the patterns of L1 and L2 planning. In our study of six adults learning English as a second language we were particularly interested in the quality of the planning each subject exhibited in his or her first and second language, with the evidence to be derived principally from think-aloud protocols. Because we needed to know the content of the plan, when particular elements entered the plan, and whether any part of the plan was modified and, if so, when it was modified, we required the sort of record provided by think-aloud protocols. Although useful, reliable data on the location of pauses for planning can be obtained from videotape records (Jones, 1982), that data doesn't tell us about the content of the plan. (We discuss our use of this research technique below.)

We hypothesized that there would be a relation between the pattern of planning in the two languages, but that possibly the quality and certainly the quantity of planning in the second would be less than in the first. In other words, the best planner in the first language would likely be best in the second as well, but his or her planning in English would not be as extensive and relevant as that in Spanish. We had no a priori assumptions about how much decrease in planning there would be or about whether the decrease would be uniform across first-language proficiencies.

In order to have some means of comparing planning from one task to another we needed some scale or hierarchy that we could use to evaluate and compare each subject.[3] As the setting of goals is a crucial element of planning as we define it, we characterized planning in terms of the kind of implicit or explicit goals that the subject was working with. In particular, we established the following hierarchy of goals:

- Simple point list of topics
- Gist of paper
- List/array of gist units
- Manipulation of genre elements
- Intentions with respect to the whole text

It is worthwhile examining each of these in some detail.

The most rudimentary, most concrete kind of goal-setting is the creation of a point list of content to be incorporated without rearrangement or deletion in the final text. This list need not be created before writing begins, but may be constructed on-line during the writing of the text. This frequently happens when writers write to a topic. Bereiter and Scardamalia (1982) have identified this kind of planning as "knowledge-telling." There is no real goal-setting involved once the specific form of the topic has been established; a writer simply decides whether a given content item fits the topic or not as he or she progresses through the text.

At a somewhat more abstract level, the goal may simply be the gist of the paper, without any specific plans as to how to implement that goal. A writer might decide, for example, to write about how difficult English is to learn when given the assignment "What has made it most difficult for you to adapt to Canada?" and may express that goal only as:

---

[3] The hierarchy discussed in this section has some of its seeds in Bereiter and Scardamalia (1982) but has been expanded by the authors.

> I thought that English was a language that could be learnt faster, but it has not been so easy. And I think that I will write the article with respect to this.[4] (212S)

The specific points that this writer made about the difficulty of learning English were considered only as he came to them and the paper he wrote, even though not planned as a list, reads like one.

A more abstract form of planning, though still topic oriented, involves the creation of a list or array of gist units, words or phrases that summarize a number of specific content items. This list/array may be rearranged and revised prior to, or during the generation of, the final text. One of our writers typically generated such lists for her Spanish compositions. When asked to write in Spanish about her adjustment to Canada she wrote a page of ideas before she started on the text. For example (these are literal translations from the Spanish original):

> to get used to the idea that I am alone in a country where everything is different (language, customs, climate, etc.)
> more than different things with respect to mine. The things that I have had to do, since I am here, have been different from those that I was used to in my country. (242S text)

In this case the text is rearranged, though not dramatically so:

> I say this because I have had to do things which I was not used to doing. These things, I do not consider difficult on the whole. They are simply different and obviously it takes me time to adapt to them. (242S text)

(Unfortunately, our translation tends to reduce the difference between the plan and the actual text.)[5]

---

[4] In addition to having to code the differences between thinking, writing, and reading in our transcription, we also must code the language used. We considered using the original language in the transcription, but we felt that that would have made the data less accessible to those readers not fluent in Spanish. Instead we opted to have the Spanish sections of the protocols of English sessions typeset in a different (sans-serif) typeface. **Boldface** is used to mark where the subject is reading and *italics* mark the places where the subject is writing. The numbers in parentheses after an example code the source; the first number is the paper within the session; the second is the subject, and the third the session, "E" indicates the composition was in English and "S" that it was in Spanish. Thus 212S marks the second paper written by subject 1 in the second session and the paper was written in Spanish.

[5] The notes in the original read:

- *a costumbrarme a la idea de que estoy sola, en un pais donde todo es diferente (lenguaje, costumbres, clima, etc.)*
- *mas que diferentes las cosas de esta pais con respecto al mio. Han sido diferentes las cosas que he tenido que hacer des de que estoy aqul a las cosas a las coales estaba habituada cuando vivias en mi pais.*

whereas the text reads:

. . . porque he tenido que hacer cosas a las cuales no estaba habituada. Estas cosas en

A still more abstract level involved the manipulation of abstract genre elements. At such a level a writer may decide what parts of the text to put where:

So first I'll do the introduction, then the pro side, then the con side. (353S)

Such writers can work with genre elements such as *introduction, pro,* and *con* in trying to visualize the form and content of the finished text.

These genre element plans may serve a number of functions. They may be used to facilitate composing by dividing the task into workable units (a writer cannot easily organize the pro side and the con side at the same time). They may also be used to organize the text to satisfy a more global intent. Writer #5 created the following plan, in order to end his text with the sentence: "This is a good point, but I still think the reasons from the other side of the argument are more important."

Now I have put my point of view about the negative things . . . or the argument, the other side of the argument, that the negative things of the woman work outside, and then I have to put the benefits of women working outside and then I decide that those benefits, from women working outside are a good point but that I continue to think that the reasons that I gave first are more important. (353S)

At the most abstract level, writers create global plans that relate to their intentions vis à vis the text as a whole, including the desired effect on the reader. This kind of goal may be as specific as the desire to convince the instructor to do something to improve the English course or as vague as the hope to think of a novel angle for a tired topic.

Although we consider this to be a hierarchy, we believe that the more abstract levels incorporate rather than supersede the less abstract ones. For our argument here it is important to note that many adults regularly operate at a relatively elementary level when writing in their first language. Flower and Hayes (1980) have similarly noted that a major difference between what they term "expert" and "novice" adult writers is that the former, but not the latter, set both relatively concrete and relatively abstract goals both before and during writing. Furthermore, experts, but not novices, assess their progress through the composing process by evaluating their texts in terms of the goals that they have set, rather than in terms of fitting the topic, a strategy employed by novices.

When we evaluated the composing behavior of our subjects using this goal-setting hierarchy our data showed quite clearly that these behaviors do transfer. Writers who set abstract goals in their first language tend to do so in the second language as well. Thus, we think our data is strong

---

su majoria no los considero difíciles. Simplamente, diferentes y absiamente eleva tiempo adaptane a ellas.

evidence in favor of inter-language transfer of abstract language performance strategies.

SUBJECTS AND METHODOLOGY

Our subjects were six Spanish-speaking students enrolled in a nine-month
intensive English-as-a-Second-Language (ESL) program. All were studying
English in order to enter graduate schools in North America; their undergraduate degrees were from universities in their home country (Venezuela).
The students' proficiency at the start of the program in October ranged
from Carroll's Extremely Limited User (Band 3) to the upper level of the
Marginal User (Band 4) group (Carroll, 1980).[6]

At the end of the study, in late April, the lowest had progressed to the
upper part of the Marginal User Band while the two best had reached the
Competent User level (Band 6) though at the lowest level (see Table 1). As
another measure of their competence, this table gives their scores on the
standardized Test of English as a Foreign Language (TOEFL). In many
universities in the United States a score of 500 is accepted for admissions;
most Canadian universities require 550 (ETS, 1978). Thus, none of our
subjects were true beginners when we began the study, though they all had

---

[6] Although only a few readers may be familiar with Carroll's system, the descriptions of
each Band make this scale informative even for those with no experience with second language
students.

Band	General Assessment Scale
9	*Expert user:* Communicates with authority, accuracy, and style. Completely at home in idiomatic and specialist English.
8	*Very good user:* Presentation of subject clear and logical with fair style and appreciation of attitudinal markers. Often approaching bilingual competence.
7	*Good user:* Would cope in most situations in an English-speaking environment. Occasional slips and restrictions of language will not impede communication.
6	*Competent user:* Although coping well in most situations he is likely to meet, is somewhat deficient in fluency and accuracy and will have occasional misunderstandings or significant errors.
5	*Modest user:* Although manages in general to communicate, often uses inaccurate or inappropriate language.
4	*Marginal user:* Lacking in style, fluency, and accuracy, is not easy to communicate with; accent and usage cause misunderstandings. Generally can get by without serious breakdowns.
3	*Extremely limited user:* Does not have a working knowledge of the language for day-to-day purposes, but better than an absolute beginner. Neither productive or receptive skills allow continuous communication.
2	*Intermittent user:* Performance well below level of day-to-day knowledge of the language. Communication occurs only sporadically.
1/0	*Non-user:* May not even recognize with certainty what language is being used.

Table 1. Some measures of English proficiency for subjects
and changes over seven months

Subject	Carroll Band November	TOEFL January	TOEFL March	Carroll Band May
1. male	3+	377	423	4+
2. female	4	467	477	5
3. female	3	353	380	4+
4. female	4+	433	513	6−
5. male	3+	500	523	6−
6. female	3	383	407	4+

some difficulty in English. By the end, several had reached a level typical of many foreign students at the start of their studies in an English-speaking university and the others were approaching that level.

Each of the subjects wrote two pieces in English and one in Spanish in November. In February they again wrote two essays in English and one in Spanish. In all six of these writing sessions the subjects were given only the topics (which had been devised by the experimenters). The topics for these tasks, which we will refer to as conventional writing tasks, are given in Table 2.[7]

Table 2. Topics used in conventional writing sessions

Language	Assignment

November Topics
English Write about an experience where something went wrong.
Spanish Tell about the celebration of a birthday or holiday.
English Compare where you live in Ottawa (your house, your apartment, or your room) with where you lived in Venezuela.

February Topics
English Write about an event in early Canadian history that would be of interest to Venezuelan students. (Be sure to include why this would be of interest.)[8]
Spanish Describe the most difficult adjustment that you have had to make living in Canada. (Do not write about the climate.)
English What is the most important difference between Canadian and Venezuelan society?

In the next set of sessions, in April, the students were assigned writing

---

[7] We have chosen "conventional" largely because the other names we tried seemed even worse. The tasks are certainly conventional in the sense that they are the kind of writing task usually set for ESL students in their writing courses or on English-proficiency tests.

[8] The subjects were taking a course in Canadian history as part of their English program at this time. The topics for the Spanish sessions were presented in Spanish, of course.

Table 3. Ending sentences and topics used in April

Narrative-ending tasks (Numbers mark constraints)

Melissa: And that is how Melissa came to be at the (1) wrong laundromat, (2) in a strange city, (3) with a million dollars (4) in her laundry bag and (5) a trail of (6) angry people behind her.

Mandria: So you see, Mandria was not only (1) mean, she was (2) dangerous and (3) clever as well, and it took a (4) tragedy to (5) get her out of the house and (6) back to where she belonged.

Argument-ending tasks (Topic in parenthesis)

Other side: This is a good point, but I still think the reasons from the other side of the argument are more important. (Should women work outside the home.)

Main point: In conclusion, my position depends on one main point, and that point is [STUDENT FILLS IN POINT.]. (Should children be allowed to choose the subjects they will study.)

tasks that were designed to produce particular kinds of planning behavior. In these sessions students were given the final sentence of the paper they were to write (see Table 3). Previous experience with similarly constructed tasks (Tetroe, Bereiter, & Scardamalia, 1981) demonstrated that this task manipulation does affect the planning behavior of the writers. We were particularly interested in whether this manipulation would have the same effect in both languages. We will refer to these sessions as the structured-task sessions.

In the November sessions think-aloud protocols were collected for the Spanish piece, but not for the two English ones due to the limited English proficiency of the subjects. Although we do not believe that verbal protocols in general affect writing, we were concerned that with students at such a low level of proficiency in English the mere act of speaking in English required such resources that interference was a serious problem. We were probably too cautious because we found that the even the lowest students had no real difficulties when we asked them to provide think-aloud reports in English in the February sessions. For all three tasks in this session, the two English ones and the single Spanish one, we collected think-aloud protocols from all six subjects.

In the four (two English and two Spanish) structured-task assignments in April, think-aloud protocols were also collected for all the papers. (In sessions in May they completed two revision tasks, but we will not report on these here.)

The instructions to the subjects at each session were simple. They were asked only to write on the topic and to say aloud whatever came into their thoughts as they wrote. Before the February sessions each subject saw a videotape of a writer modeling the think-aloud technique; this demonstration tape contained examples of different types of planning, but the subjects were not directed to notice anything particular about the tape. No special instructions about planning, audience, or rhetorical task were provided. It was necessary to answer some questions about the ending-sentence task the first time it was presented, but the subjects did not have questions at later sessions. Three of the subjects had the ending-sentence task in Spanish first and they did not have questions any different than the three whose first ending-sentence task was in English.

The quality of the papers, rated by trained raters who were experienced ESL or Spanish teachers using a primary-trait scoring system, are recorded in Tables 4A and 4B. This system was designed to be sensitive to the rhetorical demands of the task (narrative vs. argument) and the topic and to suspend judgments based on grammaticality in favor of judgments based on content.

Although the topics used in February were more abstract than those used in November, this did not seem to affect either the type of planning (comparing only the two Spanish sessions, of course, as we do not have this kind of data on the November English sessions) or the quality of the compositions (Tables 4A & 4B). Only subject #3 had a lower primary-trait score on her February Spanish composition than on the November one; for the others the rating improved or remained the same. The primary-trait scores also rose for the English compositions between November and February (Table 4A), but this may due largely to improved English proficiency.

RESULTS FROM THE CONVENTIONAL WRITING TASKS

In the conventional writing tasks (November and February) most subjects did little planning in either language. All but one, however, did plan at least one gist unit before beginning to write, typically the gist of the first paragraph. The remainder of their texts, though, were written with little comment and little evidence of extensive planning.

For example, writer #1 begins an English essay on Canadian history with this brief planning segment:

> Well, let's see, what we write here for this essay . . . I think that I should start by the conquest . . . the history of Canada is a bit different with respect to ours but . . . we will try to write something *I think that* (112E)

At the next session, writing in Spanish about the most difficult adjustment he had to make in Canada, he makes the following plan:

> that I have had to make to live in Canada . . . How could the English program have made this this adjustment easier for you . . . when I decided to come study in Canada I thought that English was a language that could be learned

Table 4A. Primary trait ratings of *English* compositions: Scale 0 (low) to 9 (high). Average of two raters.

| | Subject | | | | | |
Paper	1	2	3	4	5	6
Conventional tasks						
Nov. 1	1.5	2.5	1.5	2	2.5	1
Nov. 3	2	2.5	1	4	2.5	1.5
Feb. 1	2	3	2	4	5.5	2
Feb. 3	3	2.5	4.5	4.5	4.5	2
Structured tasks						
Narrative	2		4	2.5	4	3.5
Argument	2.5		2.5	4	5.5	5.5

Table 4B. Primary trait ratings of *Spanish* compositions: Scale 0 (low) to 9 (high). Average of two raters.

| | Subject | | | | | |
Paper	1	2	3	4	5	6
Conventional tasks						
Nov. 2	3	2.5	4	4.5	2.5	2.5
Feb. 2	6	4.5	3	4.5	4.5	3
Structured tasks						
Narrative	5		3.5	6.5	5	2.5
Argument	3.5		5	7	4.5	4

quickly, but it has not been easy. And I think that I will write this article with respect to this . . . easier . . . Canada . . . *Canada es un himoso pais* (212S)

Writer #4 typically made more detailed, although not more abstract, plans before writing. In the case of the essay on Canadian history she made a page of notes before writing the first line of her text. The writing, for the most part though, was simply converting these notes into proper sentential form. Just as there was little difference between the type of planning writer #1 did in English and Spanish, so too what writer #4 did as she wrote in Spanish was very much like her work in English. As she prepared to write in Spanish about her difficulties in adjusting to Canada, she made a page of notes which were then transformed, mostly by simply converting them to full sentences, into connected text.

Of the other four subjects, writer #3 did little planning in either language while #2, #5, and #6 planned much like #1.

In sum, we found that simply given a topic, the planning process, par-

Table 5. Number of segments other than text-generation by principle type and primary language, for each of the two conventional *English* compositions, February tasks.

Subject	Planning		Rereading		Metacomments		Evaluation	
	English	Spanish	English	Spanish	English	Spanish	English	Spanish
1	0	4	3	0	0	6	0	6
	1	2	1	0	0	0	0	1
2	2	5	0	0	0	7	0	5
	3	1	0	0	0	1	1	3
4	7	0	2	0	5	0	1	0
	9	0	1	0	0	0	4	0
5	5	0	2	0	1	0	3	0
	3	0	3	0	3	0	4	0
6	0	1	1	0	0	1	0	1
	0	4	0	0	0	1	0	3

ticularly the level of abstraction of that process, was the same in both languages. From the think-aloud protocols for the two Spanish conventional writing tasks (November and February) and from the two English conventional tasks (early and late February) for which there are such protocols (none was collected for the two November English tasks) we can identify the prewriting planning strategies of the six writers as follows:

> *Writer #1:* gist of first paragraph and sense of whole essay
> *Writer #2:* gist of first paragraph
> *Writer #3:* nothing (writes first sentence immediately)
> *Writer #4: point form notes for whole essay*
> *Writer #5:* gist of first paragraph and sense of whole essay
> *Writer #6:* gist unit to start writing with (but less than first paragraph)

Our analysis of this verbal protocol data indicated that our subjects were transferring composing patterns, answering our first question, but we were also interested in how they transferred these patterns, whether they did so by doing the goal-setting in Spanish and the text-generation in English or by some other process. Table 5 shows the type and principal language of the major segment,[9] other than text generation, of the two English compositions for all six subjects.

As the excerpt from writer #1's protocol above indicates, he did much of his prewriting planning for the English compositions in Spanish. In fact, outside of text-generation and rereading this writer had only one segment

---

[9] Although what we refer to as segments are similar to what Flower and Hayes (1981) have identified as episodes, we have chosen our own term because the segments are very short and are identified by topic. For example, a single word-search is marked as a segment in our analysis.

in these two English sessions that was not in Spanish. Writer #4 had the opposite pattern. Not a single major segment in her protocols of the English sessions was in Spanish. That is not to say that she never relied on Spanish, but she did so only when the English lexical items proved to be problematic, and even in these cases Spanish did not predominate:

> you can, you can wait a minute you can . . . you can be a . . . you can be a cult . . . a cultured person is what I want to say but I don't know how it is said in English . . . a cultured person . . . cult cultured a cult person hmm (342E)

Like #4, writer #5 had no major segments conducted entirely in Spanish, but many of the non-text-generation segments contained Spanish portions, particularly when he made meta-comments:[10]

> *the Canadian society has many ethnic* ethnic well I made a mistake again ethnic origines origines how do you say plural origines origines . . . oh no . . . I am going to put source [prettier] source because . . . this country has grown *has grown by immigration.* (352E)

Writer #6 is much like #1 in that almost all her planning while writing in English was done in Spanish. However, she made even greater use of her first language because she often, though by no means in all cases, generated a sentence or phrase in Spanish before writing its English equivalent. For example,

> *There are* there are there there are *difference* there are difference *in a party* with respect to a party in a party in a party because when when I I I am when I am when I am invited invited and when *was* when I was I was *invited* (362E)

The sixth writer, #3, does not appear in Table 5 because she did virtually no planning that is recorded in the think-aloud aside from that directly involved in text generation. Although it is difficult to believe that she did no planning at all, there are no lengthy pauses on the tape which might indicate that she was planning but not verbalizing.

It is of interest that the writers who did the most extensive planning while writing in English, did so in English, while those who did only a little did much of that little in Spanish. The two extensive planners were the most proficient in English, which may explain why they planned in the second language. But if the others, with lower English proficiency, did

---

[10] By meta-comments we mean those segments in which the writer is not focusing on the content of the paper, but on the process or some other aspect of the essay. Thus writer #5's observation here that he has made a mistake and writer #1's frequent comments (in the February sessions) on his low proficiency are both examples of meta-comments.

Table 6.   Language each subject used for each ending-sentence task.

Subject	Topic			
	Melissa	Mandria	Other side	Main point
1	English	Spanish	Spanish	English
3	Spanish	English	English	Spanish
4	English	Spanish	Spanish	English
5	Spanish	English	English	Spanish
6	Spanish	English	English	Spanish

their planning in Spanish, we cannot then claim that their limited proficiency prevented them from doing more extensive planning, because these writers could have done high-level planning in Spanish just as they did the rather low-level planning that characterizes their principle strategy. Thus it cannot be simply low proficiency in English that inhibits planning in second-language composing. This is further evidence that planning patterns in second-language composing are transferred from the patterns in the first language. The failure to plan at a more abstract level in the second language, then, is not attributable simply to low proficiency in that language.

ENDING-SENTENCE INTERVENTION

Because, as Table 5 shows, the subjects demonstrated little planning at any level of abstraction in either language, we assigned a set of tasks that compelled them to plan, if they could. Tetroe, Bereiter, and Scardamalia (1981) have shown that giving subjects a problematic ending sentence to write toward was successful in inducing means–ends planning. During sessions in March, the subjects were given two narrative and two argumentative tasks of this type. The ending sentences and topics are given in Table 3. (Although all the topics are given in English, if the paper was to be written in Spanish, the topic was presented in Spanish.) The narrative tasks each contain six constraints (or plot components) that must be integrated in the story if the given sentence is to be a sensible conclusion to it.

The arguments do not have such countable elements and the sentence will fit a number of topics; the topic we assigned is given in the table. Each subject wrote one paper of each type (narrative and argument) in each language, with the topics crossed with language. The language each subject was assigned for each topic is given in Table 6. (Subject #2 dropped out of the study at this point.)

In these tasks there was an impressive increase in the amount of planning that the subjects engaged in, compared to the conventional writing tasks. One of the most difficult aspects of writing is setting clear goals that will structure the paper. The ending sentence tasks provide readymade goals. The narrative sentences provide concrete goals in the form of gist units (money in a laundry bag), whereas the argument sentences provide more abstract goals, one at the level of genre elements (other side) and the other (main point) at the global intention level. The increase in the amount of planning, in both languages, that these tasks produced tells us that the students can, in fact, plan in more complex ways than they normally do if they are given goals to work with. They know how to plan when told what to plan for; what they appear to have trouble doing is deciding what to plan for.

Throughout these tasks all but one of the subjects spent a considerable amount of time grappling with the ending-sentence goals prior to writing (#3 continued to do little planning). Subject #1 planned only the gist of his first paragraph while working on the conventional tasks in both languages, but in the ending-sentence tasks he worked at a a higher level, as this example from his English narrative protocol illustrates:

> Ok and **that is how Melissa,** Melissa is the name of a woman **came to be in the wrong laundromat to be in the wrong laundro laundromat,** I know laundry is a place but laundromat is another name for laundry. **In a strange city . . . a million dollars in her laundry bag . . . and a trail . . . of angry . . . people . . . behind her** this, this is an essay it is a story **in a strange city . . . with a million dollars in her laundry bag . . . and a trail of angry people behind her . . . and that, and that is . . . came to be with a million dollars in her laundry bag, and a trail of angry people behind her. . . .** wow . . . I suppose that is very confused, because, if she has . . . million dollars in her laundry bag and a trail of angry people behind her wow wow wow . . . Melissa live in a small town . . . Melissa is very rich, very wealth people, very wealth person .. .but I don't understand in a strange city with a million dollars in her laundry bag . . . and a trail of angry people behind her . . . ok my plan is the following: I think that this is a young woman who had a lot of money, but who lived in a really small town. In in the countryside. She was able to have a lot of money due to her parents' inheritance. She thought of putting it, depositing it in a bank, but she had never gone to such a big city. (113E)

He makes, and announces, a similarly detailed plan for the Mandria story, which he wrote in Spanish.

Writer #5 also developed this sort of detailed plan in both languages. Writer #6 does not create as much detail in her English plan as she does in the Spanish one, but she does set out her position and the support for it in advance of text generation:

> Should women work outside? Of course they could ( ) married or not married . . . I'll put married could women work and why? They would have change **money** . . . after I speak of the money I'll speak of the . . . they can

reach with the money as a consequence a status . . . a social position . . . help
her parents (363E)

Note that while this essay was written in English, this entire planning segment was in Spanish. In this writer's case, the two Spanish tasks have plans
that are more detailed, and more to the point, than those for the two
English ones, even though the planning for all four was done in Spanish.

Writer #4 made lengthy, though primarily content-item-oriented, plans
for these tasks, as she did during conventional tasks. In the argument tasks
she did work on a point of view, though it was not extensively worked out,
something she had not done in the earlier sessions where she had been
content to be on-topic, even in her Spanish compositions. More importantly, she continued to evaluate her developing text against her goals.

In summary, the ending-sentence intervention demonstrates that the
planning behavior of second-language writers is affected by other factors
as well as the lack of linguistic proficiency. In particular, these subjects
had difficulties setting goals on their own and this constrained their performance. When provided with goal-like constraints their planning
changed, in ways we would like to consider improvements, in both the first
and the second language.

NARRATIVE CONSTRAINTS

Because the narrative tasks had a discrete number of constraints, we can
use the number integrated as an indication of the writers' success in meeting the goals we provided. That means we are able to make numerical
comparisons of their performance in the two languages. We found that
success at meeting the constraints was uniformly poorer in the second language than in the first; they met two fewer constraints in English than in
Spanish. Raters who had received training in identifying the constraints
evaluated each composition for the integration of each of the six constraints. The success of each of the subjects is recorded in Table 7. (Half
scores occurred when the raters differed on the number successfully integrated.)

The lower success rate in English appears to be due to plans that were
not as fully developed, to a failure to keep track of the plan during composing, and, most commonly, to an inability to add to the plan on-line
while writing in English. For example, in his English narrative about Melissa, subject #1 never planned how Melissa got a trail of people behind her
or why they were angry, and these never end up in the story. He spends
no more time planning for Mandria in Spanish, and his plan is less detailed, but he is able to add to it to include more of the constraints as he
develops the text.

Table 7. Number of constraints (out of 6) integrated in narrative. (Average of two judges)

Subject	English	Spanish
1	2.5	4
3	1.5	4
4	4	5.5
5	4	6
6	2.5	3.5

Writer #4 is particularly good at this on-line monitoring, finding constraints that even we had not noticed. For example, in her English story about Melissa #4 stops at one point to rework the text to make it clear that it was Melissa's laundry bag and not someone else's that had the money. However, she does not include in her plan any trail of angry people.

We can conclude that there is some decrease in performance simply due to the fact that it is in a second language, that working in an unfamiliar language does take up cognitive capacity that would be used for other tasks, such as monitoring and revising the plan, in first-language composing. In the range of proficiencies represented in this study (there were no really fluent subjects) an increase in second-language proficiency does not seem to free up cognitive space; the two most fluent subjects suffered the same sort of decrease in performance as the poorer ones.

It is essential to note that those that we had identified as the more abstract planners in the conventional writing tasks were the more abstract planners in this task as well. Further, more of the ending-sentence constraints were included by the writers who planned at a more abstract level. Finally, these generalizations apply equally to first- and second-language tasks, again providing evidence that strategies of this kind transfer from the first to the second language.

We not only found changes in planning behavior, but also found that we had altered the pattern of first-language use in second-language composing. Because we wanted to know if the subjects thought in Spanish while writing in English and whether there were intersubject differences in the use of Spanish, we counted the number of lines of the protocol transcript in each language. Because the subjects differed in total time on each task, a percent measure is appropriate for comparisons between subjects and over time.

For the two subjects (#1 and #6) who had used considerable Spanish during the planning of their two English February conventional writing tasks there was a noticeable reduction in the amount of first-language use

Table 8.   Percentage of first language during second-
language composing.

Subject	Free writing		Ending sentence	
	Canadian History	Country Contrast	Narrative	Argument
1	45%	37%	3%	2%
2	55%	37%	a	a
4	6%	1%	<1%	1%
5	1%	10%	<1%	19%
6	55%	54%	18%	32%

ᵃ Subject #2 did not complete these tasks.

in the second-language tasks. (Subjects #4 and #5 used little Spanish in the earlier English tasks.) The data in Table 8 is a measure of the percent of the protocol transcription lines by language.

This change probably is due to the structure-providing feature of the ending-sentence tasks. Because the subjects now had concrete English goals to work with, they formulated the task in English. Previously, in the conventional tasks, they had no goals to speak of, and hence drifted aimlessly along a comfortable path of familiar associations in their native language. In these ending-sentence protocols, Spanish continues to be used for meta-comments and for abstract, rhetorical goal-setting.

The use of Spanish by subject #5 is a good example. Whenever his planning included references to rhetorical or organizational details that were not directly related to content items, he used Spanish, as these excerpts from the Other side topic (Table 4A) written in English indicate:

> O.K. I have put here the argument which is supposedly my opinion, but upon which I shall support this last notion. . . . . I am writing now what I think that are my counterarguments . . . gives to refute the first argument I put forth . . . well . . . I made first a short introduction, no? o.k. and then I put as an argument that's why women shouldn't . . . and now I am putting the counterargument (353E)

It is unlikely that any of the subjects would have learned the vocabulary of English rhetoric (as we noted, ESL composition instruction is all too frequently concerned simply with sentence structure), and thus would have had to use Spanish for this sort of rhetorical planning.

The reduction in Spanish in the protocols of subject #6, however, may reflect her increased proficiency in English. She continues to do most of her planning in Spanish, but she no longer generates most of her text in Spanish as she had done in the earlier sessions.

We would summarize our conclusions about the use of first language in second-language composing as being principally a matter of vocabulary. Where writers lack second-languge vocabulary, they naturally fall back upon their native language. When we provided the vocabulary for the subjects with lower proficiency, as we did in the ending-sentence tasks, we effected a reduction in the amount of first language while composing in the second. Within these ending-sentence tasks, there was less first-language use in the one in which we provided the most vocabulary and which required the least abstract goal setting (the narrative).

SUMMARY

Second-language composing, we would argue from this real-time data, is not a different animal from first-language composing. Of course it is affected, in the texts that result, by the lack of proficiency of the writer. But that isn't the only factor. The primary trait ratings (Table 4A) do not accord exactly with the proficiency of the writer (Table 1). (There are too few cases to even suggest a formal statistical test.) We have found that the writing strategies of the writer, which we argue transfer from the first language, play a central role. With the exception of writer #3, for whom the think-aloud protocols may be misleading, those writers who can be identified as more abstract planners (#4 and #5) achieve higher primary-trait ratings in their second-language compositions.

We can identify several important conclusions. First, we think we have strong, direct, data for the transfer of first-language skill to the second language. It is direct because we have observed the actual process in real time, not inferred it from texts or scores on tests. Experimental manipulations affect the process the same way in both first and second language; indirect evidence that it is the same process. If the processes were different, the manipulation might well have different effects in the two languages. While second-language proficiency obviously affects the quality of the texts, it appears to have little role in constraining the planning process. When the writer who was most proficient in English (#5) moved to his highest level, he did so in Spanish, suggesting that those who worked at a lower level could have also used Spanish if proficiency was what was inhibiting them. We know that they showed no hesitancy in using Spanish in English composing during the conventional writing tasks and that too is evidence that the reason their planning remained at a concrete level is not because they could go no higher in English, but because they did not know how to go higher in any language.

Proficiency did seem to constrain the effectiveness of the process and reduce the quantity, though not quality, of planning. In the narrative-ending task, subjects performed less well in English than in Spanish even though the level of abstraction of planning was much the same in both languages.

The difference between languages in the results on the narrative-sentence tasks points to the possibility that planning in a second language requires more mental capacity than planning in a first language does. The ability to coordinate ending-sentence constraints has been shown to vary with working-memory capacity (Tetroe, 1984). The performance of our subjects indicates that working in the second language requires two more units of capacity than working in the native language. However, it is not clear how these units map onto more conventional measures of the writing process, or where the planning process breaks down to create this effect. It would appear that our subjects do less detailed planning in English, but that they work at the same level of abstraction in both languages. Thus, we would claim that the quality, though not the quantity, of planning transfers from L1 to L2.

REFERENCES

Bereiter, C., & Scardamalia, M. (1982). *Constructing new mental abilities: the case of reflective composition planning.* Unpublished manuscript, Ontario Institute for Studies in Education.

Carroll, B. (1980). *Testing communicative performance.* Oxford, England: Pergammon Institute of English.

Chelala, S. (1981). *The composing process of two Spanish speakers and the coherence of their texts: A case study.* Unpublished doctoral dissertation, New York University.

Clarke, Mark. (1979). Reading in English and Spanish: Evidence from adult ESL students. *Language Learning, 29,* 121-150.

Cummins, J. (1980). The cross-lingual dimensions of language proficiency: Implications for bilingual education and the optimal age question. *TESOL Quarterly, 14,* 175-187.

Cziko, G. (1978). Differences in first- and second-language reading: The use of syntactic, semantic and discourse constraints. *The Canadian Modern Language Journal, 34,* 473-489.

ETS (1978) *TOEFL test and score manual.* Princeton, NJ: Educational Testing Service.

Faerch, C., & Kasper, G. (1983). *Strategies in interlanguage communication.* London: Longmans.

Flower, L., & Hayes, J.R. (1980). The cognition of discovery: Defining a rhetorical problem. *College Composition and Communication, 31,* 21-32.

Flower, L., & Hayes, J.R. (1981). The pregnant pause: An inquiry into the nature of planning. *Research in the Teaching of English, 15,* 229-244.

Gass, S., (1979). Language transfer and universal grammatical relations. *Language Learning, 29,* 327-344.

Hosenfeld, C. (1977). A preliminary investigation of the reading strategies of successful and unsuccessful second language learners. *System, 5,* 110-123.

Jones, S. (1982, May). *Composing in a second language: A process study.* Paper presented at the annual meeting of Teachers of English to Speakers of Other Languages, Honolulu.

Jones, S. (1983, March). *Some composing strategies of second language writers.* Paper presented at the annual meeting of Teachers of English to Speakers of Other Languages, Toronto.

Jones, S. (1985). Problems with monitor use in second language composing. In M. Rose (Ed.), *When a writer can't write: Studies in writers' block and other composing process problems.* New York: Guilford.

Jones, S., & Tetroe, J. (1983, March). *Observing ESL writing.* Paper presented at the annual meeting of Teachers of English to Speakers of Other Languages, Toronto.

Kaplan, R.B. (1972) *The anatomy of rhetoric: Prolegomena to a functional theory of rhetoric.* Philadelphia: Center for Curriculum Development.

Lado, R. (1957). *Linguistics across cultures.* Ann Arbor: University of Michigan Press.

Lay, N.D.S. (1982). Composing process of adult ESL learners: A case study. *TESOL Quarterly, 16,* 406.

Lay, N.D.S. (1983). Native language and the composing process. *Resource.* City University of New York, 17–21.

Matsuhashi, A. (1981). Pausing and planning: The tempo of written discourse production. *Research in the Teaching of English, 15,* 113–134.

Raupach, M. (1980). Temporal variables in first and second language speech production. In H. W. Dechert and M. Raupach (Eds.), *Temporal variables in speech: Studies in honor of Frieda Goldman-Eisler.* The Hague: Mouton.

Scardamalia, M., Bereiter, C., & Goelman, H. (1982). The role of production factors in writing ability. In M. Nystrand (Ed.), *What writers know.* New York: Academic Press.

Tetroe, J. (1984, April). *Information processing demand of plot construction in story writing.* Paper presented at the annual meeting of the American Educational Research Association, New Orleans, LA.

Tetroe, J., Bereiter, C., & Scardamalia, M. (1981, April). *How to make a dent in the writing process.* Paper presented at the annual meeting of the American Educational Research Association, Los Angeles, CA.

Taylor, B. (1981) Content and written form: A two-way street. *TESOL Quarterly, 15,* 5–12.

Tetroe, J., & Jones, S. (1983, March). *Planning and revising in adult ESL students.* Paper presented at the annual Conference on College Composition and Communication, Detroit, MI.

Tetroe, J., & Jones, S. (1984, April). *Transfer of planning skills in second language writing.* Paper presented at the Annual Meeting of the American Educational Research Association, New Orleans, LA.

Wardhaugh, R. (1970). The contrastive analysis hypothesis. *TESOL Quarterly, 4,* 123–130.

Zamel, V. (1976). Teaching composition in the ESL classroom: What we can learn from research in the teaching of English. *TESOL Quarterly, 10,* 67–76.

Zamel, V. (1983). The composing process of advanced ESL students: Six case studies. *TESOL Quarterly, 17,* 165–187.

CHAPTER 3

Pedagogical Interaction during the Composing Process: The Writing Conference

Sarah Warshauer Freedman
University of California, Berkeley

Anne Marie Katz
Stanford University

Cee, a college freshman, receives an assignment for her writing course. She is to write a well-organized, well-developed essay supporting an unpopular opinion—either "Women should be kept barefoot, pregnant, and in the kitchen," or "All long-haired preppies should be shot." Cee chooses to argue that women are not capable of being corporate executives. What process does she follow to write this essay?

First, in a series of tape-recorded interviews about her composing process, she reports that she spent 5 to 8 hr on the assignment. She says that when the topic was first assigned, classroom discussion helped her generate her initial ideas which she recorded during that class session. The following week she continued to think about what she wanted to say as she walked around campus and as she commuted on BART (Bay Area Rapid Transit) to and from the university.

One morning at her home, five days after she received the assignment, she wrote for 25 min. This writing consisted of a list of ideas about the woman executive: "Too emotional (cry too much—?)" and "Do not want to go up the ladder (ha!)." The next morning in the student union, a noisy, active place, Cee spent 10 more min. on her list of ideas, followed by another 10 min. during her accounting class.

The following morning, again in the student union, Cee began to compose, an activity that made her late for her swimming class. In her writing class that day, she attended a peer group editing session during which she discussed her ideas with her classmates. Although she was supposed to have completed a draft, she was not ready to show her group anything she had written.

Cee did not resume writing until a week later at home, the evening

58

before the paper was due. That night she produced what she labelled a "rough draft." The day the paper was due she typed her rough draft in the basement of the library where students may borrow typewriters. After handing in what she considered her completed paper, Cee had an individual conference with her teacher.

Even this sketchy description of Cee's account of her composing process illustrates the fact that when a student faces a complex writing task, the writing process involves more than the time spent immediately before, during, and after putting pen to paper. Cee's composing process can be segmented into the three subprocesses suggested by Flower and Hayes (1980)—planning, translating, and reviewing. As Flower and Hayes note, at certain times during the process, students focus more on one subprocess than another although they frequently shift their attention back and forth between subprocesses. According to her account, Cee spends much of her composing focus on planning before she begins to write. She spends relatively little focal time translating or writing and does so only when faced with the pressure of a deadline. She also spends hardly any focal time reviewing after writing. Because she was not observed while writing, we cannot assess how she allocated her time then. For this assignment, her revising process, according to her own account, consists of cleaning up and typing her first rough draft. Although meant to stimulate reviewing, the earlier deadline of the peer-editing meeting affects Cee's process mostly by encouraging her to begin writing.

Studies of the writing process tend to focus on times when a great deal of translating or writing is occurring, but for Cee, the time spent actually writing her "rough draft" may have been a trivial part of her process in comparison with the full spectrum of her writing-related activities. In fact, while interacting with Cee during the conference, issues arise about the nature of the process itself. The teacher attempts to intervene in Cee's process; she tries to redirect and extend it. As Cee herself spontaneously comments to her teacher, with a priceless slip of the tongue, "It's good that students are able to talk to their teachers about their essays. That way students have a better idea of what's going wrong in their essay . . . And also you have a better communication gap with your teacher."

In this chapter, we will suggest how Cee's conferences with her teacher across a semester illustrate teaching as it influences and becomes part of the composing process. Some of the conferences stimulate revision; others do not. Cee's slip of the tongue signals the importance of studying pedagogical discussions that occur during the process of writing since these discussions potentially become part of the writing process itself. As Graves (1983) and Kamler (1980) illustrate at the elementary level, through examining the interaction between teaching and composing, we can uncover how teaching and learning occur and can discover more about how the writing process proceeds.

The concept of wedding the teaching and learning of writing and the writing process is not new. Experts on teaching writing from elementary through university levels suggest that the most effective teaching of writing occurs when the teaching takes place during the writing process and becomes part of that process (e.g., Carnicelli, 1980; Graves, 1978; Murray, 1979). A recent survey of directors of the sites of the National Writing Projects revealed that the directors felt that primary among what writing teachers should know about and teach was the process of writing (Freedman, 1982).

The individual conference between student and teacher, which occurs over a draft of the student's paper (Graves, 1978, 1983; Murray, 1979), is a widely recommended technique for teaching during the writing process. Conferences are thought by directors of freshman composition programs across the nation to be the most successful part of their teaching programs (Witte, Meyer, Miller & Faigley, 1982). In a national survey of exemplary teachers of writing at the elementary and secondary levels, conferences proved to be the only type of feedback during the writing process that the teachers consistently agreed to be helpful. A survey of some of the students of these teachers at the secondary level showed that students found talking to their teacher during the writing process the best technique for helping them learn to write (Freedman, 1985).

The pages of journals for teachers published by the National Council of Teachers of English contain an extensive literature on the writing conference. Practitioners of this technique describe the conference as a "student-centered" learning situation (Duke, 1975; Murray, 1979) where students "learn to express themselves" (Knapp, 1976), where "a student discovers his own ideas" (Freedman, 1981; Jacobs & Karliner, 1977), where "more 'real' teacher-student interaction" takes place (Fassler, 1978; Reigstad, 1980). These articles urge teachers to listen to students in order to teach them, to allow students to voice their own concerns about writing, and to focus on the problems they encounter when they sit down to form their ideas into coherent prose.

Strong evidence suggests that conferences "work" so effectively as part of a writing course because they allow more verbal interaction between teachers and individual students, more talk about each student's writing than is possible in classrooms where each teacher must manage the education of a roomful of students. Graves (1983) singles out the student–teacher conference as a central interactive event in the development of young children's writing skills; writing conferences permit teachers to respond immediately to students' notions about what writing is and to help them adopt strategies to improve their skills.

The assumption in the literature on conferences, thus, is that teacher–student interaction contributes to student learning. Murray (1980) points out that when teachers listen to students analyze their own writing, students are learning to react to their own work. In essence, the conference is a training ground for self-evaluative response. In the learning situation of the writing conference, then, the students' "roles" include analyzing and thinking about their writing as well as putting their thoughts into words. The teachers' "roles" include listening to the student, identifying composing problems, helping the students solve those problems, not just for the moment but for the future as well, and deciding how much higher the student can be encouraged to reach. Walker and Elias (in preparation) point out that it is not the quantity but rather the quality of the interaction that matters.

Vygotsky (1978) provides a theoretical framework to account more specifically for why this type of teacher–student interaction during the writing conference has such great teaching potential. He points out that although traditional approaches define levels of development based on what children can do alone, such measures do not adequately describe children's mental capabilities and their means of learning. He uses the phrase "zone of proximal development" to describe students' capacities to learn. He defines the "zone of proximal development" as "the distance between the actual developmental level as determined by independent problem solving and the level of potential development as determined through problem solving under adult guidance or in collaboration with more capable peers" (p. 86). Similarly, Bruner (1978) suggests that effective teachers build "scaffolds" to help students learn (also see Applebee & Langer, 1983 and Graves, 1983, for discussions of scaffolding in the teaching of reading and writing). The conference presumably can provide the guidance or scaffolds that Vygotsky and Bruner discuss.

Little, however, is known about what specifically happens in conferences that makes them effective. Certainly, not all conferences are equally effective in providing appropriate guidance or scaffolds. Scardamalia and Bereiter (1986) offer a helpful theoretical framework for judging whether a conference provides those scaffolds for students that help them reach what Vygotsky calls their potential levels of development. Scardamalia and Bereiter first suggest that in the teaching of writing, it is important to distinguish between "substantive facilitation," when a teacher responds "to what a student has said or intends to say" and "procedural facilitation" when a teacher responds not to the actual substance of a piece of writing but to the cognitive processes involved in producing a piece of writing. The intent with procedural facilitation is "to enable students to carry out more complex composing processes by themselves" (p. 796). They note that the writing conference "can include both substantive and procedural facilitation" (p. 797). However, they stress that facilitation can promote learning only if it leads to a student's "internalization" of what is being taught. Scardamalia and Bereiter worry about the dialogic nature of the conference:

> On first thought, conferencing would seem to be well designed for internalization; the thinking, carried out jointly at first, comes in time to be carried out in the mind of the student. But the form of the conference is dialogue, and there is no indication from research to suggest that the mature composing process has the form of an internal dialogue. A more readily internalizable form might be the 'assisted monologue' . . . where the talking is primarily done by the student, with the teacher inserting prompts rather than conversational turns. . . . Serious research is needed to determine what students internalize from what teachers have helped or induced them to do (pp. 797–798).

The question is: Can the conference with its dialogic properties direct students to carry out independent monologues? More specifically, what characteristics of dialogues might lead students to internalize substance and procedure so that students will independently use effective procedures to produce effective substance? Although we will not be able to answer these questions in this chapter, we will attempt to point to how the conference might assist the student in the development of effective writing.

A first step in studying teaching and learning in the conference requires the development of an analysis system for conferences that allows researchers to look carefully at the dialogic properties in the conference and then to develop a system for inferring what the teacher intends to communicate to the student and what the student understands. Such an analysis of conference conversations can allow one to observe both the student during a little studied segment of his or her real-time composing process and the teacher influencing and modifying that process.

For this chapter, using one of Cee's conferences, we will illustrate ways to analyze conference transcripts to determine the structure of the conference conversation, and we will consider how our analysis sheds light on this often-neglected pedagogical part of the composing process.

Cee was selected as the focus of this study because she was a relatively low-achieving but highly motivated student enrolled in the class of an excellent teacher of freshman composition. This teacher routinely used interactive conferences as part of her plan for writing instruction. Cee provides a typical illustration of a student who needs instruction in order to proceed as a more experienced writer would and who is motivated enough to take advantage of such instruction.

Over the 15-week semester, five naturally occurring conferences were recorded between Cee and her teacher. The first was designed to elicit information about Cee's awareness of the writing process, her feelings about writing, reading habits and so forth. The remainder focused on discussion of particular essays. The conference analyzed for this chapter, the second of the semester and the first that centers on a piece of Cee's writing, was selected because in it Cee first articulates what she considers her key composing problems and her teacher takes note of these problems. We examine one segment of this conference, a part in which the teacher interviews the student about her process for composing this particular essay about women as incompetent corporate executives. The segment illustrates those student- and teacher-initiated comments which occur early in the conference, before any discussion of the written text itself. It is the time when the student and teacher construct the topics on which teaching and learning will focus during much of the rest of the semester. It is a time that seems most unlike whole-class teaching when the teacher often has a preset agenda and when much less mutual topic construction occurs.

For background to the analysis, we will review two key studies of verbal interaction: the analysis of turn-taking operating in the conversation of adult Americans proposed by Sacks, Schegloff, and Jefferson (1974) and Mehan's (1979) description of teacher–student interaction during classroom lessons. Then, we present the analysis of Cee's conference that forms the basis of this paper. The intent of this section will be to describe the pattern of the discourse, the control and predictability of the language of that discourse in terms of its participants, and to suggest what the study of the discourse reveals about how the conference functions in the student's process of learning to compose.

Sacks, Schegloff, and Jefferson (SS&J) provide the beginning point for this description of conversation between teacher and student. Their analysis of the turn-taking system of adult American conversation outlines the underlying rules operating during verbal interaction. Because we agree to take turns at talk, discourse evolves moment-by-moment in an orderly fashion with speakers vying for turns according to a set of rules. Of particular interest to the description here is SS&J's assertion that theirs is at once a context-free system and a context-sensitive system. On the one hand, their rules for turn-taking are at a high-enough level of abstraction that they operate in a variety of situations. On the other hand, variations in the basic rules show the effect of the context and thus help to pinpoint its distinctive characteristics. Thus, an examination of turn-taking can show both how the conference is like everyday conversation and how it is different, that is, how it functions in an explicitly pedagogical setting.

Mehan (1979) examines turn-taking in the classroom. It is reasonable to suppose that, in some ways, the conference, as a pedagogical setting, abides by the rules of classroom conversation and that classroom conversations, like conference conversations, follow, in part, the general conversational rules that SS&J delineate. But each setting has its own set of appropriateness conditions that overlay a basic system like SS&J's. Probably for this reason, Mehan observes that first-grade children operate more effectively in the classroom at the end of the school year, after they have learned the context-specific rules for verbal interaction in the classroom, such as rules for asking and answering questions, getting the floor to propose their own topics for discussion, and keeping the floor.

While SS&J describe the sequence of turns in conversation as co-occurring pairs of utterances such as question–answer, request–grant, Mehan's (1979) analysis outlines a three-part sequence that satisfies the requirements of discourse symmetry, yet takes into account the instructional setting of a classroom: (a) teacher initiates, (b) student responds, and (c) teacher evaluates. The teacher initiation and student response together make up one unit that is itself "completed" by the teacher evaluation. This three-part system is a modification of the turn-allocation system described by SS&J in that one speaker, the teacher, maintains control of the discourse or the lesson. Since the teacher initiates the sequence, she may select topic and, as current speaker, select the next student speaker. After the student's response, the teacher again regains the' floor, for evaluation, topic selection, and speaker selection. Within the lesson, then, there are restricted appropriate times for speaker change initiated by the student—either when the teacher allows it, when she has not selected a specific responder, or after teacher evaluation but before her selection of another speaker and/ or before her change of topic. It could be informative also to understand how the conference is, and is not, like the classroom lesson.

SS&J suggest that speech-exchange systems can be placed along a continuum with respect to the ways turns are allocated, with conversations at one pole and debates at the other. In conversations, the speakers agree together, on the spot, on who speaks when. Turns are allocated locally. In debates, turns are preallocated, that is, there are preset rules for who speaks when, and for how long a given speaker's turn lasts. We suggest that classroom conversations and conferences fall in the middle of the continuum, with turn-allocation in classroom conversations closer to debates and, in conferences, closer to natural conversations. SS&J note that in spite of their metaphor of the continuum, "conversation should be considered the basic form of speech-exchange system, with other systems on the array representing a variety of transformations of conversation's turn-taking system, to achieve other types of turn-taking systems" (p. 730). The ways turns are allocated have implications for the function of the system. With this image of a continuum in mind, we will describe the learning situation of the writing conference in order to find its place on the continuum (see also Jacobs & Karliner, 1977).

LINGUISTIC ANALYSIS OF THE DATA

Conference Structure

We found, after analyzing not only Cee's conference but also conferences from a number of other college teachers and their students, that conferences about student writing normally consist of five sections:

1. *Opening*. Initial greetings.
2. *Student-initiated comments and questions*. The student's general talk about the writing or other issues. This talk may be about process (such as difficulties getting started, insufficient time for revision), and product (such as questions about grammar, problems with development). This talk may occur at any time during the conference between the *Opening* and *Closing* segments.
3. *Teacher-initiated comments and questions*. The teacher's general talk about the writing or other issues. Like *Student-initiated comments and questions,* this talk may occur at any time during the conference between the *Opening* and *Closing* segments.
4. *Reading*. The student or teacher reads the paper or parts of the paper aloud or silently. Often student or teacher pause to intersperse *Student-initiated comments and questions* or *Teacher-initiated comments and questions* during the course of the reading.
5. *Closing*. Good-bye, thanks-for-help statements, scheduling of future appointments, and the like.

The *Reading* segment is optional and occurs only if there is text to be read. On rare occasions, we could imagine that either the teacher's, or more likely the student's, comments and questions could be missing, but we have not found such cases in our data. Only the order of the *Opening* and *Closing* segments is fixed. However, it is possible to begin the *Closing* segment and then return to one of the earlier segments before returning to the final closing remarks. Otherwise, the segments do not occur in any fixed sequence. For example, *Student-Teacher-initiated comments and questions* are frequently sandwiched between *Reading* segments.

The analysis which follows will focus on those *Student-* and *Teacher-initiated comments and questions* which occur before the *Reading* of the text. In conferences such as Cee's, during the time before the text is read, the teacher frequently asks the student for general comments about the writing of the paper. The teacher is looking for an indication of the student's concerns about writing. With this teacher, this time during the conference is highly interactive and is a time when the student is given the opportunity to reveal most about his or her composing process and composing concerns. It is also a time when the student and teacher construct the topics on which teaching and learning will focus.

In this segment of the conference, Cee's and her teacher's talk seem to
follow the form of what Scardamalia and Bereiter describe as the "assisted
monologue"; the teacher prompts the student's thinking process. In the
"assisted monologue" the teacher or researcher always has a clear aim, a
clear sense of how a writer can solve a problem. However, in naturally
occuring conferences, when the teacher first discovers those problems that
the student has difficulty solving alone, the teacher is often less sure, on
the spot, of exactly how to lead the student. The teacher begins to construct plans.

Turn-order and turn-allocation
An analysis of turn order and allocation can pinpoint what the teacher
must do to help the student feel comfortable taking turns and initiating
topics of concern, what the student can learn through articulating areas of
concern, and what is involved for the teacher who tries to assist the learning process, on the spot.

As we stated earlier, SS&J describe the use of adjacency pairs (e.g.,
question–answer) as a basic technique to form the discourse of conversation, the current speaker selecting the next speaker. The other technique
for getting the floor in free-flowing verbal interaction is self-selection.
However, Mehan's (1979) three-part instructional sequence, Initiation–Response–Evaluation (IRE), better describes the basic structure of turn-order
and allocation in this part of the student–teacher writing conference. For
example:

```
I—│—T19:   ... Are there any things that you think I would,
    │        I would think that would be particularly good about the
    │        essay
    │        ..or that you think are good. =
R—│—S19:   = You,
    │        or me.
    │  T20:  Well,
    │        either one.
    │        Things that you think are good,
    │        // /humm/,
    │        ..let's start with that.//
    │  S20:  The paragraph,
    │        the sentence,
    │        or the .. ideas,
    │  T21:  ..anything.
    │  S21:  Anything, =
    │  T22:  = Yeah, on a sentence level, or a..paragraph level.
    │  S22:  Umm,
```

well there were some sentences,
that I..got.. from,
my,
first essay,
the one,
I forgot to turn one in,
and you told me,
to turn in an essay anyway and I wrote about,
the attitudes..of,
..Peanut's attitudes,
of Americans,
something like that.
..And let's see . . . . . . oh Lord,
... .Oh it might be in this paragraph right here. =
= /Uh hum./
I changed it around to fit my essay.
From the young man,
to the bright women.

T23:   Okay this was a sentence that you'd had in your other essay,
S23:   Uh //Hum, /and then you changed/
similar to it.//
T24:   = I see.
Okay.
And you included it..in this paper..because, =
—S24:   = It seemed to,
go in..uh..blend in well,
with it.
E-|—T25:   Okay.[1]

Essentially, the overall structure seems to follow a traditional instructional format rather than a conversational one. According to Mehan's (1979) scheme, a model of this sequence looks something like the following:

I. Teacher initiation (T19)
R. Student response (S19-S22)
   Teacher question/response (T23-T24)

---

[1] The following transcription conventions are followed: = stands for latching, that is, cases when there is no pause and no overlap between turns;
// // stands for overlap;
/ / is used when one speaker interrupts the turn of another speaker without taking a turn, generally back channel cues.
One idea unit (Chafe, 1980) is transcribed per line. Commas stand for rising intonation; periods stand for falling intonation.

Student response (S24)
E. Teacher evaluation (T25)

The teacher initiation (I) consists of a broad question or directive that allows, or rather almost forces, the student to participate actively in the discussion of her writing because the student must take responsibility for choosing the direction for development of the topic broached by the teacher. In the example just given, the teacher asks for general information, and "good" things about the essay. Searle's (1969) distinction between "real" questions and "exam" questions which are frequently used in teaching settings helps distinguish this teacher initiation in the conference conversation from the usual initiations during classroom conversation. For real questions, teachers do not already know the answer; for exam questions, they do know the answer and pose them to test the student's knowledge rather than to gather information. These initiation questions during the conference, unlike many classroom questions, are real, open-ended questions—ones to which the teacher cannot predict answers and ones which allow the student to initiate topics. Interestingly, in T19 the teacher asks both an exam question ("What would I think would be good?") and a real question ("What do you think is good?"), but in collaboration with the student in S19 shifts to the real question—"what do you think"—in T20. The student has trouble responding until this shift is accomplished. Other similar initiations with real questions are also posed by the teacher during this conference. For example, she asks, "In general, how do you feel about the paper?" and "Any other things that offhand you think made this paper good or bad?" Such real questions encourage the student to respond substantively and give the teacher important information to use in guiding the teaching-learning process.

The response part (R) is the focusing section, the part of the sequence in which the student's response indicates the direction the student wants for the discussion. The teacher's subsequent utterances are adjusted to the student's response in an attempt to track the student's thought. Here, the teacher's control of the discourse seems less directive, so that her role may be seen less as that of the teacher giving information and more as that of the manager or guide prompting the student to clarify her thoughts and ask her questions. Forty turns are analyzed in this segment of the conference data: 26 out of 40 teacher turns for Cee occur during the response part of the sequence; as in Mehan's model, this section may be extended to include several conversational turns.

In the example, after Cee is clear about the extent of the teacher's initiating question in S22 and after a cue from the teacher, she finally produces an answer and a lengthy one at that. She is concerned about how well her tactic of slipping in sentences from another essay works. She aimed to "blend" an idea from a previous essay into this one. She seemed to have had difficulty generating ideas on this topic. After Cee's lengthy answer, the teacher's questions and comments are used to help Cee finish shaping her answer; in T24, the "because" trails off, allowing Cee to complete with her own reasoning.

The teacher has learned something significant about Cee's composing. In an attempt to please the teacher, Cee takes a sentence from a previous essay that the teacher had indicated that she liked and slipped it into the current essay. The student could not abstract from the teacher's previous praise to apply it to her new piece of writing; rather she interprets the praise literally. If a sentence is good in one essay, then one should try to reuse it in another essay. The resulting text is less than satisfactory.

Teacher evaluation (E) completes the sequence and allows a shift to another topic. In the example, the evaluation is brief, a simple "Okay" (T25). As in any instructional sequence, evaluation provides feedback to the student that she is performing appropriately. Evaluation utterances also occur within the response (R) section, as markers to help the student continue her analysis of her writing, as reinforcement, and as pats on the back for her effort. Gumperz (1982) calls these conversational utterances backchannel cues. The crucial distinction between the closing evaluation (E) and the evaluation during the response (R) section is that the former closes the segment by permitting a change in topic, a change controlled by the teacher; the closing evaluation serves to redirect rather than to track the conversation.

If the data are analyzed according to the IRE sequence of turn-order and allocation, several characteristics of the teacher–student roles in the conference become apparent. Ostensibly, the teacher seems to retain a conventional role within a conventional instructional sequence, directing questions to the student. The teacher, as initiator of the instructional sequence, controls the selection of topic, broad though it may be, and so the overall flow of the conversation as well. Because she closes the sequence, she retrieves the floor and maintains that control into the text topic, the next sequence. The teacher is able to use this turn-taking system to provide help for the learner.

Yet in several important ways, this verbal interaction is more student-centered than in the usual teaching-learning situation. First, within the response part, the teacher's role as controller is modified to that of manager, as she helps Cee shape her thoughts. Because the topic is broached in such general terms in its initiation, the student is forced into an active role; she must choose a specific direction for development of the topic. Thus, although turn-order seems fairly predictable, specific topic direction in this particular segment is more affected by the student than by the teacher.

Second, the teacher-controlling parts of the sequence (I and E) occupy less time in the overall sequence than that part focused on the student (R). Most teacher turns occur during R parts of the sequence. Thus, although the student–teacher conference seems to operate with role-specific restrictions within a three-part IRE instructional sequence that affects turn-order and allocation, there also seem to be significant modifications that allow student-initiated talk.

Gaps, Overlaps, and Latching

In everyday conversational turn-taking, transitions between turns are precisely timed, resulting in brief gaps or pauses—0.40 s for adults talking on the telephone (Brady, 1968); 0.77 s for interviews with strangers (Jaffe & Feldstein, 1970); and brief overlaps—0.25 and 0.40 s—if at all, for adult conversations because over 95% of the time adults speak or listen without overlap (Ervin-Tripp, 1979). SS&J attribute rapid transition at juncture points in conversation to the predictability of those juncture points and to the pressure of a turn-allocation system in which the speaker who starts to talk gets the next turn.

Yet in the conference data, pauses, some quite lengthy, are not uncommon. This departure from the conversational norm may be characteristic of a learning situation in which thought as well as talk is considered an important part of the interchange. For example, in the conference talk discussed in the previous section, the teacher has asked Cee to pick out a particularly good feature of her essay. In her response (S22), Cee pauses in the midst of her turn, using a delaying phrase ("and let's see") characteristic of much of her conversation with her teacher throughout the semester's conferences. Rather than take back the floor, the teacher allows Cee to find the place she is searching for in her paper.

Although long pauses do not occur at every turn, their occurrence seems to indicate that this verbal interchange is operating according to criteria different from those of ordinary conversation. Because the pattern of turn-order is initiation–response–evaluation, pauses in the student's response while the student is composing her thoughts are permissible without danger of her losing the floor, and thus are more prevalent than in typical adult conversation. This conversational characteristic of allowing for pauses seems crucial to the conference that aims to assist a student to internalize the substance and procedures necessary for writing. Such lengthy pauses would also provide evidence of predictability, a pre-allocation of turns, as would occur in an instructional sequence.

Even more evidence of conversational predictability may be found in the overlap and latching patterns that occur in 16 out of 80 total teacher and student turns in an earlier section of the conference. Of the 16 occurrences, 12 are initiated by the student, the other 4 by the teacher. In general, the overlaps are brief and occur at transition-relevant points in the interchange. The single exception to this location is a student request for clarification, an acceptable variation in SS&J's system where understanding gets priority in turn selection. Again, SS&J posit that overlap at juncture points shows the predictability of such points in the discourse. And, in fact, much of the student-initiated overlap and latching, usually in turns responding to teacher questions, seems due to the student's understanding of what is coming next in the discourse. The predictability of some of these occurrences is based on standard teacher-to-student instructional patterns. For example, notice in the example below the tag question with its embedded answer (T33), the "exam" question (T34), and the sentence completion statement (T36).

T33:   Uh hum.
        It's the career that belonged to the husbands.
        Let's see it's plural isn't it? =
S33:   = It's plural, //plural
T34:   Women do not okay so.//
        Where..do you know where the apostrophe goes, =
S34:   = Would it be after the "s"? =
T35:   = Yeah.
        Good.
S35:   Okay.
T36:   So you put it there.
        Should be their husband's careers,
        I guess.
        Pluralize the two.
        Their husband's =
S36:   = Careers,
        yes.
T37:   Okay.

Clearly the student knows the pattern of the conference—the teacher asks questions in these various forms, and the student answers—and so she knows she will soon be up for her turn. When the student knows the answer or what she wants to answer, she leaves no gap in the conversation.

But not all overlap and latching may be so neatly assigned a label because other instances occur in less obviously formal teaching patterns as in T8 through S9 in the earlier discourse segment. At this point, after two teacher questions, the student in S8 is ready to answer the affirmative "uh hum," which the teacher hears and acknowledges in T9, almost a prestart to Cee's expanded response in S9 which itself is latched on to T9. Here, Cee's quick responses seem to indicate a situation in which she is being listened to, in which the questions and answers are not as predictable as in the previous pattern in which she has information to impart to the teacher.

It is worth noting here, perhaps, that the fewer occurrences of teacher-initiated latching may also indicate more willingness to listen than to speak. This sequence, in fact, is much like normal adult conversations. The student, at times, acts as an equal conversational participant when without hesitation she initiates her own topic with her contrastive "but" in S9 and when she continues her turn with the explanatory "because." Further, the teacher notes that she is listening to the student's conversation with her "humm" backchannel.

Thus although it would seem that the evidence from overlap and latching strategies supports the notion of predictability in the discourse of the conference, there may also be some support for the notion that the conference is a place where students feel their answer, their talk, is important enough to actually allow them to jump into the conversation before the teacher has completely finished her turn. Additional support for this assertion may be seen in the lesser amount of teacher-initiated overlap and latching, an indication that the teacher may be attempting to hold back from immediately reclaiming the floor and so, control.

Topic Shift
The last section of analysis focuses more closely on how teacher and student develop the discourse topic—the content of the conference. The basic outline of that development has been presented in the IRE instructional sequence. But how does the teacher manage the shifts between one IRE sequence and the next? Thus far, we have seen the teacher play the role of information gatherer. How does she make use of the information she gathers so that she can better help the student learn? How does she fit together her "agenda" and the concerns of the student? The following opening segments of the conference provide some clues.

I-	-(T1:	How did you feel about this essay?)[2]
R-	-S1:	Horrible. =
	T2:	= You did, =
	S2:	= Terrible.
		Well see it was a rush job I did the night before,
		(laughs) it was // due.
	T3:	Oh//you did. =
	S3:	= Well,
		earlier,
		I was going to start earlier in the week,
		but I, I just..every time I started on it I just couldn't think
		of anything,

---

[2] The parenthesis indicates that the talk enclosed was missing from the tape but has been reconstructed from the context.

but during the first week you gave us the assignment to us,
I did write a few things here and there.
And then I maybe about a week I left it alone,
without ever looking at it again.
Till I finally realized that I better..get going,
and I didn't feel too good about this essay.
And I feared there was a lot of little errors here and there.
And like I was reading my own copy,
about 15 minutes ago,
to see how it was.
..And there are a few errors I found,
that should have been corrected before.

T4:   ..Um, you said you sat down and you tried to do some work
        on it.
        But you just had a lot of..moments when you couldn't, =
S4:   = uh hum,
        weird thing.
        It was about the same thing I was thinking about,
E- T5:   ..Okay.
I-   ..Do you think it was the subject matter,
        that made it hard for you to write,
        or do you think,
        // /umm/
        I mean do you // have any idea why this particular paper
            was hard to write?
R- -S5:   . . . It's just that,
        ..I wanted to do the subject,
        ..but..getting the ideas out,
        and putting them out..on the paper,
        was hard to do.
T6:   Thank you (interruption).
        Sure. (Turns off recorder).
        Okay.
        Uhm
S6:   ... Now what was I saying now? =
T7:   = I was asking you why you felt it was hard to,
        to get started on this particular piece.
S7:   ... Oh yes.
        And I said something about,
        ..that,
        ... I had some ideas,
        but the ideas weren't complete,
        and putting them down on paper was hard.

	I had a lot of ideas running through my mind,
	but when I finally got to the knitty gritty.
	Writing things down,
	was hard.
T8:	Did you um,
	did you try to write them down,
	like when we talked about Trimble,
	did you try,
	..writing down an idea,
	and asking questions of it,
	or // did you.
S8:	Uh hum,//
T9:	you tried doing that. =
S9:	= But that also seemed hard too.
	/Humm,/
	Because sometimes my answer would be really long,
	and sometimes it would be short.
	But when I got down to writing it,
	..it just..wasn't there,
T10:	hum.
S10:	. . . It's sort of like half of it was blanked out.
T11:	Hmm.
	Ok,
	... hmmm.
	..Let me think.
	You were arguing about an unpopular opinion.
S11:	Yes and I felt that,
	this should have been,
	..extended more,
	but..I'm not sure how,
	/okay,/ =
	= it should be extended.
	And this should been maybe a whole paragraph right here,
	and,
	. . . there's another area,
	right here,
	and you already made a reference to it.
	.."I think" I said "women can do the job if the work were
	given to them."
	/Right./
	Because,
	women can do the job if they were given to them,
	doesn't make sense at all.

```
E- -T12:    Right.
            Right.
            That's good you picked up on that.
 - -        Right.
```

Because the teacher wants to encourage the student to talk, she begins the conference using a "real" and "open" question with a broad topic, "How did you feel about this essay?" This beginning is similar to a rather typical conversational opener about one's health—"How are you?" However, the student responds with a one-word summation of her feelings about the paper—"Horrible." Just as one would continue the conversation to get the particulars, prodding a bit with a rejoinder such as, "Oh, really?" the teacher in this conference prods the student to expand on her feelings about the paper by asking, "You did?" and so the student continues without further linguistic prompts. Her lexical choices of "horrible" and "terrible" rather than "not so good," coupled with overlap at the transition points of S1 and S2 may be indications of the student's eagerness to discuss the paper, her involvement in the conference, and her active participation in the interaction. Now she continues her explanation (S2), the marker "Well" signalling the beginning of her discourse (a prestart used repeatedly by this student).

In T3, although the surface forms may seem almost identical with T2, the meaning has changed. Here, given the information that the student does not feel good about the paper and that it was "a rush job," the teacher's utterance shifts topic slightly, focusing now no longer on how the student feels about the paper, but on why she has problems. The auxiliary "did" in T3 can be completed by the verb phrase "do the paper" rather than "feel horrible." T2 has the rising intonation of a question and is uttered quickly; T3 has the falling intonation of a statement, the vowel in "oh" is lengthened, and there is a slight pause before "you did." With these prosodic cues, the teacher is probing, asking the student to be more specific, to explain. And the student does, beginning with her marker, "Well."

In S3, the student expresses two concerns about her writing, both in broad, unfocused terms. Her first concern is with developing her ideas, "I just couldn't think of anything." Within this turn, she repeats her earlier statement of concern, the initial response to the teacher's inquiry about the essay, "I didn't feel too good about this essay," and then goes on to voice her second main concern, about grammar, "a lot of little errors here and there."

In T4, given more than she has probably counted on, the teacher focuses on one point, going back to the student's first stated concern about not being able to think of anything to say, in order to focus the student's attention and elicit more information from her. Although in S4 the student does not respond with anything more specific, the teacher tries again in T5, first prompting with a specific reason—about subject matter—then broadening the question to "any idea," although still offering a hint about topic with "this particular paper." The student, in S5, takes the hint and refers to the topic, but declines that suggestion as a reason for her difficulty, adding a restatement of her difficulty in "getting the ideas out" and "putting them . . . on the paper." Her topic initiations occur after the conjunction "but."

Additional evidence for the basic structure of the conference occurs in T6, when the conversation is interrupted. The teacher's responsibility for beginning the interaction is apparent in her self-selection for starting the conversation again, although her prestarts, "Okay, um . . ." indicate that she hasn't yet collected her thoughts to have anything to say. She is merely responding to her obligation, as the teacher, to begin the discourse, to set the stage.

The student, in S6 however, is getting warmed up again as she regains the floor though she needs the teacher's reminder (in T7) to guide her in the right direction. After a slight pause, the student (in S7) recollects her thoughts about the difficulty of putting down her thoughts, again rejecting the notion that she didn't have any ideas, rather, restating her problem as "getting them out."

In T8, the teacher tries to provide procedural scaffolding, initiating a suggestion about how to get the ideas out based on a previous class assignment. In S9, the student acknowledges the strategy for invention but claims that it, too, failed her in the clutch—"It just wasn't there." By T10, the teacher is beginning to run out of guidelines for the student. It's her turn, but she doesn't have anything to say, so she holds her place for a moment until the student returns, in S10, with yet another attempt to describe her problem in producing text. By T11, the teacher has begun to regroup. She stalls a bit, "Let me think," and returns to the topic as a possible starting point for discussing the student's problem. S11 acknowledges the return, repeats the problem about "extending" and then, perhaps tired of searching for an explanation of her problem, shifts the topic back to something more specific, a problem with the sense of a sentence. T12 finishes off the sequence, with four separate positive evaluations, perhaps as anxious for a change as the student.

Within this sequence, then, the teacher has retained a measure of control, initiating questions to the student as a way of guiding the student's discussion of her writing. But clearly the student provides the direction for the discussion, a direction that may be shaped by the teacher's list of broad questions, but which is certainly shaped by the student as to form (length of her utterance, for example) and content (problem discussed).

There is no reason to believe this sequence in and of itself will lead the student to change her process, to revise her essay, or to learn for the future. Indeed, the teacher's lack of ability to provide needed support on the spot seems frustrating. What we do see is Cee initiating discussion about, and articulating, her two major problems—idea generation and concern about mechanics. Cee will grapple with these problems during the entire semester. Throughout this conference, Cee initiates these concerns. During the rest of this conference, the teacher does not seem to provide any guidance for Cee; the teacher does not yet understand the complex relationship between Cee's focus on mechanics and her problem generating ideas.

Throughout the semester, Cee's conferences focus on Cee's two concerns with the teacher trying to "assist" but with little evidence that she is succeeding. However, in the last conference of the semester, the teacher suggests a procedure that excites Cee. The teacher suggests that Cee might have more success generating ideas if she tries to pretend that she is writing to a friendly audience and if she does not worry about grammar at the same time that she is trying to get her "ideas on the paper." Cee for the first time indicates that she sees a solution for her major procedural problem. She seems truly to understand what keeps her from generating ideas. In an "ah hah" tone of voice, she says.

> I think that's what I do. I worry too much about the grammar and how it comes out the first time around, and maybe that's the main cause I worry about that too much, that I don't really worry about how the paper would turn out in the sense of is this the right ideas, will the reader find that she can relate to this ad, can she visualize the picture.

Cee understands the importance of considering the reader as a primary part of her composing process.

CONCLUSION: WHAT DOES AN ANALYSIS OF THE LANGUAGE OF THE CONFERENCE MEAN IN TERMS OF STUDENT WRITING PROCESSES?

Although the data used in this analysis constitute a small sample of the verbal interaction in a student–teacher writing conference, there seems to be evidence of certain characteristics that place the conference somewhere between SS&J's conversational turn-taking system and Mehan's classroom interaction. The conference is a structured speech event with a predictable nature. The structure and predictability allow for ease of communication between participants who understand the rules. Students must learn conference-discourse rules just as they must learn classroom-discourse rules. When the student does not have a clear sense of the rules, there can be negative consequences for learning (Freedman & Sperling, 1985).

The nature of the structure of the conference conversation as a cross between classroom discourse and natural conversation is part of what makes the conference an optimal setting for learning to write. One of the major characteristics of natural conversation is the unpredictability of the roles of the speakers. In fact, that one speaker would mostly ask questions and the other answer them would probably seem odd unless both participants were in a context such as a TV quiz show that encouraged this behavior. Thus, a pattern of utterances, such as question-answer, usually indicates interaction in a certain kind of situation, a situation with predictable features. Many features in a student–teacher conference resemble those discussed in Mehan's (1979) analysis of classroom interaction. However, it would be too simplistic to characterize the writing conference as merely a mini-lesson between a teacher and one student at a time. If looked at in terms of predictability and the control that results, the conference may be seen as a unique opportunity for the student to talk about his or her writing and ideas.

The pattern of IRE found in the conference predicts the points at which, generally, each participant exercises control over the flow of the discourse. Because the IRE pattern involves question-answer sequences in which, usually, the teacher asks the question and the student answers, the teacher seems to carry the control of the discourse. The end of each question signals the transition point at which the teacher relinquishes her turn and her control. Yet when the student, in responding to the initial question, determines the topical course of the sequence of that talk, be it to discuss development or the use of apostrophes, she too seems to exercise control, at least until the teacher reclaims it for evaluation and a shift to another broad question. And perhaps that is more like the "given" of the situation: The teacher retains and releases control in order to encourage student talk and so gather information necessary for her to be able to encourage learning. She is the manager of the learning. She focuses the direction taken by the topics the student initiates. Importantly, in the conference, because of its regular conversational properties, the student has the rare opportunity to interact and express personal pedagogical needs.

The other characteristics discussed in the previous sections of analysis—pause, overlap, and latching, as well as topic shift—also seem to provide evidence of predictability and, as well, opportunity for the student to voice a concern, to focus on a problem. Particularly conducive to learning is the fact of the appropriateness of relatively long pauses that allow the student time to think.

In the early conference that we examined here, the teacher does a good job of probing for information about the student's problems. There are some attempts at procedural facilitation, but little evidence of collaborative problem solving. It seems to take this teacher some time to figure out how best to use her conversation turns with this student. It is encouraging, though, that across time the teacher thinks of a plan that Cee believes will help her.

When the language of writing instruction is analyzed, a post mortem of the instructional process reveals clearly the "shoulds" to teacher, analyst, and readers. We all wonder why the teacher didn't take the successful tact when the student first raised her problems about audience. However, it is important to remember that knowing what to do on the spot and after the fact are quite different. Frequently, the ideal reply comes to us long after a conversation is over and the chance to have an effect has been missed. Freedman and Sperling (1985) discuss some of the barriers to communication for this student and her teacher.

It is important to remember that the analysis begun here is merely an indication of a direction for further inquiry, an inquiry based on an interest in learning about how instruction fits into the writing process, across time and across pieces of writing.

REFERENCES

Applebee, A., & Langer, J. (1983). Instructional scaffolding: Reading and writing as natural language activities. *Language Arts, 60,* 168–175.

Brady, P. (1968). A statistical analysis of on-off patterns in 16 conversations. *Bell System Technical Journal, 47,* 73–91.

Bruner, J. (1978). The role of dialogue in language acquisition. In A. Sinclair, R. Jarvelle, & W.J.M. Levelt (Eds.), *The child's concept of language.* New York: Springer-Verlag.

Carnicelli, T.A. (1980). The writing conference: A one-to-one conversation. In P. Donovan & B. McClelland (Eds.), *Eight approaches to teaching composition.* Urbana, IL: National Council of Teachers of English.

Chafe, W. (1980). The deployment of consciousness in the production of a narrative. In W. Chafe (Ed.), *The pear stories: Cognitive, cultural, and linguistic aspects of a narrative production.* Norwood, NJ: Ablex.

Duke, D. (1975). The student centered conference and the writing process. *English Journal, 64,* 44–47.

Ervin-Tripp, S. (1979). Children's verbal turn taking. In E. Ochs & B. Schieffelin (Eds.), *Developmental pragmatics.* New York: Academic Press.

Fassler, B. (1978). The red pen revisited: Teaching composition through student conferences. *College English, 40,* 186–190.

Flower, L., & Hayes, J.R. (1980). A process model of composition. In L.W. Gregg & E.R. Steinberg (Eds.), *Cognitive processes in writing.* Hillsdale, NJ: Erlbaum.

Freedman, S. (1981). Evaluation in the writing conference: An interactive process. In M. Hairston & C. Selfe (Eds.), *Selected papers from the 1981 Texas Writing Research Conference* (pp. 65–96). Austin: The University of Texas at Austin.

Freedman, S. (1982). *A survey of writing project directors.* Mimeograph. Berkeley, CA: University of California.

Freedman, S. (1985). *The role of response in the acquisition of written language* (NIE Report No. G-083-0065). Washington, DC: National Institute of Education.

Freedman, S., & Sperling, M. (1985). Teacher student interaction in the writing conference:

Response and teaching. In S.W. Freedman (Ed.), *The Acquisition of written language: Response and revision*. Norwood, NJ: Ablex.

Graves, D. (1978). *Balancing the basics: Let them write*. New York: Ford Foundation.

Graves, D. (1983). *Children learn to write*. Exeter, NH: Heinemann.

Gumperz, J. (1982). *Discourse strategies*. Cambridge, England: Cambridge University Press.

Jacobs, S., & Karliner, A. (1977). Helping writers to think: The effect of speech roles in individual conferences on the quality of thought in student writing. *College English, 38*, 489–505.

Jaffe, J., & Feldstein, S. (1970). *Rhythms of dialogue*. New York: Academic Press.

Kamler, B. (1980). One child, one teacher, one classroom: The story of one piece of writing. *Language Arts, 57*, 680–693.

Knapp, J. (1976). Contract/conference evaluation of freshman composition. *College English, 37*, 647–653.

Mehan, H. (1979). *Learning lessons*. Cambridge, MA: Harvard University Press.

Murray, D. (1979). The listening eye: Reflections on the writing conference. *College English, 41*, 13–18.

Reigstad, T. (1980). *Conferencing practices of professional writers: Ten case studies*. Unpublished doctoral dissertation, State University of New York at Buffalo.

Sacks, H., Schegloff, E., & Jefferson, G. (1974). A simplest systematics for the organization of turn-taking for conversation. *Language, 50*, 696–735.

Scardamalia, M., & Bereiter, C. (1986). Research on written composition. In M. Wittrock (Ed.), *Handbook of research on teaching (3rd ed.)*. Skokie, IL: Rand McNally.

Searle, J. (1969). *Speech acts: An essay in the philosophy of language*. Cambridge, England: Cambridge University Press.

Vygotsky, L. (1978). *Mind in society*. Cambridge, MA: Harvard University Press.

Walker, C., & Elias, D. (in preparation). Writing conference talk: Factors associated with high- and low-rated writing conferences.

Witte, S., Meyer, P., Miller, T., & Faigley, L. (1982). *A national survey of college and university program directors (Tech. Rep. No. 2). Austin: The University of Texas, Writing Assessment Project*.

CHAPTER 4

Composing and Computers: Case Studies of Experienced Writers

Lillian Bridwell-Bowles
Parker Johnson
Steven Brehe
University of Minnesota

As computers invade writers' workplaces, we have heard numerous claims for the advantages of word processing: that writers produce more because there is less risk and the keyboards are so fast; that they revise more because their words are a fluid text on a screen until they choose to print a "hard copy"; that they are more creative because they are free to concentrate on higher order problems because the computer can handle surface problems of spelling and formatting so easily. (See Bridwell, Nancarrow, & Ross, 1984, for a review of the current capabilities of word-processing software and computer-assisted writing packages; see also Schwartz, 1982, for a review of the ways computers can be used for teaching writing.) We designed this study so that we could test some of these claims on experienced writers to see what effects learning to compose with a word-processing system on a microcomputer might have on them as writers. Their early experiences as they adjusted to word processors were important to us for several reasons. First, we wanted to describe as objectively as possible the strategies a range of sophisticated writers would find for using computers for their writing. Secondly, what we learned might be valuable as background for introducing students to word processing in writing classes. Finally, we knew we could use the computer's memory capacities to store and retrieve "real-time" writing records in absolute form, giving us a detailed record of these effects, as well as general insights into how writers produce written language.

This research was funded in part by grants from The Graduate School of the University of Minnesota, Lillian Bridwell, Principal Investigator, and from The Fund for the Improvement of Postsecondary Education, Lillian Bridwell and Donald Ross, Co-Principal Investigators. The information and interpretations in this report are those of the authors and do not necessarily represent those of the funding groups.

RELATED STUDIES

Computer Composing

We found no studies of the effects of word processing on writers, other than a few in office environments (Gould, 1981) or with younger children (Daiute, 1983). While we were conducting our study, we learned of Richard Collier's since-published (1983) account of a study to learn whether text editors would improve the revisions of freshmen writers in a computer lab. His study was inconclusive because he used sophisticated equipment that was too complicated for his students, but he did find that the "superior" students in his study used the text editor most successfully and that, over-all, his subjects added more words and edited more often with the computer than they did with traditional methods. The text editors seemed to make the students more efficient with their own habits and composing styles, but there was no clear evidence that their writing improved. In an-other of our studies (Bridwell, Sirc, & Brooke, 1985), we found that com-puters did not significantly improve the revising abilities of selected college juniors and seniors. (See Nancarrow, Ross, & Bridwell, 1984, for an ex-tensive bibliography of research on word processing and writing with com-puters.)

Composing Process Research

We also examined composing-process studies (Daiute, 1981; Flower & Hayes, 1981; Matsuhashi, 1981, 1982; Scardamalia, Bereiter, & Goelman, 1982) for general production patterns that might be altered as a result of using computers for composing; however, because most of these studies also involve case study data, we were unable to predict "average" values for production factors for experienced writers. We sought, instead, to com-pare general patterns in other studies with those we found in ours. We will argue that some of our findings are characteristic of the writers' processes in general, whereas others are effects of writing with a computer.

One of the patterns we see in the methodologies used to study compos-ing processes is a focus on text *production,* apart from careful analyses of the texts themselves. Some of this work reflects the influence of studies done on the production of spontaneous speech, but so far those interested in written-discourse production have shown varying degrees of dissatisfac-tion with speech-based models (see Daiute's work, 1981, for example).

Most recent research on written language production reveals processes that reject linear models of production. We now have sufficient evidence that drafting does not follow in a straight line from planning, nor does it always result in revising followed by editing. Flower and Hayes (1981), for example, have discounted "prewriting" as an accurate representation of an actual stage in the writing process. Recent evidence showing that a greater amount of global, strategic planning goes on during actual production has been confirmed in their studies of writer's protocols—spoken records of what writers are doing as they produce written language. In these protocols, they distinguish between the text itself, which they claim is "eventual" rather than "actual" (p.243), and planning or problem-solving statements. Their desire to find the processes underlying writing sends them past actual writing production and into the protocol's realm of metaproduction: "It is not enough to think of writing as simply a process of text production or deciding what to say next" (p.242).

Matsuhashi (1981, 1982) is not so willing to divorce planning from the actual utterance produced. She has chosen to study events in writing processes—such as pauses—with videotapes, as opposed to oral protocols, within the context of specific discourse tasks. Global and local strategies become equally important in her text-production model. She proceeds beyond the lexical and clause boundaries of the earlier speech-based research to explore the role of pauses in the larger rhetorical realm. Although her research lacks the richness of Flower and Hayes's studies of protocols, it may be a more valid record of written-language production because it avoids the double demands of composing aloud for protocols and writing.

Writer's Retrospective Accounts of Composing

Richard C. Gebhardt (1982) has considered recent composing process research in the light of his own experiences as a writer and those of fiction writers such as Styron. His point is that two conflicting views of composition, the linear "thought-comes-first" school and the "discovery" school, are inadequate to account for composing. He argues, "Writing is—for some people, some times—an act that is linear and controlled by prior thought, just as it is—for some people, some times—a process of discovery through the physical act of moving pen or typewriter keys" (p. 624).

Interviews with fiction writers suggest that they often see themselves as falling into one of the camps Gebhardt describes. Thomas Wolfe, for example, said of his writing process. "It seems to be an element of my creative faculty that it has to realize itself through the process of torrential production" (Schreiber, 1936, p. 165). Wolfe's manuscripts were heavily revised and edited by Maxwell Perkins, who said of their collaboration, "There never was any cutting that Tom did not agree to. He knew that cutting was necessary. His whole impulse was to utter what he felt and he had no time to revise and compress" (Wolfe, 1957, p. x). Wolfe wrote to discover and left the "problem-solving" part of composing to his work with Perkins.

On the other hand, there are many accounts of writers who plan extensively before they write. Dorothy Parker reported that it often took her 6 months to write a story: "I think it out and then write it sentence by sentence—no first draft. I can't write five words but that I change seven" (Cowley, 1958, p. 10). Sinclair Lewis, lamenting his "chaotic mind," recalled seeing the manuscript of Arnold Bennett's *The Old Wives' Tale:* "He had each sentence clear in mind before he put it down—and it was his best book" (Dembo & Pondrom, p. 80). (See Bridwell, 1979, for other accounts of fiction writers' writing rituals.)

Although many interviews with writers are notoriously inaccurate—either because they aren't aware of what they *really* do or because they want to create some mystique about the way they work—we should not discount them as we gather information about composing. Neither should they suggest that a writer *always* writes in a certain way, for surely factors such as the writer's familiarity with the ideas, the audience for the text, and the context within which the writer works influence what happens. But we might ask whether writers find markedly different patterns or rituals for composing. As we studied experienced writers, we watched to see whether they did report such rituals and whether they changed as they used new technologies for composing.

THE DESIGN OF THE STUDY

We wanted to determine whether computer composing altered patterns of text production, planning and revising, and the writers' views of their writing. We asked them to write four essays for us—one using their "typical" ways of working with pen or typewriter and paper, and three with computers. Because we wanted to establish a consistent context for the study, we gave them all the same assignments, had them write in the same places (rooms on our campus) and scheduled 4 hr, in 2-hr blocks, for each essay.

Using procedures described in detail below, we compared their composing processes for the first essays with those they used when they moved to the computers. We also watched for changes in the computer sessions as they became more comfortable with the particular word-processing software we selected (WordStar from MicroPro, Inc., chosen because it is a very widely known, commercially popular package). Finally, we interviewed them every 2 hr as they wrote and analyzed their self-reports about their work.

When we began, we were interested in three kinds of information: (1) the writers' typical composing "styles"—how they worked; (2) the characteristics of their writing and how the writers viewed the quality of their own writing; and (3) changes in the writers' styles of composing, the writing they did, or their perceptions of their work that could be attributed to using a computer for composing.

The Writers

Over a 10-week period, 8 "experienced" writers—4 females and 4 males who ranged in age from 26 to 42—wrote essays in response to four articles on composition theory. Our writers were all graduate teaching associates who had written extensively both within and outside academia. Because we had a number of volunteers for the study, we used the criterion of non-academic publishing to select these 8. Their publications included scores of newspaper stories, magazine feature articles, scientific and technical manuals, advertising copy, bibliographies, fiction, and poetry. All were competent typists, but none had ever used a word-processing system before. They volunteered for the project because they wanted to learn to use computers for their own writing.

The Writing Tasks

The writers wrote four essays in 8 2-hr sessions (4 hr for each essay). Before they began each essay, we gave them an article on composition theory[1] that might have implications for teaching composition and asked them to report implications to an audience of peers, other writing instructors at the University of Minnesota. All of the writers had participated in training seminars for composition instructors and were familiar with the expectations their readers would have for "theory into practice" reports. We chose to control the kind of writing they did in the study for two reasons. First, their current writing projects were quite diverse, ranging from dissertations on children's literature and legal philosophy to newspaper reviews and magazine feature stories. Writing a report for the training seminar was a task that was familiar to all of them. They received a new article 3 days before they began an essay, and they were free to plan or write ahead of time, if they so desired. A second reason for using uniform writing tasks was to determine whether their individual approaches differed with this particular kind of writing.

For the first of the four reports, they used their usual writing tools, generally pen and paper, although one writer brought her typewriter to the sessions because she nearly always used it in composing. We refer to these sessions as "scribal sessions" in this chapter. For the remaining three re-

---

[1] We selected the following four articles for the four tasks (listed in the order all the writers received them): Linda Flower and John Hayes' (1981) "A Cognitive Process Theory of Writing." *College Composition and Communication, 32,* 365–387: Janet Emig's (1977) "Writing as Mode of Learning," *College Composition and Communication, 28,* 122–127; Richard E. Young and Alton L. Becker's (1981) "Toward a Modern Theory of Rhetoric: A Tagmemic Contribution;" in Gary Tate and Edward P.J. Corbett (Eds.). *The Writing Teacher's Sourcebook.* (Eds.), New York: Oxford University Press, 129–148; and Richard Ohmann's (1981) "Use Definite, Specific, Concrete Language," also in *The Writing Teacher's Sourcebook,* 379–389.

Table 1.   Schedule of Sessions for the Writing Tasks

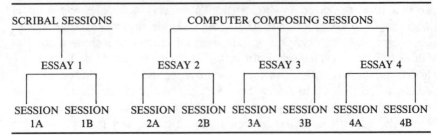

ports, they used microcomputers and word-processing software. We refer to these sessions as "computer sessions." We gave them a 2-hr introduction to the computers and the word-processing package. Although all the writers reported that they felt comfortable enough to begin composing with the computer, they also reported that they learned more word-processing commands and became more successful with the task as the study progressed. Aside from the common assignments and scheduling constraints we imposed, the writers were free to do what they wanted. They did not have to produce finished texts, although some did; they could use as much of the 2-hr session (and in some cases, more) as they needed; they could use the word processor in combination with handwriting if that proved more convenient. Table 1 shows the labels we have used for these sessions.

The Data

We collected two kinds of data during the study: information from interviews and observations of the writers' composing processes. After each 2-hr session, we interviewed the writers for about 20 min, following a standard set of questions about what they recalled doing or thinking. We synthesized the information from these interviews in the narratives that appear later in this chapter.

To analyze composing processes in the scribal sessions, we computed deletions of words and sentences per 15 min, as well as the total number of words in the final version of their reports. For the computer sessions, we were able to collect a more detailed, timed record of their composing processes on the computer by using special programs developed in cooperation with the University of Minnesota's Computer Center. These records contain all keystrokes (both characters in the actual texts themselves and control key commands for word-processing operations) reported in 1-s intervals.

To synthesize the patterns of production from the keystroke data, we developed a classification scheme for keystrokes that would give us a larger picture of what each writer was doing across a session. Table 2 lists these

Table 2.   Process Categories for the Keystone Record

Pause: 15-s interval during which fewer than two words are produced.

Text production: Two or more words produced during a 15-s interval; fewer than 5 consecutive seconds' pause

Editing: two or more character deletions or insertions without pauses of 5 s or more; fewer than two words produced (character changes, often typographical corrections)

Revision: two or more consecutive deletions of units beyond the character; a formatting command; a "block" command to move or delete (word, sentence, or block changes)

Cursor movement: line, word, or block moves of the cursor (always occurred in combination with some other category)

Scrolling: changing the text that appears on the screen

Combinations: more than one of the operations above within a 15-s interval

Note: Our keystroke interpretations of these categories are specific to the word-processing program we used, WordStar (MicroPro, Inc.). They are available upon request.

categories. Working inductively from the record of the keystrokes, we defined the major ways the writers used their time: pausing and planning, producing text, revising (deleting words, phrases, or sentences; formatting, moving or deleting "blocks" of text), moving the cursor around (always associated with some other category), editing (minor changes; often typographical corrections), rereading (scrolling through their writing on the screen), or combinations of these processes.

We chose to analyze the keystrokes ourselves, rather than to use the computer to classify them, because we, as readers, were more accurate at assessing the processes than our models for computerized analysis. Using one of our codings of a keystroke record as a basis, we compared two other sets of independent codings; the other two investigators achieved 93% and 91% agreement, respectively, for a 2-hr session.

In addition to the interviews and the process classifications, we counted the total number of words preserved at various points, deletions, and notes made by hand as they composed during the scribal and the computer sessions. Finally, we found that our writers' concepts of "drafts" differed so much that we had to describe how their processes varied, depending upon how they viewed the texts they were producing. For example, the processes we observed when they were writing passages that they considered "salvageable" for the final version were different from processes in "discovery drafts" that would probably not be preserved at all in the final texts.

THE WRITERS' DESCRIPTIONS OF THEIR COMPOSING PROCESSES

The poet Stephen Spender (1970) has described two kinds of poets, the "Beethovians" (those who compose to find out what they have to say) and the "Mozartians" (those who plan extensively and then execute).[2] In our study, we observed that our writers fell along a continuum marked by these extremes, at least for this particular kind of task. Because we found that their "general styles" influenced the way they wrote for us, both with and without the computer, we have grouped them into these two categories, plus a middle one, "The Combinations."

The Discoverers: The "Beethovians"

Mike. An academic writer, Mike had written some poetry, but his primary writing topics included composition theory and ideas for training other writing teachers. He, of all the writers, seemed most concerned with his audience for these reports. He reported that he typically spent "quite a bit of time pre-writing," an understatement, as we discovered. During his first session, he wrote 17 pages of what he called "talking to myself on paper" about who his readers were and what they might want to know. He produced several "trees" of his ideas, and ended the session with a real concern about the "honesty" of what he was doing because he really wanted to write to an audience of peers rather than to new teachers.

In the second scribal session he continued to report his reactions to the theories in what he had read, but was still struggling with his audience, vacillating between a need to discuss theory with those who would be interested in it and a need to say something helpful to new teachers. Through an alternating process of writing and planning with visual "trees" and diagrams, he finally arrived at a goal he wanted to reach: to write a report reassuring new teachers about a discovery and problem-solving approach to teaching. At this point, he ended the session, but said he had found a paper worth sharing with the staff. Mike told us that this was not entirely typical of his writing style. He said that the articles he usually wrote were scholarly, "academic" papers or, if they were directed toward teachers, more clearly "practical" than what he found himself writing in this essay. He was pleased with the task, however, because he had been able to reconcile his two competing goals—to argue at a theoretical level (for peers) and to inform with practical ideas (for new teachers). Writing the essay was a real struggle for him, and, despite pages and pages of writing, he did not have a "draft" to show for the time he had spent. He did finally find a plan for a piece of writing he could value, one that would allow him to salvage parts of what he had written if he ever finished this essay.

---

[2] Janet Emig, among others, has also noted Spender's descriptions of "Beethovians" and "Mozartians." In her 1964 article, "The Uses of the Unconscious in Composing," *College Composition and Communication, 15,* 6–11, she discusses ways to help students, who may be "Beethovians" more often than they are "Mozartians," develop successful rituals in their composing processes.

When he moved to computer composing, he expressed much displeasure because he could not see all the pieces of writing he had produced at once: "I kept losing sight of my text, what I'd already written . . . I kept trying to find stuff." After several sessions, he was able to identify specifically what was bothering him: "Scrolling is frustrating . . . I'm much more aware of rereading now . . . [I miss the] quick access with the pen and paper process." Even though he became more comfortable with scrolling as time went on, he did not learn, at least during the period of the study, how to make the screen work for him as easily as paper and pen did when he wanted to diagram his ideas with a tree or jot lists of notes to himself.[3]

Another problem that Mike faced quite early was that he missed paper. During the study, we printed copies of the drafts for those who requested them at the end of each session. This did not satisfy Mike's need for quick, visual access to his ideas. We noted in his scribal sessions that he often alternated between diagramming or treeing his ideas on paper and writing. Diagrams mingled with sentences on the pages of his scribal draft, but he did not find a way to do this easily on the screen. During his computer sessions, he tried to compose without paper because he thought this was the way to use the computer efficiently. During the second computer session, he shifted his focus from the task to the machine, experimenting with new ways to use the screen: "I felt free to take more risks this time . . . changing things just to learn the machine." However, he did not succeed in changing his methods or in finding a way to make the computer replicate his scribal processes during the study. To do so, he would have required graphics features, a light pen, or a mouse—features our word-processing package did not have. For this writer, the computer interfered with his successful writing practices, but he did see clear advantages for editing or for preparing reference lists on a computer. After the study ended, he became convinced that the computer might help him with the preparation of his PhD dissertation, so he typed the hundreds of pages of his final manuscript onto floppy disks and did his final editing on the screen.

Brian. Brian came to us with a newspaper and legal writing back-ground and was working on a dissertation on philosophy and the law. He described his current writing as "argumentative and philosophical" and directed toward scholars. He was clear about his composing process: "rough planning, more detailed plans, execution, scrap, rough plan, re-fined plan, execution, scrap and repeat." He said he usually wrote on legal pads but occasionally composed at a typewriter. Knowing how quickly he

---

[3] We should point out here that our word-processing software did not have a split-screen feature that might have allowed Mike to see his notes or diagrams at the same time he had a draft file on the screen—clearly an advantageous feature for a writer like Mike, but one that is not available on the widely used word-processing package we chose for the study.

had produced many essays as a scholar, we were surprised by the way he worked. We had expected that he would value logical, a priori planning and efficiency over repeated revisions of his ideas.

Like most of the other writers in the study, he knew his own patterns and gave us an example of them in his first sessions. He made extensive notes that he used as "an initial springboard," but then he "abandoned them" as he wrote because his writing led him to many "new starts." Once he began drafting, he made very few new notes, preferring to hold what he was doing in memory. He said he "discovered a lot" in what he wrote, but decided to reread the article so he would have it more thoroughly "analyzed" before he started again. He, like Mike, was concerned about his audience, but, Brian wondered, "Just how pedantic can I be?"

At the beginning of the second scribal session, he completely abandoned all of what he had done earlier because he had decided what his audience would want: a thorough review of the theoretical ideas, a genre he knew well from legal writing. With almost no planning on paper, he finished a "whole draft," but said if he had more time he would "start from scratch" again because he had some additional insights, consistent with his practice of "routinely junking all the old writing." In this session, he was more concerned with the quality of the ideas in the article he had read and with expressing them well than he was with his audience. He reported that the writing he had done in these sessions was very typical because he had only "one mode for how I work."

Brian reported some of the same difficulties Mike had when he moved to the computer for composing—scrolling, planning on paper—but his habit of starting completely over once he'd had an insight helped him adjust more quickly to the screen. He seemed to have a less pronounced need for a visual representation of his planning, but at one point he said, "I didn't do any prewriting on the screen, but [if he'd been working with paper] I would probably scrawl on paper." Several times he abandoned his old files or deleted large blocks (41 lines in session 4B, the last one), replicating his "traditional" processes. Despite these major deletions, he reported that he felt less free to abandon his writing during computer sessions, even though deleting is relatively easy with a word-processing system: "The computer has a tendency to make you want to salvage too much." We speculated that the polished quality of the writing on the screen lured him and some of the other writers to preserve writing they might otherwise have abandoned.

Unlike Mike, however, he had less difficulty discovering the shape of his ideas with the computer. He liked the keyboard because its speed allowed him to see his ideas quickly. He nearly doubled his rate of text production in first sessions (1A compared to 4A). The difference seemed to be that he did not require diagrams for his planning as Mike had. Brian used the emerging text as a cue for his planning process.

Jane.   Jane had worked as a freelance writer before returning to graduate school and had diverse experiences—from "about a dozen" articles on nuclear energy to neighborhood newspaper features on topics ranging from a development project to "a mushroom-picking group." She reported that she composed longhand and typed only after she got some distance from her ideas. She said she liked to "think for a long time" before she began to write. She said she wrote slowly, with what she called "drafting" taking most of her time. She also said she liked to revise what she had written—at least twice—before she was comfortable that she had found what it should be.

Jane was one of the writers who had difficulty in adjusting to the setting for the writing—a room with at least three other writers present for the study, and, for the later sessions, a room with four microcomputers with people talking occasionally and walking in and out. She was distracted in her planning by this, and often produced "only prewriting." It was difficult to determine how much of her long "incubation" period was typical and how much was caused by the conditions we imposed. Her problems are interesting, however, in that they are similar to those many of us have experienced when we were forced, because of our addiction to word processing, to work in a communal computer lab.

Jane never succeeded in producing what she called a finished draft on the computer. She reported her problems to us in a variety of ways: "All of today was prewriting, but I might use chunks because what I've done is in complete sentences. . . . On the word processor I'm writing more notes to myself, notes on thoughts." In contrast to both Mike and Brian, she found herself almost exclusively planning in words on the screen, but the planning was different from her "typical" processes in that it was in complete sentences. She was pleased with this change, commenting, "Just getting thoughts down on the screen helped me get into the writing," an observation she made several times during the study.

Executors: The "Mozartians"

Bill.   Bill had written reviews and scholarly, analytical articles about scientific and technical writing, particularly in medical journals. If any of these writers was "self-aware," Bill was. He described his nearly invariant process for us before he began, and we watched it unfold each time he wrote:

> When writing about a text, I read and annotate carefully, getting a general idea of what I'll say. Then I outline (or rather, *assemble* points into an

argument) in *specific* terms; this can take 2 hours or 2 days. By the time I begin to write, I'm confident of my purpose and content, and I worry mainly about audience, especially as it concerns voice and style. I bang out *one* heavily worked on draft (cross-outs, arrows within paragraphs, etc.), spending 60 to 120 minutes per 250 words. Rarely do I undertake major revisions or even tamper with paragraph order. Proofreading is for mechanics only.

Although he said he worked differently when he wrote letters or "when working from data," all of our reports were "writing about a text," and we observed amazing consistency in his approach throughout the study.

Bill began his first scribal session by making a list of "potentially remarkable things" from the article, followed by a note to himself to cut and paste them in the order he would include them when he wrote, a step he did carry out. About halfway into the session, he produced an outline, writing on the page: "OUTLINE: not immutable, esp. toward the end, but I am *fairly* committed to it." At the bottom of this outline, he wrote, "One hour has now passed—used it for task definition, gathering, organizing. Now to drafting." He wrote these notes to himself, monitoring his own process. We observed later that he had cut up strips of paper, each with a point he would cover, and had taped them in the order he finally produced for his outline.

On the computer, Bill was determined to find a way to make the computer emulate his cut-and-paste outlining process. He began with "points possibly worth mentioning," followed by an "outline" he spent much time evolving on the screen. In the keystroke record, we discovered that he had initially written out points in a different order and had used "block commands" to rearrange these points. Referring to his "typical" outlining step, he said after the first computer session, "I spent an hour trying to find the word processor version of this" because he could not cut and paste electronic images without printing them out. He liked being able to replicate his ritual and seemed more pleased initially than most of the other writers.

Beyond his planning, which he reported was nearly all over before he ever began to write complete sentences, Bill found another advantage in word processing. He could perfect each sentence as he went along without retyping. This activity, he said, "displaced my frustration" with formulating each idea as he drafted. He told us that while he was tinkering with surface details he was building momentum for the next sentence. Toward the end of the study, he reported that he wanted to "try to compose in a different style . . . the word processor may make this break possible." He told us he wanted to feel freer to compose more rapidly without so much crafting. Now that he has his own microcomputer, he tells us that he is not so "compulsive" about his need to plan things in advance. Clearly, in his case, our study covered only the initial effects of using a computer for composing.

Teresa.   Teresa was accustomed to "clocking in" as a writer because of her writing in an advertising agency and for newspapers. She said she almost always worked under a deadline and was aware of "cost efficiency"; her pen "should always be moving." She told us before she began writing for us that she did very little "pre-writing" or pre-planning. Her experience had taught her to make quick decisions about purpose and audience, a quick plan for how to execute a piece of writing, and then get on with it.

In her first scribal session, she made a one-page topical outline immediately and then proceeded to execute it. During this session she said she forced herself to "Go, go, go!" even when she didn't know where she was headed; she made notes to herself in the margins to monitor what she was doing so that when she came back to her raw material she would recall her thoughts about it as she went along. The only sentence she recalled changing was the first one because she knew immediately it would take her in the wrong direction. During the second session, she reread the article she was reviewing and decided to "take the easy way out"—to summarize the article and then respond with implications for teachers in a list form. She avoided a more complicated approach because, she said, "Ignorance is speed." She used the time she might have to report her paper to her peers as a way of limiting her list of implications.

She used scissors and tape to piece together her "final" draft—using nearly all of what she had produced the first day, but rewriting some sections with minor wording changes and a few added examples. Her quick judgments at the beginning were closely in line with what she decided to do with her essay.

Teresa reported that she found the time limits distracting because she usually wrote in "long stretches" until she got a whole draft out. She quickly adjusted during the second session, however, rereading and finishing her first draft and piecing together the second one within about 20 min.

When she moved to the computer, Teresa found that learning the word-processing commands slowed her down, that "it really changes things." Although she managed to produce as much or more finished "copy" with the computer, she was not totally sold and told us at the end of the study, "Longhand seems more secure." We had to ask ourselves if, in her case, she might not have reacted differently had she not had so many successes with paper, pen, and typewriter. She did not seem to have a strong reason to abandon her successful practices in favor of a machine that took some concentrated time to learn, perhaps because she knew she would not have unlimited access to one in the foreseeable future.

The Combinations

Didi. For her academic writing, Didi reported to us that she spent much time planning her first paragraph ("3 to 8 hr"), then "a slow first draft followed by a faster one," and finally "tinkering and proofreading." In her first session, she planned on paper throughout the session, telling us she needed "the first paragraph or the draft dies." In the second session she continued this process until she was generally satisfied with the beginning and then produced a rough draft.

Didi's response to the computer was mixed. Initially she said, "I'm surprised. I thought I was hooked on pen and paper, but I liked being able to play on it [the computer]." As the study progressed, however, she found herself going back to paper. We would often find notes in the computer files that told us she was "off in another room writing on paper." She found she was drawn toward editing before she even knew what she wanted to say: "Misspellings drive me crazy . . . I keep tidying up, tidying up." On not following her usual process of making many lists of words and phrases on paper: "I felt a linear need to string sentences together." Finally, toward the end of the study, she found more abstract problems: "I feel a distance from the writing because of the screen . . . I'm a private writer in the early stages . . . I like to have everything hidden . . . not on the word processor." Some time after the study ended, we learned that Didi had not done any more composing with the computer (we were not surprised), but that she had begun to use it for her extensive bibliographies.

Sue. Primarily an academic writer, Sue reported that she had some rituals for writing. She reported that she would plan on paper, draft unconnected ideas in a "free-writing" form, type a "free-writing" draft and edit it as she went along, make pen-and-paper changes, retype, revise again, retype individual pages, edit and polish, and then deliver her manuscript to a typist. When she wrote her initial report for us, she brought in a typewriter. She followed her rituals faithfully: a handwritten list of ideas, followed by seven pages of handwritten free-writing, several pages of which she described as "a decent working draft," but "mostly notes about what should be done." She ran into a block after about three-quarters of the first session and attributed that to her need for an introduction and a plan that would satisfy her description of herself as a "beginning-to-end writer."

Once she had an overall plan worked out, she said, she proceeded rapidly through its execution—exactly what she did in the second session. She was much more satisfied after this session because she had found the "shape of the essay," even though the text itself was far from finished— four typed pages that followed from four previously typed draft pages and five pages of handwritten inserts. She reported that one of her problems during this session was deciding where her new material would go in relation to chunks she had already produced. She used a methodical system of labeling parts and marking points for insertion to set up the last version she typed.

Throughout both sessions, she worked on wordings and phrasings because "surface details never escape me." Although she said she couldn't compose on a typewriter, she had to have the typed form to "tinker on," a need many of the writers expressed. They wanted to see their ideas on paper so they could perfect them or judge them for shape and coverage.

Sue adjusted fairly rapidly to the word processor, even though she had her doctoral exams in the middle of the study and claimed this really affected one of her sessions (3B). She liked the speed with which she could produce a more polished draft to read and revise: "This is not as messy as my typewriter version would have been." Like Didi, she found the screen lured her to corrections, commenting. "I take care of commas I never noticed before." But, unlike Didi, this did not slow her down. She claimed she was more "prolix" on the word processor, saying at one point, "I wouldn't normally try to write without putting more thought into it." At the end of the study, however, she didn't think this had been detrimental at all, and promptly went out and bought the same system we used in the study. She also mentioned a new awareness we have seen in many computer composers. She commented that she just "loved to fool with formatting."

Lance.   Although Lance had published scholarly articles on child psychology, his current writing was prose fiction and literary criticism, including dozens of reviews for newspapers. He told us he did *all* his composing on a typewriter after he had made extensive notes, outlines, or diagrams to work from. Some of this planning he did with a pen, but he could also do it at a typewriter. Once he had a plan, he said he composed and typed "quickly and cavalierly" on cheap yellow paper. After the first complete draft, he said he liked to do "moderate" revision of nonfiction and "wholesale rewriting" of fiction. He reported that he took great pleasure in typing all of his final drafts on white bond paper.

When he wrote the first report, he followed his description of himself. He spent about a quarter of his time reviewing his marginalia on the article and planning before he began. He struggled with what his readers would want to know, but settled that question very quickly: They were very much like him, and they would want a translation of the ideas he got from the article. He went on to make an outline and began drafting in the first session and finished what he called a "decent working draft." He said he knew where he wanted to go from the beginning but went through a "midcourse correction" when he "stumbled on" a better way to organize it. His second draft amounted to shaping up the parts so that he would have the right "balance"; he found his outline didn't work as his focus became

Table 3.   Average, Across Sessions, Of Percentage Of Time Spent In Process Categories By Each Writer During Computer Sessions

Operation	Sue	Brian	Didi	Bill	Mike	Teresa	Jane	Lance
Pause	17.60	34.39	43.81	42.69	42.05	24.88	40.74	22.42
Text Production	13.96	17.88	14.27	13.56	14.92	21.45	11.32	15.50
Text Production—Pause Combination	7.11	8.18	6.34	13.40	8.32	14.92	9.67	8.46
Text Production—Editing Combination	18.32	13.91	9.10	3.80	5.11	9.73	6.70	12.64
Other Editing Combinations	32.96	18.15	19.41	20.59	16.64	18.05	20.58	22.72
Scroll Combinations	4.98	2.38	5.10	4.51	12.12	8.45	8.83	11.48
Revising Combinations	5.32	4.45	1.91	1.40	.79	2.43	2.14	6.70

clearer and he cut much of what he had written earlier. The pressure to shape up the essay within the time period, once he had found his structure, was the only difference he noted from his "normal" routines, but he described his draft as "very good" and "finished."

Lance's reactions toward computer composing were also mixed. Early on, he told us it was "easy to revise [with the word processor], but crippling to compose." He reacted to the pressure he felt to produce, saying there was "less sitting back and staring." He also missed other rituals, "paper shuffling, which I like to do," visual diagramming, his yellow paper for early drafts and bond paper for final drafts. As the study progressed, however, he seemed to adjust, saying "I write faster than usual," something he was pleased about. At the end of the project he quipped, "I've made my peace with that machine!" and indeed he had if the amount of writing he was able to produce is any indication.

THE KEYSTROKE RECORD OF THE WRITERS' COMPOSING PROCESSES

From our analysis of the keystroke record, we were able to compute average times spent in various "operations" during composing: pausing, producing text (text production), producing text slowly with pauses interspersed (text-pause), producing text and editing (text-edit), primarily editing (editing combinations), scrolling—or reading "screenfuls" of text—while performing other operations (scroll combinations), and revising units, at least at the word level (revising combinations).

Table 3 shows how each of the writers spent their time during the computer sessions. Bill, the "preplanner," and Mike, the "discoverer," show overall similarities in the percentages of time spent in pausing and produc-

Table 4. Average, Across Writers, Of The Percentage Of Time Spent In Process Categories In First And Last Computer Sessions

| | First Computer Sessions | | Last Computer Sessions | | |
	2A	2B	4A	4B	Mean
Pause	33.53	31.56	34.47	34.71	33.56
Text Production	17.75	12.69	16.98	14.01	15.35
Text Production—Pause Combination	8.75	10.12	12.02	7.31	9.55
Text Production—Editing Combination	11.61	7.96	26.59	6.79	13.23
Other Editing Combinations	19.43	24.40	15.72	24.86	21.10
Scrolling Combinations	6.93	9.46	11.87	7.66	8.98
Revising Combinations	1.94	3.75	2.28	4.60	3.14

ing text. These similarities, however, mask important differences between writers, illustrating the important relationship between composing processes and the text being produced. The major difference between these two was that Bill paused to plan initially and Mike stopped for long periods throughout his sessions to question where he was going with his ideas and to reformulate what he had already written. Their time spent in scrolling through their writing on the computer's screen also differed. Looking forward and backward from the places where he stopped, Mike scrolled more than twice as often as Bill. Bill's scrolling went from start to finish as he edited what he had written.

Teresa, Sue, and Lance valued the speed with which they could enter their ideas on the screen with the computer, and their pause times show that they spent much less time planning than did their counterparts. Teresa, true to her "time is money" philosophy, changed very little of what she wrote so quickly. Sue and Lance, however, were much more likely to delete and rewrite whole chunks of what they had written at later points as they reread and revised.

Table 4 shows the combined average time these writers spent in each of the process categories during the first and last computer sessions. No other operation involved more time in our writers' composing processes than did "pausing," significant planning time at all stages during composing. Fully a third of the time we recorded (an average of 12 hr for each subject) was coded in the pause category. These pauses followed two significant patterns: (1) They nearly always came at the end of paragraph breaks in the text, no matter whether the writer was producing the draft for the first time or rereading and editing an existing text; and (2) in many cases, they came after the writer produced a high-level abstraction and searched for the examples to illustrate it. Bill, for example, wrote that writing involves making connections, saying, "Writing forces us to do this at various levels:" After the colon, there is a full three min pause before he fleshes out the levels, "lexical, syntactic, and rhetorical." Other significant pauses come as the writers read and reread their texts, in combination with scrolling.

Text production, the operation in which words simply spill out, occupies a surprisingly small portion of their time—an average of 15%, without much variance depending on the particular session—about the same in first and second sessions for each task. Similarly, the combination of producing text and pausing shows a uniform average time, around 9%. Composing combined with editing, however, it is the most common operation when the writer is producing new text. It occupies 12% of the time in the first computer session (2A), 8% in the second (2B), and then skyrockets to 27% for the first session of the last task (4A) in contrast to 7% for 4B.

At first glance, one might attribute the abundance of superficial editing to problems with typing on a computer keyboard, to the likelihood that they make many errors, and certainly novices do make more typographical errors; however, by the fourth writing task, all the writers had stopped commenting on this problem, and it is at this point that the jump in "text-edit" occurs. Our interpretation of this is that they can produce text faster, but they are continually editing to perfect their expressions as they go along. This is particularly interesting in that it comes in the *first* sessions for each writing task, rather than the second when one might expect more editing. Indeed, the "editing combinations" category is much higher in the second (B) sessions, and it is from the start. This category does not include much text production, however, but rather more deliberate searching for typos, misspellings, and infelicitous phrasings.

Scrolling—changing what is visible on the screen—is just as predominant in first sessions as it is in second sessions, indicating that even early on, they had a need to read and reread what they had written to pick up forward momentum.

Tables 5 and 6 show the patterns of deletions the writers used in their scribal and computer composing sessions. Bill and Teresa did not revise in major ways as they wrote manually because many of their rhetorical decisions were made in advance and they had little need to. Mike, who had not yet written the draft he had discovered by the end of these sessions, did not need to tinker at the word level either. These patterns did not change for them as they used the computer. With the exception of Lance, all of the other writers made more word-level changes during the second sessions, clearly using them as editing sessions.

By the fourth set of sessions, most of the writers had found ways to

Table 5. Deletions In Scribal Sessions For Each Writer

Units	Sue	Brian	Didi	Bill	Mike	Teresa	Jane	Lance
Words per 15 min								
1A	5.75	13.5	a	3.13	8.25	5.13	a	40.5
1B	18.13	61.88	0.63	3.63	3.63	4.50	5.50	39.5
Sentences per session								
1A	0	2	a	0	b	1	a	15
1B	7	19	0	0	b	1	0	11

a All "prewriting" lists, etc.; no "text" or actual sentences.
b Whole passages abandoned in favor of new starts, some of which incorporated earlier material; difficult to count accurately.

Table 6. Deletions In Computer Sessions For Each Writer

Units	Sue	Brian	Didi	Bill	Mike	Teresa	Jane	Lance
Characters per 15 min[a]								
2A	4.9	5.8	3.2	1.7	2.6	2.8	0.4	3.0
2B	2.8	4.5	2.0	1.9	2.6	2.3	0.1	2.2
4A	4.2	6.8	0.9	2.0	2.9	1.2	0.3	1.6
4B	2.5	3.8	2.6	1.3	1.2	1.4	0.6	2.2
Words per 15 min[a]								
2A	4.0	6.7	5.9	0	0	0	0.43	4.1
2B	7.6	2.2	9.9	0.11	0.16	0.25	5.09	26.5
4A	3.12	2.37	0.33	0	0	2.00	2.00	19.12
4B	27.25	19.43	9.43	0.30	0.29	5.00	2.00	11.33
Lines per session								
2A	3	1	6	10	0	0	0	12
2B	5	1	22	3	8	5	0	27
4A	6	1	0	5	3	0	2	27
4B	5	41	8	24	5	12	26	18
Blocks per session								
2A	1	0	0	0	0	0	0	0
2B	0	0	0	0	1	1	0	3
4A	0	0	0	6	1	0	0	1
4B	0	1	0	0	5	0	0	5

[a]Character and word frequencies divided by each writer's time.

approximate their familiar revision patterns with the computer, but with several notable differences. All of the writers deleted lines with the computer far more frequently than they had deleted sentences as they wrote manually. Brian, for example, deleted 41 lines and a whole block in his final computer session. Mike, by this time willing to gamble with the computer to make his "Beethovian" changes, deleted five blocks of writing as

Table 7. Average, Across Writers, Of Words Preserved In Texts At The End Of Each Session

	Scribal Sessions	
	M	**SD**
1A	1096.85	545.73
1B		
(final)	1309.12	484.98
	Computer Sessions	
	M	**SD**
2A	938.25	362.06
2B		
(final)	1091.12	383.89
3A	891.00	383.89
3B		
(final)	1612.75	350.81
4A	1008.62	401.11
4B		
(final)	1506.38	548.20

Note: The mean for the second scribal session includes only new words written during the second session. In most cases, these were additions made at end of the draft produced on the first day, or pages marked "insert." The means for the computer sessions are simply counts of the words in each essay at the end of the sessions. These procedures mean that the figures for scribal and computer sessions are quite comparable.

he pulled together his draft. Very clearly, they revised more with the computer than they did when they wrote or typed their essays.

THE TEXTS THE WRITERS PRODUCED

Total Words Preserved

As the writers moved to the computers, we observed something we could have predicted. They were affected by the demands of the new system, and most of them produced less writing. The mean number of words preserved in the first essay (1,309 words at the end of the second session), compared to the mean for the second essay (1,091 at the end of the second session), demonstrates this reduction (see Table 7). However, the difference was not as pronounced as it could have been, partly because those writers who prolonged note-taking in the first scribal sessions (e.g., Didi and Jane) moved more quickly into producing text during the first word-processing session. (See Table 8 for word totals for each of the writers.) One explanation they had for this was that the computer encouraged them as they began writing because the information looked so "polished" on the screen.

Table 8.   Total Words Preserved in Texts By Writers In Each Session

Writer	1A	1B	2A	2B	3A	3B	4A	4B
Sue	1221	1925	1318	1503	878	1924	1545	1685
Brian	774	1056	824	1516	1361	2068	1333	1436
Mike	1548	1161	1005	1200	1106	1301	763	1210
Didi	429[a]	1328	746	1494	1144	1586	272	704
Bill	244	595	315	662	452	1161	803	1867
Teresa	2048	1347	966	628	921	1957	1174	1233
Jane	[b]	996	828	898	535	1245	932	1357
Lance	1414	2065	1502	826	732	1657	1246	2559

[a]Excluding many planning notes; text only
[b]All planning notes, no text

Even though a large part of Bill's first computer session (2A) included crafting an outline, he spent much time correcting and editing these notes. The writers who were most fluent in the first scribal session (e.g., Teresa and Sue), however, produced much less on the computer. Teresa's production was cut by more than half (from a total of 2,048 words in Session 1A to 966 in Session 2A). These two writers "recovered" by the fourth report, but their final texts were still not quite as long as their first ones had been.

Across the board, however, the texts produced in the final computer session (4B) were longer by an average of 200 words than those the writers produced with scribal methods (see Table 8). Even Jane, who never wrote what she called an "essay" with the computer, produced many more ideas on the screen than on paper. One explanation seems reasonable: They did more planning that was not recorded on the screen as they composed with the computers; in contrast, when they composed on paper, they were more likely to record text that resembled planning notes to themselves ("come back to this"; "write out summary here") in their first attempts to draft. A few, particularly Didi, continued to write to themselves on the computer because they could not, or would not, jump to preparing final drafts ·quickly, even if what they were producing "looked" like final copy. Didi interspersed comments like these with her text on the screen in Session 2B:

> [Why can't I see all of my essay at the same time? . . .] . . . [I can't stand this! I need to scribble before I write. How can I go forward if I can't make notes about what I'm going to talk about?] (taking a break) . . . (going downstairs for coffee . . .)

In the middle of her final computer session (4B), she wrote a note to us on the screen, "[off to use conventional (old-fashioned) methods . . .]." our final bit of evidence that she had a definite need to plan on paper. She did this, however, very effectively, because with a combination of notes on paper and final draft on screen, she produced much more in two of the computer sessions than she had for the first report.

The increased average length of the third and fourth essays may simply be a function of their adjustment to the context for writing, even though several of them were reporting that they felt freer to compose with the computer. Whatever the explanation, they had at least recovered from the losses in the first computer sessions.

Bill's texts reveal the most consistent pattern: planning in the first sessions, whether on paper or on the screen, and over double the production in the second sessions as he "executed" his plan. He seemed to make the transition to screen planning most successfully. It should come as no surprise that he was one of two who bought a personal computer immediately after the study was over. The other writers used a combination of planning and text production in more recursive patterns.

The Writers' Perceptions of Word Processing
In every session we asked the writers to reflect on the quality of what they had produced, and often their opinions hinged on their perceptions of the quality of the article to which they were responding. Nearly all felt they had to go beyond mere reporting to produce some insight that might be of interest or use to their colleagues. At the end of the study, however, we asked them to reflect specifically on how the computer had affected their writing ability. Their responses were mixed and tentative.

The "discoverers" were least satisfied. Mike, still unable to drag the text around on the screen the way he would if he could draw circles and arrows and trees, had resorted to what he called "rush-writing," saying, "Everything now is a rush-write." He was not able to adapt his processes to the screen, had changed his pattern, and did not like what he produced. Brian complained that his writing had "no coherent feeling to it." He felt "obligated" to salvage too much, as opposed to abandoning whole drafts, and blamed this problem on the word processor. He told us he doubted he could overcome this habit if he continued to compose on the screen, despite the number of deletions he made in his final session. Jane, too, found herself indulging in long passages that she might have formerly abandoned. "I pursued an odd connection [in the final task] and left it in." She, like the other discoverers, liked about half of what she had. The rest she just left.

The "executors" were split in their opinions, probably because they chose different paths as they accommodated to the machine. Bill had early on discovered a way to replicate his typical process, and chose, toward the end of the study, to write more freely. He said he thought his text was "sloppier," and didn't trust his impression of it because the method by which he had produced it was so radically new for him. He had earlier been quite satisfied with what he had produced. Teresa, on the other hand, was generally pleased with everything she produced, finding it easy to make her quick judgments about audience, tone, and purpose, and then proceed. She never deviated from her usual methods when she used the computer. However, she was clear in her preference for longhand as a more "secure" way of writing the first draft.

All three of the "combinations" were pleased with their writing at the end of the study. When asked if his writing were typical of his quality, Lance responded emphatically that it was not, that it was "inspired . . . much smoother, more fluent." Although he noted that he was much more accustomed to the context for writing in the study and that this might have had something to do with it, he also said that he felt he had picked up "good forward momentum" with the computer and that this might have allowed his prose style to flow. Sue, too, remarked about the speed with which she could produce something she was pleased with, noting that the time from start to polished product was cut in half because she did not have to contend with a "messy typewriter." She did, however, think that the computer lured her to write sometimes too quickly, noting that she was "not spending enough time in a gestation period." Didi, although she felt she had not "adjusted to the computer," was pleased with the combination of planning and drafting on paper and transcribing and editing on the computer.

CONCLUSIONS AND IMPLICATIONS

Computer Composing

Our study concluded with mixed reviews from the experienced writers who attempted to use a computer for composing. Although they were uniformly impressed with the capabilities of the computer for editing, their reactions to taking their writing from start to finish on a screen varied, particularly as a result of their varied composing "styles." Those who planned initially and then executed a draft were most satisfied with what the computer could do for them, probably because their style of composing meant that large-scale problems were solved in advance, leaving chiefly editing and surface-level planning for their drafting stage. Those who used the forward progress of their words appearing on paper as "discovery drafts" were least pleased. These writers were accustomed to constant rereading and planning as they wrote and were bothered by the never-never land of the computer's memory. Unless they could see their writing, what they had composed was lost as an aid to invention and discovery. Those who were able to work out "combinations" of planning, executing, drafting on paper, and entering their texts on the screen were most successful.

These findings are not unusual when one considers that we were working with writers whose composing processes and rituals were already firmly established. Those who had methods close to what the word processor was initially designed for—transcribing composed texts for final editing—had no difficulty in making the computer do for them what they normally did. Those who wrote to find what they had to say did not find analogies for their desks covered with paper and their bold lines and arrows marking the direction a final draft might take. They could not, or would not, change their processes sufficiently to use the machines productively, at least, and this is important, in the early stages of their introduction to the computer as a composing tool.

We should point out that one of us—as well as Mike in the study—has since shifted to complete, on-screen composing, indicating that there are changes beyond those we studied. Quick access to a printer helps the writer who must see her text spread out before her to judge the shape of it. Other word-processing features such as light pens, split screens, and "print a screenful" keys, tools that were not available to these writers, can help the "Beethovian" to replicate her processes on the computer, but the difficulties are greater than for the executor.

One point to make about implications for computer composing is that students, for whom composing on a computer may be a commonplace in the future, may develop altogether different styles of composing as a result of what the machine can do for them. It will be important to watch the kinds of word-processing systems to which young writers are introduced to see if they allow enough freedom for a range of problem-solving patterns. If, for example, the computer does not make it easy for a writer to change her mind about large sections of a piece of writing, and encourages her instead to preserve something less than satisfactory merely because it "looks" polished on the screen, the computer may inhibit creative processes. On the other hand, those who praise word processing claim that it makes revision easier. The size of the revision is the critical issue, however. There is no question that revising the surface features and format of a text is easier; but to use the computer for large-scale revision, real "re-seeing" and "re-composing," may require word-processing features that do not yet exit on most popular word-processing systems (e.g., integrated graphics for planning; multiple, high-resolution screens that allow the writer to see several pages at once; the ability to print parts of a file while working on other parts of it). Adults who work at it hard enough (ourselves included) can make the transition with almost any system, but we may have to take special pains to encourage large-scale revision and risk-taking on a screen that makes even the most trivial writing look polished.

Written Language Production

This study also raised some important questions about the production of written language in general. First of all, the time the writers spent in pausing differs from other reports—there was more of it, over a third of the total time spent for all writers. Further, the way they used their time differed. Every one of our writers reported doing "pre-writing," a stage that Flower and Hayes have rejected. They had a need to plan by writing and often this writing did not resemble finished texts, but rather notes to themselves about what they would do as they composed or what they should do to revise if they had already produced a text. This "pre-writing" did not necessarily come at the beginning of the writing process—in fact, it could occur at any time—but it differed in kind from the production of the actual text. Perhaps a better term for this writing about writing might be "discovery writing." Pause time across sessions for a particular writing task remained relatively constant, indicating that whether they were creating or revising text, they had a need for planning and evaluating.

The points at which significant pauses occurred also differed somewhat from Flower and Hayes' (1981) findings with experienced writers. Our results were more similar to Matsuhashi's (1981) study of skilled high school writers. She found that subjects required more planning time for highly abstract sentences and paused at paragraph breaks. We found that the most frequently occurring pauses came at the ends of paragraphs and statements containing high-level abstractions that were then expanded with details and illustrations. Pauses at the ends of paragraphs may occur most often with experienced writers because they can hold a "text-level" chunk of ideas in long-term memory and stop to reread and judge a series of statements rather than individual units. Because we did not do protocol analyses, we did not measure planning in terms of talk about problems in process. When writing is not interrupted by talking about what one is doing, planning seems to occur at logical breaks in the development of a series of ideas, namely, the paragraph for these writers. We doubt that the results would be the same for less experienced writers who do not have such a well-developed sense of written text conventions.

Finally, our study shows us that for these experienced writers there is not "one right way" to solve writing problems, even those associated with the same kind of writing task. We could not make qualitative distinctions in the final texts when we considered the "executors' " results compared to the "discoverers' " texts. Although their attitude toward the usefulness of the computer certainly hinged on this distinction, their overall success as writers did not. We believe this adds to the accumulating evidence that standard advice to solve problems and organize one's writing before one begins just does not adequately describe the reality of successful composing for all writers.

Research on Computer Composing

Case studies on composing cannot give us definitive answers about how written language is produced, about how one should be taught to produce it, or, for that matter, about how computers can best be used as writing tools. They can, however, lead us to the unanswered questions that can then be asked on a large scale, across many writers, writing tasks, and communicative contexts. The technology we now possess makes collecting such data relatively easy because we can depend on the computer's memory to store and retrieve in incredible detail all the behaviors that contribute to composing. As we become more sophisticated with computer programming, we can begin to define questions in a form that will allow the computer to analyze more and more data for us. The computer cannot interpret these data, nor can it speculate about the connection between these performance behaviors and an underlying competence model of written language production. But, for the first time, we have access to information that can lead us to more questions and better answers. In mathematics and physics, to name only two fields, the computer has enabled researchers to ask questions that could never be asked before because it can manipulate and calculate with lightning speed. In writing research as well, we should be able to study ways writers produce written language with a breadth and precision never before possible.

REFERENCES

Bridwell, L.S. (1979). *Revising processes in twelfth grade students' transactional writing.* Unpublished doctoral dissertation, The University of Georgia, Athens.

Bridwell, L.S., Nancarrow, P.R., & Ross, D. (1984). The writing process and the writing machine: Current research on word processing relevant to the teaching of composition. In R. Beach & L. Bridwell (Eds.), *New directions in composition research.* New York: Guilford.

Bridwell, L.S., Sire, G., & Brooke, R. (1985). Revising and computing: Case studies of student writers. In S. Freedman (Ed.). *The Acquisition of written language: Revision and response.* Norwood, NJ: Ablex.

Collier, R.M. (1983). The word processor and revision strategies. *College Composition and Communication, 34,* 149–155.

Cowley, M. (Ed.). (1958). *Writers at work: The Paris Review interviews.* (Vol. 1). New York: Viking.

Daiute, C. (1983). The computer as stylus and audience. *College Composition and Communication, 34,* 134–145.

Daiute, C. (1981). Psycholinguistic foundations of the writing process. *Research in the Teaching of English, 15,* 5–22

Dembo, L.S., & Pondrom, C.M. (1972). *The contemporary writer: Interviews with sixteen novelists and poets.* Madison: University of Wisconsin Press.

Flower, L., & Hayes, J.R. (1981). The pregnant pause: An inquiry into the nature of planning. *Research in the Teaching of English, 15*(3), 229–243.

Gebhardt, R.C. (1982). Initial plans and spontaneous composition: Toward a comprehensive theory of the writing process. *College English, 44,* 620–627.

Gould, J.D. (1981). Composing letters with computer-based text editors. *Human Factors, 23*(5), 593–606.

Matsuhashi, A. (1981). Pausing and planning: The tempo of written discourse. *Research in the Teaching of English, 15*(2), 113–134.

Matsuhashi, A. (1982). Explorations in the real-time production of written discourse. In M. Nystrand (Ed.), *What writers know: The language, process, and structure of written discourse.* New York: Academic Press.

Nancarrow, P.R., Ross, D., & Bridwell, L.S. (1984). *Word processors and the writing process: An annotated bibliography.* Westport, CT: Greenwood Press.

Scardamalia, M., Bereiter, C., & Goelman, H. (1982). The role of production factors in writing ability. In M. Nystrand (Ed.), *What writers know: The language, process, and structure of written discourse.* New York: Academic Press.

Schreiber, G. (1936). *Portraits and self-portraits.* Boston, MA: Houghton Mifflin.

Schwartz, H.J. (1982). Monsters and mentors: Computer applications for humanistic education. *College English, 44*(2), 141–152.

Wolfe, T. (1957). *Look homeward, angel.* New York: Charles Scribner's Sons.

CHAPTER 5

Writing as Language Behavior: Myths, Models, Methods *

Sabine Kowal
Technical University, Berlin

Daniel C. O'Connell
Loyola University of Chicago

CONCEPTS OF WRITING

In the introduction to his book *Zur Psychologie des Schreibens* the German psychologist W. Preyer (1895) writes:

> While speaking has frequently and successfully been engaged as a topic of scientific research, writing has only seldom and inadequately been given similar attention. (p.1 [authors' translation from the German])

Not only does this statement well describe the research situation in psycholinguistics nine decades later, it is also of interest because it leaves the term *writing* indeterminate. Preyer actually approaches writing in the tradition of *Ausdruckspsychologie* from the viewpoint of the graphologist who studies features of handwriting as clues to personality characteristics of the writer.

Graphology has since fallen into disrepute (though quite undeservedly) as an area of scientific investigation. In part perhaps because of this disrepute, writing—even when conceived more broadly than handwriting—has been thoroughly disregarded in research through the intervening years. Current textbooks of psycholinguistics do not refer to writing at all in their subject index (e.g., Hörmann, 1981; Palermo, 1978), delimit it to the notion of an abstract system (e.g., Paivio & Begg, 1981), or exclude writing deliberately from their consideration. According to Clark and Clark (1977), for instance,

> One of the principles that gives the field coherence is that psycholinguistics is fundamentally the study of three mental processes—the study of listening, speaking, and of the acquisition of these two skills by children. (p. vii)

---

* The first author has received support from the German Research Foundation for the present research.

They go on to state: "Communication with language is carried out through two basic human activities: speaking and listening" (p. 3).

Writing has been included in research on story recall—but only indirectly and without any specific interest in writing itself. Sometimes recall has been tested on the basis of written stories (e.g., Owens, Bower, & Black, 1979), sometimes oral (e.g., Mandler & Johnson, 1977); but the possible effect of modality has been disregarded.

The neglect or exclusion of writing as language production in the written (by comparison to the oral or visual–manual) mode in mainstream psycholinguistics may also reflect the preoccupation of linguists with oral language. Hockett (1966), in determining the "design features" of language which are shared by all human language, asserts: "The channel for all linguistic communication is vocal-auditory" (p. 8). He explicitly excludes writing because of some basic differences between spoken and written language which demand "detailed consideration of the two taken separately" (p. 15). It would appear that this second step of detailed consideration has not yet been taken by psycholinguists, but that instead an intermediate stage has become permanent. Paivio and Begg (1981) have acknowledged this limitation explicitly but have not moved beyond it.

A similar limitation characterizes Foss and Hakes (1978), who refer to reading and writing as inventions but to speaking and listening as natural: "evolved in the history of the species" (p. 323). They consider writing only insofar as they distinguish "between the processes involved in the production of language . . . and those involved in the production of speech" (p. 170). The former, according to Foss and Hakes, refer to the planning aspects of production, including the formulation of ideas and choice of semantic and syntactic frameworks. The authors hypothesize: "Very likely, these sentence production processes are much the same whether the thought is eventually expressed in speech or in writing" (p. 170). A similar statement regarding the role of thinking common to both speaking and writing is expressed by Smith (1982):

> The "thinking" part of writing—the describing, exploring, explaining, arguing and constructing in words—is also fundamentally no different from that of speech, indeed from the kind of thought the brain is engaged in all the time. (p. 122)

Foss and Hakes (1978) characterize speech production processes as follows:

> Speech production processes, on the other hand, are peculiar to speaking, for they involve the construction of a program of skilled motor movements to produce the speech sounds corresponding to the intended sentence and,

of course, the realization of that program, the actual generation of a sound pattern. (p. 170)

The authors seem to overlook the fact that writing also entails the *act* of writing, "when words flow from the hand" (Smith, 1982, p. 103), an act which certainly requires "a program of skilled motor movements" though a different set from those involved in speaking. Hence, Foss and Hakes simply omit a treatment of writing as language behavior.

In the educational context of the teaching of English, the term writing is frequently used synonymously with composition. Black (1982), for instance, in his article on psycholinguistic processes in writing, is concerned with the processes "involved in composing written discourse" (p. 199) in a school context. Frederiksen and Dominic (1981), in a similar vein, state: "A major goal of research on writing is to help schools and teachers increase their effectiveness in providing writing instruction" (p. 1). Such research emphasizes the need for educators to know about the internal cognitive processes involved as a text is being composed (e.g., Flower & Hayes, 1981; Nold, 1981).

Still another notion of writing has been proposed by Frase (1981) who determines the following goals for empirical research in writing:

1. Develop a better understanding of the elements of written discourse that control reading process.
2. Characterize the psychological processes that mediate discourse effects.
3. Develop methods for observing reading outcomes. (p. 209)

Not only composition of a text but composition of an effective text is the topic of research on writing in this case, and consequently the investigation of the reader—as the one who decides about the effectiveness of the text—becomes the research focus.

It should be clear by now that a considerable amount of vagueness prevails in the current usages of the term *writing*. In research reports it may mean an abstract system of symbols, the product of the activity of writing; or the process of composition or skill therein; or the act of writing or skill of producing linear sequences of graphemes in time.

In what follows we would like to approach writing from a psycholinguistic viewpoint as language behavior unfolding in time, open to direct observation and therefore to systematic empirical investigation. Conceptually we will consider it as language production in one modality, the written mode. In order to learn about the internal psychological processes involved in the act of writing, we propose that two viable methods of analysis can be adapted from research in speech production: the systematic investigation of the temporal aspects of writing including production rate and pause time, and the study of the processes of revising, editing, and correcting as they are related to ongoing writing. In this approach analyses of the written product are also of concern but only insofar as they pertain to temporal aspects of the production itself.

The application of such methodologies demands that the writer be studied *in action,* that a careful record of his writing behavior as it evolves in time be made with the aid of instrumentation, and that such records be analyzed according to explicitly stated criteria. The methodological approach adopted here specifies the characteristics of neither the writing task nor of the writer himself. In principle it allows observation of writings as varied as a second grader copying sentences from a reader, a professor typing the first draft of an essay on the application of catastrophe theory, or someone making up a shopping list. The choice of an appropriate task or several tasks for comparative purposes and of suitable experimental subjects is determined entirely by the empirical logic of the research design. There is no a priori reason for limiting research to school or other developmental settings, although such settings have an obvious priority. In view of our present lack of knowledge about both the behavioral characteristics and internal processes involved in the act of writing, however, it seems advisable to choose writing tasks which allow for as much external control as possible.

ASSUMPTIONS ABOUT TEMPORAL CHARACTERISTICS OF WRITING

Three assumptions about the temporal course of writing appear repeatedly in linguistic research and in research on composition. They have been made in an attempt to explain the psychological processes involved in the act of writing as well as the characteristics of the produced text. The three pertain to the on-time of writing, the off-time of writing, and to revisions during the act of writing; they emphasize the contrast between speaking and writing. As will be evident in the following sections, little actual research has been carried out to support these assumptions with empirical evidence. The specific assumptions concern respectively the rate of text production during on-time (articulation rate), pause time, and revisions.

Articulation rate. Writing as a physical activity is performed at a relatively slow rate. By comparison to speaking, reading, and listening, it is the language mode with the slowest pace. This assumption focusses on the articulation rate of writing, i.e., exclusive of all off-time or nonwriting time.

As early as 1900, Wilhelm Wundt (cited in Freud, 1904/1954) used the difference in speed of articulatory movements in writing and speaking to explain the higher incidence of anticipatory slips of the pen (relative to slips of the tongue):

> In the execution of normal speech, the control function of the will is continuously directed toward the synchronization of concurrent imagination and articulatory movement. Such anticipations occur particularly when the movement of expression following upon the images is slowed down, as in writing, due to mechanical causes. (p. 107, [authors' translation from the German])

The possibility of conflict between the processes of composing and transcribing during the act of writing has also been pointed out by Smith (1982) and has been attributed to the different time courses of the physical act of writing and the act of thinking. According to Emig (1978; cited in Smith, 1982), however, the very slowness of writing must be considered an advantage for composition because the slow pace allows time for careful thinking. Chafe (1982) has also emphasized the benefits rather than the drawbacks of the slow pace of writing. He contrasted the " 'integrated' quality" of written language with the "fragmented quality" of spoken language (p. 38) and attributed the observed characteristics of writing to its slow pace:

> As we write down one idea, our thoughts have plenty of time to move ahead to others. The result is that we have time to integrate a successsion of ideas into a single linguistic whole in a way that is not available in speaking. (p. 37)

Despite the apparent unanimity about the slow pace of writing, all of the above descriptions of the relative speeds of speaking and writing are based on speculation and informal observation. The unanswered questions concern the accurate measurement of ongoing writing and speaking under comparable conditions. Chafe (1982) in fact acknowledges that he is basing his description on comparison of *formal* written language on the one hand and *informal* spoken language on the other. The apple–orange effect here is precisely the following: The integrated or fragmented quality of discourse can be legitimately compared only when the temporal constraints during text production are themselves comparable. Integration may be a product of prewriting and revision rather than of the slow pace during the act of writing.

The empirical challenge raised by these speculations involves the careful collection of data on articulation rates of writing. Such normative data for various settings could then be compared with similar data for speaking.

Pause Time. Writing as a "private" activity (Ong, 1981) allows for more extensive periods of planning between writing spurts, whereas speaking as a "public" activity is characterized by rapid turn-taking and other social constraints on time. This assumption focusses on *pause time* in writing as an off-time characteristic.

Pause duration, frequency, and location as observable indicators of internal planning are by now well established in research on speech production. Research on pause time in the act of writing opens up an altogether new area of inquiry. There is an important difference in the conceptualization of planning in speech and writing research. Historically, speech-production models began with relatively narrow notions of planning, largely restricted to the word and phrase level (e.g., Goldman-Eisler, 1958; Lounsbury, 1954). Pauses were interpreted in terms of proximal, rather than distal, planning. Models of the process of writing, by contrast, have incorporated not only local planning but also more remote planning on the level of paragraph and text. In fact, the concept of planning has included the process of *inventio* antecedent to the act of writing. This planning is sometimes referred to as "pre-writing"; it includes such procedures as sentence outlines (Nold, 1981) and even "the stage, untouched by pen, paper, or rhetorical purpose, in which you discover your ideas" (Flower & Hayes, 1980, p. 32).

The application of pause analysis to writing research will require that the construct of planning be exactly specified in its temporal dimensions. The only way in which off-time can genuinely be considered pause time and the only way in which pause time may meaningfully point to planning is by reference to proximate overt behavior in which the off-time is embedded; off-time is not *eo ipso* pause time, and pause time is not *eo ipso* planning time.

Revisions.   Writing results in a permanent record whereas the spoken word is only momentarily available: *Verba volant, scripta manent.* The writer thus has a text available not only for focal but also for more global *revisions* in the attempt to successively approximate his or her communicative intentions.

In research on spontaneous speech, various aspects of revision or correction have from the very beginning been considered part of the descriptive analyses of the corpus under investigation. They have been classified as "hesitation phenomena" (Maclay & Osgood, 1959) or as "speech errors" (Clark & Clark, 1977). Despite their consideration in empirical analyses, they have not been incorporated as stages of speech production models (e.g., Cooper & Paccia-Cooper, 1980; Foss & Hakes, 1978).

By contrast, models of writing have typically incorporated revisions as necessary stages of production. Such a difference in model construction may be due to the fact that in speech research revisions (often referred to as false starts) are conceptualized as flaws whereas in writing research they are considered to be improvements. The fact is that in both they are both;

in both speaking and writing revisions are signs of improvement when considered as part of the process, but are flaws when considered as part of the product. The advent of both word processors and voice recorders made it imperative that we rethink what is process and what is product.

WRITING IN REAL TIME: EMPIRICAL STUDIES

Temporal Aspects

The studies on temporal aspects of writing are reviewed in the following section according to their chronological order. Our decision reflects the disparate nature of the research tradition in this area and the difficulty of relating the various studies to one another thematically.

van Bruggen. In view of the scarcity of process studies on writing, a fact which is certainly related to the enormous methodological problems involved, an early study on the "regularity of the flow of words during written composition" by van Bruggen (1946, p. 133) deserves special mention.

Using a time recording kymograph, van Bruggen kept a temporal record of the on–off pattern of the same junior high school students writing under three different conditions. Recordings were made by the experimenter while he observed the subjects writing. Although the accuracy of this method of measurement depends partly on the reaction time of the experimenter, it surpasses some of the methods used in later studies. The measurement of pauses was to 0.10 seconds.

During a first writing period, the subjects were asked to write down the first seven sentences of Lincoln's Gettysburg Address. The correctness of their memorization was previously ascertained from perfect recitation. The subjects then reproduced the story of Androcles and the Lion which they had read just before writing. Finally all subjects wrote a composition on a topic of their choice selected from six topics. Three dependent variables were included in the data analysis: flow of words (measured by mean pause duration of all pauses above the median pause duration), writing speed (measured by mean seconds/word), and thought units (not defined operationally).

van Bruggen found that writing speed was slower in the first task (writing from memory) than in either of the composition tasks; writing on selected topics was slower than reproducing a story. He interpreted these results as indicating that the decrease in writing speed was due primarily to memory demands when the writer has to retrieve the exact wording. Such an explanation not only seems implausible in view of the relatively difficult planning involved in the composition tasks compared to the relative ease of retrieving overlearned material from memory, it also appears unlikely, though certainly open to further investigation, that retrieval problems would decrease the rate of writing movements rather than increase pause time.

Another problem with this interpretation is the fact that van Bruggen failed to control for mean word length across the several tasks. Our analysis of the Gettysburg Address and of the topical compositions reported by van Bruggen yielded the following means: 1.37 and 1.25 syllables/word, respectively. Given the small range of variability for this index, this difference could well have been responsible for the significant differences found by van Bruggen in writing speed. If so, they must be thought of as an artifact of his analytic method rather than a reflection of true differences in cognitive processing.

van Bruggen further found that the flow of words was reduced in writing on selected topics as compared to reproducing a story: Longer pauses occurred in the former composition task. No pause data were reported for writing from memory. Compositions were also judged to be of superior or inferior quality and subsequently analyzed in terms of pause location according to "thought units." Apparently these units are somewhat equivalent to major syntactic units but this relationship is nowhere spelled out. van Bruggen found that in the better compositions pauses occurred more often between groups of words representing thought units, whereas in poor compositions pauses broke up these units. He also observed that the poorer compositions contained on the average longer pauses than the good compositions (2.3 seconds > 1.6 seconds). In other words, the flow of words was faster when the text was composed in thought units. van Bruggen interpreted the results in terms of the uncertainty of expression which manifests itself in longer and more irregular pausing.

For purposes of comparison with data on temporal aspects in speaking, it is of interest to note that van Bruggen found an increase in the rate of word flow with chronological age, as did, for example, Sabin, Clemmer, O'Connell, & Kowal (1979) for spoken discourse.

Horowitz and Berkowitz.   A study by Horowitz and Berkowitz (1964) emphasized biologically determined differences in articulation, i.e., in the rapidity of motor movements involved in speaking and writing. They varied the ease of writing (handwriting vs. typewriting vs. stenotyping) and found that it took nearly eight times as long in handwriting or about six times in typing and more than three times as long in stenotyping to produce approximately the same amount of words as in speaking. The respective results in terms of tokens/second as derived from their data in Table 2 (p. 623) are 0.33, 0.43, 0.92, and 2.39, respectively. Horowitz and Berkowitz concluded that one of the major factors influencing differences between spoken and written language is "the facility of the different organs of use"

(p. 624). It is difficult to imagine any alternative to their general conclusion as stated. The authors might have been better able to discriminate empirically between the "organs of use" in writing and speaking had they isolated articulation rate as we have described it above—exclusive of pause time. Writing speed or rate with pause time included does not reflect the motoric components of writing accurately or specifically.

Tannenbaum, Williams, and Wood. Hesitation phenomena in both language modes were compared by Tannenbaum, Williams, and Wood (1967) in a factor analytic study. Subjects were asked to describe TAT (Thematic Apperception Test) cards both orally and by using a special typewriter for their responses. The typewriter recorded key striking, spacing, backspacing, and carriage return and was linked to a chronograph for temporal measurement. Controls for levels of proficiency in typewriting are not mentioned by Tannenbaum et al. On the basis of the distribution of their pause data they selected cutoff points of 0.30 seconds for speech and 3.0 seconds for typing.

Tannenbaum et al. found that oral descriptions were produced significantly more rapidly than typewritten descriptions; speech and writing rates were 1.62 and 0.24 words/second respectively. Pause patterns for the two modalities were quite different. Whereas speaking was characterized by a frequent alternation of the on-off pattern and by brief pauses, typing was characterized by longer but fewer pauses. The authors suggested that such difference in pause patterns may be due to differences in social context and short-term memory constraints in speaking by comparison to writing. The speaker who pauses too long may not only receive negative reactions from his audience, he may also lose his train of thought; by contrast, "the writing situation affords the encoder the luxury literally to 'stop and think'—without fear of losing his audience, and without the hazard of losing track of his sequence of expression" (p. 214).

Intuitively acceptable as Tannenbaum et al.'s conclusion may be, it should be noted that their findings cannot but be distorted by the differential cutoff points themselves. The arbitrary adoption of cutoff points of different duration for pauses in writing (typing) and speaking is not justified given the present state of our scientific knowledge. Such adoption renders the respective sets of data completely incomparable.

Blass and Siegman. Blass and Siegman (1975) analyzed interview answers in three different modes—oral, dictated, and written—on a number of syntactic, content, and extra-linguistic variables, including the silence quotient (percentage of pause time/total time). In writing, Blass and Siegman assessed pauses from tape recordings of pen scratchings on paper. No reference to earlier attempts at measuring pauses in writing is made. Pauses in both speaking and writing were measured by means of a stopwatch. A cutoff point of 2 seconds determined the minimum duration of pauses. The authors' hypotheses were presented as follows:

> The less pressure the subject experiences, the greater his freedom to take his time, to think before and during his responses, and to plan and construct his responses more carefully. Lowest silence quotients should, therefore, occur in the speaking condition, higher in dictation, and highest in the writing condition. . . . Similarly, production rate (number of words per second) should be the highest when speaking, lower in dictation, and lowest when writing. (p. 23)

As hypothesized, the authors found production rates (in standard terminology, speech and writing rates, not articulation rates) for speaking, dictating, and writing of 3.03, 2.92, and 0.43 words/second respectively. The silence quotient was significantly greater for dictating than for speaking. Contrary to expectation, writing yielded the lowest silence quotient:

> The explanation for this unexpected finding probably has to do with the basic differences in the mechanics of production between writing and the other two modes. It takes much longer to write a word than to utter it. Hence, while the person is writing one word, he can already formulate the next one. He, thus, has less need to pause between words. In speaking and dictating, however, the articulation of words requires such little time, and therefore, the person relies more on pauses to plan what he is going to say next. (pp. 29–30)

Important as the above consideration is, the experimental results have been overinterpreted in view of a number of methodological deficiencies. Blass and Siegman's (1975) measurement devices were inexact, there is no evidence that planning was a salient component of the task, and finally revision was differentially allowed from condition to condition. How much formulating or other planning a writer can do while writing remains an unanswered and important question.

Shulansky and Herrmann.   Shulansky and Herrmann (1977) found that rate of typing was slower for nontouch-typists as compared to touch-typists. They also showed that nontouch-typists decreased their typing rate considerably when typing meaningless or both meaningless and ungrammatical sentences from dictation. No such difference was observed for touch-typists. The authors suggested that touch-typists encode sentences as linear strings of letters or words regardless of syntactic and semantic cues.

Gould.   In a series of publications, Gould (1978, 1979, 1980) and Gould and Boies (1978) reported research on composing letters. Composition modes included speaking, dictating, and writing. The basic assumption was that there are four psychological processes involved in composing: planning, generating, reviewing, and acquiring external information. The processes were identified with their operational definitions in terms of time components. A theoretical basis for these concepts independent of their empirical assessment has not been spelled out.

Gould's experiments were intended to assess among other things the proportional time required for each of the four processes, and in particular to determine the relative amounts of planning and generation time. Letters were composed as replies to business letters of inquiry, and the entire sequence of composing was videotaped. Whereas Gould (1978) sampled the videotapes at 6-second intervals to assess duration of the ongoing processes, Gould (1979, 1980) used a more sensitive method of temporal measurement. The videotapes were sampled at 0.10-second intervals (Gould & Quinones, 1978). The use of different methods of measurement makes any direct comparison of the earlier and later results impossible.

Gould (1980) summarized his results regarding planning time across modalities as follows: "Planning time was a constant *proportion* of total composition time" (p. 112). He further clarified his findings as follows: "When total composition time was less for one method than another, as it generally was for speaking versus writing . . . then planning time was also less" (p. 113). In his various studies he found that a constant amount of about two-thirds of composition time was devoted to planning. No effort was made to reconcile this finding with Blass and Siegman's (1975) findings reviewed earlier in this section.

Between the first 1978 article and his 1980 summary of his research, Gould shifted his methodology in a number of ways which make the coherence and intelligibility of his findings less than satisfactory. His methods of measurement were changed midstream; his conviction that a 40-word-per-minute generation rate should be considered a maximum for writing shifted to a conviction that the same rate was to be considered an average. His allocation by formula of a part of generation time to planning time was used and then discarded for the notion of planning time as pause time. However, his findings regarding proportion of planning time remained remarkably stable.

Nonetheless it should be noted that Gould's (1980) aim "to identify and understand cognitive processes in composition " (p. 97) has not been substantively accomplished. Planning remains for him operationally nothing other than "the time spent pausing" (Gould, 1979, p. 4). The logical inference from pausing to cognitive processes in composition is not even attempted:

> Our model is more of a theoretical framework for investigating composition than a detailed description of what goes on in the head during composition. It makes no prediction about the transitions from one process to another. (Gould, 1980, p. 111)

Matsuhashi. Matsuhashi investigated the relationship between the time course and content aspects of composition writing by several high school students with good writing skills and reported data from the same study in a number of publications (Matsuhashi, 1981, 1982; Matsuhashi & Cooper, 1978; Spittle & Matsuhashi, 1981). Her research has been based on the assumption that the composition process varies in different types of text and that pauses are indicative of the processes involved in composition.

Subjects were instructed to write reporting, persuading, and generalizing texts. They were provided with the specific topics for their compositions two days ahead of the experiment and were encouraged to rehearse and plan, but not allowed to take notes. In view of this procedure it seems at least an open question whether the compositions produced during the experimental sessions were in fact, as Matsuhashi and Cooper (1978) maintain, an early draft, reflecting the "actual workings of the composing process" (p. 18). No controls on the amount of preexperimental planning are reported. It is in principle possible that a subject may have come to the experiment with a ready-made composition memorized to a point where further planning on the level of composition was unnecessary, whereas another subject may have strictly adhered to the instructions given or indeed may have made no preparation whatsoever. These subjects would not be comparable to one another in their writing performance. The validity of data regarding temporal aspects of performance is reduced correspondingly. In view of the strong interest in planning processes on the one hand and our meager empirical knowledge of their behavioral manifestations on the other hand, it seems all the more important to exert careful control over those variables which would plausibly have an effect on these very processes.

For each composition the subjects were allowed a maximum of one hour of writing time. They were videotaped with two cameras with a split screen while writing their compositions. Pause measurement was from the videotapes, played back in slow motion. Real time was recorded continuously by a clock integrated into the video display and yielding accuracy to 0.10 seconds. Onset of pause time was operationally defined as the point in time when the writer lifted pen from paper. However, there is no a priori reason to assume that a writer may not as well stop writing with his pen resting on the paper. Matsuhashi and Cooper (1978) do not report observations of this alternative. It will be of importance for future writing research to explore this question further. Finally, no mention is made of a minimum cutoff point for pause duration.

Matsuhashi and Cooper (1978) reported results on pause duration and writing rate for one subject. The total of 4,000 pauses ranged in duration from 0.10 seconds to 95.30 seconds. This maximum would be approximately 20 times the most liberal estimate of a maximum pause in ordinary spoken discourse. A frequency distribution of pauses ranging only from 0.10 to 3.50 seconds in duration yielded a median pause duration of 1.00 second for the various composition tasks. Mean pause durations of this restricted sample of pauses for reporting, persuading, and generalizing, respectively, were 1.76, 2.12, and 2.70 seconds. The respective figures for the entire corpus of pauses were 3.79, 4.73, and 4.70 seconds (Matsuhashi, 1981, p. 123). Mean writing rates for the three tasks were 0.25, 0.22, and 0.18 words/second respectively (Matsuhashi & Cooper, 1978).

In order to assess pause duration and writing rate in the absence of original composing, Matsuhashi and Cooper (1978) analyzed data on a copying task of one subject; mean writing rates under this condition increased to a rate of 0.37 words/second and mean pause duration dropped to 0.87 seconds. The authors concluded that pauses shorter than 1.00 second are necessary for transcribing only; they are indicative of the time needed to lift the pen at the end of a word and immediately go to the next word. It would appear that a better control condition for the assessment of such "articulatory" pauses without planning functions would have been the task of writing from memory. Such a task would not include delay in writing due to changes in eye fixation from the text to be copied onto the text being written. It is at least conceivable that in the absence of such extraneous behavior, both pause duration would decrease and writing rate would increase even more. Clearly the question of the empirical determination of "articulatory" pauses (necessary to lift the pen from paper in order to write the next word) by contrast to "planning" pauses deserves further investigation with more appropriate control conditions.

Matsuhashi (1981) studied the relationship between pause duration, location of pauses in terms of T-units (Hunt, 1965) and a variety of linguistic features. Of importance for comparisons with speech-pause analyses is her finding that pause duration varied according to location between or within T-units. Mean pause duration within T-units was 3.79 seconds, with no significant differences due to discourse type; mean pause duration between T-units was 7.56, 10.87, and 12.56 seconds for reporting, persuading, and generalizing, respectively, with a significant difference between reporting and generalizing. The longest pauses occurred before T-units beginning a paragraph, with a significant difference between overall mean pause duration at paragraph boundaries (15.10 seconds) and nonparagraph boundaries (9.00 seconds).

A more selective analysis of data from only one speaker was performed by Matsuhashi (1982). The 10 longest pauses in a generalizing and a reporting composition were located at either sentence boundary or internally and two concomitant behavioral aspects were recorded: visual focus of the writer (rereading a given part of his composition or gazing away from the text) and pen location (either near the previously written word or far re-moved). The purpose of including hand and eye movements in the analysis was to investigate a variety of motor activities indicative of internal cog-nitive activity.

Matsuhashi observed that in generalizing 5 and in reporting as many as 7 out of the 10 longest pauses occurred within, rather than between, sen-tences. She concluded that planning does not necessarily correspond to the units defined by grammarians; psychological processing units seem instead to be determined by underlying conceptual content. Multiple decisions on a global as well as on a local level are made at points of text composition where long pauses, gazing or rereading, and pen removal coincide.

At some point, Matsuhashi's emphasis on underlying conceptual con-tent as determinant of longer pauses must be integrated with her previous emphasis on the determination of longer pauses by T-unit structures.

In a semantic analysis of the same two composition samples Spittle and Matsuhashi (1981) coded the data in terms of propositional text bases after Turner and Greene (1977). They found support for their hypothesis that predicate propositions contain more pause time than do modification prop-ositions. Their interpretation of this finding maintains that producing predicate propositions is more demanding (and therefore more time-con-suming) because this type of proposition forms the ideational core of the text whereas modification propositions are more peripheral.

However, their examples of modification and predication suggest an-other possible explanation for the observed differences in pause time. As is clear from Figures 1 and 2 in Spittle and Matsuhashi (1981), each word in the running text is followed by a pause of some duration. If no cutoff point for minimum pause duration is used in order to distinguish articu-latorily necessary pauses from planning pauses—and Spittle and Matsuha-shi do not give such a cutoff point although its necessity was indicated by Matsuhashi and Cooper (1978)—amount of pause time per text segment covaries with the length in words of a given segment. Because predications tend to consist of more words, Spittle and Matsuhashi's findings of more pause time for predication propositions is influenced to an unknown extent by this characteristic rather than by the cognitive difficulty involved.

To sum up the studies on temporal aspects of writing we can state that the designs have included comparisons of various writing tasks on the one hand and comparisons of writing with speaking on the other hand in terms of the overall time course. In only one study (Spittle & Matsuhashi, 1981) were comparisons made between temporal aspects within a given text. All of the studies were concerned with writing rate or pause time or both; all neglected articulation rate and revising. The prevalent aim of the research has been to obtain clues to the internal processes of planning as they differ according to language modality or writing task. Our critique of the methodological approaches used in the design of the studies as well as in data analyses has made it clear that for the most part the research questions have not been settled.

Protocol Analysis

The studies we have reviewed up to this point have all had in common a concern with the temporal organization and sequencing of writing as it proceeds. Another approach to writing has sought to analyze it indirectly through other behaviors proceeding concomitantly in real time, verbal reports of what the writer thinks he is doing.

In the following section, we wish to concentrate on several recent studies that approach writing as language behavior in this way: Flower and Hayes (1980), Flower and Hayes (1981), and Hayes and Flower (1980). Black (1982) has already described their work as a promising new research method that will provide a component of "the eventual theory" (p. 213). Black's own presuppositions are not without interest in this forecast:

> Prerequisite for a widespread improvement in the teaching of writing is a better understanding of the psychological processes used by writers. The lines of research described in the following promise to provide this basic knowledge. (p. 200)

He adds that the results of some of the recent research are already "amenable to direct application in the classroom" (p. 213). One hardly has to be cynical about scientific research to recognize here an act of faith. Some recent researchers would strongly agree with Black. Emig (1981), for instance, voices a sweeping censure of all the adults involved in the back-to-basics movement for their "magical thinking" (p. 22) and calls for a conversion experience to a developmental view strongly suggested by her own research.

It is refreshing, however, to find in the same volume with Emig's chapter a more modest approach on the part of Nold (1981): "We do not understand the subprocesses of writing enough to plan research-based curricula for the elementary and secondary schools" (p. 78).

We juxtapose the above viewpoints deliberately here by way of introduction to our own critical comments. We find much of the heady optimism over new methods premature and uncritical. With that brief and perhaps ominous *apologia,* let us examine Flower and Hayes' protocol analysis of writing.

Their basic premise appears to be that protocol analysis is "a powerful tool for the identification of psychological processes" (Hayes & Flower, 1980, p. 3). A protocol is defined as *"a description of the activities, ordered in time, which a subject engages in while performing a task"* (p. 4):

In a verbal, or "thinking aloud" protocol, subjects are asked to say aloud everything that occurs to them while performing the task, no matter how trivial it may seem. (p. 4)

Newell and Simon's (1972) use of protocol analysis was originally to identify processes in problem-solving tasks, and writing can indeed be viewed as problem solving—but not simply as problem solving. Here is the first stumbling block for the model. Let us pursue the logic of Hayes and Flower more closely: "The degree to which the processes identified through protocol analysis correspond to the processes identified by the writer provide a test of the model" (p. 10). Apart from the intrinsic circularity of their test, we must note here the assumptions that serve as necessary, though completely implicit, premises in their use of protocols. Their use logically requires that what the writer says he is doing and what he is doing be related—veridically, nontrivially, and proximally in time. Moreover it is logically required that the engagement of the protocol in no substantive way disturb the true process of writing. It is, however, perfectly obvious that at the very least the temporal organization and sequencing of the writing process are thoroughly altered. Common sense and the methods of experimental design concur in indicating caution: A protocol which involves 14 pages and 5 additional pages of notes for "a page of completed essay" (Hayes & Flower, 1980, p. 20), for example, cannot but alter the process of writing by sheer dint of task processing other than the processing dictated by the goal of writing. Black (1982), Gould (1980), and Frederiksen and Dominic (1981) all acknowledge the possibility of such interference, but do not seriously pursue it.

What Hayes and Flower (1980) have actually presented is about half of the data of one subject for the first half of the logically required *pilot* experiment. At the very least a control group is required, the process of whose writing would be observed without the intrusion of a protocol. All the rest is speculation. In view of these problems, the "objectivity" (p. 21) and "reliability" (p. 23) reported are not cogently related to the empirical logic.

The model is "a model of competent writers" (p. 29). Even a brief look at the evidence presented by Gould (1980) from the Paris Review Interviews (1963, 1967) would counterindicate Hayes and Flower's assertion. The acute sensitivity of good writers to the disruptions occasioned by self-conscious analysis is common literary knowledge. Perhaps more important as a distortion of their empirical logic than they might imagine is Flower and Hayes' (1980) insistence that "the act of writing is best described as the act of juggling a number of simultaneous constraints" (p. 31). That may indeed be one way for the psychologist to look at writing; it is most certainly not what the competent writer is focally processing. He or she has mastered a whole set of overlearned skills that now *quietly subserve* a closely concentrated, intentionally determined communicative language task. Hence, their assertion that "one of the important things protocol analysis reveals is that a great part of skill in writing is the ability to monitor and direct one's own composing process" (p. 39) has a hollow ring to it. Flower and Hayes already knew that before engaging protocol analysis; it is one of the basic assumptions underlying its use. Nor is their assertion that "contrary to some traditional notions, the writing process is not a neat, additive sequence of stages" (p. 44) anything more than the dumping of a straw man. The starts and stops, the saltatory leaps, the desert wastes and verdant gardens of the creative spirit are all knowledge common to youngster and creative artist alike; but they are also one very important reason why Flower and Hayes should not have completely neglected—indeed distorted—the temporal aspects of the process of writing with their protocol analysis. What we need is precisely data about what people "*do* do under typical composition-writing circumstances" (Bereiter, 1980, p. 90). Only the phrase is from Bereiter, however, not the conviction of need; he feels that we already have such data available—because, once again, the process is confused with the product. Only thus could he make the statement that "the available data mostly relate to what children *do* do under typical composition-writing circumstances" (p. 90).

Unexpected support for our conviction of the importance of research concerned with on-going temporal factors in writing appears in the same volume with Flower and Hayes. Bartlett and Scribner (1981), in commenting on children's writing problems, found that:

> Difficulties arose not so much from any lack of basic awareness of the referential requirements inherent in these contexts or from any basic inability to choose appropriate linguistic devices, but rather from more momentary and transient performance factors specific to the context in which referencing occurs. (p. 165 f.)

Whatever else may be said, Flower and Hayes (1981) have not succeeded in describing "the heuristic procedures writers use during the act of composing" (p. 40); what they have actually described is a set of *orally* produced data completely other than the writing process insofar as they reflect a task of introspecting and reporting, not the task of planning and executing writing.

There is, finally, a very basic reason why protocol analysis is inadequate for the investigation of writing. Smith (1982) has put it very simply: "Introspection is a poor guide in such matters" (p. 105):

> None of this word-generating is conscious. Words come. They are shaped as James Britton (1970) says, "at the point of the utterance" on the tongue, the pen, or in the voice we hear in the mind if we rehearse them mentally.

But we cannot inspect the source of the words or the procedures by which they come; we let them come, and they arrive. (p. 108)

Matsuhashi (1982), in commenting on similar testimony on the part of well-known professional writers, concluded that the process of writing is for the most part not available to conscious introspection. Commentaries on the limitations of introspection have long been part of the history of psychology. James (1890) was one of the early commentators:

> The main end of our thinking is at all times the attainment of some other substantive part than the one from which we have just been dislodged. And we may say that the main use of the transitive parts is to lead us from one substantive conclusion to another.
>
> Now it is very difficult, introspectively, to see the transitive parts for what they really are. (p. 243)

Boring (1950) has summarized Külpe's criticism as follows:

> Contents are analyzable in consciousness, whereas functions are not, for analysis alters the function but not the content. Thus contents are observable by introspection, but functions only by retrospection. Moreover contents are relatively stable and functions are relatively unstable. In these characteristics one comes to see just what has been meant by the impalpability *(Unanschaulichkeit)* of the functions or acts. (p. 451)

Nisbett and Wilson (1977) have reviewed the evidence "that there may be little or no direct introspective access to higher order cognitive processes" (p. 231). Ericsson and Simon (1980) are more specific:

> Verbalizing information is shown to affect cognitive processes only if the instructions require verbalization of information that would not otherwise be attended to. From an analysis of what would be in STM at the time of report, the model predicts what can reliably be reported. The inaccurate reports found by other research are shown to result from requesting information that was never directly heeded, thus forcing subjects to infer rather than remember their mental processes. (p. 215)

Regarding inferences of processes, Ericsson and Simon (1984) add:

> Many procedures attempt to encode the *processes* that generate heeded information, rather than the information itself. But the processes can only be implied from the information in STM, which does not, as we have seen, usually include information about process. (p. 227)

Waldrop (1984) puts it quite bluntly: "Little human expertise is really codified, and . . . the experts are not necessarily doing what they say they are doing" (p. 1282). Because of these limitations in our ability to introspect and report verbally, protocol analysis must be said to generate a great deal of data about something other than the process of writing.

WHAT WE KNOW AND WHERE TO GO

Our review of empirical studies on writing in real time has been deliberately critical. The intention is not to discourage further research in this area but quite the opposite. Our own involvement in research on temporal aspects in speech production over the years has led us to the conviction that the careful empirical investigation of time aspects and hesitation phenomena in oral discourse production is a viable approach to the investigation of the intricacies of internal psychological processes. Our contention is that writing research and speech research are necessary complements to one another.

Our primary concern is that the issues raised in writing research, important as they undoubtedly are for the long-term progress of research and theory, have been formulated too ambitiously and engaged prematurely at a point in time when there is hardly any research tradition in this field, very little basic knowledge about the behavioral phenomena serving as indicators for highly complex internal processes, and a deplorable lack of methodological sophistication. The preoccupation with planning (however elaborately the construct may be defined) as well as the interest in the applicability of research findings are evident in most of the studies reviewed; but the lack of conclusive findings about such planning processes in writers is equally evident. In various studies, observed behavioral differences manifested the likelihood of contamination by methodological artifacts.

It is encouraging to observe that one major obstacle to empirical research on writing in real time seems to have been largely removed: the problem of data collection with dependable instrumentation. In particular, the methods described by Gould and Quinones (1978) and by Matsuhashi and Cooper (1978) allow for the recording of the moment-to-moment details of writing behavior.

In this last section we would like to outline some directions for further research on writing behavior in real time based on our literature review and on research available from speech production. Essentially we suggest three priorities: refinement of basic methodologies for the assessment of temporal variables, comparisons of writing tasks varying in amount of planning, and comparisons of writing with speech behavior.

Assessment of Temporal Variables

Let us return for a moment to our preoccupation with articulation rate, pause time, and revising. It will be remembered that writing can be divided into on-time (production of text including revisions) and off-time (pauses).

Articulation rate. In the research tradition to date, the speed of writing has been largely determined by dividing total amount of text produced by the total amount of time used. We have referred to this measure as writing rate analogously to speech rate for oral discourse. Such a measure provides rough comparisons of production rates for various writing tasks just as it does for speech tasks. It does not provide detailed information regarding the writer's use of articulation rate and pause time. Even in studies where pause time has been isolated, articulation rate has not been investigated separately. van Bruggen (1946) has come closest with his measure of writing speed in seconds/word. At one point in time Gould and Boies (1978) entertained the hypothesis that a variable amount of planning could go on concurrently with articulation (generation) depending upon the rate of articulation, thus implying that a fast writer had less additional planning time at his disposal while writing than a slow writer. However they did not study articulation rate.

There is in fact no standard method of measuring articulation rate in writing in use today. Unless we are to assume that articulation rate in writing does not vary—and such an assumption would imply that Shulansky and Herrmann's (1977) finding of a faster rate of typing for touch-typists was due to a reduction in pause time only—or that its variation is unimportant for the actual course of writing, it is imperative that such a standard method of measurement be developed and adopted.

We have pointed out the possible artifact in the use of words/unit of time consequent upon the considerable variation of word length from corpus to corpus. Syllables or even graphemes/unit of time would seem much better suited for writing research.

The status of punctuation poses yet another methodological question: Should punctuation marks be considered part of the text and thus included as equivalent to a syllable or grapheme unit? We would favor such a convention on the grounds that punctuation is graphemic, that it requires production time, and that it reflects planning. Nor is there any consensus regarding the inclusion of revisions as part of the written corpus. In speech-production research, confusion has resulted from the fact that some studies have included all hesitation phenomena as part of the text (and therefore in the calculation of articulation rate) whereas other studies have determined articulation rate exclusive of such hesitations, as Kowal and O'Connell (1983) have noted.

Pause time. Despite recent progress in instrumental methods of pause analysis, some measurement problems regarding pause time in writing research remain. The simple problem of measuring pause time from the time a writing instrument is removed from the writing surface *or* from the time its movement ceases has not been solved. Some researchers have also included a variety of extraneous activities in pause time, e.g., reading or rereading source material (Gould, 1979), or rereading the composed text (Matsuhashi, 1981). It is imperative that a more exact and detailed taxonomy of off-time activity be adopted, that these activities be instructed, allowed or controlled from study to study in systematic ways, and that they be carefully timed, recorded, and analyzed in keeping with the specific purposes of each study.

Matsuhashi and Cooper (1978) have raised the question of a minimum pause duration in writing research. In the research reviewed above, such cutoff points ranged from 6 to 0.10 seconds. An analogy to research on speech production would indicate that pauses measured to a small fraction of a second are psychologically useful *(tempus utile)*. There exists the additional problem of the adoption of a standardized convention in this regard; without such a convention, studies remain mutually incomparable.

Again by analogy to research in speech production, it is necessary to analyze both pause time and articulation rate, since they have been found to vary independently and indeed differentially under various conditions (e.g., Grosjean & Deschamps, 1975).

In addition the separate analysis of the two components of pause time (pause duration and pause frequency) should be encouraged. Such an analysis allows the researcher to relate pause patterns to the characteristics of the concurrent text. Matsuhashi's (1981, 1982) research can be considered a first step in this direction. Such research will have to engage methodological problems such as the treatment of excessive variability of pause duration and the determination of appropriate criteria for pause location, relative, for example, to syntactic characteristics of the text.

Revising. Revising has not been studied systematically in any of the research reviewed above. Matsuhashi and Cooper (1978) indicated some possible first steps toward a temporal analysis of revising but did not pursue the matter.

Revising has been extraordinarily resistant to a real-time processing approach because of the wide variability in the stylistics of revisions; some writers revise a word at a time, some a paragraph at a time. Methods of shrinking this variability by instruction, by limitation of time, and by level of difficulty of the writing task must be used. Methods of revision of unskilled and skilled writers (e.g., editors) must be compared. Units of revision must be standardized. Only then will we be able to engage important research topics regarding revising. These, we feel, would include: semantic, syntactic, and stylistic comparisons of revised and original text; distance (in time and amount of text) of revisions from original text; and the temporal course of revising in itself and in comparison with original text production.

Writing and Planning

In research on speech production, it has become customary to distinguish between spontaneous speech on the one hand, i.e., speech that is being "organized at the moment of utterance" (Rochester, 1973, p. 51), and reproductive speech on the other hand, including reading aloud and reciting from memory. Most of the research on writing clearly involves spontaneous text production, although amount of preplanning and task demands vary. Writing a memorized text, copying from a written text, and writing from dictation are the equivalents in writing of reproductive speech. They have rarely been studied for their own sake. In fact, the preoccupation of recent research with composition has minimized interest in basic writing tasks involving no creative planning.

Initial research regarding the assessment of temporal variables might best be carried out with writing tasks requiring as little planning as possible. Simple tasks provide a normative baseline in research and are the more necessary as we move toward analysis of very complex behavior.

Comparing writing with speaking

All three of the basic assumptions about temporal characteristics presented in the second section of this chapter are based on comparisons of speaking with writing. But our review of empirical writing research has indicated that our present knowledge of similarities and differences between speaking and writing in real time does not surpass the truism that speech rate is indeed faster than writing rate. Specific answers will all require further research. But the research must be characterized by methods of temporal analysis common to both modalities so as to permit comparisons of articulation rate, pause patterns, and revision strategies in both writing and speaking. Because research in speech production has indicated that pausing and hesitations may be highly idiosyncratic, within-subject designs will be needed.

Our final word on writing as language behavior must be that we know very little even about what goes on overtly during the process of writing. But on the other hand, we have hardly begun to investigate the ways of finding out. As to internal cognitive processes, they can be considered largely virgin territory. Let no one restrict the human uses of writing:

> Then they made signs to his father, asking him what name he would like the boy to have. Zechariah asked for a writing pad and wrote, "His name is John." (Luke 1:62–63)

REFERENCES

Bartlett, E.J., & Scribner, S. (1981). Text and context: An investigation of referential organization in children's written narratives. In C.H. Frederiksen & J.F. Dominic (Eds.),

Writing: The nature, development, and teaching of written communication (Vol. 2). Hillsdale, NJ: Erlbaum.

Bereiter, C. (1980). Development in writing. In L.W. Gregg & E.R. Steinberg (Eds.), *Cognitive processes in writing*. Hillsdale, NJ: Erlbaum.

Black, J.B. (1982). Psycholinguistic processes in writing. In S. Rosenberg (Ed.), *Handbook of applied psycholinguistics*. Hillsdale, NJ: Erlbaum.

Blass, T., & Siegman, A.W. (1975). A psycholinguistic comparison of speech, dictation and writing. *Language and Speech, 18,* 20–34.

Boring, E.G. (1950). *A history of experimental psychology* (2nd ed.). New York: Appleton-Century-Crofts.

Chafe, W.L. (1982). Integration and involvement in speaking, writing, and oral literature. In D. Tannen (Ed.), *Spoken and written language: Exploring orality and literacy: Vol.9. Advances in discourse processes*. Norwood, NJ: Ablex.

Clark, H.H., & Clark, E.V. (1977). *Psychology and language*. New York: Harcourt Brace Jovanovich.

Cooper, W. E., & Paccia-Cooper, J. (1980). *Syntax and speech*. Cambridge, MA: Harvard University Press.

Emig, J. (1981). Non-magical thinking: Presenting writing developmentally in schools. In C.H. Frederiksen & J.F. Dominic (Eds.), *Writing: The nature, development, and teaching of written communication* (Vol. 2). Hillsdale, NJ: Erlbaum.

Ericsson, K.A., & Simon, H.A. (1980). Verbal reports as data. *Psychological Review, 87,* 215–251.

Ericsson, K.A., & Simon, H.A. (1984). *Protocol analysis. Verbal reports as data.* Cambridge, MA: MIT Press.

Flower, L., & Hayes, J.R. (1980). The dynamics of composing: Making plans and juggling constraints. In L. Gregg & E. Steinberg (Eds.), *Cognitive processes in writing: An interdisciplinary approach*. Hillsdale, NJ: Erlbaum.

Flower, L., & Hayes, J.R. (1981). Plans that guide the composing process. In C.H. Frederiksen & J.F. Dominic (Eds.), *Writing: The nature, development, and teaching of written communication* (Vol. 2). Hillsdale, NJ: Erlbaum.

Foss, D.J., & Hakes, D.T. (1978) *Psycholinguistics: An introduction to the psychology of language*. Englewood Cliffs, NJ: Prentice-Hall.

Frase, L.T. (1981). Writing, text, and the reader. In H.C. Frederiksen & J.F. Dominic (Eds.), *Writing: The nature, development, and teaching of written communication* (Vol. 2). Hillsdale, NJ: Erlbaum.

Frederiksen, C.H., and Dominic, J.F. (Eds.). (1981). *Writing: The nature, development, and teaching of written communication* (Vol. 2). Hillsdale, NJ: Erlbaum.

Freud, S. (1954). *Zur Psychopathologie des Alltagslebens*. Frankfurt: Fischer Taschenbuch-verlag.

Goldman-Eisler, F. (1958). The predictability of words in context and the length of pauses in speech. *Language and Speech, 1,* 226–231.

Gould, J.D. (1978). An experimental study of writing, dictating, and speaking. In J. Requin (Ed.), *Attention and performance* (Vol. 7). Hillsdale, NJ: Erlbaum.

Gould, J.D. (1979). *Writing and speaking letters and messages* (IBM Research Report No. RC-7528). Yorktown Heights, NY. Thomas J. Watson Research Center.

Gould, J.D. (1980). Experiments on composing letters: Some facts, some myths, and some observations. In L.W. Gregg & E.R. Steinberg (Eds.), *Cognitive processes in writing*. Hillsdale, NJ: Erlbaum.

Gould, J.D., & Boies, S.J. (1978). Writing, dictating, and speaking letters. *Science, 201,* 1145–1147.

Gould, J.D., & Quinones, A. (1978). Handwriting and speech signal analyzer. *IBM Technical*

Disclosure Bulletin. Disclosure Number Y0878-3045. Yorktown Heights, NY. Thomas J. Watson Research Center.

Grosjean, F., & Deschamps, A. (1975). Analyse contrastive des variables temporelles de l'anglais et du français: Vitesse de parole et variables composantes, phénomènes d'hésitation. *Phonetica, 31*, 144–184.

Hayes, J.R., & Flower, L.S. (1980). Identifying the organization of writing processes. In L.W. Gregg & E.R. Steinberg (Eds.), *Cognitive processes in writing*. Hillsdale, NJ. Erlbaum.

Hockett, C.F. (1966). The problem of universals in language. In J.H. Greenberg (Ed.), *Universals of language* (2nd ed). Cambridge, MA: MIT Press.

Hörmann, H. (1981). *Einführung in die Psycholinguistik*. Darmstadt: Wissenschaftliche Buchgesellschaft.

Horowitz, M.W., and Berkowitz, A. (1964). Structural advantage of the mechanism of spoken expression as a factor in differences in spoken and written expression. *Perceptual and Motor Skill, 19*, 619–625.

Hunt, K.W. (1965). *Grammatical structures written at three grade levels*. Urbana, IL: National Council of Teachers of English.

James, W. (1890). *The principles of psychology* (Vol. 1). New York: Henry Holt & Co.

Kowal, S., & O'Connell, D.C. (1983). Practice makes fluent—but how? *Rassegna Italiana di Linguistica Applicata, 15*, 161–168.

Lounsbury, F.G. (1954). Transitional probability, linguistic structure, and systems of habit-family hierarchies. In C.E. Osgood & T.A. Sebeok (Eds.), *Psycholinguistics: A survey of theory and research problems*. Baltimore, MD: Waverly Press.

Maclay, H., & Osgood, C.E. (1959). Hesitation phenomena in spontaneous English speech. *Word, 15*, 19–44.

Mandler, J.M., & Johnson, N.S. (1977). Remembrance of things parsed: Story structure and recall. *Cognitive Psychology, 9*, 111–151.

Matsuhashi, A. (1981). Pausing and planning: The tempo of written discourse production. *Research in the Teaching of English, 15*, 113–134.

Matsuhashi, A. (1982). Explorations in the real-time production of written discourse. In M. Nystrand (Ed.), *What writers know: The language, process, and structure of written discourse*. New York: Academic Press.

Matsuhashi, A., & Cooper, C. (1978, March). *A video time-monitored observational study: The transcribing behavior and composing processes of a competent high school writer*. Paper presented at the meeting of the American Educational Research Association, Toronto, Ontario.

Newell, A., & Simon, H.A. (1972). *Human problem solving*. Englewood Cliffs, NJ: Prentice-Hall.

Nisbett, R.E., & Wilson, T.DeC. (1977). Telling more than we can know: Verbal reports on mental processes. *Psychological Review, 84*, 231–259.

Nold, E.W. (1981). Revising. In C.H. Frederiksen & J.F. Dominic (Eds.), *Writing: The nature, development, and teaching of written communication*. Hillsdale, NJ: Erlbaum.

Ong, W.J. (1981). *Fighting for life: Contest, sexuality, and consciousness*. Ithaca, NY: Cornell University Press.

Owens, J., Bower, G.H., & Black, J.B. (1979). The "soap opera" effect in story recall. *Memory and Cognition, 7*, 185–191.

Paivio, A., & Begg, I. (1981). *Psychology of language*. Englewood Cliffs, NJ: Prentice-Hall.

Palermo, D.S. (1978) *Psychology of language*. Glenview, IL: Scott, Foresman.

Paris Review Interviews. (1963). *Writers at work*. Second Series. New York: Viking Press.

Paris Review Interviews. (1967). *Writers at work*. Third Series. New York: Viking Press.

Preyer, W. (1895). *Zur Psychologie des Schreibens*. Leipzig: Leopold Voss.

Rochester, S.R. (1973). The significance of pauses in spontaneous speech. *Journal of Psycholinguistic Research, 2,* 51-81.

Sabin, E.J., Clemmer, E.J., O'Connell, D.C., and Kowal, S. (1979). A pausological approach to speech development. In A.W. Siegman & S. Feldstein (Eds.), *Of speech and time: Temporal speech patterns in interpersonal contexts.* Hillsdale, NJ: Erlbaum.

Shulansky, J.D., & Herrmann, D.J. (1977). The influence of linguistic structure on typing. *Language and Speech, 20,* 80-85.

Smith, F. (1982). *Writing and the writer.* New York: Holt, Rinehart and Winston.

Spittle, K.B., & Matsuhashi, A. (1981). Semantic aspects of real time written discourse production. In M. Hairston & C. Selfe (Eds.), *Selected papers from the 1981 Texas writing research conference* (pp. 137-164). University of Texas at Austin. Department of English.

Tannenbaum, P.H., Williams, F., & Wood, B.S. (1967). Hesitation phenomena and related encoding characteristics in speech and typewriting. *Language and Speech, 10,* 203-215.

Turner, A., & Greene, E. (1977, April). *The construction and use of a propositional text base.* (Tech. Rep. No. 63). Boulder: University of Colorado, Institute for the Study of Intellectual Behavior.

van Bruggen, J.A. (1946). Factors affecting regularity of the flow of words during written composition. *Journal of Experimental Education, 15,* 133-155.

Waldrop, M.M. The necessity of knowledge. (1984). *Science, 223,* 1279-1282.

CHAPTER 6

Children's Development of Prosodic Distinctions in Telling and Dictation Modes*

Elizabeth Sulzby

Northwestern University

In this chapter I report a study comparing kindergarten children's language when they were asked to tell and to dictate stories in preparation for writing their own stories. Since story telling and dictation are modes that have potential for children (and adults) to display their understandings of oral and written language relationships, I introduce the chapter, first, with a discussion of oral and written language relationships broadly, then focus on both storytelling and dictation as modes of communication. In the final section of the introduction, dictation is portrayed as a research tool that is of theoretical interest for literacy studies of both children and adults, as well as being a practical means of dealing with difficulties from the mechanical aspects of writing.

ORAL AND WRITTEN LANGUAGE RELATIONSHIPS

Attention to features of oral and written language in both oral and written delivery forms is a relatively new development within linguistics and psycholinguistics. Influential linguists in the early twentieth century treated language as if it consisted of oral language and dismissed written language as a secondary coding system not important or relevant to language itself (cf. Bloomfield, 1933; Jesperson, 1921, 1924, 1938). Even more contem-

* The research reported herein was supported by a grant from the National Institute of Education (NIE-G-80-0176). The opinions expressed are the responsibility of the author and not of NIE. This chapter is an expansion of a paper titled, "Children's Development of the Ability to Distinguish Telling and Dictating Modes," presented at the American Educational Research Association, Montreal, April 1983. The author is grateful to the children, teacher, and school district involved; to Beverly Cox, Beverly Otto, and Susan Anderson, Research Assistants on the project; to numerous undergraduate research assistants, but particularly to Harriet Rabenovets; and to Dr. Norman Bowers of Northwestern University for his advice on data analysis.

porary linguists who have discussed the topic typically dismissed written language as nothing more than a secondary form. Pyles (1971) treated written language as simply the development of writing systems. Chomsky (1957, 1965) made little of the relationships between oral and written language except as historical changes in orthography affected phonology (Chomsky & Halle, 1968). The recent trend has been to reconsider written language, including both its impact on the totality of language and its distinction from oral language (Cook-Gumperz & Gumperz, 1981; Martlew, 1983; Ong, 1982; Sulzby, 1985, 1986a, 1986b, in press; Tannen, 1982).

Historians of language are also beginning to change their treatment of written language. Rather than treating it as a mere mechanical coding system laid upon oral language, historians of language are beginning to point out the impact of written language or of a "written standard" upon the development of language. Strang's (1970) history of English in Great Britain traced the development of both written and oral standards and their mutual impact on the totality of British English as a language. She distinguished between the historian's use of written records in order to infer the oral characteristics of English at different historical points and the use of such records in order to ascertain characteristics which were taken to be appropriate to written language.

Many of the records the historian uses include the work of scribes who filled carefully defined roles which could be examined separately in relation to oral and written language. Such roles could be that of a scribe in a monastery copying a text as close to "verbatim" as possible, of a scribe translating and interpreting one dialect of English into another during a period in which writing was not highly conventional, or of a scribe filling more commonplace roles in the community, keeping chronicles or writing letters for acquaintances. From differentiating characteristics of oral language from those of written language found in surviving written documents, Strang claims that, by the period of 1370–1570, London was a cultural center in which there were both clear written and clear oral standards (even though written standards had existed earlier in various times and regions of Great Britain).

Two conclusions can be drawn from the historical methodology: First, oral and written language developed together and had a mutual impact on the totality of language and, second, literacy affected individuals differently. I return to this second point from a historical standpoint in the section on dictation.

Now, however, let us turn to think a bit about the child in a contemporary, highly literate culture. I conceive of the young child who grows up in a middle-class home in a highly literate society as developing both oral and written language long before the child is literate in the conventional sense.

Some evidence about the impact of oral and written language relationships in modern societies, including the children growing up in those societies, comes from the work of linguists, psychologists, sociologists, and anthropologists who investigate discourse-level interactions between people in contemporary social situations. In their ethnography of Athabaskan speakers in Canada and Alaska, anthropologists Scollon and Scollon (1981) argued that their 2-year-old daughter Rachel was more literate than an 11-year-old Athabaskan girl who could read school texts, write simple sentences, and use the typewriter passably. Rachel was not reading from print nor was she writing conventionally. Yet in her speech, delivered orally, she used the wording of written language and the prosody of reading. Scollon and Scollon stressed that Rachel had a literate attitude toward storytelling; she fictionalized herself as author and seemed to address a fictionalized audience, even when the physically present audience was one of the participants she put into her stories. At age 2, Rachel had been socialized strongly into her parents' world which included using a tape recorder as a surrogate scribe for dictation.

The Scollons treated their daughter's speech as a storytelling, yet the storytelling was elicited in what I would judge to be a written context, including the use of a tape recorder from which her parents transcribed written text. In my own research, I have begun to use the terms *emergent reading, emergent writing,* and *emergent literacy* to describe the literacy behaviors of young children that develop into conventional literacy; this term and other similar terms (like *print awareness, linguistic* or *metalinguistic awareness, invented spelling*) are being used increasingly by researchers to emphasize the nature of early literacy development (see Teale & Sulzby, 1986).

In my research (Sulzby, 1981a, 1983, 1986a, 1986b, in press), I have used a task paradigm designed to elicit children's speech in situations in which oral and written language relationships can be compared. The tasks range from those situations that are most typically oral and interactive to situations that appear to be written—in which the interaction is deferred from face-to-face to an internalized interaction between a nonpresent author and reader. The tasks were conversation, storytelling, story dictation, and handwritten stories. When samples from each type of task were requested, we watched to see whether and in which ways children would "adapt" these modes, either toward more typically oral or written conventions. In the part of that research that I report here, I focused just upon the two modes of storytelling and dictation.

STORYTELLING AS A MODE OF COMMUNICATION

Storytelling can take many forms and has been investigated as an adult practice within various cultures by numerous researchers from many disciplines. Much attention has been paid to the notion that story schemata (or structured expectations for what counts as a story) are widespread phenomena cross-culturally (Applebee, 1978; Kintsch & Greene, 1978; Mandler & Johnson, 1977; Propp, 1968; Rumelhart, 1977; Scollon & Scollon, 1981; Stein & Glenn, 1979). For now, I only report on some characteristics of storytelling as they differ from those of dictation.

Storytelling (or the broader category of oral narrative about both real and imagined events) is typically a form of face-to-face communication in which a teller narrates directly to a listener or listeners. In many cultures, particularly Western literature cultures, storytelling is taken to be an oral monologue, even though listeners may ask occasional questions or chime in with reactions. In other cultures, like the Athabaskans studied by Scollon and Scollon (1981), storytelling is interactive but the interaction is highly structured by cultural expectations around the "genre" and event of storytelling. Athabaskan listeners are supposed to participate in the telling of the story by commenting or otherwise signalling their interpretations at points in the narrative, signalled by features such as structure and pauses.

Even though storytelling is ideally an oral monologue in mainstream America, adults often "help" young children tell stories by asking them questions that are designed to help the child give enough information to be clear to the adult's satisfaction. In school settings, this help reaches an extreme level in rituals like "rug time," "circle time," or "sharing time" (Green & Wallat, 1981; Markowitz & Moses, 1981; Mehan, 1979; Sulzby, 1983) in which a teacher may ask questions designed not to help the teacher understand but instead to help other members of the audience, other children, understand the event being narrated. This kind of help by the teacher also appears to have a teaching effect upon the child storyteller, intended to help the child learn how to maintain an oral monologue that is sufficiently clear (or decontextualized, to use Olson's 1977 term) for other people to understand. When adults furnish this kind of help, they appear to be leading children away from the face-to-face character of storytelling and away from the expectation that the child should entertain the listeners with a well-told tale toward a way of speaking that is more like written language in both its interpersonal aspects and in its wording.

When children tell stories in the ritualized setting of the school or in experimental studies of story production, their output is often quite scanty and relatively uncomplex (Sulzby, 1981a, 1983, 1985). When children tell stories spontaneously or with elicitations that are structured more like casual, out-of-school conversations (cf. Botvin & Sutton-Smith, 1977; Peterson & McCabe, 1983), they create complex stories, filled with the markings of high personal involvement and other features of oral language. Here is an example taken from near the end of a long narrative told by a 9-year-old rural Midwestern boy, given in the Peterson and McCabe research. The boy and his father are chasing each other around the house after a series of catastrophes ending in half-play, half-earnest flight.

and he went down the stairs
and down the stairs.
He got so excited,
he said, "I'm gonna go one way,"
So, I kept on running that-a-way,
and he that-a-way,
and I stopped at the corner
when he was at that corner,
and he started coming back there,
and he went around there,
and he went around there,
and on in the house,
and kept going round and round and round.
Finally I was up on there,
and here he come.
He had went behind the cars
and I had had a bucket of water
and threw the bucket of water at him.
Ooooooooohhhhh.
It was cold that day too.
He went brrrrrr,
'Cause this hot water I threw at him?

Although Peterson and McCabe (1983) did not report the speed of this narrative, the reader can almost infer a rapid speed of speaking. The written transcript shows that the boy uses deictic references (*that-a-way, that-a-way, the corner, that corner; back there; around there; up on there,* etc.). He also uses the simple conjunctions *and* and *so* most typically found in oral language, particularly in informal settings.

Chafe (1982) recently has been involved in a study of what he refers to as written and spoken language. That study has partially replicated older research examining the surface features most typical to oral and written language situations. Chafe gathered data from adults in informal and formal speaking situations (dinner-table conversations and lectures) and in informal and formal written tasks (letters and academic papers). He found, like Gould (1980), that speaking is faster than writing. In fact, the average speed of speaking in English that he reported, including pauses, was approximately 180 words per minute (or approximately 3 words per second).

Other surface features of speaking that Chafe found included a preference for simple conjunctions like *and* or *so,* as the boy in the example above used abundantly. Chafe classified this feature under a more general category of fragmentation of ideas units in contrast with devices used to integrate ideas in written language. He also found evidence that speakers involve themselves more directly with their listeners through the use of self-references and references to their own thought processes and to the understanding of the listener, often breaking up idea units with comments like, "I think," "you know," or "really." Each of these features has some relevance for the distinctions that young children make between storytelling and dictation, as we shall see.

As we see throughout this volume, speed and pausing are emerging as important variables in language study. Speed of speaking and length of pausing are receiving increased attention by sociolinguists and anthropologists (Gumperz, 1982; Scollon & Scollon, 1981). Scollon and Scollon attribute differences in inter- and intra-clause pausing to difficulties which Athabaskans and English speakers have in conducting conversations and in delivering and interpreting longer stretches of discourse. A difference of about ½ second between utterances signals a quite different intention. When intending to continue speaking in a conversation, English speakers wait only about 1 second between utterances; Athabaskans wait about 1½ seconds. So while Athabaskans are waiting their normal pause time, English speakers often think they have received a signal that it is their turn to speak. In relating narratives, Athabaskans use stylized pauses along with intonation and lexical markers to signal parts of the narrative, including points at which the listeners are expected to take part. Narratives proceed not as oral monologues driven by the intentions of the speaker alone, but as an interactive process in which the responses of the listeners affect what the speaker will say next. Athabaskans, according to Scollon and Scollon, are subtly repelled by the written language orientation that English speakers have imported into their orally delivered narrative discourse. English speakers say a lot and say it rapidly, without allowing their listeners to signal their understandings of the narrative. In conversation, on the other hand, English speakers do not realize how pauses are used by Athabaskans to "hold the floor," and they interrupt when they should be listening patiently. In these situations, speakers from the different cultures have great difficulty telling stories to each other, either in face-to-face interactive conversation or in oral monologue.

DICTATION AS A MODE OF COMMUNICATION

Historical Development of Writing Systems

As written forms of language developed, literacy spread gradually among individuals of a given culture (just as there was variation in literacy's spread across cultures). In cultures in which literacy was not yet widespread, dictation and oral reading were common practices for pragmatic reasons. A literate member of a community would write and read letters and other documents for other members who were either illiterate or marginally literate. This practice continues in modern-day cultures which have widespread effects of literacy but also have members who are not yet literate. Such practice may include social routines and genre schemata which are well-established for all participants—composer, scribe, and recipient. Scribner and Cole's (1981) study of the Vai culture in Liberia is a good example of a modern-day people's use of community scribes. Of their sample of 107 Vai literates, 94% reported that they wrote and received letters themselves. Sixty-one percent of these literates acted as scribes for nonliterate relatives and friends. Although the letters typically are to people well-known to the persons dictating, dictators used specific genre characteristics that are not typically oral in character. "Analysis of our [Scribner & Cole's] letter collection made it clear that Vai letters are more than talk written down; they are a new, written form of discourse" (p. 204).

Research With Very Young Children

Very young children are in a somewhat similar position *vis à vis* literacy in the home. Because children appear to be not yet fully literate, parents often encourage children to dictate letters to relatives or friends. The parent will serve as the child's scribe. However, as with the Vai "illiterates" of Scribner and Cole's research, the modern-day child in a literate society also is surrounded by literacy; such children seem to begin to understand the role of the scribe, of the print, and of the writer-as-(oral) composer even before they are themselves independently literate. In an extreme example of how widespread literacy and its associated schooling practices are, kindergarten and preschool teachers have reported receiving "dictations" of stories or descriptive prose that parents of their students have sent to school for "show and tell"—even though the teachers were not using dictations as an instructional technique.

Three major longitudinal studies of children's literacy development have made systemic use of dictation as an important language mode. In King and Rentel's (1981, 1982; Rentel & King, 1983) research on children's writing, they gathered samples of children's story retellings after books had been read to them; of children's dictations; and of children's handwritten compositions. The major focus of this project was children's abilities to create coherent and cohesive English texts during the period from first through second grades. Harste, Burke, and Woodward (1981, 1982) gathered six major types of language samples, including reading from environmental print, dictating and rereading a dictated story, samples of uninterrupted writing and drawing, reading a familiar storybook, writing and reading letters, and, finally, writing and rereading a story. Children from whom these samples were drawn ranged from 3 through 5 years old. In Sulzby (1981a, 1983, and elsewhere) I have reported studies of groups of kindergarteners in which I compared samples of conversation, storytelling, dictation, and writing, along with rereading and editing of the two handwritten forms. Sulzby (1981a) used experimental techniques to compare these language modes with 24 kindergarteners. The study reported herein used these same techniques with 9 children selected for intensive case study during their kindergarten and first-grade years.

The King and Rentel studies and the Sulzby (1983) study included very specific guidelines about the role of the scribe in dictation sessions. In both studies tape recorders were used to record the entire session but scribes were present to take dictation. These scribes wrote at a specified speed and interacted verbally and nonverbally only in specific ways. In contrast, the earlier Sulzby study (1981a) used less specific guidelines governing when the scribe could take part in conversational exchanges with the child. Harste, Burke & Woodward (1981) indicate that they noted that children negotiated the dictation task demands toward conversation but they did not conduct in-depth analyses of this phenomenon.

Like King and Rentel, I have treated dictation as being an intermediate step between oral language and written language, at least potentially. Thus far, however, only the Sulzby project has included systematic comparisons of the forms of the orally delivered language in the tasks of storytelling and dictation. One reason for this maybe that both the King and Rentel project and Harste et al. used different topics in the different language modes. I used the same topic across the modes, using a randomized and counterbalanced order in the first study (1981a) and using the same order across children in the later work (1983). I will return to the details of these studies in the section reporting the comparisons selected for discussion in this chapter.

Research With School-Aged Children
Dictation was used as a contrast to writing by Scardamalia, Bereiter, and Goelman (1982) in order to study what they call production factors associated with writing. They posited a short-term memory loss due to the slow speed and mechanics of handwriting. They wanted to find out if children would write more and write higher quality compositions if the hindrances of handwriting were removed through dictation and if the inequal time

were removed by using slow dictation, dictation at the speed the child typically wrote. They collected samples of writing, slow dictation, and regular dictation from fourth- and sixth-grade children, using different topics for each mode. Regular dictation was collected with a tape recorder and no scribe. In slow dictation, a scribe sat beside the child and avoided both eye contact and conversational exchanges while writing at the speed the child had used in the writing sample. After each production, the child was encouraged to dictate or write even more and the two portions were analyzed separately.

Scardamalia et al. found that children continued to produce more in regular dictation than in writing but that slow dictation was intermediate in quantity, measured as the number of words written. Following the encouragement prompt, however, the quantity advantage of normal dictation over writing disappeared. Quality analyses of clarity and cohesion indicated that there were no significant mode differences before the encouragement prompt but that writing was rated significantly higher in quality for the portion produced after the encouragement.

Research With Literate Adults

Adults use dictation in the workplace, most typically to dictate letters into a tape recorder or transcribing machine for someone to transcribe and type later. A few still dictate to secretaries who sit and take shorthand in person. Dictation is a different task from simply recording and transcribing speech that was not intended to be dictation. For the literate adult in the modern business office, dictation requires that the speaker be aware of the scribe's needs, either immediately or via the tape recorder, so the dictator's speech may include meta-statements referring to the body of the dictation. As an extreme example: "Capital D dear sir colon paragraph indent Capital I insurance costs have been climbing. . . ."

Dictation in the workplace is an innovation in the history of language development in that the dictator is typically not a novice writer but a fairly accomplished writer (producing, if not artful, at least readable, prose). In contrast, we have found that some young children do not seem to be aware of the role of the scribe or of a tape recorder. When asked to dictate, they take the request (or the context) as an invitation to talk, either as an oral monologue or as interactive conversation.

Adult dictators vary in their considerateness for the scribe or secretary. Dictators who are business "bosses" often depend heavily upon the scribe to make them appear more literate than their dictation might sound; they depend upon their secretary (often called the "executive secretary") to translate oral characteristics of their speech into standard written form. Such dictators show that they are literate by having such expectations even at times when they themselves do not want to use the effort to compose acceptable written discourse. Other dictators require that the scribe simply transcribe as carefully as possible, "What I said," occasionally failing to realize that some features of written language are not expressible in oral speech without specific metalinguistic translations (like those in the facetious example of the insurance letter above).

In the workplace, the scribe or secretary can wield considerable power by the obvious or subtle translations that go on when people transcribe written text from orally delivered discourse. Such translations also occur in dictation taken from young children. In instructional practice with children, teachers are often advised to write down what children dictate and then to have children reread those dictations—presumably rereading their own oral language. These teachers often import features of written language, such as quotation marks or periods, into speech in which the child did not give clear signals about what should be written. But let us return to consider research with literate adult dictators.

John Gould and his associates at IBM's Watson research center (see Gould, 1980, for a summary) have studied literate adults doing office-related tasks in which different modes of composition were used. Most of their studies have compared speaking with dictation and writing. The primary task has been to convey business information either as a "letter," which may be spoken (as in giving information over a telephone), or dictated into a tape recorder or dictated person-to-person to a secretary, or handwritten, or typed. Two findings from this project are of importance to the current study. First, literate adults have no difficulty differentiating between these tasks, even though there are expert and novice differences. Second, Gould's research indicates that adults do not use the maximum speeds possible in these modes, probably because the tasks differ in the physical and cognitive complexity involved in preparing information for a listener or a reader under these different circumstances.

Gould (1980) began with the hypothesis that the maximum speaking speed would be about 200 words per minute (wpm) for dictating and that writing would occur at a speed of about 40 wpm. The dictating figure he suggested is a bit faster than the speed which Chafe reported but Chafe's figures were taken from adults retelling stories under experimental conditions. Gould found that, when subjects conveyed business information, speaking was indeed faster than dictating which was again faster than writing but that actual composers using business information fell far below the maximum times he had suggested. He reported composing rates (consisting of words divided by total composition time, which includes pauses) of 13 wpm for writing, 23 wpm for dictating, and 30 wpm for speaking (when speaking was giving a letter orally to a listener who was not a scribe). (These rates in words per second are 0.22, 0.38, 0.50, respectively.) In the study that follows, I investigated whether or not children would distinguish between the two modes of dictating and storytelling and how speed and pauses, along with other variables, could be used to detect such distinctions in young children over time.

Questions Raised by Instructional Practices

In schools, dictation is often used as an instructional technique for beginning reading instruction. This technique is most closely identified with the language-experience approach (Stauffer, 1970) which holds that children will learn to read most easily from their own language about topics which they have experienced personally. Books and articles concerning the language-experience approach often suggest that teachers should have groups of children dictate joint stories or accounts. The teacher often asks questions about wording or about the scribal duties, such as how a word might be spelled or about whether a capital letter or punctuation mark is needed. In addition to "group dictations," teachers also take dictation from individual children, often using parent volunteers, paid aides, or older students as scribes for individual children.

Language-experience theorists are particularly responsible for teachers and educators of young children beginning to attend a linguistic and psycholinguistic research in oral and written language relationships. Unfortunately, however, the writings of many language-experience theorists preceded their awareness of such research. Teachers following language-experience approaches often use the dictum that reading/writing is "talk written down." Russell Stauffer (1970) actually put that comment in a broader intellectual framework, drawing on the work of Dewey, but the catchphrase sticks out:

> It would seem that the most functional way to show children that reading is *no more than speech written down* is to do a great deal more than we do about using their language-experience-cognitive wealth to share each other's intellectual life. (p. 16) [author's emphasis]

The language-experience approach led to debates about whether or how closely the teacher should transcribe exactly what the child said during dictation. Such debates included the argument that reading (I assume this should mean writing) is *not* talk written down; writing is an interpretation process even when the raw oral speech is encoded into writing. When thought is transformed into what Olson (1977) calls autonomous text able to be understood by a nonpresent audience, it requires major overhauling from its immediate oral expression as Flower (1979) has shown with adults and as other researchers (King & Rentel, 1981; Sulzby, 1981a, 1982) are showing with the oral and written expressions of young children.

Some language-experience theorists like Stauffer and Henderson (Henderson, personal communication, July 1982) have suggested that children's oral speech during dictation is a useful diagnostic tool that teachers can use to understand the concepts about reading that children hold. Until recently, however, linguistic tools were lacking to investigate this claim. Current research is beginning to reexamine this claim and also to reexamine the use of dictation during the development of the child as a writer and not just as a reader.

One important step in conducting such research is to begin to separate the notions of oral and written language from the notions of oral and written delivery forms (Rubin, 1980; Sulzby, 1981a). Thus researchers are beginning to examine children's orally delivered speech for characteristics of written language and to examine their written forms for characteristics more appropriate in oral language. Dictation appears to be an intermediate form in which the child is asked, implicitly or explicitly, to compose written language and to deliver it orally. Storytelling appears to make an important contrast with dictation, but may or may not, depending upon the child's concepts.

THE STUDY

The language modes of telling and dictating seem to offer important contrasts that relate to children's knowledge about oral and written language. Both modes seem to be conditions in which the person does essentially the same thing: tells a story. However, children differ in how much they are aware of characteristics of written language. Children with little awareness of written language should treat both modes as situations for "regular talking," or oral monologue in a face-to-face situation. The child with growing awareness of how written language works should make a distinction in the wording of the two modes, suiting telling to a present audience and dictating to a nonpresent audience (Cox & Sulzby, 1984). Additionally, the child who is increasing in awareness of how writing works should adapt to the needs of the scribe and should use pauses aligned with the graphic segmentation of the writing system as used by the scribe. In other words, dictation should be slower overall and should contain pauses between words and longer phrases keyed to the scribe's writing speed.

In Sulzby (1981a), we collected samples of told and dictated stories from 24 middle-class kindergarteners as part of a larger study of emergent literacy. In that study, two replications of told, dictated, and handwritten stories, with rereading and editing of both the written modes, were collected from all 24 children, with topic and mode orders counterbalanced and assigned at random. I found that slightly over half of the children clearly distinguished between dictating and telling modes. This finding was based upon analyses of responses of naive judges listening to tape recordings of the children's speech. Evidence that the judges used in order to say that children distinguished between the modes varied widely. For example, some children used word-by-word dictation, with steady, monotonous pitch, and voice pausing between words and then spoke in an animated, fluent conversational tone for storytelling. We also analyzed and described the characteristics of each mode separately and found that children who were judged to be more advanced in emergent literacy showed more adaptation toward the needs of the scribe in dictation; children who were judged to be low in emergent literacy tended to adapt storytelling toward conversational interaction.

A difficulty with the Sulzby study described above was that the tapes contained clues to composition mode which the judges had to ignore. The study reported herein was designed to replicate the Sulzby (1981) study with more consistent elicitation procedures, to standardize the kinds of comparisons judges were asked to make, and to gain more information about the bases upon which such comparisons were made. Additionally, speed of speech in comparable stretches of discourse was calculated. Four questions were addressed: (1) What evidence does prosody offer that children distinguish between the modes of telling and dictating? (2) Do children of different ability levels differ in the distinctions they make? (3) Are there differences over time? and (4) When judgments are made by naive linguistic judges listening to tape recordings, what criteria are used in making the judgment that a child did or did not distinguish between the modes?

Method

Subjects. The subjects for the study were 9 children selected for intensive case study during kindergarten and first grade. An interview that allowed children to display their knowledge about reading and writing was administered to all 24 children in one classroom in a middle-class suburban school district near Chicago, IL; this was a new class of the teacher involved in the Sulzby (1981a) study. From the 24 children, 3 children were chosen who were judged on the basis of a reading and writing interview to be high, 3 moderate, and 3 low in the construct we called "emergent literacy." (The specific procedures used to make these judgments are explained in detail in Sulzby, 1983, in press.)

The primary focus of the full study was the children's kindergarten year, during which time weekly classroom observations were also included to document the instructional content. The observations confirmed the teacher's statement that neither writing nor reading was taught formally during kindergarten. In first grade, the children were distributed into three classrooms and all were taught by teachers using a basal-reader approach. Telling stories or events was a typical classroom activity in both grades but dictation was not used. In addition to the data reported in this study, other kinds of data were collected from the 9 case-study children and from the total group (see Sulzby, 1983).

Procedures. Four sets of told and dictated stories were collected, with three trials in kindergarten and one at the beginning of first grade. In all trials the same order and procedures were used but topic was varied. In each trial the child was asked to write a story and was told that the examiner would help. Then the child was asked to tell the story to the examiner who would listen, with the explanation that people sometimes do this when writing to be certain that the story is "just the way you want it to be." Dictation was described as a second way people prepared to write. Following dictation the child was asked to reread the dictation and make any changes he or she wished to (editing task). Finally, the child was asked to produce the handwritten composition, with rereading and editing again elicited. The topic for trial 1 was specified as a "real story about you [the child] and how you learned to ride a Big Wheel" [or bicycle, or other child vehicle]. In trial 2, the child was asked to write a "make-believe story about how Little Prince [or Princess] Charming learned to ride a Big Wheel." For trial 3, children took part in a race with silly wind-up toys and then wrote about that activity. In trial 4, the children were asked to select the topic.

The examiner acted as a listener in the telling condition and as a scribe in the dictating condition, taking dictation on unlined paper. In the telling task, the examiner looked at the child's face and responded with facial interest but no verbal comments. In dictation, the examiner wrote with a pencil at a speed described to be like that of a first-grade teacher taking dictation. The child was seated beside the examiner on the side opposite the examiner's writing hand at an angle so the print could be viewed easily. The examiner was not allowed to interact with the child until after a set number of pauses and encouragements had elapsed. After that point, the examiner could elicit responses conversationally, but the child was judged to have made an adaptation toward the mode of conversation; speech prior to that point was treated as unaided dictation and speech that was part of the conversational exchanges was treated as aided dictation. The examiner-scribe was allowed to use two, and only two, interruption prompts when the child spoke too fast for the examiner to write what was said: "Wait. I can't keep up with you. Here's where I am," with the examiner rereading the last sentence. When such prompts were used, the unaided dictation was judged to have ended, with the child adapting the dictation again from written to oral conventions. The full sessions were tape recorded, transcribed, and checked carefully for accuracy. All written products like the scribe's copy of the dictation and the child's writing were collated with the typed transcripts.

Analysis.   First, comparable units of speech with no clue to composition mode were selected from session audiotapes. All samples were taken prior to interruption prompts. Master tapes were then prepared with pairs of telling and dictating samples for each child. The order of the child on the tape was assigned at random, as was the order of the two modes for each child. Judges naive to the study but acquainted with young children then listened to the master tapes and made three types of judgments, after having been told that the samples were taken from children dictating and telling stories. The judgments were (1) Are the samples the same or different? (2) Which is dictation and which is telling? and (3) What was the basis for the judgment? Judges were urged to mark "guess" when the judgments were difficult but to go ahead and make a choice.

Second, using the tapes and the typed transcripts, two research assistants calculated the speech density in number of words per second. All pauses of over 1 second duration were inserted into copies of the typed transcripts.

Finally, full transcripts of entire sessions were analyzed for the number and type of interactions that the examiner engaged in with the child, including interruption pauses and conversational exchanges. This descriptive analysis was done by the author and double-checked by research assistants.

Results

Auditory judgments and criteria.   The judgment that the two samples were different was taken as one piece of evidence that children distinguished between dictating and telling. Overall, 85% of the samples were judged to be different. Percentage of trials in which children made distinctions varied by ability level (high = 92%, moderate = 72%, low = 70%). The difference increased over trials to the extent that 100% of the children were judged to distinguish in trial 4, in December of first grade.

The same/different judgments probably overestimate the degree of distinctiveness between samples, however. The judges were forced to decide which sample was telling and which was dictating and when uncertain to decide anyway, marking the response "guessed." Judges correctly identified the mode most easily for the high group, again 92% of the time, and the moderate and low groups less easily, 63% each. Guesses were spread fairly evenly across groups (5-7-5) and between correct and incorrect judgments.

Another ability-level difference had appeared at the outset of this analysis, however. One moderate child and 1 low child were removed from trial 2 and 1 low child from trial 3, due to clues on the tape that prevented a long-enough comparable passage being used for the judgments, reducing

Table 1.   Mean Number of Words Per Second in Telling and Dictating Modes

Emergent Reading Ability	Storytelling				Dictation			
	Trial 1	Trial 2	Trial 3	Trial 4	Trial 1	Trial 2	Trial 3	Trial 4
High[a]	2.18	2.17	2.11	1.74	1.40	.48	.37	.47
Moderate	1.15	1.38	.78	3.04	1.37	1.44	.69	.95
Low	2.15	3.43	1.71	1.90	1.90	2.22	1.80	.54

[a]$N = 3$ in each group

the sample to 7 children in trial 2 and 8 in trial 3. (This sample reduction applied only to the auditory judgments.)

Criteria used by the judges fell into three major categories: (1) rate, (2) intonation, and (3) content or wording. Rate was described in terms of pauses, "as if for the scribe to write" and speaking slowly. Mention of intonation referred primarily to within-sentence intonation but there was one mention of a difference in clause or sentence-final intonation. In dictating one child used a rising elongated intonation at the end of clauses and used a falling, sentence-final intonation at the same places in telling. The content or wording category included comments that dictating was "more of a story," "worded more clearly," and was more organized "in expression."

Rate was mentioned with the greatest frequency (44 out of 64 times) with only 14 uses of intonation and 6 of context or wording. When responses included multiple responses, rate and intonation were mentioned together but no content or wording mentions were part of multiple responses. I suspect that the content/wording criterion was underrepresented because the samples were incomplete parts of the total stories. Finally, it must be remembered that these were subjective judgments by naive judges so we moved to an analysis of speech density to further explore children's distinctions between telling and dictating.

Speech density.   Words spoken per second were calculated for both the comparable sections used in the auditory judgments and for the child's total speech production. Table 1 shows the mean words per second for the comparable sections used in the auditory judgments and also includes times for the children not included on those tapes due to clues to mode (like conversational exchanges initiated by the child or questions about the scribe's writing).

The children's speech density in words per second for the comparable sections were analyzed in a 3 (ability) $\times$ 2 (mode) $\times$ 4 (trial) mixed analysis of variance for repeated measures. Children's distinctions between telling and dictating were confirmed by a significant main effect for mode, $F(1,6)$

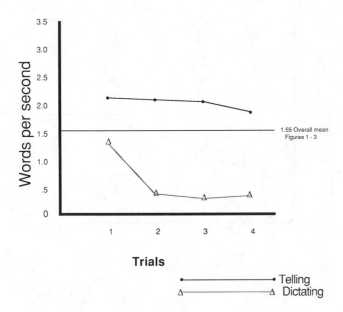

FIG. 1.   Rate of Speaking, High Group

$= 6.27$, $p < .05$. There were also significant interactions of mode by trial and mode by trial by group. The mode by trial interaction, $F (3, 18) = 4.52$, $p < .025$, indicated that difference between dictation and telling speeds was greatest at the fourth trial.

The mode by trial by group interaction, $F (6, 18) = 6.68$, $p < .001$ reveals a complex developmental pattern. I have chosen to graph this interaction in three steps, first beginning with the pattern of the high group (Figure 1).

In Figure 1 it can be seen that the high group distinguished between telling and dictating over all four trials, with all telling speeds above 1.5 words per second and all dictating speeds below that speed, beginning at 1.4 words per second and dropping to < 0.5 words per second for the last three trials. The high group's only change over time was to increase the speed differential.

The moderate children (Figure 2) did not differentiate between telling and dictating speed until trial 4 but they show an interesting contrast to the low children (Figure 3). The moderate children were slow in both dictating and telling until trial 4, whereas the low children were fast at both telling and dictating until trial 4.

The moderate children look like good dictators and the low children

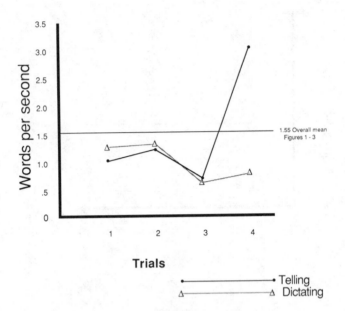

FIG. 2.   Rate of Speaking, Moderate Group

look like good tellers no matter what the task until trial 4. It is possible that the exaggerated slowness of the moderate children shows their growing awareness of the features of writing paired with a lack of knowledge of the specific situations in which speed of talking is an important factor. The low children appear not to have such awareness in kindergarten, treating both tasks similar to normal talking situations.

The movement of these two groups between trial 3 (end of kindergarten) and trial 4 (beginning of first grade) forms a dramatic disordinal interaction with the moderates speeding up in telling and the lows slowing down in dictation. By trial 4, the three groups look approximately alike, all using a fast speed for telling and slow speed for dictating.

The above comparisons applied only to partial stories, omitting all instances in which the adult spoke. The total productions were also analyzed. Using child talk time alone as the measure, we found that it takes children two to three times as long to dictate as to tell a comparable stretch of discourse. Children engaged the examiner conversationally or were interrupted more often in dictation. That is, children directed conversational exchanges at the examiner even though it was not appropriate. Interruption prompts were not appropriate in telling, unless the child spoke inaudibly. On the other hand, they were appropriate in the dictation when the child

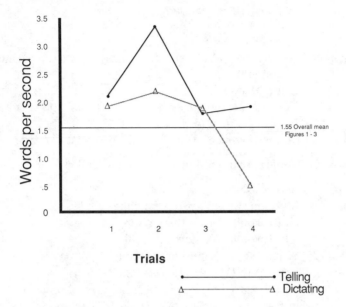

FIG. 3.   Rate of Speaking, Low Group

spoke too rapidly. Such interruptions were more frequent for the lower children (as could be inferred from the speed analyses). Conversational exchanges with children of higher ability tended to be clearly signalled asides (see Sulzby & Otto, 1982). Exchanges with lower children often caused some confusion about whether or not the child intended the speech as an aside or as part of the discourse.

Pausal appropriateness.   Children's pauses tended to become more regular over trials. Here are examples of comparable stretches from two children: Douglas from the moderate group and Richard from the low group. These examples are taken from trial 4, in December of first grade. In these following examples only pauses of 1 second or longer duration are shown. By trial 4 the children were making such vivid distinctions between telling and dictating that judges often laughed at the task of making judgments.

Richard is telling the story of the Elves and Shoemaker and Douglas is telling how he learned to ride a bicycle, because in this trial children were asked to select their own topics.

Example 1—Richard (content almost same)—Trial 4

> *Told:*   (No pauses over 1 second)
> And then one man came in
> and he bought 'em

and then the shoe—um,
and he said, um,
and how much money does it cost?

Dictated: And (3 seconds) then (4 seconds) a (2 seconds) man (3) came (3)
and (3) said (3)
I (4) will (2) buy (3) those (3) pair (3) of (2) shoes
(4) and (4) then (4) he (2) asked (3)
ho-ow (5) much (4) money (4) does (4) it (3) cost?

Example 2—Douglas (content highly similar)—Trial 4

Told: (No pause over 1 second)
My mom would get out my bike
and I would get up there on my bike
and I would ride down the hill.

Dictated: When (3) my (2) mother (4) taught (4) me (2)
how (2) to (2) ride (2) a (2) bike (2)
we (2) started (3) on (3) a (2) hill (3)
in (2) in (2) my (2) front (3) yard.

Children varied in the skill with which they paused for the scribe but they tended to move toward an exaggerated word-unit pausing, and then to more finely attune their speech to the scribe's rate of writing, seemingly judged by phrases, clauses, or some notion of "idea spurts" (see Chafe, 1980, 1982). The transcripts were examined to select the child judged to differ most vividly over time. Here are examples from Nicole, a child from the high group, showing that vivid sorting out of the distinction between telling and dictating modes over time, from the January of her kindergarten year to December of first grade.

Example 3.1—Nicole—January, Trial 1 (topic: real story about learning to ride a Big Wheel)

Told: I don't know (2 seconds)
what I did (9 seconds)
at first when my daddy when we didn't have the training wheels
on my bike. At night time after dinner we (1 second) we went outside and daddy was teaching me how to ride my bicycle . . .

Dictated: Um (4 seconds)
when I felt like I wanted to um (9 seconds)
like I wanted to (9 seconds)

I wanted to ride I mean I wanted to ride a bicycle by myself
without training wheels (4 seconds)
but I couldn't do it.

**Example 3.2—Nicole—February, Trial 2 (topic: make-believe story about
Little Prince/Princess Charming learning to ride a Big Wheel)**

Told: She learnt (3 seconds)
from her big sister (1 second)
when she rided her bike she copied her and then (2 seconds)
when she didn't know how to ride she tried but she couldn't
do it (2 seconds)
But her sister gave her a big push and she did it and she
was proud of herself (2 seconds)
At first she was really scared.

Dictated: When her sister (9 seconds)
was riding her bike (23 seconds)
she tried to do it (10 seconds)
but she couldn't. (9 seconds)
She was very scared (11 seconds)
when her um sister pushed it (10 seconds)
but when she pushed it (11 seconds)
she wasn't afraid anymore.

Example 3.3—Nicole—April, Trial 3 (topic: a race with wind-up toys)

Told: Once it was no once it was a very nice day out (1 second)
and this little boy and his friend were outside planning a
race (1 second)
and the race they put some tape down (1 second)
to make the lines and then they raced and who won was
the little boy he had a tie (2 seconds)
and then (3 seconds)
they made theirselves ribbons and decorated them with cra-
yons (3 seconds)
That's all.

Dictated: There (4 seconds)
was (3 seconds)
a lit + tle boy (5 seconds)
and (3 seconds)
his (3 seconds)
friend (5 seconds)
and (4 seconds)
the(y) were (5 seconds)
planning (5 seconds)

a race. (4 seconds)
So (3 seconds)
he (4 seconds)
put (3 seconds)
down (3 seconds)
some (4 seconds)
tape (4 seconds)
and he (3 seconds)
had (3 seconds)
a (2 seconds)
race. (6 seconds)
And they had a tie. (12 seconds)
And they made two ribbons otherwise it wouldn't be fair.
   (25 seconds)
The end.

Example 3.4—Nicole—December, Trial 4 (topic: child's choice)

Told: I like doing math (3 seconds)
             and I like to (9 seconds)
             talk to the teacher (9 seconds)
             And that's all.
Dictated: I like to talk to the teacher (22 seconds)
             and I like to do math (17 seconds)
             The end.

The average pause duration for each of these examples is shown in Table 2. In example 3.1 Nicole's pauses may be planning pauses in both telling and dictating conditions. At this time her average time per pause is closest across conditions, 4.0 versus 6.5 seconds per pause. By trial 2 (example 3.2) her pauses show the largest contrast, 2.0 versus 11.8 seconds, and her pauses are primarily between individual clauses in dictation. In telling, in contrast, she tended to emit multiple clauses between pauses. In example 3.3, April of kindergarten year and Nicole's third dictation experience, she showed the same kind of dictating behavior seen in Richard (example 1) and Douglas (example 2), word-by-word dictation with only small variation in pause duration. She appeared to be watching the scribe's writing closely and timing her pauses to the scribe's writing time. In example 3.4, however, Nicole went back to pausing between clause units. Now, though, her pauses appeared to be tied to a fairly realistic estimate of the adult's writing time. Unfortunately, this sample is brief. We have, however, seen a similar pattern with other children. They distinguish little between telling and dictating in pause time with pause seeming to be used more for their own convenience than for the scribe's. Then they begin to make exagger-

Table 2. Nicole's average pause
length in seconds per pause

Trial	Telling	Dictating
1	4.0	6.5
2	2.0	11.8
3	1.8	5.1
4	7.0	19.5

ated word-by-word pauses, then to pause between larger meaning units for an appropriate length of time for the scribe.

DISCUSSION

From the results reported above, it appears that kindergarten children who are not yet reading conventionally or writing conventionally are beginning to make distinctions between the modes of storytelling and dictating and that these distinctions can be detected in prosodic features. Furthermore, these distinctions can be related to ability differences between children and traced developmentally over time.

All of the children were distinguishing between the modes by the beginning of first grade. Even though they distinguished to the degree that naive judges listening to their taped speech could detect the differences and even though the measure of words per second confirmed the auditory judgments, the children were not yet all performing the same nor were they performing like adult composers, at least from the comparative data available. Gould's (1980) adults, working in a different genre and setting, dictated at a rate of 23 wpm. Children in the high group approached that rate, dictating at 28.4 wpm. Their speaking was far more discrepant from Gould's adults, but Gould's adults were passing information to other adults. Children told stories at a rate of from 95.4 wpm (moderate group) to 123 wpm (low group), with the high group's last trial being the slowest telling in the first grade at 104.4 wpm.

Certainly, variables like rate in words per second or minute are uninteresting unless they help us understand more important phenomenon. Naive judges could make judgments more easily as children grew older and could make judgments more readily for the high-performing children. The rate analyses suggest that the moderate group had more awareness of written language than did the low group and that both groups were progressing toward a level of understanding that they signalled in first grade, a level that high-performing children had attained at the beginning of kindergarten. Moderate children seemed to use both tasks, telling and dictating, as tasks in which speech should be more deliberate or slower. Low children, on the other hand, spoke rapidly for both tasks all the way through kindergarten, acting as if they had little awareness of the task dimensions.

From this study, we do not know what happened between April of kindergarten and December of first grade that led to the moderates and lows beginning to treat telling and dictating as different tasks. We do know that there was no formal instruction in reading and writing and that the tasks themselves did not seem to have an effect, unless it was a cumulative one after three trials. Furthermore, the children reacted to the tasks differentially, according to our judgments about their emergent literacy levels. However, in addition to telling and dictating, the children were writing as part of our study. In another analysis of the data (Sulzby, 1981b; see also 1986a), I suggested that the moderate and low children were showing characteristics in the writing tasks of our study that have previously been reported for precocious young readers and writers. These children, rather than the high children, were asking questions about reading and writing and were eliciting aid and information from the adults. It is possible that we are seeing an effect of this exploration, of other forms of literacy like the teacher's storybook reading sessions, or even of first-grade reading instruction.

The pause data may shed some light on what is happening (if not why) during this period of development. In the examples from Nicole, which were reflected in the performances of other children, we tracked a child's ability to interrupt a line of thought that had been translated into a composition. I suggested that Nicole's early pauses were simply the kinds of pauses speakers use in order to generate their next meaning units. Nicole paused, then emitted a number of related clauses. Later, she began to make pauses between individual words while watching the scribe. I think this is an important point in development.

Children who are at a very low level of awareness of the task demands of dictation dictate rapidly. More importantly, they dictate so rapidly that an adult cannot keep up and must interrupt. When these children are interrupted, they often begin again at the point where they left off, not giving the scribe the material he or she missed. Another response is to begin again, but inaccurately, repeating the words differently. A third response is to begin again with very different ideas. These behaviors I take to indicate that the child is not treating the orally delivered text as a stable, memorable, retrieval entity but rather with the evanescent nature that we attribute to oral language and to what Ong (1982) calls primary oral cultures, cultures in which memory is used differently because of the difference in oral, as compared with written, language. This is not to imply that the children do not have memory—rather, they are using it differently and treating different things as memorable.

On the other hand, speakers typically do not pause between words with the frequency that the advanced word-by-word dictators pause. Such pauses, in the length of 3 to 5 or more seconds, typically would lead to memory loss. Yet we see children seeming to hold on to their ideas and utter the composed unit. I think this ability to segment the utterance while holding on to the whole idea is an important point in development.

It should be noted that children's dictation at this point is somewhat frustrating to the adult who is expecting meaningful speech and gets speech that goes word by word rather than by larger, meaningful units. Hence, there is the likelihood of semantic ambiguity and the loss of the prosodic information of connected speech. This is a period that almost seems regressive but is quickly left behind as the child moves on to have a better estimate of what adults can write and how fast they can write. Thus Nicole's fourth trial is more exemplary of high-level performance than is her third trial with its word-by-word dictation. It should be noted that the moderate and low children who were used as the first two examples gave just this kind of behavior at the beginning of first grade. At that point Nicole was reading and writing conventionally but the two boys were not yet reading conventionally from print, even though they had been placed in formal reading instructional groups. The low child was described by his teacher at that point as performing poorly and having "almost no memory"; yet he could hold onto utterances while pausing between each word. The moderate boy was reading in a laborious letter-by-letter fashion that I call "aspectual with a letter-sound emphasis" (see Sulzby, 1983). This "reading" resulted in his emitting nonsense syllables for most words. At that time, he was writing using quite full invented spelling. He seemed to be working on understanding segmentation and its relationship to the text.

I have been using comparisons between telling and dictation as research techniques. Teachers of young children could also take a research stance and use similar techniques for similar purposes. More likely, however, teachers would use these techniques for the closely related diagnostic value that they potentially hold. I am not suggesting that children should be encouraged to pause in dictation; indeed, I think that might be detrimental. It appears that they learn to pause from their growing awareness of the needs of the scribe. I do suggest, however, that teachers (and researchers) carefully analyze the situations in which they ask children to produce language. If the situation is dictation and teachers or researchers interrupt with questions, that situation has been changed drastically from a situation in which the child is expected to produce all of the speech as a monologue. If the situation is storytelling and the audience is focusing on correcting the child's expression rather than listening for the content, then the situation is again changed drastically.

When dictation is used in teaching situations, the teacher often wishes to introduce new understandings to the child. What I draw from the research I report here is that teachers need to be aware that they are not introducing new ideas into a vacuum. Children already have concepts about oral and written language and will integrate (or reject) new information developmentally. We have far to go to understand the rationales teachers would give for some of the teaching techniques they use and to understand the effects of those techniques upon children with differing amounts of knowledge about literacy.

In the research I report here, we analyzed the performances of 9 children from many different perspectives, using many related techniques. Certainly, prosodic distinctions between the modes of storytelling and dictation are only a part of the many ways researchers are beginning to examine children's developing literacy. At this point, looking at prosodic distinctions makes us aware that children have more knowledge and reveal it in more ways than teachers and researchers have been aware of heretofore and this growing body of research makes us more aware of many more questions that we can ask about early literacy development.

REFERENCES

Applebee, A.N. (1978). *The child's concept of story: Ages two to seventeen.* Chicago: University of Chicago Press.

Bloomfield, L. (1933). *Language.* New York: Holt, Rinehart and Winston.

Botvin, G.J., & Sutton-Smith, B. (1977). The development of structural complexity in children's fantasy narratives. *Developmental Psychology, 13,* 377–388.

Chafe, W.L. (1980). The deployment of consciousness in the production of a narrative. In W.L. Chafe (Ed.), *The pear stories: Cognitive, cultural, and linguistic aspects of narrative production.* Norwood, NJ: Ablex.

Chafe, W.L. (1982). Integration and involvement in speaking, writing, and oral literature. In D. Tannen (Ed.), *Spoken and written language: Exploring orality and literacy.* Norwood, NJ: Ablex.

Chomsky, N. (1957). *Syntactic structures.* The Hague: Mouton.

Chomsky, N. (1965). *Aspects of the theory of syntax.* Cambridge: M.I.T. Press.

Chomsky, N., & Halle, M. (1968). *The sound pattern of English.* New York: Harper & Row.

Cook-Gumperz, J., & Gumperz, J.J. (1981). From oral to written culture: The transition to literacy. In M. Farr Whiteman (Ed.), *Variation in writing: Functional and linguistic-cultural differences.* Hillsdale, NJ: Erlbaum.

Cox, B., & Sulzby, E. (1984). Children's use of reference in told, dictated, and handwritten stories. *Research in the Teaching of English, 18,* 345–365.

Flower, L. (1979). Writer-based prose: A cognitive basis for problems in writing. *College English, 41,* 19–37.

Gould, J.D. (1980). Experiments on composing letters: Some facts, some myths, and some observations. In L.W. Gregg & E.R. Steinberg (Eds.), *Cognitive processes in writing.* Hillsdale, NJ: Erlbaum.

Green, J.L., & Wallat, C. (1981). Mapping instructional conversations—A sociolinguistic ethnography. In J. Green & C. Wallat (Eds.), *Ethnography and language in educational settings.* Norwood, NJ: Ablex.

Gumperz, J.J. (1982). *Discourse strategies: Studies in interactional sociolinguistics 1.* Cambridge, England: Cambridge University Press.

Harste, J.E., Burke, C.L., & Woodward, V.A. (1981). *Children, their language and world: Initial encounters with print* (Final report to the National Institute of Education [NIE-G-79-0132]. Bloomington: Indiana University.

Harste, J.E., Burke, C.L., & Woodward, V.A. (1982). Children's language and world: Initial encounters with print. In J. Langer & M. Smith-Burke (Eds.), *Bridging the gap: Reader meets author.* Newark, Delaware: International Reading Association.

Jesperson, O. (1964). *Language: Its nature, development, and origin.* New York: W.W. Norton. (Original work published 1921)

Jespersen, O. (1965). *The Philosophy of grammar.* New York: W.W. Norton. (Original work published 1924)

Jespersen, O. (1968). *Growth and the structure of the English language.* New York: The Free Press. (Original work published 1938)

King, M.L., & Rentel, V.M. (1981). *How children learn to write: A longitudinal study.* Final report to the National Institute of Education (NIE-G-79-0137 and G-79-0039). Columbus: Ohio State University.

King, M.L., & Rentel, V.M. (1982). *Transition to writing.* Final report to the National Institute of Education (NIE-G-079-0137 and G-79-0039). Columbus: Ohio State University.

Kintsch, W., & Greene E. (1978). The role of culture specific schemata in the comprehension and recall of stories. *Discourse Processes, 1,* 1–13.

Mandler, J.M., & Johnson N.S. (1977). Remembrance of things passed: Story structure and recall. *Cognitive Psychology, 9,* 111–151.

Markowitz, J., & Moses, R. (1981). What is rugtime? In *Papers from the Parasession on Language and Behavior.* Chicago: Chicago Linguistic Society.

Martlew, M. (Ed.), (1983). *The psychology of written language: Developmental and educational perspectives.* Chichester, England: Wiley.

Mehan, H. (1979). *Learning lessons.* Cambridge, MA: Harvard University Press.

Olson D. (1977). From utterance to text: The bias of language in speech and writing. *Harvard Educational Review, 47,* 257–281.

Ong, W.J. (1982). *Orality and literacy: The technologizing of the word.* London: Metheun.

Peterson, C.L., & McCabe, A. (1983). *Three ways of looking at a child's narratives: A psycholinguistic analysis.* New York: Plenum.

Propp, V. (1968). *The morphology of the folktale* (2nd ed.). Austin: University of Texas Press.

Pyles, T. (1971). *The origins and development of the English language.* New York: Harcourt Brace Jovanovich.

Rentel, V.M., & King, M.L. (1983). *A longitudinal study of coherence in children's written narratives.* Final report to the National Institute of Education (NIE-G-81-0063). Columbus: Ohio State University.

Rubin, A. (1980). A theoretical taxonomy of the differences between oral and written language. In R.J. Spiro, B.C. Bruce, & W.F. Brewer (Eds.), *Theoretical issues in reading comprehension.* Hillsdale, NJ: Erlbaum.

Rumelhart, D.E. (1977). Understanding and summarizing brief stories. In D. La Berge & J. Samuels (Eds.), *Basic processes in reading: Perception and comprehension.* Hillsdale, NJ: Erlbaum.

Scardamalia, M., Bereiter, C., & Goelman, H. (1982). The role of production factors in writing ability. In M. Nystrand (Ed.), *What writers know: The language, process, and structure of written discourse.* New York: Academic Press.

Scollon, R. & Scollon, S.B.K. (1981). *Narrative, literacy, and face in interethnic communication*. Norwood, NJ: Ablex.

Scribner, S., & Cole,M. (1981). *The psychology of literacy*. Cambridge, MA: Harvard University Press.

Stauffer, R. (1970). *The language-experience approach to the teaching of reading*. New York: Harper & Row.

Stein, N.L., & Glenn, C.G. (1979). An analysis of story comprehension in elementary school children. In R.O. Freedle (Ed.), *New directions in discourse comprehension* (Vol. 2). Norwood, NJ: Ablex.

Strang, B.M.H. (1970). *A history of English*. London: Metheun.

Sulzby, E. (1981a). *Kindergarteners begin to read their own compositions: Beginning reader's developing knowledges about written language project*. Final report to the Research Foundation of the National Council of Teachers of English. Evanston, IL: Northwestern University.

Sulzby, E. (1981b, December). *Kindergarteners deal with word boundaries*. Paper presented at the annual meeting of the National Reading Council, Dallas, TX.

Sulzby, E. (1982). Oral and written mode adaptations in stories by kindergarten children. *Journal of Reading Behavior, 14,* 51–59.

Sulzby, E. (1983). *Beginning readers' developing knowledges about written language*. Final report to the National Institute of Education (NIE-G-80-0176). Evanston, IL: Northwestern University.

Sulzby, E. (1985). Kindergarteners as writers and readers. In M. Farr (Ed.), *Advances in writing research, Vol. 1: Children's early writing development*. Norwood, NJ: Ablex.

Sulzby, E. (1986a). Children's elicitation and use of metalinguistic knowledge about "word" during literacy interactions. In D.B. Yaden & W.S. Templeton (Eds.), *Metalinguistic awareness and beginning literacy: Conceptualizing what it means to read and write*. Portsmouth, NH: Heinemann Educational.

Sulzby, E. (1986b). Writing and reading: Signs of oral and written language organization in the young child. In W.H. Teale & E. Sulzby (Eds.), *Emergent literacy: Writing and reading*. Norwood, NJ: Ablex.

Sulzby, E. (in press). *Emergent writing and reading in 5–6 year olds: A longitudinal study*. Norwood, NJ: Ablex.

Sulzby, E., & Otto, B. (1982). "Text" as an object of metalinguistic knowledge: A study in literacy development. *First language, 3,* 181–199.

Tannen, E. (1982). *Spoken and written language: Exploring orality and literacy*. Norwood, NJ: Ablex.

Teale, W.H., & Sulzby, E. (1986). Emergent literacy as a perspective for looking at how children become writers and readers. In W.H. Teale & E. Sulzby (Eds.), *Emergent literacy: Writing and reading*. Norwood, NJ: Ablex.

CHAPTER 7

The Influence of Syntactic Anomalies on the Writing Processes of a Deaf College Student

Leonard P. Kelly

Gallaudet College
Washington, DC

INTRODUCTION

Deafness does not enhance literacy. Yet is is not uncommon for those who are inexperienced with the deaf to expect the diminished capacity to hear and speak language to be balanced by refined skills in reading and writing. After all, the deaf get extensive practice spelling words with their fingers, and their opportunity to write notes to non-signers ought to promote formal writing skills. Although such an expectation may be consistent with some benign order of compensation, it represents a naive view of the way in which deafness actually affects literacy in English. Far from enjoying enhanced writing skill, those who suffer a profound hearing loss frequently endure obvious limitations in the way they write the language that they cannot hear.

Immediately apparent to a native, literate speaker of English is the presence of syntactic errors. When many of the profoundly deaf, who lose their hearing early in life, are required to write, they deviate in obvious ways from the conventions of standard English. Persistent errors include the misuse of pronouns, determiners, inflections, copulas, and prepositions. It is not uncommon to find such errors in the prose of even those deaf people who have succeeded in earning advanced academic degrees.

The literature cites a number of causes: inability to hear an acoustically based language; the inappropriateness of prevalent instructional practices; inexperience in writing; and interferences from the first language of the

I would like to express my thanks to a number of people who have contributed substantially to this study: Veda Charrow, John Convey, Kathleen Crandall, Carolyn Ewoldt, The Gallaudet College Instructional Development and Evaluation Center, The Gallaudet College Research Institute, Jaclyn and Patricia Kelly, Stephen Kerst, Ann Matsuhashi, Thomas Nolan, David Snyder, Jana Staton, Tonona Taylor, and Peter Yurkowski.

deaf, manual (signed) communication. And with regard to the effects: It is almost certain that these errors mislead, confuse, or irritate the reader. Skepticism of the writer's intellectual capacity is sometimes aroused. Beyond these effects on the reader, there is also reason to suspect that the tendency to make frequent errors may adversely affect certain deaf writers during the writing process.

Research into the writing processes of college-age writers with normal hearing suggests that the difficulty of making linguistic choices imposes on the writer a persistent concern for sentence-level correctness. The work of Shaughnessy (1977), Perl (1978), and Pianko (1979) reveals a preoccupation with errors that virtually monopolizes the unskilled writer's attention for long periods, disrupting the flow of composition and limiting the amount of short-term memory available to address more sophisticated writing constraints such as rhythm, organization, and sense of audience.

Research on the language of the deaf (Charrow, 1974; Stokoe, 1971) suggests, however, that the deaf might not be as sensitive as hearing writers to certain forms of anomalous syntax. Certain anomalies that appear consistently in compositions of the deaf may actually be the performance of a nonstandard dialect. And, ironically, the influences that perpetuate such anomalies in the prose of even highly educated deaf adults may also reduce the vulnerability of their short-term memories to concern for these mistakes. It follows that their minds are hypothetically free, if sometimes not adequately skilled, to address higher level writing tasks.

The chapter that follows describes the case of a single deaf student, one of the subjects in a dissertation study currently in progress at the Catholic University of America and Gallaudet College. The study is being conducted to determine the manner in which syntactic anomalies affect the deaf writer during composition. The background and methodology of the study are described below. This study uses pause time—suspensions in the graphomotor act of inscribing text—as the primary indicant of attention and short-term memory. Writers are being observed while composing and later revising narratives to determine whether their pause times seem to fluctuate in a manner related to the appearance or presence of syntactic anomalies in the writer's text. The writing performance of this one subject, Molly, provides the basis for beginning a discussion of both the writing processes of deaf students and consequent implications for instructional practice. As a special case of the category of students called Beginning Writers by Shaughnessy (1977), Molly's performance may also help us to better understand the writing processes of native English speakers and English as a Second Language (ESL) students who can hear normally but who have not mastered the conventions of standard written English.

They had a nice meeting, but one things that disappointed them was

that there was no Gallaudet's approved. So they went back to Gallaudet

College and had discussed with a president, Dr. Hall. Dr. Hall was

turned down with his reasons. So Dr. Hall's son, Jon, came to Eric to

asked him for letting him helping. Eric sent many information to the

faculty and staffs. they liked his idea and supported his idea. He

made it and was thanked to Jon for helping Eric out.

FIG. 1.   An Example of writing by a deaf college freshman

THE ANOMALOUS ENGLISH OF THE DEAF

The sample of student writing displayed in Figure 1 is an excerpt from a deaf college freshman's written retelling of a story that had been signed manually on videotape. The typed copy is the student's original work. The handwritten notations are a scorer's corrections needed before the excerpt would accurately represent in standard form the information presented on the videotape.

This sample exhibits some of the more prevalent kinds of anomalies that surface in the writing of people who suffer a profound hearing loss before the age when they begin to use spoken language. Present in the excerpt are errors in use of verb and noun inflections, articles, auxiliary verbs, infinitives, and pronouns.

Charrow (1981) provided another instance of such anomalous English, a portion of a message sent by teletype, which is a device used by the deaf to send typed messages via telephone.

> I am very happy about what the kids have done but wow, it put hard on poor English teachers . . . we had two hours meeting, discussing our problems about (high school) . . . Really it is a big exciting among the kids and the teachers . . . I know that the mess will be solved soon or later. (p. 18)

This example is dramatic because its author is a college-educated deaf person, approximately 27 years old, who used English frequently in the course of his daily work. Although this conversation was an informal one, in which the writer had little time to find and edit errors, the anomalies are not unique. Even in more formal writing contexts, highly educated deaf writers both commit, and are unable to detect, anomalies in their prose.

Perhaps because the writing problems of the profoundly pre-lingually deaf are so obvious, they have attracted considerable comment in the literature (Bochner, 1978; Bunch, 1979; Charrow, 1974, 1981; Crandall, 1978; Goldberg & Astley, 1983; Goldberg & Bordman, 1974; Goldberg, Ford, & Silverman, 1982; Kates, 1972; Kretschmer & Kretschmer, 1978; Myklebust, 1964; Quigley, Power & Steinkamp, 1977; Taylor, 1969; Wilbur, 1977). Much of the work has focused on describing and classifying the surface features of the language. As early as 1940, Heider and Heider observed that the average length of sentences written by 17-year-old deaf students was a 10.2 words, reflecting the syntactic maturity of an 8-year-old child with normal hearing. Studies by Charrow (1973, 1974) found that the deaf made consistent errors in use of relative pronouns, determiners, prepositions, compound tenses, inflected tenses, tense agreement, modals, copula markers, and plural markers. Taylor (1969) and Kates (1972) found similar errors in studies of deaf writing.

Quigley is perhaps the largest contributor to the literature that describes the English language processes of the deaf. He and his colleagues conducted a series of studies of deaf students, ages 10 through 18. Quigley et al. (1977) summarize the results of those studies and show examples of the different kinds of errors consistently found in the writing of deaf students.

Kathleen Crandall (1980) provides a system for classifying the anomalous English of the deaf. As a way to promote homogeneous grouping and systematic instruction, she developed a procedure for classifying the diverse array of errors that appear in the writing of deaf college students. The errors are classified into one of nine categories, depending on the judged impact of the errors on the intelligibility of the student's written passage. The categories of errors are as follows:

- *Type 9, Mechanical* includes spelling and punctuation errors.
- *Type 8, Inflectional Morpheme* includes noun and verb inflection errors.
- *Type 7, Bound Derivational* includes errors related to prefixes, suffixes, and infixes.
- *Type 6, Free Functor* includes pronoun, preposition, and auxiliary verb errors.
- *Type 5, Semantic Contentive Stem* includes use of incorrect content words.
- *Type 4, Structural* includes word-order errors and omission of major constituents.
- *Type 3, Multiple Structural* errors indicate more than one structural error in a T-unit (minimally terminally unit [Hunt, 1965]).

- *Type 2, Unconnected English* indicates more than two structural errors in a T-unit.
- *Type 1, Unrecognizable English, Word Listing, or Naming.*

Crandall's taxonomy shows the wide range of errors that appear in the writing of deaf students. Error Types 6 and 8 appear to be the most chronic.

The problems that the deaf encounter with written English are not confined to production of their own compositions. They also have difficulty with standard English when they read it. Quigley et al. (1977) reported deaf students' problems comprehending written texts that make frequent use of the passive voice, relative clauses, and certain auxiliary verbs. This research also revealed the tendency of the deaf to impose a Subject Verb Object pattern on sentences and to interpret them as such regardless of the actual wording of the sentences. Trybus and Karchmer (1977) reported that only 10% of young deaf adults can read at or above the eighth-grade level.

The anomalies that appear in the writing of the deaf can produce a number of unfavorable consequences. At worst, the anomalies affect the written message in a way that either misleads, frustrates, or confuses the reader. The deviations from standard English pose distractions that severely drain the reader's time and energy. When the reader is not familiar with deafness, such writing can be interpreted as the reflection of an inferior intellect. In addition, a recent survey (Zambrano & Kelly, 1984) of the faculty at Gallaudet College, the only liberal arts college for the deaf in the world, indicated that anomalies in student prose tend to discourage professors' use of writing assignments in their courses. Students' severe limitations circumscribe teachers' willingness to provide opportunities to practice and develop those skills. Hence, the problems are perpetuated.

These errors, as they have been discussed so far, manifest themselves primarily at the sentence level. They do not necessarily indict the quality of development, organization, and coherence of the full passages of discourse that include anomalous English. Research on the writing processes of writers with normal hearing, however, raises the possibility that sentence-level concerns may frustrate the achievement of discourse goals.

Writers engaged in the composition process have been characterized by Hayes and Flower (1980) as "jugglers" of the constraints, knowledge, language, and rhetoric. Each sentence must accurately represent what the writer knows about the topic, it must conform to the conventions of written language, and it must contribute to the rhetorical strategy of the full composition. Before actually inscribing an element of text, the writer must make a set of decisions (one at a time), preserve those decisions in short-term memory, and then inscribe a text segment that conforms to those decisions. All this must be done quickly before any of the decisions are forgotten. When treatment of any single constraint is relatively swift or automatic, its processing requires little attention, freeing short-term memory for more careful decision making relative to other constraints. On the other hand, when the processing of a single writing constraint attracts the writer's attention for a relatively long period of time, that constraint monopolizes short-term memory and circumscribes the attention available for other constraints that require focal attention.

Studies by Shaughnessy (1977), Perl (1978), and Pianko (1979) have demonstrated the result when the language constraint draws substantial attention. In studying college-level writers with normal hearing who made frequent grammatical errors in their writing, the researchers observed that these writers tended to manifest acute concern for errors during the writing process. At least partly as a result, the writers produced fragmented, egocentric, stilted discourse.

These findings have ostensible implications for deaf writers whose prose—even that of highly educated adults—contains nonstandard English. Like unskilled writers with normal hearing, the deaf may be vulnerable to an excessive concern for syntactic errors, which circumscribes the capacity to visualize the intended audience, to organize ideas, and to crystalize meaning. Plagued by anomalous syntax, the short-term memories of the deaf may be prone to worrying about errors, while higher order rhetorical concerns remain neglected. Writing samples of deaf students offer little evidence to the contrary. A discussion of the purported causes of the anomalous English of the deaf also illuminates the issue.

CAUSES OF ANOMALOUS ENGLISH IN COMPOSITIONS OF THE DEAF

The literature attributes the anomalous written English of the deaf to a number of interactive influences. For purposes of this presentation, they will be discussed in four categories: causes directly related to the inability to hear, causes related to the instruction that is routinely offered to the deaf, causes common to unskilled hearing writers, and causes related to sign language.

Causes Related to the Handicap

Crandall (1978) noted that English is, after all, a language that is rooted in sound. She wondered how you teach an acoustic language system to individuals who cannot easily develop an auditory referent. She observed further that deafness severely hampers the development of both syntactic and morphologic coding and that the typical child with a profound hearing impairment is faced with the task of learning to read without having developed an internal language symbol system.

Studies of deaf children with deaf parents demonstrate their superior language competence and imply a limitation to which the vast majority of deaf children are exposed. Because most deaf children have parents with normal hearing, who rarely know sign language, these children spend their preschool years, so critical to language acquisition and cognitive development, in an environment that is linguistically bankrupt (Crandall, 1978; Bochner, 1978). In addition to having been deprived of communication with their parents, such children have a considerably more difficult time learning English than their peers whose parents are deaf (Bonvillian, Nelson, & Charrow, 1976).

Many of the errors in English that the deaf exhibit are in those features described by Charrow (1974) as redundant or nonessential; features such as articles and tense markers do not contribute substantially to meaning. Because these features are less informative, Charrow reasoned, they are difficult to learn, hard to retain, and easy to overlook for a person who cannot hear them. The very fact that the deaf cannot hear spoken English and, in that way, acquire it naturally (instead of learning it through formal instruction) is to their disadvantage according to Schmitt (1969).

It is true that the deaf who reach college have been reading standard English prose for years. There is evidence, however, that, because of their auditory isolation from standard syntax, deaf readers may rely primarily on semantic understanding, as opposed to syntactic understanding, in order to get meaning from print, further reducing their attentiveness to syntactic conventions. This position is supported by Sarachan-Deily (1980) and Ewoldt (1981) who said, "There is anecdotal evidence suggesting that there are occasions when the print-to-meaning leap is unmediated by syntax" (p. 76).

These observations suggest that the deaf read with limited appreciation of the nuances of conventional syntax. It also means that when reading their own writing, the deaf may be more sensitive to errors that distort meaning than to those that violate correct form but preserve the substance of the communication.

Causes Related to the Educational System

Whatever the initial obstacles that the deaf encounter in learning English, with few exceptions, it is to the schools that they turn for help. Yet, according to the literature, the educational system has not been totally successful in responding to their needs.

Kretschmer and Kretschmer (1978) said that deafness is not the whole problem. While acknowledging the sometimes extensive years of formal education, they described the deaf as inexperienced in reading and writing English. Charrow (1974) suggested that some of the writing limitations of the deaf may be due simply to no exposure and consequent misunderstanding of the functions of certain grammatical constructions. She noted that, although teachers of the deaf may emphasize the importance of certain rules, their students do not acquire the intuitions to guide appropriate use of those rules. Many students are aware that the instruction hasn't "taken." Consequently, as Crandall (1978) noted, ". . . One of the reasons that many students make very little progress in English during adolescence is because they no longer have any real motivation in this area" (p. 324).

What are the characteristics of the instructional system that trains the students who write such obviously anomalous English? For one thing, teachers may have limitations in either their own sign communication skills or they may have limited expectations of their students (Meath-Lang et al., 1982). Crandall (1978) elaborates on how teachers' zeal to establish classroom communication may constitute an insidious impediment to language acquisition.

> Young children learn by experiencing the positive and negative effects of their linguistic behaviors. Conversely, the deaf child is usually led to form his or her utterances correctly. The teacher guesses (from context) what the child wishes to say and formulates the expression in standard English. The child is asked to jump over most of the acquisition process and formulate his or her utterance according to the teacher's symbol system for standard English. The child is rarely allowed to experience any self-imposed hypothesis testing behavior. Furthermore, the child may be led to incorrect conclusions about the language system when the teacher's guess about his or her intention is incorrect. (p. 325)

Several sources also assert that instruction routinely places undue emphasis on the formal correctness of individual, unrelated sentences. Wilbur (1977) said, "The problem with pronoun usage, determiner usage and conjoined sentences most likely arises from the heavy emphasis that is placed on the proper structure of the single sentence in language training program for the deaf" (p. 91). She expressed concern that writing has been taught to the deaf in isolation from its discourse function.

Meath-Lang et al. (1982) gathered students' perceptions of the English programs to which they had been exposed. Some of the students' comments: "In the past I learn to write nouns and verbs, subject and write composition and have vocabulary word also have term paper" (p. 6). And another: "I learned grammar and also English" (p. 6). The researchers' conclusions from these responses:

> The word "English" seems to have become an academic shopping bag crammed with forty-five minute learning packages as opposed to a living language (p. 6). . . . Many students allude to "learning about English" instead of learning English . . . They examine language microscopically as if to view its parts (p. 14) . . . English is viewed as separable from words, talking, listening, and signing. (p. 16)

Meath-Lang et al. also said,

> [The student] utterances give an impression of programs oriented toward
> form and correction. . . . However, it appears that prioritizing form and
> correction has not allowed students to perceive English skills in a positive
> developmental sense. (p. 12)

Causes Shared With Unskilled Hearing Writers

As Kretschmer and Kretschmer (1978) said, deafness is not the whole problem. And because the deaf usually get limited writing experience, it is likely
that they commit errors for some of the same reasons that unskilled hearing writers commit them.

Shaughnessy (1977) cited limited vocabulary as one cause of the frequent syntactic errors of unskilled hearing writers. Forced to depend on a
limited fund of words, the student must sometimes attempt convoluted
syntactic structures in order to express the intended meaning. The risk of
error is thus increased. Shaughnessy quoted Moffett (1968), who said, "The
person who has not learned the word 'dregs' . . . must speak of 'what is
left in the cup after you finish drinking' " (Shaughnessy, p. 74). The risk
of making a syntactic error is far greater for students like the deaf whose
lexicon is relatively small.

There are other characteristics that the deaf writer seems to share with
people like Shaughnessy's students, who reached college age without experiencing a reasonable opportunity to communicate through written English. Because of this inexperience, both kinds of writers—the deaf and the
unskilled hearing—have limited fluency in the process of creating the complex structures that writing calls for. Also, as a result of that inexperience,
both kinds of writers do not seem to know, in Shaughnessy's words, "how
writers behave." They are unaware how writing is different from face-to-
face communication. Shaughnessy (1977) reported how one of her students
reacted to a draft page of Richard Wright's *Native Son,* with all its deletions and substitutions still visible. Wright could not have been much of a
writer, according to the student, because of all those "mistakes."

Finally, Shaughnessy felt that unskilled hearing writers make errors
partly because they do not have a firm grasp of the meaning that they wish
to express through their writing. And because they do not really know what
they mean, they are missing a necessary criterion for evaluating whether
their prose is faithful to that meaning. If, as Wilbur (1977) and Meath-
Lang et al. (1982) have argued, the English instruction of the deaf has
emphasized sentence-level correctness, minimizing the opportunity to develop full discourse, it is likely that the deaf too are inexperienced in crys-
talizing meaning through the composition process.

Causes Related to Sign Language

It has become widely held that the problems that the deaf exhibit when writing English are in large part similar to those of any learner of a second language. According to Goldberg and Bordman (1974), "Although most of these students are native and were born into homes where Standard American English is spoken, none of them is in any sense a native user of that language" (p. 263). Goldberg and Bordman compared passages written by students enrolled in ESL classes with the writing samples of deaf students. The similarities among the passages suggested that the deaf students too are ESL students. Charrow and Fletcher (1973) complemented these observations with quantitative analytical evidence that English is the second language of the deaf.

Crandall's (1978) instructional experience with the deaf also supports the notion that English is the second language of the deaf. She said, "When grammatical structures and vocabulary were taught in a developmental sequence designed for second language learning, greater gains were observed than when grammatical structures were controlled but not presented in a developmental order" (p. 330). Bockmiller (1981) observed that reading instruction of the deaf can be enhanced once the ESL concept is accepted by the teacher.

The role of sign language as the first and native language of the deaf has had some unfavorable effects on English learning according to the literature. Goldberg and Bordman (1974) said,

> . . . these manual systems which are such an advantage in the early schooling of these deaf children and which continue to be a very great tool for the imparting of information and for making easy communication among the students themselves turn out to be the very thing which ultimately stymies their education (p. 266).

For one thing, according to Goldberg et al. (1982), sign language, especially forms of sign that resemble American Sign Language (ASL), interfers with the learning of correct English because its forms are so remote from English. These authors asserted that in contrast to foreign students with Indo-European backgrounds, the deaf use a language that is incompatible with English. The messages conveyed through some sign languages (there are more than one) are hardly the equivalent of English sentences, signed manually. American Sign Language (ASL), a version of sign language which may be the first language of some deaf children, illustrates possible differences between English and sign language. According to Charrow (1981),

> ASL lacks many of the features that make English what it is: articles, plural markers, tense markers, certain prepositions, passives, heavy use of subordinate clauses . . . ASL has many syntactic features that English lacks: si-

multaneous signs, tense and number inflections on time words, inflections for habitualness, for repetition of action, the ability to 'spatialize'—to set up a scene in space—and many others. (p. 112)

Meath-Lang et al. (1982) quoted a student's perception of the interfering influence of sign language: "That was impossible for me to built (English) back to normal while in high school because my sign language (I learned it in high school) confused it" (p. 17).

The opinion that sign language interferes with English acquisition is not held unanimously. Children of deaf parents, who are more active as users of sign language, tend to demonstrate English competence that is superior to children of hearing parents (Bonvillian et al., 1976). One of Meath-Lang et al.'s (1982) informants blamed late acquisition of sign skills for more current difficulties in English: "I wanted to learn the sign language when I was a child. Maybe my English would be very good and improved" (p. 17).

Problems of interference aside, the literature cites a second way in which sign language may indirectly influence the written English of the deaf. Charrow (1974) noted that when exposed to certain linguistic environments, second-language users will produce dialects or pidgins that are altered versions of the standard language. She described the written English as well as the linguistic environments of the deaf to show that what she called "Deaf English" seems to meet the six criteria of a pidgin as proposed by DeCamp (1971) and Hall (1966). Charrow noted a stabilization in the English of the deaf. "Except in rare cases, the English that the deaf know at age fifteen or sixteen is the English they continue to use throughout their lives" (p. 42). She tested empirically for the presence of a pidgin and found some evidence to support her theory.

Her assertions of a pattern and stability to these errors are corroborated by other researchers who concluded that the anomalies of the deaf are systematic and predictable. Quigley et al. (1977) observed the presence of ". . . distinct syntactic structures, apparently rule ordered, that appear consistently and persistently in the language comprehension and production of many of the deaf subjects" (p. 79). Bunch (1979) said that the deaf draw on two or more parallel sets of rules to produce written English. Lenneberg (1967), as quoted by Bunch, described the English of the deaf as a meta-language. Finally, Goldberg et al. (1982) lent support to the notion of not only the consistency, but also the permanence of the anomalous English of the deaf when they wrote: "[If] left completely to their own devices . . . we see again and again that the language of these students fossilizes, and with relatively few exceptions becomes permanently fixed except for some increase in vocabulary" (p. 8).

Because of the persistent and pervasive nature of these anomalies, which are quite different from Standard English, it is possible that these are the overt performance associated with a unique version of written English competence. Stokoe (1971) pointed out that the deaf may exhibit those stable linguistic intuitions believing all the while that they are producing Standard English. The deaf may be fluent in these anomalous constructions; because certain errors reflect true language intuitions—competence—the deaf may produce them with a high degree of automaticity. And if the anomalies are produced automatically, it would mean that their production does not encroach on short-term memory during composition.

The notion of fluent production of certain anomalies by the deaf is further supported by Krashen's Monitor Model, a prominent theory in second-language learning. Krashen (1977) argued that second-language learners draw on two kinds of competence when using the second language. One form of competence, which Krashen calls "Learned" competence, is a set of formal rules, the result of explicit instruction, feedback, and error correction. This Learned competence constitutes a psychological "monitor" that guides correction of partially formulated utterances so that they conform more exactly to the conventions of the second language. Krashen emphasizes that the Monitor can be used only when conditions are optimal: most notably when there is adequate processing time available. Otherwise, the speaker will have to rely on the second form of language, Acquired Language.

Acquired Language, according to Krashen (1977), is the intuition that language learners develop without formal, explicit instruction. These are skills that are "picked up" by the student rather than taught directly through a teacher's error correction and feedback. The Acquired Language focuses on, and is produced by, the pursuit of meaning rather than correct form. According to Krashen, the Acquired Language is what is used to produce utterances quickly, when there is not time for the language user to invoke the Monitor of conscious, learned rules. Acquired intuitions produce language automatically without regard for form, in the same way that the language intuitions of the deaf seem to generate deafisms.

The English produced by the deaf seems to have much in common with Acquired Language, the basis of fluent, automatic, if not error-free, performance in a second language. Acquired Language is not taught directly, just as misuse of inflections and omission of necessary definite articles are not included in the English curriculum of the deaf. Also, Acquired Language is meaning centered; and, as Charrow (1974) pointed out, the most common and persistent deafisms represent reductions in the features of English that fail to contribute substantially to meaning. Acquired Language develops where there is a minimum of explicit feedback and correction; Charrow (1974) and Crandall (1978) have explained how the deaf student, even in English class, becomes insulated from correction, either by the handicap of deafness or the communication-skill limitations of the classroom teacher. The similarities between Deaf English and Acquired Language, which is fluent intuition, suggest that deafisms are also produced automatically.

It is not surprising that Acquired Language should surface during writing, even though composing is an apparently ponderous act, ostensibly affording ample opportunity for Monitor use. Recalling that writers must quickly inscribe their texts, before their propositions are lost from short-term memory, it seems that the conditions for Monitor use during composition are not altogether optimal, especially for inexperienced writers. Hence, writers must rely heavily on Acquired Language to form the substance of much of their texts. Again, this implies anomalies written by the deaf are produced automatically.

The combined research presents a dilemma: Studies of unskilled hearing writers suggest that the short-term memories of the deaf will be absorbed by concern for syntactic anomalies. But research on the anomalies of the deaf provides reasons to believe that their nonstandard English may actually be produced fluently. When some deaf writers attempt to compose in English, their concern for grammatical correctness might not be as severe as that endured by unskilled college-age writers who hear normally. Thus it is unknown whether concern for errors occupies the attention of the deaf for relatively long periods of time during the writing process.

There has been discussion of this issue in the literature, but it has been conflicting and somewhat anecdotal. Some say that the deaf do attend to errors. According to Charrow (1974), because of their instructional experiences, the deaf may know that certain grammatical functions belong in English prose, but they lack the competence to identify where the functions belong. Aware of this personal limitation, many deaf are ashamed to write, according to Charrow. The words of one of Meath-Lang et al.'s (1982) informants suggest a more focused concern for mistakes. "When I have write something, I have to stop and think to see if my language are right" (p. 7). Also consistent with these sentiments, Goldberg et al. (1982) do not encourage free written communication in the classroom because ". . . Encouraging [deaf] students to express themselves 'freely' is to plunge them into a morass of uncertainty from which the chances of emerging successfully are very small" (p. 8). These comments are reminiscent of the terms used by Shaughnessy (1977), Perl (1979), and Pianko (1979) to describe the hyperconcern of unskilled hearing writers.

Yet consistent with the theory presented earlier, there is also comment to support the position that certain anomalies in the writing of the deaf do not draw their attention. Ironically, Goldberg et al. (1982) are one source of this. As an alternate justification for not encouraging free writing, they observed that "[The deaf students] feel no limits upon their English expression. Even the most unlikely utterances seem perfectly acceptable" (p. 8). If the utterances seem perfectly acceptable, it follows that they do not draw excessive attention. And "feeling no limits" suggests that the deaf devote little attention to the language constraint, which reputedly dominates the short-term memory of the unskilled hearing writer. If not contradictory, these comments suggest a position that is uncertain. The uncertainty is dramatized by the fact that Goldberg et al. made both statements within the space of three sentences.

Although appearing contradictory at first, their observations may indeed be accurate. As teachers of the deaf, Goldberg et al. (1982) may have observed both trends in their students. Some deaf writers may be highly self-conscious of their writing . . . sometimes. Other deaf writers may be oblivious to their anomalies . . . sometimes. The prior research suggests that the deaf will be more sensitive when their errors are the kind that severely affect intelligibility; alternately, they will be less sensitive when the errors have a somewhat limited effect on meaning. As yet, however, there is little direct evidence to verify this theory.

RESEARCH QUESTIONS

This apparent gap in the literature gave rise to the following research questions. In the description of methods, results, and implications that are discussed below, these questions are limited to a single subject.

1. Does pausing during composition seem to be a measure of within-sentence decision making for this student?
2. Do patterns of pausing and revising suggest concerns related to specific syntactic difficulties? To what extend do these concerns impose severe interruptions in the writing process?
3. What instructional guidance can be derived from this student's pausing and revising performance?

Though prompted by the writing problems of deaf writers, these questions may have broader applicability, because many of the deaf are members of a larger population of writers who are labeled unskilled. Emig (1978) encouraged our attempts to make generalizations to broader populations when she wrote:

> The major recommendation here is that we study, through the available literature and through direct observation, persons with specific and generalized disabilities, such as the blind, the deaf, and the brain-damaged . . . attempting to infer the whole from the fragmented, the normal from the aberrant, the functional from the dysfunctional, is a classic research approach. (p. 60)

METHODOLOGY

Summary of Methodology

The subject produced a written account of a short story, viewed as it was signed, on videotape. In a later session, she revised and recopied the draft version of her story account. While she was writing under both conditions, the subject's pauses were monitored and recorded. After the session, her pausing episodes were timed and written on the text locations where they actually occurred. Subsequently, the texts were segmented into T-units (Hunt, 1965), and T-units were appraised for the presence of different kinds of syntactic anomalies and for any alterations in the anomalies originally produced. These procedures represent a subset of the procedures used in the full dissertation study mentioned earlier. The sample of the full study also includes 10 additional deaf subjects as well as a sample of unskilled college writers with normal hearing.

Subject

Molly is a 20-year-old profoundly deaf freshman who was born deaf. She has no additional handicaps beyond hearing loss. She had attended secondary school at a residential school that used sign language for classroom communication. Immediately after high school, Molly's performance on the Gallaudet entrance exam required her enrollment in the Gallaudet School of Preparatory Studies for one year before her entrance as a freshman. As a first-semester freshman, she had failed the initial English composition course which she was taking (successfully) at the time that the data for this study were gathered. Molly's written compositions contained an assortment of anomalies classified as types 4, 5, 6, 7, 8, and 9 according to Crandall's (1980) system. She was paid $5.00 for each writing sample produced and received a letter of recommendation documenting her performance.

Experimental Procedures

Task Level: Reporting. Molly completed writing assignments that were on the Reporting level according to Britton's (1975) paradigm for classifying writing tasks. In essence, she was asked to recount in writing a description of the people, places, and events of a story that was told her in sign language on videotape. The videotaped story lasts for approximately 14 min and presents a total plot consisting of several integrated episodes.

Composing Conditions. This chapter discusses Molly's processing of text under two separate composing conditions that theoretically impose different degrees of cognitive strain.

Generating: Under this condition, she generated an original first draft after viewing the story. Because she was "writing from scratch," Molly was required to manage all of the constraints related to composing: Knowledge, Language, and Rhetoric. This condition did not completely preclude her reviewing and revising of text as she wrote, but she was told of a later opportunity to revise her original text. The Generating condition was the relatively high constraint condition.

Revising: Studies of writers in the act of writing have for the most part been confined to observations of the writer processing one text during a single session during which the composition conditions were kept standard throughout. In the present study, the processing of a single text was extended to a second session when the student returned to edit and recopy the original draft. Although editing could and did occur during the Generating session, these instances are different from sustained periods of reviewing and revising. According to Hayes and Flower (1980) this ". . . is not a spur-of-the-moment activity but rather one in which the writer decides to devote a period of time to systematic examination and improvement of the text. It occurs typically when the writer has finished a translation process rather than as an interruption to that process." (p. 18)

Molly reviewed and revised her original draft during a session that occurred subsequent to the original Generating session. She was instructed to inspect her text and make changes that she thought would improve the grammar of the original version. She recopied each sentence of the original composition after having separately inspected it and decided on any necessary changes. According to Applebee (1982) and Nold (1981), sentence-level changes such as these are the kinds customarily made by inexperienced or unskilled hearing writers. Wilbur's (1977) observation that writing for the deaf is often a sentence-by-sentence (vs. discourse) process suggests further that this condition did not impose unrealistic conditions.

Because Molly was not forced to generate a complete original draft during Revising, this condition was considered a low constraint condition. As Humes (1983) pointed out, cognitive strain on the writer is most severe during the original Translating (Generating) phase of composition. Nold (1981) said that revision places much less of a burden on short-term memory. It was expected, therefore, that anomalies that had been produced during the earlier Generating session would be considerably more detectable and perhaps correctable during Revising, if such errors truly draw attention.

Methods of Recording Pauses. There were two methods for recording second-by-second accounts of pauses during each writing session. In the first, a black-and-white camera was focused on Molly's page and connected to a videotape recorder. Before recording began, the paper was secured in a comfortable location. Once the paper was positioned, the camera was adjusted in such a way that the entire page was in focus, making it unnecessary to move or refocus the camera in the midst of the writing session. Molly was instructed to remove completed pages and to place them in a designated location on the writing desk.

The subject's stationery was positioned on a pressure-sensitive electronic tablet that was connected to an Apple II computer. This provided the second account of pausing behavior. The pressure created by Molly's pen point was recorded as a series of impulses in the computer's memory. Meanwhile, the computer's internal time-keeping system monitored the passage of time in increments of approximately $1/10$ second. The computer was programmed to produce later a printout of both the exact tablet and page locations (the Cartesian Coordinates: X,Y) where interruptions in writing, and the duration of those pauses, occurred. This method is similar to the procedure used by Martlew (1983).

Both of these methods were used so that the duration of pauses, as measured by the more traditional videotape method, could be used to validate the information gathered by the computer tablet. The computer monitoring resulted in accurate measurement. Although the methodology is still under refinement, it promises to simplify the somewhat onerous task of timing pauses on videotape.

Coding of Session Results.   Each composition was processed in the following ways:

1. The compositions were segmented into units that are roughly the equivalent of T-Units.
2. Pauses, timed in seconds, were transferred from the computer printout to the location on the page where they were initiated. Each T-Unit would therefore be accompanied by a pause that came before it (Pause Before), one that occurred after it (Pause After), and frequently one or more pauses that occurred when the T-unit was only partially completed. Those pauses that occurred within the T-unit were summed to produce Pausing Within. Adding the Pause Before and Pause After to Pausing Within yield the Total Pausing associated with the T-unit. All interruptions in writing that were at least $1/2$ second in length were used in the statistical analysis.
3. All anomalies in the T-unit were identified and rated for their impact on intelligibility according to Crandall's system (1980). This meant that each error was rated at some value from 9—the least impact on intelligibility—to 4, the greatest impact.
4. Each anomaly was classified as altered or unaltered depending on whether it was changed by Molly either during the original Generating session or, as happened more frequently, during the Revising session.

Table 1. Number of Anomalies Committed
Altered and Corrected in Student Narrative

Error Type	Number of Anomalies	Number Altered	Number Corrected
9	21	12	12
8	47	17	16
7	5	2	2
6	64	31	28
5	24	9	8
4	19	12	12
Total	180	83	78

RESULTS

The data that follow are the results of a Generating session, 50 minutes in duration and a Revising session, which was 59 min long. The student produced a 900-word narrative during the Generating session and revised it in the Revising session.

Anomalies
Molly's writing included virtually all of the chronic errors that have been observed and discussed in the related literature. Table 1 lists the frequencies of anomalies made by Molly, classified according to Crandall's system. The column labeled "Number of Anomalies" lists the types of errors produced during the Generating session.

These data indicate a total of 180 syntactic errors produced in the initial text. The most frequent were Type-6 errors which are free functor errors related to use of pronouns, prepositions, conjunctions, determiners, and auxiliary verbs. The least-frequent errors occurred in error Type-7; these included incorrect substitutions, omissions, or additions of prefixes, suffixes, and infixes. There were only five such errors. The total number of Type-6 and Type-8 errors, the categories that seem most persistent and prevalent in the writing of the deaf, was 111 or 62% of the total errors.

Table 1 also shows considerable activity by the writer in attempts to improve the correctness of the sentences. She altered 83 of the original errors during the Revising session. Almost all of these changes (78 out of the 83) resulted in elimination of the errors. These results suggest that careful inspection strategies (here, the student completely recopied the narrative) may promote error correction. This indicated that the student was eventually able to attend to many errors during Revising.

Table 2. Average Duration (Seconds) of
Pauses That Occurred under Two Composing
Conditions

Position	Generating	Revising
Pauses between T-units	8.5	14.6
Pauses within T-units	17.5	18.3
Total Pausing	34.5	47.6

Descriptive Statistics on Pausing

Table 2 displays the average pause times produced for each T-unit under the two different composing conditions.

Molly paused for an average of 8.5 seconds between each T-unit during the Generating condition. The average Within T-unit-Pausing duration was substantially larger than that, 17.5 seconds. During the Revising session, pauses between T-units were on the average almost double the duration of pauses that occurred at those same points during the Generating session. Although the student was instructed to inspect each T-unit thoroughly before making revising decisions, it was surprising that this difference was that dramatic because during the Generating session it was necessary for the student to devote at least some time to remembering the content of the videotape and deciding what to write. Apparently, deciding how to eliminate errors, the stated focus of the Revising session, induced more ponderous decision making. The Revising-session pauses indicated further that not all of these decisions relative to correctness are made before inscription of a T-unit begins, because Pausing Within was virtually the same during the Revising session as it was during Generating. Within-T-unit decision making seems to be a substantial component in the composing pattern of this student.

Pausing, Revising and Anomalies

Summary statistics provide a concise overview of composing performance but at the sacrifice of informative textual detail. The nature of composing is better revealed by combining the quantitative pausing data with the qualitative descriptions of text. To this end, a second type of analysis inspected the separate text elements in a methodical fashion, tracing Molly's progress through the passage, noting pauses and the nature of the text adjacent to pauses. Matsuhashi (1982) and Jones (1981) have demonstrated that it is possible to make reasonable inferences about the cognitive activity occurring during a specific pause by analyzing the text that is adjacent to the pause under scrutiny. They inferred the source of the burden on short-term memory from the nature of the tasks executed subsequent to the pause. In the present study, the availability of the pauses and text alterations produced during the Revising session permitted yet another source of evidence for inferring cognitive activity. The combination of the pauses and text from the Generating session with the pauses and text from the Revising session strongly suggest the text location and nature of constraints that were burdening short-term memory during composition.

The data from the two separate sessions were first merged in a way that would promote convenient inspection. Figure 2 shows the format used to combine the unique pausing and textual information from each of the two composing sessions for an excerpt at the beginning of the student's composition.

Text produced during the Generating session appears on the numbered lines. Pauses (in seconds) associated with that text appear below the line proximate to the places in the text where writing was interrupted. Words eventually deleted during the Revising session appear in parentheses, and words crossed out by the student in either session are indicated by overstriking. Words added or substituted during the Revising session when the student recopied the original text appear above the numbered lines as do the pauses that occurred during the Revising session.

The following discussion focuses exclusively on pauses that occurred within sentences. Because of the extended comment in the literature on "shaping at the point of inscription" (Britton, 1978; Matsuhashi, 1984; Scardamalia, Bereiter, and Goelman, 1982; and Shanklin, 1982), I decided that within-sentence pauses would be a much more direct indicator of a writer's sentence level (vs. discourse) concerns. A pause between T-units can be associated with the sentence before it or the sentence after it, blurring interpretation of the reason for the pause. To relieve some of the density of information, only relatively long within-sentence pauses are displayed in Figure 2 and discussed below.

The clearest evidence of sentence-level concerns in Figure 2 is related to the spelling of certain words. On line 1, Molly demonstrates uncertainty regarding the spelling of the name, Malzhuln (the correct spelling is Malzkuhn). During the Generating session she paused twice within the word, once for 1.8 seconds and once for 1.2 seconds. Although it is difficult to imagine that her halting progress through "Malzhuln" is anything other than a reflection of spelling uncertainty, that conclusion is supported further by inspecting the evidence from the Revising session, during which Molly again paused in the middle of the word, this time for 2.7 seconds. Another clear example of spelling concerns appears on line 14, where the writer is entangled in the production of the word "costume." In addition to the pausing, crossing out, and revising that occurred during the Generating session, we see that, during the Revising session, Molly paused for 6.3 seconds after writing the letter "c" and before revising the spelling into its correct form. In some cases, as in "costume," she shows the focus of

```
                       was            2.7
 1.        A man name (is) Eric Malzhuln.  Anyway, (Ħ) when
                          1.8   1.2
                    in                        and he
 2.   he was sophomore (at) Gallaudet College (in) 1942(.  He)

                                                        7.1
 3.   himself loved to play on the stage.  One day, he got
                                                12.0
      a job for helping                                  7.2
 4.   (to help)^people who worked in the auditorium.  He worked
                                      2.2    2.2          4.9
      pulling           8.3                —
 5.   (as pull) the rope for opening (or) closing the curtain.  Then
         4.7 | 3.3
         7.9      6.0    in the play    Øne            reading 9.9
 6.   he got himself involved playing.  (One day), he was (read)
      12.0                                               5.6
                  script#
 7.   several kinds of (script).  One that he really liked to know

                                      became
 8.   about was "Arensa and the Lace".  He (himself was) a director

           that              N       T     in Broadway
 9.   of (the) play so he asked the (n)ational (t)heatre^(if) to see if

      they were                    23.0 from National Theatre 21.3
10.   (it) approved his idea.  Several days later, he got a letter ^

      and it          they weren't
11.   (which) said that (national theatre in Broadway was not)

      approved 16.0 which     they        him
12.   (accepted.  That) mean (it) turned^down.  Eric was disappointed

            he
13.   and^had found (the reason why was was) that they didn't

          enough               c(6.3)ostume
14.   have (any) money, and (dønt cústóne contume) for the play.  So Eric
                                            7.6,3.2 4.8
            a          that he 9.1 earned          and
15.   had^better idea(.  His idea was to earn) the money(,) supplies,
                                                4.6
      for themselves.           6.3 N              T
16.   etc. ^ Then he sent his idea to (n)ational (tíréA) (t)heatre.

                                      it, but none
17.   He was waited and wanted (tø) to hear from^(there).  His

          4.1 was
18.   heart (had) broken soon.
          4.5
```

FIG. 2. Selected pauses and text produced in a Generating session and a Revising session by a deaf college student

covert concern by physically altering the text. But even where revisions were not made, the combined pausing patterns of the Generating and Revising session could have led to reasonable conclusions.

Beyond spelling, this same strategy can be used to infer the location and nature of grammatical decisions. During the Generating session Molly stopped writing for a substantial 12 seconds after writing the word "got" on line 3 and before writing the infinitive "to help" on line 4. When considering this pause alone, it is uncertain which constraint is interrupting inscription. The writer could have been trying to remember where Eric had worked. Or she could have been puzzling over the conventions related to the production of any of the words "people who worked in the auditorium." The Revision session information, however, suggests strongly that "help" was the focus of the decision making. First, during revising Molly paused again immediately after "got" for 7.2 seconds. She was probably not formulating what to say after "help" because, during revising, she was gazing at her complete original composition. This is supported by the alteration of the text to produce a new form of "help." The additional decision making ironically led to an ungrammatical construction of what had been correct in its original form. But the revised version was closer to the meaning of the story since Eric continued to work as a curtain puller beyond the "One Day."

The passage in Figure 2 offers other instances of how the nature of decision making can be inferred from pausing, as confirmed by the writer's actual revisions. On line 4, Molly paused for 4.9 seconds after inscribing "worked" and made three additional pauses proximate to the words "as pull." The difficulty of producing that phraseology seems clear. These Generating pauses suggest a search for how to cast the verb "pull." A pause of 7.2 seconds immediately after "worked" during the Revising session provides further evidence that "pull" is the source of the interruption. Finally, the conversion of "as pull" to the participle "pulling" confirms the source and nature of the problem.

Line 6 demonstrates a similar accumulation of evidence, culminating in the correction of "read" to form the obligatory "reading." Later, lines 14 and 15 show that, during the Revising session, Molly merged two independent clauses, a major change that was probably formulated during a 25-second pause that occurred before the first clause. But her use of the infinitive "to earn" during Generating, a possible source of some concern as suggested by the pause of 4.6 seconds, was undermined by the subordination of the second clause, and she once again returned to "earn," during Revising, pondering its correct form for 9.1 seconds before writing it. The new version includes the past-tense marker "ed," possibly an attempt to compensate for the loss of the tense designation of "was."

Line 18 shows further concern related to verb syntax that occurred at the same location during the two separate writing sessions. In the Generating session, the writer paused for 4.5 seconds before writing "had broken." Then, during the Revising session, she paused for slightly longer than 4 seconds after inscribing "heart" before substituting the auxiliary "was" for the original "had." In this case, either of the auxiliary verbs would have been syntactically acceptable and appropriate for expressing the meaning of the story.

The five instances of Generating/Revising pauses cited above suggest that Molly is concerned with the form of her verbs. She seems to know that the unavoidable use of verbs is accompanied by ample opportunity to err. In this one rather limited excerpt of text, the student displayed five verb-related interruptions in fluent inscription. There may have been concern for additional verbs but these may have been pondered during the pauses between T-units, blurring the true focus of the student's concern.

DISCUSSION

Sensitivity of Pausing to This Student's Decision Making

John Gould (1980) has expressed some skepticism about whether the duration of a specific pause can be attributed to the production or pondering of adjacent text. Incorporation of the pausing data from a subsequent revising session seems, however, to produce another source of evidence from which to infer covert cognitive activity. Generating pauses and Revising have a synergistic relationship; their combination makes them both more potent. The Generating pauses signal when attention has been drawn in the realistic situation when all composing constraints are competing for attention. The Revising pauses do not share this in-context validity, because availability of the student's original text reduces substantially the Rhetoric and Knowledge constraints, especially when the writer has been directed to concentrate on improving the grammar of individual sentences. But Revising pauses that occur at text locations that are proximate and sometimes identical to Generating pauses serve to corroborate and refine a judgment of where attention was focused during the Generating pause. When an actual revision of the text occurs, the evidence becomes even more compelling. It is important to note that, in order to produce Revising pauses, the student needs to recopy, and not just edit, the original text.

The Impact of Syntactic Anomalies on Attention

What made Molly stop and think? Was it the mental "drafting" of an incorrect form temporarily suspended in her short-term memory that stimulated attention even before an error was inscribed? Was it the actual appearance on the page of an anomalous verb that prompted a reexamination to see how the attempt "sounded"? Or was it merely the arrival at a point in text production where the need for a verb—with all its pitfalls of auxiliaries, particles, and inflections attendant—became unavoidable and the student entered a realm where she had experienced frequent failure and uncertainty in the past? Was the student's attention drawn by choices among specific textual alternatives, or was it the mere experience of entering a context requiring a verb that stimulated the concern?

A closer examination of the five cases of pausing and revising discussed above suggests that Molly's pauses were not stimulated by the explicit syntactic "wrongness" of what was produced. Two of the five verb constructions ("got to help" on line 3 and "to earn" on line 15, Figure 2) were originally correct but still drew attention and eventually were revised. In contrast, two of the five verbs were incorrect originally ("worked as pull" on line 4 and "was read" on line 6) but attention and revision concluded in the correct forms, "worked pulling" and "was reading" in both cases. In the case of the fifth example (line 18), either the original auxiliary "had" or the revised "was" would have been correct with "broken." The student seems equally likely to attend to, and tinker with, correct verb forms as incorrect verb forms. Further, in an interview conducted after her writing was concluded, Molly expressed a chronic weakness with "helper" verbs and tense. This student seems to know that she is vulnerable to error. And because she knows that there are a finite number of ways to manipulate verbs, in her uncertainty she seems at times obligated, if not compelled, to manipulate them until something looks right. Although not quite ensnared in a "morass of uncertainty" (Goldberg et al., 1982 p. 8), neither at times is she completely fluent in verb production.

In contrast, she doesn't seem willing to invest her time pondering the hopeless. (At one point, after hesitating for 50 seconds trying to remember the name of a famous actor (Boris Karloff), she finally settled on "Robert Moore" to fill the slot and never hesitated again during Generating or Revising when the name was used.) Moreover, Molly didn't attend to the form of her verbs in every proposition. In several places, she wrote rather deviant English with apparent fluency. While writing the following segment (Figure 2, line 10) during the Generating session, she demonstrated almost no within-sentence pausing. "Several days later, he got a letter which said that national theatre in Broadway was not accepted. That mean it turned down." Further, on line 17 of Figure 4 she wrote, "He was waited and wanted to hear from there." She wrote this without substantial interruptions in her inscribing. Molly doesn't seem driven by uncertainty to continuously reflect on the form of each of her verbs. Like the language of students observed by Goldberg et al. (1982, p. 8), certain "unlikely utterances" are at times produced without hesitation.

Because the deaf are second-language users, it is appropriate to consider Molly's performance in the context of Krashen's (1978) theory that second-language users sometimes invoke a Monitor of explicit, learned rules to modify the correctness of their productions in the second language. Krashen has discussed individual variation in Monitor use, identifying several categories of individuals: Monitor overusers are those who make excessive use of learned rules to the point that they impair communication; underusers, on the other hand, rarely make use of learned rules and, instead, rely almost exclusively on acquired competence to produce language which may deviate substantially from standard form. Appropriate Monitor use is somewhere between these two: occasional use of rules to make refinements in language produced.

Jones (1981) has studied the writing performance of both overusers and underusers. Monitor overusers or "heavy" users, as he calls them, plan text in very short segments because only a limited amount of information can be held in short-term memory for review and correction. He found that appreciable pausing occurred after relatively short segments of text in the writing of the heavy user in his study. He noted also that heavy users would be likely to polish up one piece of text before moving on to plan the next and, for that reason, would have little need to return later for revisions because they have made all possible refinements at the time that they had initially inscribed the text. Monitor underusers, on the other hand, would plan in much larger segments, pause and polish less frequently, and would therefore have more opportunities to revise after completion of a first draft.

In the present study, did Molly demonstrate the traits of a Monitor overuser, a writer who devotes excessive concern to correctness much like the students in the studies by Perl, Pianko, and Shaughnessy who endured severe interruptions in the writing process as a result of the preoccupation with correctness? Based on this pausing and revising performance, this student seems to be neither an overuser nor an underuser. She stops periodically to explore the possibility of refining her output but even when she doesn't succeed in producing correctness, she pushes on with regularity so that her production of ideas sustains its momentum. Other times she produces somewhat anomalous text fluently. Also, unlike an overuser, she returns to the text (albeit under explicit instructions to do so) and under the Revising condition produces ample and appropriate changes in the original text. She has not exhausted all possibilities for change by engaging in excessive monitoring during the Generating stage.

Monitor use seems to help performance as indicated by the correction of 78 of the 180 anomalies that were produced in the original passage. But when a revision encompassed substantially more than a single word, Molly sometimes produced additional anomalous language, because even though she was operating in the sustained Revising condition, production of an extended text segment forced her into the Generating mode in which she relied primarily on her intuitive acquired competence, which was frequently the source of nonstandard text. Examples of new errors inserted during Revision appear on lines 4, 10, 15, 16, and 17 of Figure 2.

Though Molly often demonstrated an ability to postpone her concern for errors until the Revising condition, it is important to recall that she was completing a less-demanding Reporting task. She was retelling a story that was rather predictable in its structure and rich in details. The student apparently had very few "dry spells" when she had nothing to write about what happened in the videotape story. So when she found herself temporarily deliberating on a syntactic choice (perhaps not totally satisfied with her first attempt) she routinely had other business competing for her attention. She could tolerate the flawed syntax and engage productively in delivery of the next character, event, or setting of the story. The relatively brief period between T-units during Generating (8.5 seconds) suggests that she was rarely lacking for something to say.

One wonders whether a more complex Generalizing writing task, in which a writer discovers what is known during the act of writing, would allow her to put aside grammar concerns so easily. During a Generalizing task a student might encounter considerably more instances of having nothing to say. As an alternative to the more strenuous engagement in the creation of discourse, the student might resort to a monitoring and correction of the syntactically flawed text that had already been produced. During the Reporting task, on the other hand, especially when the information is well known, the knowledge constraint may compete more successfully for attention than it does during a Generalizing task. This might be a fertile topic for future research.

Instructional Implications

In research of this type, meaningful results are dependent on the student's production of mistakes. No errors, no analyses. Hoping for errors is not a comfortable sentiment and suggesting the implications of these findings for instruction is a task with considerably more appeal.

Much has been written about how to help students reduce their errors and to improve their composition. I will limit this discussion to ideas that are derived from this student's writing performance. Her traits will dictate the treatments.

A summary of the student's traits will facilitate a discussion of the techniques that are designed to help this student. Her performance suggests the following trends:

- Use of the Monitor to correct errors more often during the Revising condition than during the Generating condition.
- The ability to detect and correct anomalies may have been promoted

to a large extend by a clear mental representation of the meaning that was intended. This may have been the result of the less-demanding Reporting writing task.

- The student attends to the correctness of her verbs, a concern indicated during both the Generating and Revising conditions and expressed by Molly herself during an interview at the conclusion of the study.
- The student's writing exhibits a substantial number of anomalies even after a sustained period of systematic inspection and revising.

This student might benefit from an explicit explanation of the dynamics of the writing process, especially its multiconstraint nature which makes writing so difficult. With this knowledge applied as a conscious set of procedures, the student could intentially manage her writing in the most prudent fashion possible, saving in-depth editing for a systematic reviewing session. The form of this advice would be critical: rich enough so that the essential elements of the writing dynamic are included, yet simple enough to avoid confusion.

The most meaningful source of "props" for explaining the nature of the writing process might be a record of the student's own writing performance. Although its form might be slightly different from the dense array in Figure 2, the student would find out what happens when she writes. The student would learn a salient aspect of her performance and then receive composing advice based on that observation of herself.

Observation 1: Molly would be told that she seems better able to find errors by conducting a sustained review and recopying of her completed first draft several days after the original is composed.

Advice:

1. Instead of trying to produce perfect copy during the first writing, sacrifice perfection initially and be satisfied with getting ideas recorded in rudimentary form. (Molly already demonstrates a certain tendency to compose in this manner).
2. Write the first draft early enough so that several days can pass before revising. The passage of time will promote the "distancing" from the ideas in the original text that Bartlett (1982) claims will enhance error detection.
3. Recopy the second version as part of the revising process instead of after the first draft has been edited. The process of writing the text in longhand will promote error detection because it slows inspection in the same way that reading text aloud aids the scrutiny of professional proofreaders who have normal hearing.

Observation 2: Molly seems able to detect errors when the meaning that she wishes to communicate is clear.
Advice:

1. Do more planning. Flower and Hayes (1980) distinguish among several kinds of planning that help a writer to crystalize the direction that they want their texts to take.
2. Read what is already written to give guidance in formulating the meaning of later text. Although, through writing, writers acquire a progressively more refined sense of what they know about a topic (Perl, 1979; Shanklin, 1982) the writer in the present study might fit Pianko's (1979) description of remedial writers who tend to lose the benefit of interacting with completed text. ". . . Remedial writers do not pause as often during the writing for additional planning or rescan as often to take stock of what they have written to aid in the next formulation as do traditional writers" (p. 20).
3. Defer a systematic error search until the first draft is completed and the intended meaning of the whole passage is clear.

Each of these pieces of advice assumes that the student is becoming involved in writing experiences that are potentially meaningful. Observations by Applebee (1982) and others suggest that this has not always been the case in our schools. Pianko (1979) urges that writing ". . . should begin with an idea developing out of students' confrontations with life; it should necessarily brew in students' minds for a while then be tentatively explored and re-explored on paper until students feel that they are ready for a final version" (p. 18).

These techniques may help this student make optimal use of consciously learned rules—the Monitor. It is sobering to note, however, that although the student was reasonably prudent in the way she treated her errors, resulting in many corrections, the passage was still fraught with anomalies at the conclusion of the Revising session. When any of the corrections of an original error involved more than a single word it was not unusual for the student to jeopardize adjacent text that had been correct in its original form. Because she was obligated to "put out fires" so repeatedly, she created ample tinder for additional syntactic flareups. Hence, this student's performance suggests that need for an additional kind of strategy: modification of her Acquired Language so that language is produced fluently in standard form, reducing somewhat the need for extensive monitoring.

Krashen (1977) asserts that Acquired Language focuses on, and is produced by, the pursuit of meaningful communication as opposed to the explicit polishing of correct form. Others, however, recommend a more direct approach to improving form. Gould (1980) wrote that pedagogical emphasis upon syntax and mechanics is necessary to prevent people from being so hampered by lack of these abilities as to give up writing. He stated that the teacher needs to make grammatical or linguistic aspects of sentence generation more automatic, thus freeing attention for other aspects of composition. In this same spirit, Scardamalia (1981) derides certain instructional systems for their "benign" acceptance of student errors.

Shaughnessy, however, was less certain of whether instruction should explicitly emphasize correctness. According to her,

> . . . if error becomes a subject for instruction it will quickly loom in the writer's consciousness as a central problem in writing . . . [S]uch a concentration is believed to impede the writer's development, even in relation to the reduction of error, producing highly self-conscious and hypercorrected writing that moves him [the unskilled writer] even further from his resources as a native speaker of English. (p. 118)

Those who educate the deaf have not abstained from this controversy. Goldberg (1983) is representative of those who advocate an emphasis on correct form, a "bottom-up" approach to competence. When he teaches grammar, "If a given sentence is 'meaningful' (communicate a picture of some sort) and grammatical, it is accepted without question. It does not matter to me that the sentence does not follow what was said before, nor lead 'naturally' into the sentences which follow . . ." (p. 7). In contrast, Wilbur (1977), Meath-Lang et al. (1982), and Gormley (1981) criticize emphasis of sentence-level correctness, which is widely used in the education of the deaf, and hold it partly responsible for the fragmented discourse and even some variations of the anomalous syntax that so many deaf students produce. Their comments support a "top-down" approach, an emphasis of meaning even though form has not yet been perfected. Advocates of the "top-down" approach want to avoid wounding students further by confronting them with their inadequacies, a process which is, in their opinion, counterproductive because acquired competence is not enhanced while the threat of promoting Monitor overuse is increased. In contrast, the "bottom-up" advocates want to focus on the students' most glaring weaknesses so that the sources of the students' eventual embarrassment can be expeditiously eradicated from their prose.

It may be possible to wed such a selective treatment of errors to the kind of emphasis on meaning that promotes acquired competence. Suppose it was decided to enhance Molly's use of the continuous form of verbs: The three errors on lines 3, 4, and 5 of Figure 2 demonstrate the student's limitations in this area. Instead of pointing out the errors explicitly, however, the instructor might make the following marginal notation on the first draft: "Did Eric work for only a single day or did he continue to work in the role as a curtain puller?" The student would be signalled that her choice of words, whatever its grammatical merits, was not conveying the picture that Eric held a job as a curtain puller for a sustained period. And if the student was at a loss as to how to express the continuous action, the instructor could point out places in the student's own text where the appropriate form was used correctly to express the intended meaning. Nystrand's (1982) distinctions among the different types of reader confusions and misunderstandings that flawed writing sometimes produces can guide teachers in responding creatively to their students' prose.

The density of this student's errors requires discretion in deciding which errors to emphasize when taking this meaning-centered approach to promoting better syntax. If all errors were addressed simultaneously the instructor would quickly saturate the margins with questions, and the student would be placed again in a position where there was an extremely heavy burden on short-term memory. Burt and Kiparsky (1969) recommend working first on those "goofs" that seriously impair communication. They seem to be (rightly) concerned about how error affects the reader. But research on anomalous writers suggests an additional criterion for assigning priorities.

Anomalies that draw the greatest attention (the longest pauses) also warrant the most expeditious instructional intervention. Two reasons for this are proposed. First, devotion of substantial attention suggests that the writer is at the first stage of Bartlett's (1982) three-stage text revision process, which includes detection, identification, and, finally, correction. The deaf writer's concern for a certain type of anomaly may suggest the emergence of a kind of competence: the development of the internal criterion needed to find mistakes. The student writer is thus ready to learn ways to eliminate the errors that he or she is able to detect.

Second, immediate instruction is also indicated when attention draw is relatively high, because the writer's processing space is being monopolized by those errors, limiting the capacity to execute more sophisticated writing tasks. Conversely, anomalies that seem to draw little attention may warrant commensurate instructional time, as they are not impeding the student's concern for higher level discourse tasks. In addition, minimal attention draw by subsets of anomalies may actually advise against investment of substantial instructional time. Insensitivity to certain anomalies suggests that classes of errors may be uniquely resistant to change. Reflecting on such instructional choices for the teachers of hearing writers, Shaughnessy (1977) wrote,

> The stubbornness of these problems and the economics of getting rid of them (the cost of the letter 's' in remedial writing programs, for example, would be worth exploring) raise questions about the nature of the errors and the wisdom of trying to clear them completely from a student's writing before moving on to other things. (p. 90)

In instruction of the deaf, it may be necessary to acknowledge the resistance of certain anomalies and to divert instructional energies more judiciously elsewhere. Although the revisions in Figure 2 demonstrate that Molly is capable of correcting many of the problems herself, her attention to the formation of verbs suggests that teacher reactions to her writing should emphasize refinements in meaning that would result from an improvement in the grammar of her verbs.

In each examination of this student's writing one is jolted by the density of errors. And any contemplated systematic exchange between teacher and student, though focusing on meaning and making some improvement in acquired competence, could probably best be described as a war of attrition. There is so much to be done and the costs to teacher and student seem so high.

Frank Smith (1984) fortunately recommends marshalling strategic resources that may have the impact of megatonnage on student errors. And in the language of the computer programmer, Smith's advice is elegant: It promises substantial results while requiring a minimum of additional resources. Smith argues that the subtle skills of writing are so complex and numerous that it would be impossible to teach each of them explicitly. Moreover, most of the rules of grammar "are circular and meaningless to anyone who cannot already do the operations that are 'explained' by the rule" (p. 48). He says further that practice and feedback help to polish writing skills but cannot account for their initial acquisition. Smith concludes that people learn to write well, applying all the linguistic intricacies correctly and effectively, by reading the work of other authors provided that they *read like a writer*.

Smith makes the analogy between a writer learning from reading and a child learning to talk from listening. Few will dispute the notion that listening helps develop a child's speaking ability. Borrowing an expression from Miller (1977), Smith describes the burgeoning speaker as a "spontaneous apprentice" closely observing the "master" adult speaker with the anticipation of himself becoming a "journeyman." Smith describes how this apprenticeship functions in writing:

> To read like a writer we engage with the author in what the author is writing. We anticipate what the writer will say, so that the writer is in effect writing on our behalf, not showing how something is done but doing it with us. . . . The author becomes an unwitting collaborator. Everything that the learner would want to spell the author spells . . . Every nuance of expression, every relevant syntactic device, every turn of phrase, the author and learner write together. Bit by bit, one thing at a time, but enormous numbers of things over the passage of time, the learner learns through reading like a writer to write like a writer. (p. 53)

Smith also points out, however, that students do not automatically think of themselves as writers, so the spirit of spontaneous apprenticeship sometimes has to be cultivated. Teachers must help students to envision themselves as writers by demonstrating the uses of writing and by helping students to use writing themselves. Teachers, through the judicious selection of reading materials and orchestration of writing activities, can show that writing is for real purposes: "stories to be read, books to be published, poems to be recited, plays to be acted, songs to be sung, newspapers to be shared, letters to be mailed, jokes to be told, notes to be passed, cards to be sent, cartons to be labelled, instructions to be followed . . ." (p. 55) and many other meaningful and satisfying purposes. By involving students in projects such as these—both reading and writing—the teacher will increase the students awareness that they should and can be "members of the writers club" (Smith, p. 53). And then they can more easily read like writers, enhancing their own writing competence as a result.

Smith points out also that "writing is not for having your ignorance exposed, your sensitivity destroyed or your ability assessed" (p. 55), and "Emphasis on the elimination of mistakes results in the elimination of writing" (p. 56). Teachers have the power to discourage membership in the writers' club, and in that way sever access to what may be the single-most potent resource for reducing the errors that rivet teachers' attention and fuel their aggression.

The number of deaf students who consider themselves members of the writers' club is probably quite small. As stated earlier, the emphasis of sentence-level correctness has been an instructional staple in schools for the deaf. Students have been given little reason to think of themselves as writers. As a result, students have been largely unable to capitalize on what may be the most potent tool for helping them to acquire—instead of learn— writing competence. This student's (Molly) performance has demonstrated that efficient use of a linguistic monitor can help eliminate many errors without disrupting the flow of composition. But the final form of her text shows that the monitor is not enough. This student also needs a large dose of acquired competence. Frank Smith (1984) has explained how this might be achieved. His advice should strike an optimistic cord with educators of the deaf. He has identified a resource that has probably gone unused but which is potentially accessible in schools for the hearing impaired.

CONCLUSION

"Bit by bit, one thing at a time." Frank Smith's (1984, p. 53) description of accumulating competence reminds one of another test of endurance and guile, the marathon. Slow but steady progress toward a goal. Also, like a marathon, the expansion of writing competence—the kind that comes from reading like a writer—is accomplished alone: No coaches, no seconds, *no teachers* are allowed to enter the arena directly. These terms will probably be repugnant to many teachers of the deaf. Few enter deaf education to wait by idly as students learn by themselves. Fewer still choose inertia once they are jolted by a series of encounters with their student's anomalous language.

If these teachers were entering their students in any race, it would be the dash. They want to dispatch them to the destination of writing competence without delay. In few places is their haste more apparent than on the Gallaudet campus, where there is an elementary school and a high school as well as a college for the deaf. Teachers at the upper grades of the demonstration elementary school hurry to prepare their students for the secondary school. Teachers of upper classmen in the model secondary school focus on preparation for the tasks of the Gallaudet entrance examination. Professors at Gallaudet college strive for real-world competence. Not all of them, however, consider graduation a day for rejoicing.

Aware of the need to prepare their students to cross the next threshold of academia, teachers of the deaf have been in a hurry. They therefore routinely choose what appears to be the most expeditious path to their goal: They tell the students exactly what they did wrong, they tell them what is correct, and they give them a rule both to understand why it is correct and to avoid future mistakes. Molly described her English experience, until this year, as similar to this: finding errors and correcting them with a rule. It is doubtful that this experience helped her to feel at one with members of the writers' club. Not surprising then are the apparent gaps in her acquired syntactic competence when she is required to write English. She demonstrated plenty of willingness, ability, and good sense in making use of rules during revising, but her learned competence was not sufficient to correct a substantial number of errors.

Instead of hurrying to expunge errors, teachers might better serve their students by altering their instructional strategies. They should work to contain their predilection to banish syntactic flaws immediately from their students' writing. Because their students cannot acquire language by hearing it in natural contexts, they need to acquire it by reading it in natural contexts. As mentioned earlier, selected errors can be emphasized by the teacher. Smith (1984) does not forbid feedback. But the focus on a specific kind of anomaly should remain the teacher's hidden agenda, and, overtly, emphasis should focus on opportunities to improve meaning. Molly's reasonably regular production tempo suggests that such tactics are appropriate. Her short-term memory does not seem totally absorbed, nor her attention to meaning completely preempted by her nonstandard English.

Resisting the temptation to reveal mistakes to students will not come easily. In our zeal to help, the first instinct for many of us is to pounce.

But knowing the effect of our unbridled exposure of flaws, we would be prudent to preface our reactions to students' writing with a systematic, tempering safeguard: a long and thoughtful pause.

REFERENCES

Applebee, A. (1982). Writing and learning in school settings. In M. Nystrand (Ed.), *What writers know: The language process and structure of written discourse.* New York: Academic Press.

Bartlett, E. (1982). Learning to revise: Some component processes. In M. Nystrand (Ed.), *What writers know: The language process, and structure of written discourse.* New York: Academic Press.

Bochner, J. (1978). Error, anomaly, and variation in the English of deaf individuals. *Language and Speech, 21,* 174–189.

Bockmiller, P., (1981). Hearing-impaired children: Learning to read a second language. *American Annals of the Deaf, 126(7),* 810–813.

Bonvillian, J.D., Nelson, K.E., and Charrow, V.E. (1976). Language and language related skills in deaf and hearing children. *Sign Language Studies, 12,* 211–250.

Britton, J. (1978). The composing processes and the functions of writing. In C. Cooper and L. O'dell (Eds.), *Research on composing: Points of departure.* Urbana, IL: National Council of Teachers of English.

Britton, J., Burgess, T., Martin, W., McLeod, A. & Rosen, H. (1975). *The development of writing abilities: (11–18).* Urbana, Illinois: National Council of Teachers of English.

Bunch, G. O. (1979). Degree and manner of acquisition of written English language rules by the deaf. *American Annals of the Deaf, 124,* 10–15.

Burt, M., and Kiparsky, C. (1969). *The gooficon: A repair manual for English.* Rowley, MA: Newbury House.

Charrow, V. (1974). *Deaf English—An investigation of the written English competence of deaf adolescents.* (Unpublished doctoral dissertation, Stanford University).

Charrow, V. (1981). The written English of deaf adolescents. In M.F. Whiteman (Ed.), *Writing: The nature, development, and teaching of written communication (Vol. 1), Variation in Writing.* Hillsdale, NJ: Erlbaum.

Charrow, V. and Fletcher, J.D. (1974). English as the second language of deaf children. *Developmental Psychology, 10,* 463–470.

Crandall, K. (1978). Reading and writing skills and the deaf adolescent. *Volta Review, 80,* 319–32.

Crandall, K. (1980). *Written language scoring procedures for grammatical correctness according to reader intelligibility.* Rochester, NY: National Technical Institute for the Deaf.

De Camp, D. (1971). Introduction: The study of pidgin and creole languages. In D. Hymes (Ed.), *Pidginization and creolization of languages.* Cambridge, England: Cambridge University Press.

Emig, J. (1978). Hand, eye, brain: Some 'basics' in the writing process. In C. Cooper & L. O'dell (Eds.), *Research on composing: Points of departure.* Urbana, IL: National Council of Teachers of English.

Ewoldt, C. (1981). A psycholinguistic description of selected deaf children reading in sign language. *Reading Research Quarterly, 1,* 58–89.

Flower, L. & Hayes, J. (1980). The dynamics of composing: Making plans and juggling constraints. In L. Gregg & E. Steinberg (Eds.), *Cognitive processes in writing.* Hillsdale, NJ: Erlbaum.

Goldberg, J.P. (1983). The grammar angle. *Teaching English to Deaf and Second-Language Students, 1,* 4–11.

Goldberg, J.P., & Astley, R. (1983). *Revising your writing: Solutions to common grammar and usage problems for college students.* Washington, DC: Gallaudet College.

Goldberg, J.P., and Bordman, M. (1974). English language instruction for the hearing impaired: An adaptation of ESL methodology. *TESOL Quarterly, 8,* 263–270.

Goldberg, J.P., Ford, C., & Silverman, A. (1982). *Deaf students in ESL composition classes: Challenges and strategies composition classes.* Paper presented at the 16th Annual TESOL Convention, Honolulu.

Gormley, K. (1981). A functional strategy for writing: A case study of Tom. *Volta Review, 83* (1), 5–13.

Gould, J. (1980). Experiments on composing letters: Some facts, some myths, and some observations. In L. Gregg & E. Steinberg (Eds.), *Cognitive processes in writing.* Hillsdale, NJ: Erlbaum.

Hall, R. (1966). *Pidgin and creole languages.* Ithaca, NY: Cornell University Press.

Hayes, J. & Flower, L. (1980). Identifying the organization of writing processes. In L. Gregg and E. Steinberg (Eds.), *Cognitive processes in writing.* Hillsdale, NJ: Erlbaum.

Heider, F. & Heider, G. (1940). A comparison of sentence structure of deaf and hearing children. *Psychological Monographs, 52,* 52–103.

Humes, A. (1983). Research on the composing process. *Review of Educational Research, 53,* 201–216.

Hunt, K. (1965). *Grammatical structures written at three grade levels* (Research Rep. No. 3). Champaign, IL: National Council of Teachers of English.

Jones, S. (1981). *Observing monitor use during the composing process.* Unpublished manuscript, Carleton University, Ottowa, Canada.

Kates, S.L. (1972). *Language development in deaf and hearing adolescents.* Northhampton, MA: The Clarke School for the Deaf.

Krashen, S.D., (1978). Individual variation in use of the monitor. In W. C. Ritchie (Ed.), *Second language acquisition research.* New York: Academic Press.

Krashen, S.D. (1977). The monitor model for adult second language performance. In M. Burt, H. Dulay, & M. Finocchiaro (Eds.), *Viewpoints on English as a second language.* New York: Regents.

Kretschmer, R.R., & Kretschmer, L.W. (1978). *Language development and intervention with the hearing impaired.* Baltimore: University Park Press.

Lenneberg, E. (1967). *Biological foundations of language.* New York: Wiley.

Martlew, M. (1983). Problems and difficulties: Cognitive and communicative aspects of writing development. In M. Martlew (Ed.), *The psychology of written language: Developmental and educational perspectives.* New York: Wiley.

Matsuhashi, A. (1982). Explorations in the real-time production of written discourse. In M. Nystrand (Ed.), *What writers know: The language, process, and structure of written discourse.* New York: Academic Press.

Matsuhashi, A. (January, 1984). Personal Communication.

Meath-Lang, B., Caccamise, F., and Albertini, J. (1982). Deaf persons' views on English language learning: Educational and sociolinguistic implications. In H. Hoemann and R.B. Wilbur (Eds.), *Interpersonal communication and deaf people.* Washington, DC: Gallaudet College.

Miller, G. (1977). *Spontaneous apprentices: Children and language.* New York: Seabury.

Moffett, J. (1968). *Teaching the universe of discourse.* Boston: Houghton Mifflin.

Myklebust, H.R. (1964). *The psychology of deafness.* New York: Grune and Stratton.

Nold, E. (1981). Revising. In C. Fredericksen and J. Dominic (Eds.), *Writing: The nature, development, and teaching of written communication (Vol. 2), Process development and communication.* Hillsdale, NJ: Erlbaum.

Nystrand, M. (1982). An analysis of error in written communication. In M. Nystrand (Ed.), *What writers know: The language, process, and structure of written discourse.* New York: Academic Press.

Perl, S. (1978). *Five writers writing: Case studies of the composing processes of unskilled college writers.* Unpublished doctoral dissertation, New York University.

Perl, S. (1979). The composing processes of unskilled college writers. *Research in the Teaching of English, 15* (4), 317–336.

Pianko, S. (1979). A description of the composing processes of college freshmen writers. *Research in the Teaching of English, 13,* 5–22.

Quigley, S.P., Power, D.J., & Steinkamp, M.W. (1977). The language structure of deaf children. *Volta Review, 79* (2), 73–83.

Sarachan-Deily, A.B. (1980). *Deaf readers' comprehension of individual sentences.* Albany, NY: College of St. Rose. (ERIC Document Reproduction Service No. ED 214 325).

Scardamalia, M. (1981). How children cope with the cognitive demands of writing. In C. Fredericksen and J. Dominic (Eds.), *Writing: The nature, development, and teaching of written communication: (Vol. 2), Process, development and communication.* Hillsdale, NJ: Erlbaum.

Scardamalia, M., Bereiter, C., & Goelman, H. (1982). The role of production factors in writing ability. In M. Nystrand (Ed.), *What writers know: The language, process, and structure of written discourse.* New York: Academic Press.

Schmitt, P. (1969). *Deaf children's comprehension and production of sentence transformations and verb tenses.* Unpublished doctoral dissertation, University of Illinois, Urbana.

Shanklin, N. (1982). *Relating reading and writing: Developing a transactional theory of the writing process.* Bloomington, IN: Indiana University School of Education.

Shaughnessy, M. (1977). *Errors and expectations.* New York: Oxford University Press.

Smith, F. (1984). Reading like a writer. In J. Jensen (Ed.), *Composing and comprehending.* Urbana, IL: ERIC and NCRE.

Stokoe, W.C. (1971). *The study of sign language.* Silver Spring, MD: National Association of the Deaf.

Taylor, L.T. (1969). *A language analysis of the writing of deaf children.* Unpublished doctoral dissertation, Florida State University.

Trybus, R., and Karchmer, M. (1977). School achievement scores of hearing impaired: National data on achievement status and growth patterns. *American Annals of the Deaf, 122,* 62–69.

Wilbur, R.B. (1977). An explanation of deaf children's difficulty with certain syntactic structures. *Volta Review, 79* (2), 85–92.

Zambrano, R., and Kelly, L. (1984). *Potentially favorable components of a campus-wide writing program and the climate for implementation.* Washington, DC: Gallaudet College.

CHAPTER 8

Revising the Plan and Altering the Text

Ann Matsuhashi
University of Illinois at Chicago

"Shaping at the point of utterance" is the phrase James Britton uses to describe the moment-by-moment invention process that occurs as we speak. "When we start to speak," he explains, "we push the boat out and trust it will come to shore somewhere—not *anywhere,* which would be tantamount to losing our way—but somewhere that constitutes a stage on a purposeful journey" (Britton, 1980). That speakers hem and haw, umm, urgh, and ahh their way to the end of a sentence is an obvious fact made use of by actor Jimmy Stewart playing the role of Elwood P. Dowd in the 1950 movie *Harvey.* Although working from a carefully scripted text, Stewart bumbled his way so convincingly through conversations with an invisible rabbit that this halting pattern of "composing aloud" became Stewart's trademark throughout his career.

Certainly, in creating the character, Stewart had taken into account that which *separates* speech from writing: gesture, intonation, pitch, and stress. Beyond these obvious differences, however, lies a greater and more substantial similarity, because speech and writing may be thought of as "different realizations of the same underlying language system" (Stubbs, 1980, p. 116). Stewart seems to have realized that there is a rhythm, a tempo, a measured quality to language produced anew.

When a writer begins to inscribe a text, the line of text sometimes emerges as a steady flow of words but more often in spurts, stutters, and slips of the pen punctuated by pauses of various lengths. This process of shaping at the point of utterance (or at the point of "inscription," in the parlance of this chapter) can differ radically for beginning, inexperienced writers and for professionals who write daily. Mina Shaughnessy (1977) described the composing process of a practiced professional writer who begins a text with an almost infinite number of options:

> . . . With each word he writes down, the field of choices narrows. The sentence seems to take its head and move with increasing predictability in the

directions that idiom, syntax, and semantics leave open. The experienced
writer responds to these constraints unconsciously, providing the words or
structures that different contexts allow. (p. 44)

For the inexperienced writers who Shaughnessy described with such acuity,
this "semantic engine" (Haugeland, 1981, p. 31) often derails under a
variety of pressures. These writers may lack a familiarity with the social
uses and functions of writing and with the formal conventions governing
written English. Beyond this, they may lack a general memory for "unheard sentences" (Sternglass, 1980) and during sentence production lack a
memory for the grammatical structures just committed to print (Daiute,
1984).

It is just this marked disparity between the successful composing strategies of the practiced writer and those of the halting, error-conscious be-
ginner that has motivated much of the current interest in research on writing
processes. While Stewart seemed to be composing aloud, most writing is
done privately, concealing the process of shaping at the point of inscription. Writing, Frank Smith (1982) observes, "covers its own traces. The
record is erased of the false starts, the dead ends, the deletions, and the
rearrangements. The seams do not . . . show" (p. 2).

In this chapter, studying revision helps to uncover the "traces" of the
writing process of Edna, a reasonably competent high school writer. I have
chosen to observe Edna precisely because of the variability that the phrase
"reasonably competent" implies. Edna revises using a wide range of strategies, but her success at revision is irregular. Sometimes a construction is
improved, but sometimes an error appears where none existed before. The
focus of this paper is on the thinking process that gives rise to the final
text, imperfect as that text may be.

Traditionally, revision has been linked to repair. Revisions were studied,
not for the "window" they might provide on a writer's thinking processes,
but for their impact on the relative quality of the final text. When one
revises, one unquestionably intends to improve the text in some way, but
the observation of both failed and successful attempts at revision can also
be quite instructive. Thus, current studies of revision stress the relationship
between revision and higher order thinking processes. This emphasis on
revision "strategies" or "thinking processes" has resulted, in some measure, from research on reading comprehension, which, for some years now,
has focused on the construction of a mental representation of the text as
a meaning-making strategy.

A brief review of these current trends in research will provide a context
for studying revision as shaping at the point of inscription—a strategic,
goal-oriented, cognitive activity. My own aim here is to argue that observ-

ing revisions as they occur in real time can illustrate a writer's shifting focus of attention and pattern of decision-making.

CONTEXTS FOR STUDYING REVISION

Revision as Repair

In large part, the current interest in revision grew in reaction to narrow, pedagogical views of revision as the final stage of a three-part "think-write-rewrite" process which often equated revision with editing. Yet, in most current revision studies, researchers still feel compelled to evaluate the success of revisions in terms of the quality of the text. This evaluation process is appropriate when the research is motivated by pedagogical questions. In cognitive-based, exploratory research projects, however, such as the one reported in this chapter, the success of the revisions ought not to be the only criterion. In the selected review below, we can see how patterns of errors and repairs reflect cognitive strategies in a diverse group of subjects.

Elsa Bartlett (1982) studied revision as repair for the purpose of examining the cognitive strategies of young writers. She found that young writers were capable of correcting errors of referential ambiguity in others' texts but were unable to do so in their own. Bartlett surmised that when these writers reviewed their own texts, they were "blind" to errors of correctness because they read with a focus on meaning.

Ellen Nold (1982) makes the distinction between revising to fit conventions—matching the text against accepted rules of correctness—and revising to fit intentions—matching the existing text against goals defined in terms of meaning, audience, and purpose. When writers attend too frequently to rule-governed revisions (revising to fit conventions), their behavior might be characterized as premature editing (Rose, 1984). In observations of blocked writers and unblocked writers, Mike Rose noted that the unblocked writers often avoided premature editing by, for example, circling a word with questionable spelling and returning to the larger writing task.

Cazden, Michaels, and Tabor (1985) studied the spontaneous repairs of first- and second-grade children in oral narratives produced during classroom "sharing time." Unlike earlier studies, which only characterized these spontaneous repairs as lexical replacements (e.g., substituting "ramp" for "thing"), Cazden's study classified a special type of repair called bracketing—the insertion of a chunk of material into an otherwise syntactically intact sentence. This additional, bracketed material demonstrated a rather sophisticated use of syntactic resources. Beyond this, however, the additional material was taken as evidence of the children's ability to make "repairs for the listener at the level of organization of thematic content of the narrative as a whole" (p. 7). In this and other studies such as the ones reviewed above, the notion of repair extends far beyond a narrow definition of correctness and reintegrates notions of error and repair within a more complex view of the writing process.

Revision as Reading

Often, revision is equated with reading in an overly simple manner. With a narrow, reading-based view, how can we explain the evaluation processes of a blind writer who writes without revising or rereading (Gere, 1982)? Or, similarly, how can we explain a writer who makes a revision not after reading a portion of the text, but after gazing away, or who, on the third page of a text returns to the first page and crosses out a line without rereading (as does the writer discussed later in this study)?

We have seen, on the one hand, that the continual rereading or rescanning in basic writers seems to inhibit evaluations of anything but the current grammatical, mechanical, or lexical problems (Perl, 1980), and yet when the text was removed during the invisible writing experiences of Sheridan Blau's (1983) graduate students, they claimed that the "absence of visual feedback from the text they were producing actually sharpened their concentration . . . enhanced their fluency, and yielded texts that were more rather than less cohesive" (p. 298). In Blau's invisible writing experience students could not and did not revise. In a study I conducted with Eleanor Gordon (Matsuhashi & Gordon, 1985), students who planned their revisions after rereading and listed ideas for revision on the blank back pages of their paper were able to produce substantial revisions in the argument structure of the text, whereas those who revised while looking at their texts made an overwhelming percentage of surface corrections.

If the role of reading during the writing process has been oversimplified, current reading theorists may be of some help. Nancy Shanklin (1984) suggests that reading during the writing process and writing itself may involve similar mental processes. In both reading and writing, revisions occur if one has lost sight of "the meaning potential under construction" and if one "wants to confirm or disconfirm the meaning network already created" (p. 12).

This emphasis on a mental representation of a text is reiterated by Teun van Dijk and Walter Kintsch (1983) in their definition of discourse processing (comprehension), "a strategic process in which a mental representation is constructed of the discourse in memory, using both external and internal types of information, with the goal of interpreting (understanding) the discourse" (p. 6). For discourse production, the task is the construction of a mental representation of a discourse plan which can, strategically, be executed with an end goal of a syntactically formatted, coherent text. Although comprehension and production are not simply inverse processes, they are related. The broader notion of revision suggested by Shanklin above allows us to think about how we evaluate the evolving mental representation of the text during production and comprehension.

REVISION AS SHAPING AT THE POINT OF INSCRIPTION

Revision is clearly a complex phenomenon, initiated by a range of creative impulses, reflecting not only repair but a constant reevaluation of the evolving text and the writer's mental representation of that text. In most writer's work, it is the very *potential* for revision that allows the process to move forward efficiently. Without the option to revise—to evaluate the evolving plan and the text—progress in producing any but the most facile, rote texts would grind to a halt.

Studying Goal-Oriented Behavior

Just as James Britton describes the process of "shaping at the point of utterance" as a purposeful journey, Herbert Simon (1969/1981) in his chapter, "The Psychology of Thinking," focuses on the path of an ant in order to highlight purposeful, goal-directed behavior. Picture, he suggests, from above, the path of an ant making its way across the dunes and valleys of a windswept beach:

The ant is moving toward its colony, but, because it cannot anticipate the obstacles in its path, it adapts to the terrain of the environment. Looking at the path alone, not knowing whether it represents the path of a skier or the route of an elevated train, Simon asks, "Why does it [the path] not aim directly from its starting point to its goal?" (p. 63). Simon's answer has to do with the relation of the behaving organism to the outer environment. Turning, then, to the study of human cognition, Simon proposes:

> A thinking human being is an adaptive system. . . . To the extent that he is effectively adaptive, his behavior will reflect characteristics largely of the outer environment (in light of his goals) and will reveal only a few limiting properties of the inner environment—of the psychological machinery that enables a person to think. (p. 66)

In Simon's example the outer environment is clearly external—a windswept beach. For studying human cognition, he contrasts the notion of an inner environment (our psychological machinery) with an external environment to highlight the flexible nature of our goal-oriented, information-packed memory and consciousness.

Writing in Real Time

The information about the outer environment for this study comes largely from textual and rhetorical analysis (Cooper, 1983; Matsuhashi & Quinn, 1984). In a recent essay, Charles Cooper and I (Cooper & Matsuhashi, 1983) identified an incomplete but staggering list of possible considerations during sentence production. After constructing a discourse-level plan for the text, the writer searches long-term memory to identify an appropriate chunk of information, formulates a proposition, chooses a predicate for the proposition, determines the speech act for the proposition, decides which information will be treated as given or new, makes specific lexical choices, and formats the sentence in syntactically acceptable form. These decisions—guided by global plans for audience, goals, and schema—occur at the point of inscription. Subject to the constraints of real-time processing, they require the writer to align a complex set of cognitive processes with a forward-moving time line.

The inner psychological machinery, discussed by Simon above, places a small number of limitations, or parameters, on an otherwise highly adaptable cognitive system during real-time processing. Simon isolates two limitations which apply to all sorts of cognitive activities, including writing and revising. First, it takes about 5seconds to fix a chunk of information in short-term memory. Second, short-term memory can hold only a limited number of chunks.

Writers must function within these constraints. Fortunately, though, memory and planning operate strategically, grouping related bits of information in response to intentions and goals (Simon 1969/1981; Hayes-Roth & Hayes-Roth, 1979). For the study of writing, this means that, even though one has limited focal attention to devote to any particular aspect of the writing task, one can relegate some well-learned activities to an automatic mode, while focusing one's attention on the areas that need it (Cooper & Matsuhashi, 1983). Also, the writer must make scheduling decisions about what will be done in what order (de Beaugrande, 1982). Revision, then, offers a strategy for reducing complexity during writing by allowing the writer to shift focal attention to an evaluation mode, revising the plan for the text and perhaps by altering the text itself.

Methods for Facilitating Revision

For inexperienced writers, it is these limitations coupled with inefficient and ineffective writing strategies that make success so difficult to achieve. Revision, for these writers, is a trap, not an opportunity (Shaughnessy, 1977). In order to study cognitive processes during revision, writing researchers such as Marlene Scardamalia and Carl Bereiter (1983) and Eleanor Gordon and I (Matsuhashi & Gordon, 1985) have developed procedures to help the writer orchestrate his or her divided attention.

Although these studies diverge in many ways, they share the assumption that young and inexperienced writers do not revise effectively because, under the pressure of real-time processing, their attention is consumed by the low-level problems of generating and inscribing the text:

> Attention to one thing means neglect of another, and so one can never be sure that the child's failure to do something in writing indicates a lack of competence. It may merely reflect an inability to direct cognitive resources to that aspect of writing when it is needed. (Scardamalia & Bereiter, 1983, p. 68)

Using a simplified model of the revision process called CDO (Compare, Diagnose, and Operate), Scardamalia and Bereiter arrived at a procedure which, they believed, could lift the burden of scheduling and allow the child to shift his or her attention to the revision process at the end of each sentence. Children in grades 4, 6, and 8, after writing a sentence, engaged in the CDO process by first choosing an evaluation statement which suited that sentence (compare); second, telling why that statement was appropriate (diagnose); and third, deciding what change to make in the existing sentence (operate).

This procedure, carried out after each sentence was written, was used for the "on-line" group. Another group (the "evaluation-after" group) carried out the CDO process on each sentence only after the text had been completed. In both treatment groups, children in grades 4 and 6 produced compositions of the same length, although grade-8 compositions in the "on-line" group were significantly shorter than those in the "evaluation after" group. It may be that as the eighth-graders' ability to produce longer texts developed, the CDO process presented new scheduling difficulties by focusing attention on evaluation to the exclusion of generation processes.

In interviews following the study, students largely agreed that the CDO process helped them review their texts in ways they never could before. Although the students revised more than would normally be expected, the revisions did not improve the quality of the texts. Further analyses, though, suggested that students were quite accurate in evaluating (compare) their sentences, that is, in "detecting mismatches between intended and actual text, when prompted to look for them" (p. 92). They were unable, however, to correct the difficulty at the diagnose and operate stages.

Eleanor Gordon and I (Matsuhashi & Gordon, 1985) designed a study to test the hypothesis that the typically low-level revisions by college students resulted not so much from a lack of competence but from an inability to look beyond the local span of text to consider a mental representation of the text as a whole. In addition, we suspected that the direction, "Revise!" elicited a schooled response pointing only to a limited range of surface-structure corrections.

Working with three groups of college students, we asked a first group to reread and revise an essay they had written during the previous class. We asked a second group to "add five things" to an essay after rereading but while still looking at the text. The third group was asked, after rereading, to list five additions on the back of the essay and then to insert the additions into the text. This third group produced significantly more high-level additions to the texts than did the second group, which, in turn, produced significantly more high-level additions to the text than did the "revise" group.

We concluded that, when the writer adds to the text while looking at it, to some extent he or she has been freed by the instruction to add (only one of many possible revision strategies). The presence of the text, though, can still distract the writer and interfere with attempts to focus on high-level revisions. When the writer plans additions to an unseen text, as in the third group, the plans are based on a mental representation of the text. The opportunity to plan—free from both the presence of the text and from the efforts of prose production—offers an incentive to work exclusively with the idea structure of the text.

Both of these studies developed techniques to facilitate revision based on assumptions about cognitive processing during writing. Scardamalia and Bereiter's (1983) CDO procedure helped students focus attention, initially, on a wide range of possible problems in a text, while my research with Eleanor Gordon shifted the writers' attention to only one revision strategy—addition.

Shaping (But Not Revising) at the Point of Inscription

Presumably, as the writer "pushes the boat out," she has some idea of where the text is headed. At the point of inscription the writer continually makes decisions, pushing the text forward, evaluating the plan for text, revising the plan, or altering the text.

In a two-sentence example (taken from Matsuhashi & Quinn, 1984), we observe one writer composing two contiguous sentences from a report on a play about Daniel Webster. What is especially interesting about these sentences is the way in which John, the writer, adjusted the underlying semantic content of the sentence to the real-time demands of producing syntactically correct, coherent prose. In writing the first sentence, the pattern of pauses reveals the process of shaping at the point of inscription. I have separated each word by periods (each period reflects 1second) to display, graphically, John's continued indecision as the "field of choices narrows" (Shaughnessy, 1977, p. 44):

.....Once.we...had....everything..figured...as. to.........
what.we.wanted.to.do.......,.........there.was..now.........
the.matter.of..researching.this..remarkable.man.

Although one doesn't usually plan sentences completely and then transcribe the thought into language, it would seem that John had begun writing prematurely, before he had a clear enough plan to carry him through.

In sharp contrast, the next sentence seems to flow from idea to inscription with little hesitation, reflecting the ease of reporting a well-practiced agent/action format. Notice that in the following sentence the longest pause appears before John begins to inscribe the sentence:

.....Each.of.us.laid.our.hands.on.every.book.we.could.find.
on.the.man ... and..read.eagerly.

In the first example, John did not revise, even though doing so could have repaired some of the sentence's faultiness. As we see in Edna's revision patterns, when a writer does revise, we obtain striking evidence of the process of shaping at the point of inscription.

OBSERVING REVISION AT THE POINT OF INSCRIPTION

The Research Problem

Theoretical Perspectives. The key phrase, "shaping at the point of inscription," suggests that cognitive processes during writing are flexible and that writing is produced as it is organized, in response to goals (Matsuhashi, 1982). Several current theoretical models present detailed accounts of the sequencing and organization of decisions during writing, and although they may differ on details, they all describe written language production in a way that accounts for real-time constraints and the complexity of the final product (de Beaugrande, 1980, 1982; Chafe, 1977; Cooper & Matsuhashi, 1983; van Dijk & Kintsch, 1983; Flower & Hayes, 1981; Frederiksen, Frederiksen & Bracewell, this volume; Scardamalia & Bereiter, 1983; and Scardamalia, Bereiter, & Goelman, 1982).

Of continuing interest to these theorists is the relation of the underlying semantic content to its syntactic representation in the surface text. Wallace Chafe (1977) uses the term verbalization to cover "all those processes by which nonverbal knowledge is turned into language" (p. 41). Through a process of successively refined chunking activity, the speaker identifies relational groups of case frames (e.g., agent, action) which are amenable to expression in surface structure.

Teun van Dijk and Walter Kintsch (1983), too, describe the strategic, goal-oriented nature of production processes:

There exists a flexible mechanism which at the same time constructs semantic representations, lexical expressions, and their syntactic and phonological structures, taking into account various kinds of information, such as knowledge, goals, local and global constraints at various levels, and other contextual information of the communicative setting. (p. 264)

Robert de Beaugrande (1980) uses the concepts of "conceptual and sequential connectivity" to explain production processes. Sequential connectivity refers to the arrangement of elements in the surface text, and conceptual connectivity refers to the network of underlying concepts and relations. During production, the writer's focus of attention can shift from a concern with the conceptual nature of the ideas to a concern for their expression in the surface structure.

The distinction between conceptual plans and sequential plans is central to this study. During real-time production processes, conceptual plans do not necessarily precede sequential plans. Instead, the writer moves from thought to language in a highly flexible manner defined by the current goals for the text. Yet, when a writer interrupts a relatively fluent production process to evaluate the plan for the text, he or she has an option to revise. The content of that revision suggests whether the writer's focus is primarily on the conceptual or sequential nature of the plan. The research problem for this study, then, is to find a way to document the nature of one writer's revisions from this real-time perspective.

Limitations of Existing Revision Taxonomies.   This perspective casts doubt upon several of the recent coding schemes or taxonomies devised to study revision patterns. Taxonomies, such as Sommers' (1980) or Bridwell's (1980), identified revision operations (e.g., addition, substitution) or levels (e.g., word, phrase, clause). Incidences of these revisions, tallied over several drafts or compared among groups of varying skill, often obscure what we can learn by watching a writer revising the text at the point of inscription.

Consider, for instance, a revision in which the writer substituted the transition "conversely" for "and." Under the product-oriented taxonomies mentioned above, this change would have been classified as a single-word revision, a category which suggested to Bridwell and Sommers low-level, relatively unimportant revisions. Yet, in this case, the substitution of one highly specific transition for an overused, general one suggests that the writer has discovered a logical relationship in the text.

We might ask whether this single revision occurred within a constellation of related revisions that corroborate inferences about the writer's focus of attention and plans for the text. We might also ask whether that revision occurred at the time "and" was originally written or whether it occurred later, after the writer had completed more of the text. This real-time information supplements what can be learned from revised drafts alone.

Questions for Research

The purpose of this study is to develop and apply a "process-oriented" taxonomy to on-line revision data. This taxonomy will examine revisions from three perspectives:

1. *Content.* By examining the revised segment of text, what can we learn about the writer's focus on conceptual and sequential aspects of text production?
2. *Process.* By tracking the temporal order of revisions and by charting the kinds of revisions which are made literally at the point of inscription and those which involve forays back into the text, what can we learn about the recursiveness of the writing process?
3. *Discourse.* Because this is primarily a study of sentence production set in a well-defined discourse context, what can we learn about the influence of discourse on revision and sentence production?

Data Analysis

The data for this observational study consists of the first drafts of one generalizing essay and two reporting essays, all written by Edna, the competent high school senior we are studying. The data for this study—timed videotapes of Edna's writing—were selected from material collected in a case study based on four writers (Matsuhashi, 1981). Descriptions of the writing tasks are included in Appendix I.

Subject. At the time the data for this study was collected, Edna, a black, middle-class, 16-year-old, was a senior in a suburban Buffalo high school, majoring in math and science and planning to attend the State University of New York at Buffalo following her graduation.

Edna was 1 of 4 students chosen from the 20 top writers in her high school to participate in a study of writing processes (Matsuhashi, 1981). Although revision was not explored in that study, it was readily apparent that 2 of the writers in the study rarely revised and 2 (1 of whom was Edna) revised quite often, making their revisions a rich subject for inquiry.

The material from Edna's initial interview, largely recollections of her writing experiences, provides a backdrop for further study of her writing processes. Barbara Tomlinson (unpublished manuscript) argues that writers' recollections and interpretations of their writing processes, such as Edna's, provide a definition of their writing situation, which, in turn, guides behavior. This information has often been disregarded by writing researchers because of its apparent lack of veridicality. Tomlinson explains:

Reviewing past writing experiences, and anticipating future writing experiences, writers must talk about, think about, make sense of the seemingly inaccessible reality of their composing; they must bring structure and shape to those inchoate experiences. To do so they construct interpretations of the composing process and their own engagement in it. (p. 6)

A writer's interpretations, Tomlinson argues, are not veridical by a psychologist's standard, but they do, indeed, reflect reality—the writer's "interpretive reality." If, for instance, students define their writing situation as one "in which they are to produce neat, grammatically correct summaries of derived information . . ." (p. 18), and if that view is supported and encouraged by teachers, it is unlikely that they will experience writing as a meaning-making enterprise. Edna's view of writing is quite different; and, during an initial interview, she eagerly recounted memories of writing experiences in school and out.

Edna's comments suggest that her attitudes about writing do not result solely from her experiences in school. She is independent; when a teacher advised her to write an outline, she evaluated that advice against her experience. She understands writing as a way of exploring ideas and feelings, not simply as a way of communicating or as a way of achieving a high grade for an error-free composition. Given Edna's comments, I felt I could proceed with an analysis of her revisions, confident that she did not cling to a narrow definition of revision as correction and repair.

A Notation System for Tracking Revisions.   For purposes of unambiguous data analysis, the following behavioral definition of a revision was used: A revision is an episode in which the writer stops the pen's forward movement and makes a change in the previously written text. The writer may then either resume the pen's forward movement or make another change at another location. Pauses associated with revisions were counted from the time the writer stopped the pen's forward movement until the writer moved to another location or resumed the forward inscription of the text.[1]

The notational system displayed in Figure 1 allowed me to track Edna's revisions. In the scripted portion of the example, we can see that John (another writer from Matsuhashi, 1981) deleted the word "other" and substituted the word "first."

Because, by looking at this example alone, it is not possible to determine when the revision was actually made, I developed the notation system displayed in the second portion of Figure 1. The circled 5 indicates that this

---

[1] Because pauses were counted before and after each word in a revision episode the number of pauses in the study is higher than the number of revisions. No pause, however, was counted twice.

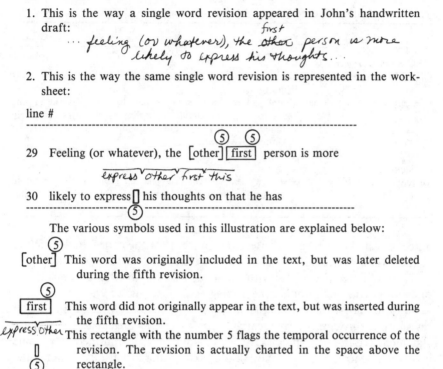

1. This is the way a single word revision appeared in John's handwritten draft:

2. This is the way the same single word revision is represented in the worksheet:

line #

The various symbols used in this illustration are explained below:

[other] This word was originally included in the text, but was later deleted during the fifth revision.

first This word did not originally appear in the text, but was inserted during the fifth revision.

This rectangle with the number 5 flags the temporal occurrence of the revision. The revision is actually charted in the space above the rectangle.

FIG. 1. Worksheet for Indicating the Location and Time of Revisions

was John's fifth revision. It occurs in line 29 of the text, but John did not actually revise until after he had written the word "express" on line 30.

Edna's generalizing essay, coded in this way, is included in Appendix II.

Content of the Revision. A coding scheme was necessary that would support the theoretical assumptions of this study. This scheme aimed to uncover whether, during revision, the focus of the writer's attention was on primarily conceptual or sequential concerns (see Table 1).

I established this coding scheme after working with several graduate students.[2] After trying several more elaborate versions of this scheme, we decided to maintain only the most crucial distinctions between conceptual and sequential plans. I found that, through discussion, we could readily

[2] The graduate students who worked with me on the coding scheme are B.J. Wagner, Marianthe Karanikas, Reginald Johnson, Brenda Nash, and Katie Witek. I also want to thank Anne Doyle for her help as a research assistant on an early segment of this project.

Table 1. Content Coding Scheme for Revisions

Category	Explanation
(1) Conceptual Plans	
Global Discourse Plans	Evaluating the plan for the text and evaluating the extant text against goals.
Conceptual Sentence Plans	Chunking idea units; testing the verbalizability of an idea as the basis for a grammatically complete assertion; successively detailed decisions regarding semantic relationships (e.g., cohesion, given-new).
(2) Sequential Plans	
Textual Sentence Plans	Assigning lexical items and clausal structures to semantic relationships; sequencing; grammaticality; correctness; and inscription.

agree on whether a revision reflected a concern for the conceptual structure at the global or sentence level or for the sequential surface structure.

To familiarize the reader with the data, I'll describe the revisions in the opening portion of Edna's generalizing essay (see Figure 2).

In Edna's first three attempts at an opening sentence (lines 1 through 7; revisions 1 through 3), she searches for a way to articulate the general statement required by the task: ". . . reasons or ways that people become involved in sports. . . ." Although the juxtaposing of various sentence elements could be described in terms of their surface syntax, the elements reflect conceptual concerns about whether "people" or "sports" will be the causal agent in her argument.

By lines 8 and 9 Edna had committed her essay to an opening that was similar to her first try in line 1. Because, during the first three revisions, Edna was framing an initial generalization for the essay, these revisions were each coded as conceptual revisions at the sentence level (see Table 1).

Revisions 4 and 5 (adding "emotionally" and "to" to line 9) were classified as sequential revisions because they fill out an established clausal structure and do not significantly alter the meaning of the sentence. (Line 9, however, was later deleted during the 16th revision).

During the 6th revision (line 11), Edna stopped the inscription of an appositive series to cross out lines 1 through 7 again. This conceptual revision, reflecting the global discourse plan, confirmed that she was on the right track and could proceed with the development of her general statement.

Revisions 7 and 8, classified as sequential plans, add team names to the T-shirts and helmets that spectators buy. Revision 9, also classified as a sequential plan revision, corrected an inscription error, adding an "r" to the end of "whatever."

FIG. 2.   The First Page of Edna's Generalizing Essay

Two revisions on this page (revisions 16 and 18, lines 9 and 15, respectively) occurred, temporally, much later in the text. Edna was on the second page and had just begun a new paragraph. Suddenly, in the middle of a word, she turned back to page 1 and, without rereading, inserted a period after "together" (line 9), and crossed out the remainder of the sentence. Later, in an interview, she explained, "I felt it [line 9] was unnecessary and confused the direction of the piece. I didn't want to go on—in that paragraph—and talk about getting emotionally involved." This conceptual revision reflected Edna's global discourse plans.

After completing a paragraph near the bottom of page 2 Edna put her pencil down, sat back, and lifted page 1 to a comfortable reading position.

Table 2.   Percentage of Time Used by One Writer in Three
Activities: Inscribing, Pausing while Drafting, and Pausing while
Revising

	Inscribing the Text	Pausing During Forward Drafting	Pausing During Revision Episodes
Generalizing (43:00)[a]	26.5	42.9	30.6
Reporting #1 (27:32)	22.2	52.9	24.9
Reporting #2 (45:11)	32.1	56.1	11.8

[a] Total writing time in minutes and seconds.

She put the page down when, by the puzzled expression on her face, she
had found a sentence which did not read well (lines 14 and 15). First, she
added the word "team" at the end of the sentence; still unsatisfied,
she crossed out everything after "but" and added "communities team
win." She didn't reread the sentence and didn't notice that she was still
missing an article and that she had gotten the possessive wrong. In her
mind's eye she had corrected the problem.

Distance of the Revision from the Point of Inscription.   In view of the
fact that when we look at a finished text or even a copy of a rough draft,
we forget the fluidity of its production, it seemed to me important to
number the revisions according to their temporal occurrence. I further
noted the distance of the revision from the point of inscription. If Edna
revised the word or unit of language she had just completed, the revision
was coded as *Si* (Sentence-immediate revision). If she revised elsewhere
within the current sentence, the revision was labeled *Sd* (Sentence-distal).
If she revised beyond the current sentence, the revision was labeled *T* (text
revision). With this coding category, I hoped to discover what "shaping at
the point of inscription" meant for the recursive quality of writing. At any
one point in the text, what impelled Edna to revise beyond the current
word or sentence?

Summary Data for Revisions
Summary information about revising helps determine its relative temporal role in each of the three essays. Table 2 indicates that in each of
the three essays Edna spends no more than one-third of her time with
her pen in hand, actually inscribing the text. The remaining two-thirds
(or more) of the time she spent during writing was taken up by pauses
which resulted in the continued forward inscription of the text or by

Table 3. Pause Time Summary

Mean Pause Length	Pauses During Inscription	Pauses During Revision
Generalizing (333 words)[a]	2.9s ($N = 380$)	12.2s ($N = 65$)
Reporting #1 (248 words)	3.4s ($N = 253$)	16.5s ($N = 25$)
Reporting #2 (566 words)	2.7s ($N = 572$)	14.5s ($N = 22$)

[a] Total number of words in the completed draft.

pauses which resulted in a revision. She spent the highest percentage of time revising the generalizing essay and successively less time in each of the two reporting essays.

The large difference in the mean length of pauses during writing and pauses during revision stays relatively constant for all three essays (see Table 3). The low mean for pauses during inscribing reflects, for the most part, fluent production and some longer pauses during which revision might have been contemplated. The smaller number of pauses which result in revision are, for the most part, lengthy pauses.

Results

Comparing Conceptual and Sequential Revisions. Because the central theoretical distinction informing this revision study concerns conceptual plans and sequential plans, I looked for differences in the amount of pause time associated with each type of revision in three essays taken as a group. However, the mean pause length is nearly the same for conceptual revision ($M = 14.5$, $N = 32$) as for sequential revision ($M = 13.2$, $N = 80$).

Differences by Discourse Type. As I explored further, I discovered that, in fact, there were pause-time differences between the two revision categories when viewed in a discourse context. As Table 4 indicates, Edna uses her time differently when revising the generalizing essay and the reporting essays (see also Table 4A).

In writing the generalizing essay, Edna pauses for longer periods of time, on average, for revisions reflecting conceptual plans than for revisions reflecting sequential plans (16.5 vs. 10.1). In writing the reporting essay, a very different pattern appears. Here, Edna spends less time on revisions reflecting conceptual plans than on revisions reflecting sequential plans (10.6 vs. 17.3).

These results are quite striking and I explore their significance for Edna's writing process in the discussion section.

Table 4.   Mean Pause Length[a] of Conceptual and Sequential Revisions in Generalizing and Reporting

	Generalizing	Reporting[b]
Conceptual Revision	16.5 ($N = 21$)	10.6 ($N = 11$)
Sequential Revision	10.1 ($N = 44$)	17.3 ($N = 36$)

[a] Pause time reported in seconds.
[b] These results reflect the combined data from two reporting essays with roughly parallel results. The results for each reporting essay are shown in Table 4A.

Table 4A.   Mean Pause Length[a] of Conceptual and Sequential Revisions in Two Reporting Essays

	Reporting #1	Reporting #2
Conceptual Revision	11.00 ($N = 6$)	10.2 ($N = 5$)
Sequential Revision	16.7 ($N = 16$)	17.3 ($N = 20$)

Note: The results of both reporting essays displayed below were averaged together to achieve a higher number of revisions. This table reveals that the patterns in both essays are parallel.
[a] Pause time reported in seconds.

Table 5.   Percentage of Pause Time during Revisions at Three Locations

	Revising at the Point of Inscription (Si)	Revising within the current sentence (Sd)	Revising beyond the current sentence (T)
Generalizing	9.6	54.3	36.0
Reporting No. 1	24.3	44.3	31.3
Reporting No. 2	7.5	37.4	55.0

Revising at the Point of Inscription.   Table 5 surveys the percentage of pause time used by Edna at the three revision locations identified in the research questions: at the precise point of inscription (Si), within the current sentence (Sd), and beyond the current sentence (T).

At first glance, these percentages suggest what is obvious to anyone who observes his or her own writing practice: That revising, literally, "at the *point* of utterance" is only one of several locations for revision. For Edna, this requires the least amount of time. Further, the phrase "shaping at the point of utterance" ought to be revised to "shaping at the *moment* of utterance." A real-time approach to revising asserts that at any *moment* during composing the writer reevaluates the text as a mental representation and as a written artifact.

The data reported here raise questions about the nature of the revisions that absorb various percentages of pause time. For instance, what kind of revisions (conceptual or sequential) comprise the 24.3% of time spent at the point of utterance in the first reporting essay? In the second reporting essay, what kind of revisions absorbed 55% of Edna's revising time? Do these data reflect patterns related to the discourse task?

Table 6.   Location of Revision[a] in Conceptual and Sequential Revisions for Generalizing and Reporting

	Generalizing	Reporting[b]
Conceptual Revision	S—10	S—11
	T—11	T— 0
Sequential Revision	S—41	S—28
	T— 3	T— 8

   [a] The categories of Si (Revising at the Point of Utterance) and Sd (Revising Within the Current Sentence) have been combined to heighten the comparison between revisions within the current sentence and revisions in other portions of the text.

Revising at the Point of Inscription in a Discourse Context.   Table 6 displays the revision categories (conceptual or sequential) that occur at two locations in the generalizing and reporting essays. As the table indicates, I have combined the revisions which occur at the point of utterance and within the current sentence (under the heading "S") to heighten the contrast between relatively local revisions and revisions which involve forays back into the text.

With this additional data, different revising patterns emerge for generalizing and reporting. In composing the generalizing essay, Edna uses her forays back into the text for a substantial number of conceptual revisions (11 vs. 3 sequential revisions). Referring back to Table 4, these conceptual revisions are the time-consuming ones. By contrast, in composing the reporting essay, all of Edna's conceptual revisions are completed "on-line," within the current sentence, taking less time than the sequential revisions.

In response to the questions posed about Table 5, during the first reporting essay, Edna spent 24.3% of her time making six conceptual plan revisions. In the second reporting essay, Edna spent over half (55%) of her revising time reading through the text, but making only sequential plan revisions.

Discussion

The single most important observation from these data is that Edna adjusts her revision strategies for the discourse requirements of the two tasks. Below, I'll describe how she manipulates the possible range of revision strategies for the generalizing and reporting essays.

The Logic of Generalizing.   These results suggest that Edna's revising patterns are strongly influenced by the discourse requirements of the task. The logic of the generalizing task requires that Edna construct the layout of her argument within the first paragraph and elaborate on it in the succeeding text.

The real-time record of Edna's revising activity helps us to document this process. She reviews sentences locally, revising, for the most part, on the basis of sequential plans (see Table 6). These revisions require less time ($M = 10.1$ s) than the conceptual revisions, most of which are completed while reviewing her plan for the entire text. When she reviews the text and her mental representation of that text, she invests more time, revising conceptually the layout of the argument. As Table 4 indicated, conceptual revisions in generalizing require, on average, 16.5 seconds, and many of these revisions are carried out beyond the current sentence (see Table 6).

Here is an example from Edna's generalizing of a time-consuming conceptual revision which occurred beyond the current sentence (see lines 20–41 in Appendix II).

Edna had written the following, making several local, sequential revisions which I will not discuss here:

> People will sit in bars together or at home to watch team sports on television and comment on calls the referee has made. They'll discuss over super-star players and why or why don't they think that person deserves the money he or she is being paid. If a basketball team is playing at home, they know they will have what is called a home team advantage. The people will root and holler everytime their team makes a basket but will become silent when the other team shoots.

Edna read the essay up to this point, stopping only to make one sequential plan revision. In a post-writing interview she explained that she was unhappy with the section about what "super-star" players are paid:

> I just left the idea of super-star players hanging in mid-air. I just left it open and went on to a new subject that made this seem weak because I didn't name any reasons. I was thinking about doing the whole thing over and then I decided not to. I just blocked this [If a basketball team . . .] as a separate paragraph and then put an arrow down here, because I just felt that I had to continue the thought.

Edna circled the section about the home-team advantage, holding it in abeyance, while continuing the section about super-star players in a way that supports her initial generalization (that sports cause people to come closer together):

This makes a good conversation piece and helps people to relate to one another. It aids in "breaking the ice" between persons who may have otherwise not been able to communicate.

Finally, Edna returned to the point about a home-team advantage, citing an example of a fight in which the fans had participated on behalf of the home team.

Facing the incongruity of the two sections, Edna nearly gave up and started all over again (a common, but often unsuccessful strategy among beginning writers); but she resisted. Instead, she seemed, on her own, to summon up the same sort of strategy imposed by the Matsuhashi and Gordon study (1985) on the third group: adding to the unseen text. In order to make the initial revision, which moved the "home team" section to another location as a paragraph opener, and then to add the necessary detail filling out each of her claims, Edna had to manipulate a mental representation of the text and did so successfully.

The Logic of Reporting. Because of its event-based narrative format, the reporting task required that Edna remember only one segment of that report at a time. Without having to keep the complex road map of generalizing in memory all at one time, she is free to compose in a sentence-by-sentence fashion.

All of Edna's conceptual revisions in reporting are made on-line, within the current sentence. She makes sequential revisions, however, both within the current sentence and throughout the text (see Table 6). Temporally, Edna uses her time quite differently in the reporting pieces than in the generalizing piece. In reporting, the time-consuming pauses occur during sequential revisions ($M = 17.3$ s) which take place as she reviews the entire text. In these instances, she appears to be making what Flower and Hayes (1981) call "editing interrupts," low-level corrections and repairs. Edna might have given her generalizing essay such a last-minute reading, but time (or, perhaps, energy) did not allow. She had already used up 43 of her 50 min when she reached the end of the essay.

Here is an example, in the 7th revision below, of an on-line, conceptual revision that illustrates Edna's struggle to align an idea unit with a sequential, syntactic structure. (Revisions 8 and 10 are sequential revisions.) She had been describing in great detail the food and treats at a Halloween party her brother had once given. She must have had a mental picture of the candy's presentation but was unsure how to articulate that picture. Here is how her struggle to move from idea to language progressed:

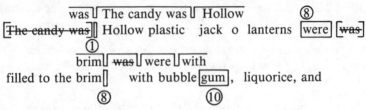

assortments of candy.

In this example, Edna found that she could better articulate her memory of the candy by describing the containers first and then the contents. Through this revision we obtain a trace of her attentional focus and decision-making process. When Edna reviewed the text as a whole, she made only low-level editing changes, one of which was to add the word "gum" to the above example.

Implications for Research and Teaching.   These results are important for a number of reasons. First, they confirm the importance of close textual analysis and what it can suggest about the writing process. Second, this close-grained, observational account stands as a caution against ready-made categories such as "expert-novice" differences, which in Edna's case would have obscured the contrast between her reporting and generalizing revision strategies. We need to continue to observe, firsthand, what reasonably competent writers actually do when they revise.

These observations inform both research design and pedagogy. In reviewing the Scardamalia and Bereiter (1983) study and my study with Eleanor Gordon (Matsuhashi & Gordon, 1985) we must question the a priori logic of both research designs. The logic of the Scardamalia and Bereiter design favored "on-line" revision processes and my research with Eleanor Gordon favored an "addition-after" process. The new information suggested by this study is that a competent writer might choose to schedule his or her revision activity differently (on-line vs. addition-after) depending on the discourse demands of the task. Likewise, the results of this study suggest that instruction in revision should take into account the demands that the discourse task makes on scheduling and focus of attention.

APPENDIX I

Generalizing Task

Think of a general statement that seems true to you about the various reasons or ways that people become involved in sports—whether as spectators or as participants. Organizing carefully, illustrate the generalization with examples from among the things you have observed, experienced, seen in movies or on T.V., or read about that led you to make this generalization in the first place. Write this piece for a "The Way People Are" section of the *Spectrum*. Your purpose is to inform your readers in a sincere, calm, reasonable way about your views on the general statement you have chosen.

Reporting Task #1

Choose an incident that you were involved in during elementary school or while you were very young. Write about the incident for the "Nostalgic Times" section of the *Spectrum*. Use a sincere, reasonable, informative writing voice. Your purpose is to inform your readers about what happened to you on that day in your past.

Reporting Task #2

Choose an incident that you were involved in during your first two years of high school. Write about the incident for the "Nostalgic Times" section of the *Spectrum*. Use a sincere, reasonable, informative writing voice. Your purpose is to inform your readers about what happened to you on that day in your past.

APPENDIX II: LOCATION AND TIME OF REVISIONS IN EDNA'S GENERALIZING ESSAY

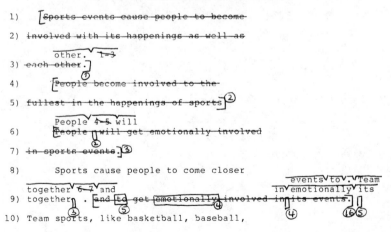

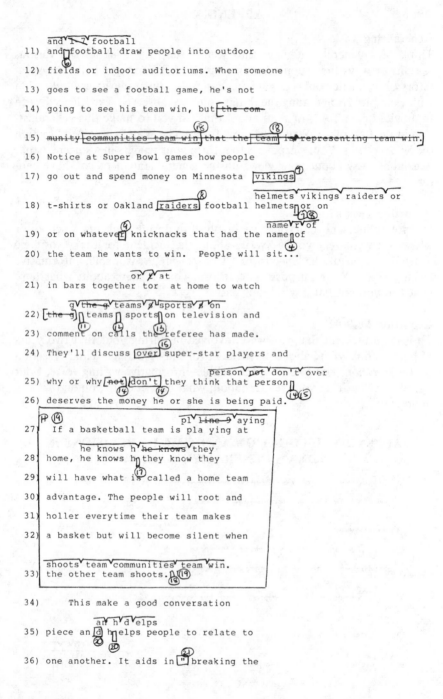

11) and football draw people into outdoor

12) fields or indoor auditoriums. When someone

13) goes to see a football game, he's not

14) going to see his team win, but the com-

15) munity communities team win that the team is representing team win.

16) Notice at Super Bowl games how people

17) go out and spend money on Minnesota vikings

18) t-shirts or Oakland raiders football helmets or on

19) or on whatever knicknacks that had the name of

20) the team he wants to win. People will sit...

21) in bars together tor at home to watch

22) the g teams sports on television and

23) comment on calls the referee has made.

24) They'll discuss over super-star players and

25) why or why not don't they think that person

26) deserves the money he or she is being paid.

27) If a basketball team is pla ying at

28) home, he knows h they know they

29) will have what is called a home team

30) advantage. The people will root and

31) holler everytime their team makes

32) a basket but will become silent when

33) the other team shoots.

34)   This make a good conversation

35) piece an d h elps people to relate to

36) one another. It aids in " breaking the

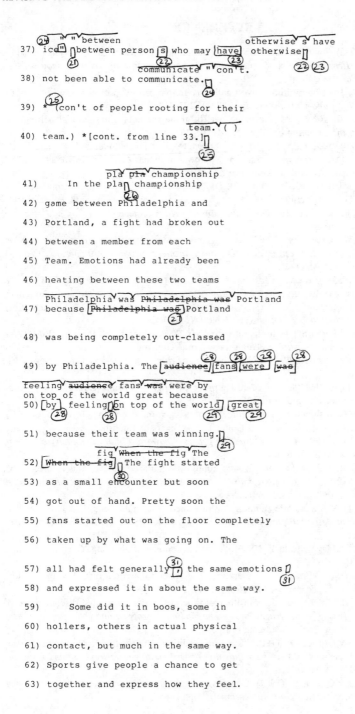

37) ice between person s who may have otherwise

38) not been able to communicate. con't.

39) * (con't of people rooting for their

40) team.) *[cont. from line 33.]

41)   In the plan championship

42) game between Philadelphia and

43) Portland, a fight had broken out

44) between a member from each

45) Team. Emotions had already been

46) heating between these two teams

47) because Philadelphia was Portland

48) was being completely out-classed

49) by Philadelphia. The audience fans were was

50) by feeling on top of the world great because

51) because their team was winning.

52) When the fig The fight started

53) as a small encounter but soon

54) got out of hand. Pretty soon the

55) fans started out on the floor completely

56) taken up by what was going on. The

57) all had felt generally the same emotions

58) and expressed it in about the same way.

59)   Some did it in boos, some in

60) hollers, others in actual physical

61) contact, but much in the same way.

62) Sports give people a chance to get

63) together and express how they feel.

REFERENCES

Bartlett, E. (1982). Learning to revise: Some component processes. In M. Nystrand (Ed.), *What writers know: The language, process, and structure of written discourse*. New York: Academic Press.

Blau, S. (1983). Invisible writing: Investigating cognitive processes in composition. *College Composition and Communication, 34* (3), 297–312.

Bridwell, L. (1980). Revising strategies in twelfth grade students' transactional writing. *Research in the Teaching of Writing, 14,* 197–222.

Britton, J. (1980). Shaping at the point of utterance. In A. Freedman & I. Pringle (Eds.), *Reinventing the rhetorical tradition*. Ottowa, Canada: Carleton University, L & S Books for the Canadian Council of Teachers of English.

Cazden, C.B., Michaels, S., & Tabors, P. (1985). Spontaneous repairs in sharing time narratives: The intersection of metalinguistic awareness, speech event, and narrative style. In S.W. Freedman (Ed.), *The acquisition of written language: Revision and response*. Norwood, NJ: Ablex.

Chafe, W. (1977). Creativity in verbalization and its implications for the nature of stored knowledge. In R. Freedle (Ed.), *Discourse production and comprehension* (Vol. 1), Norwood, NJ: Ablex.

Cooper, C.R. (1983). Procedures for describing written texts. In P. Mosenthal, L. Tamor, & S. Walmsley (Eds.), *Research on writing: Principles & methods*. New York: Longman.

Cooper, C., & Matsuhashi, A. (1983). A theory of the writing process. In M. Martlew (Ed.), *The psychology of written language*. New York: Wiley.

Daiute, C. (1984). Performance limits on writers. In R. Beach and L.S. Bridwell (Eds.), *New directions in composition research*. New York: Guilford.

van Dijk, T.A., & Kintsch, W. (1983). *Strategies of discourse comprehension*. New York: Academic Press.

Flower, L., & Hayes, J. (1981). A cognitive process theory of writing. *College Composition and Communication, 32* (4), 365–387.

Gere, A.R. (1982). Insights from the blind: Composing without revising. In R. Sudol (Ed.), *Revising*. Urbana, IL: National Council of Teachers of English.

de Beaugrande, R. (1980). *Text, discourse, & process: Toward a multidisciplinary science of texts*. Norwood, NJ: Ablex.

de Beaugrande, R. (1982). Psychology and composition: Past, present, and future. In M. Nystrand (Ed.), *What writers know: The language, process, and structure of written discourse*. New York: Academic Press.

Haugleland, J. (1981). Semantic engines: An introduction to mind design. In J. Haugleland (Ed.), *Mind design: Philosophy, psychology, artificial intelligence*. Cambridge, MA: MIT Press.

Hayes-Roth, B., & Hayes-Roth, F. (1979). A cognitive model of planning. *Cognitive Science, 3,* 275–310.

Matsuhashi, A. (1981). Pausing and planning: The tempo of written discourse production. *Research in the Teaching of English, 15* (2), 113–134.

Matsuhashi, A. (1982). Explorations in the real-time production of written discourse. In M. Nystrand (Ed.), *What writers know: The language, process, and structure of written discourse*. New York: Academic Press.

Matsuhashi, A., & Gordon, E. (1985). Revision, addition, and the power of the unseen text. In S.W. Freedman (Ed.), *The acquisition of written language: Revision and response*. Norwood, NJ: Ablex.

Matsuhashi, A., & Quinn, K. (1984). Cognitive questions from discourse analysis: A review and a study. *Written Communication, 1* (3), 1984.

Nold, E. (1982). Revising: Intentions and conventions. In R. Sudol (Ed.), *Revising*. Urbana, IL: National Council of Teachers of English.

Perl, S. (1979). The composing processes of unskilled college writers. *Research in the Teaching of English, 13* (4), 317–336.

Rose, M. (1984). *Writer's block: The cognitive dimension*. Carbondale: Southern Illinois University Press.

Scardamalia, M., & Bereiter, C. (1983). The development of evaluative, diagnostic, and remedial capabilities in children's composing. In M. Martlew (Ed.), *The psychology of written language*. New York: Wiley.

Scardamalia, M., Bereiter, C., & Goelman, H. (1982). The role of production factors in writing ability. In M. Nystrand (Ed.), *What writers know: The language, process, and structure of written discourse*. New York: Academic Press.

Shanklin, N.L. (1984). *Writing as creation of a cybernetic system*. Unpublished manuscript (Available from Dr. Nancy L. Shanklin, University of Colorado at Denver, 2115 S. University Blvd., Denver, CO 80210.

Shaughnessy, M. (1977). *Errors & expectations*. New York: Oxford University Press.

Simon, H. (1981). The psychology of thinking: Embedding artifice in nature. In H. Simon (Ed.), *The Science of the Artificial*. Cambridge, MA: MIT Press. (Original work published 1969)

Smith, F. (1982). *Writing and the writer*. NY: Holt, Rinehart, and Winston.

Sommers, N. (1980). Revision strategies of student writers and experienced adult writers. *College Composition and Communication, 31,* 378–388.

Sternglass, M. (1980). Creating the memory of unheard sentences. In A. Freedman & I. Pringle (Eds.), *Reinventing the rhetorical tradition*. Ottowa, Canada: Carleton University, L & S Books for the Canadian Council of Teachers of English.

Stubbs, M. (1980). *Language and literacy: The sociolinguistics of reading and writing*. London: Routledge & Kegan Paul.

Tomlinson, B. (1983). *The interpretive reality of the composing process: Notes toward the study of writers' retrospective accounts*. Unpublished Manuscript (Available from Dr. Barbara Tomlinson, Director, Muir College Writing Program, C-006, 2346 Humanities, University of California at San Diego, La Jolla, CA 92093).

CHAPTER 9

Idea Generation in Writing

Donna J. Caccamise

Essex Corporation
Goleta, CA

Idea generation is perhaps the most important process in a concatenation of processes that create the written word. To write, not only must we generate ideas that constitute the message, but we must also generate ideas to govern how we organize the content of that message in order to achieve some desired effect.

People who are good at this sort of thing seem to have developed the knack through some magical combination of intuition and practice. Can we somehow translate what we know of memory processes into a prescription that can enhance a writer's efforts? Is there some systematic way to teach this skill? Can anyone recall a composition teacher ever taking this approach?

According to Humes (1983), our traditional teaching methods conveniently focus on products rather than processes because, until recently, research has placed emphasis on measurable aspects of written products rather than on the elusive behavior of writers. The shortcoming of this product approach for teaching is that the approach specifies, in a linear fashion, *where* some written element should exist, but they say little or nothing about how these elements came to be. In contrast, a process approach focuses on the underlying cognitive mechanisms which give rise to the written product.

If our goal is to understand and eventually model how written discourse is achieved, we should set aside this product-based approach and adopt a process-based approach to guide our research. The emergent discipline of cognitive science, in which emphasis is placed on process rather than product, provides a promising foundation for investigating production processes in the writing task (e.g., Atlas, 1979; Black, 1980; Flower & Hayes, 1979; Meehan, 1976).

Flower and Hayes (1981) provide a useful description of the component behaviors of the writing task. The Flower and Hayes model divides writing into three interacting processes: planning, translating, and reviewing. Writers can reduce the cognitive strain involved in juggling these three processes by paying special attention to planning. Perhaps, then, the most interesting and important phase identified by Flower and Hayes, but the least understood psychologically, is the planning process, during which ideas are generated and integrated in response to the writer's goals. For this reason, the research reported later in this chapter focuses on this phase of writing.

Flower and Hayes (1981) claim that idea generation is influenced by the writer's long-term memory (LTM) as well as by the task requirements. Thus, items are retrieved from the writer's memory based on information available at the time of retrieval, but this retrieval process is constrained by the topic and the intended audience. Before we can study how a writer selects and organizes ideas, we need to understand something more about how information is represented and stored in memory and about how it is retrieved.

The processes involved in idea generation and the processes of memory organization and retrieval actually underlie several related cognitive tasks. Speaking, problem solving, and writing all have in common a similar reliance on idea generation. For instance, in order to produce speech, the speaker must retrieve information from LTM which will provide the substance of his or her comments. This retrieval process is motivated by the current context for communication. Likewise, the problem solver must generate information from LTM in order to form a plan (or several plans) to guide him or her toward a problem solution. The nature of this problem is established by the goals of the task at hand. Both of these cognitive tasks proceed by generating information from LTM and therefore rely on retrieval process which are influenced by the specific task environment.

As with speech production and problem solving, when faced with a writing task, one must determine the ideas appropriate for successful communication. To achieve this, the writer generates (as does the speaker and problem solver) a solution plan based on the task requirements. This plan, among other things, includes the relevant ideas generated from LTM in anticipation of the text to be produced. Once again, LTM retrieval emerges as a fundamentally important element in the task performance.

The research project to be described in this chapter combined the task analysis model of the writing process proposed by Flower and Hayes (1979) with the psychological theories of information processing incorporated in the text comprehension model of Kintsch and van Dijk (1978) and in the model of recall proposed by Raaijmakers and Shiffrin (1980). The results from this research demonstrate how these models, reviewed briefly below, can help us learn about idea generation.

Current psychological theories of memory organization and retrieval can provide some guidance in determining the nature of these cognitive processes, but the application of these theories is ultimately limited by the methods of the research upon which they were based. For instance, Raajimakers and Shiffrin (1980) base their probabilistic retrieval model on an epidosic memory task—free recall of lists of words. Yet we are interested, in the present study, in the production of ideas rather than words. The Raajimakers and Shiffrin model may also fail to account for tasks, such as the ones in this study, which involve free generation of ideas in a complex writing situation. Even so, in the absence of more suitable models, the Raajimakers and Shiffrin model can provide a standard from which to measure possible differences between idea-generation tasks and more traditional recall tasks.

TEXT COMPREHENSION, RECALL, AND RETRIEVAL

Early experiments on semantic memory which attempted to pinpoint the organization of LTM as one particular type (Anderson & Bower, 1973; Collins & Quillian, 1969) have since been disputed. It is currently believed that those results stemmed from the nature of the artificial task which actually reflected decision processes in short-term memory (STM) rather than LTM representation of information, as originally believed. A more recent model by Raaijmakers (1979) and Shiffrin (1970, 1976) assumes that memory is an associative network, a large collection of nodes with complex associations between these nodes. However, they do not make any specific assumptions as to the nature of this network. Other models go a step further, assuming a propositional representation (e.g., Anderson, 1976; Kintsch, 1974). A propositional approach specifies the nature of information units. Perhaps the most formalized of these approaches is that of Kintsch. Essentially, a proposition consists of a predicate and relational terms: Each proposition states some relationship among concepts.

More recently, Kintsch (1980) has provided a description of LTM which synthesizes much of this previous work. LTM is viewed as a huge propositional network that is loosely organized in two ways. First, certain relationships exist among propositions (e.g., they share common arguments). Second, the proximity of one proposition to another is a function of their relatedness.

We can observe that people's ability to retrieve information from LTM is limited, but just how and why is this so? Memory retrieval has been extensively studied in list-learning tasks, and is most popularly described as a generate–edit process where retrieval cues lead one to generate all possible relevant information in LTM, and an edit process decides whether or not to "keep" each received piece of information based on the goals of the task.

Raajimakers and Shiffrin (1981) have proposed a recall model which updates earlier work in the field (Atkinson & Shiffrin, 1968). They begin by assuming that LTM is an associative network where item-to-context and interitem associations exist. In order to tap LTM for information, the subject makes a retrieval plan which includes search strategies based on the demands of the task. The subject assembles probe cues[1] which could take into account context and all other information available in STM. Next is the search phase: all information in STM (probe cues) will automatically activate associated, related information in LTM—a search set. Only some portions of this activated information will be attended to, due to the capacity limitation of STM. Finally, context and item features are recovered from LTM so that they can be compared with the context cues in STM to determine whether the correct information has been recovered.

Raaijmakers (1979) formally describes this retrieval process in terms of the probability of sampling a given item. This probability is assumed to be proportional to the product of the associative strengths of the sampled item to the probe cues. The probability of recovery is described as a function of the sum of the associative strengths. The probability of sampling an item, then, decreases if the search set is large (not well constrained by the probe). Conversely, a small search set will improve the sampling probability.

The probability of finding a match of information in LTM with any given probe cues and therefore generating a response in their list-learning experiments is based on the outcome of two processes, sampling and recovery. This phase of the search process is thought to be a pattern completion process: the greater the overlap in features between probe cues and sampled information, the higher the probability of recovery. This overlap is determined by both contextual as well as interitem association.

Raaijmakers and Shiffrin's (1980) description of their search model can be recast within the idea-generation process. First, the subject is given a task (e.g., text topic, text type, and intended audience are specified). A memory-retrieval probe is generated from these constraints and placed into STM. A search set is then selected, based on this probe information. This search set consists of a number of information units which are closely interassociated and stored as groups. Retrieval of one of these information units will tend to lead to retrieval of the associated information units. At least three factors should influence the size of the search set: the specificity of the topic, the intended audience, and the knowledge of the writer.

---

[1] Information which will trigger recollection of related information residing in LTM. The amount of information that can be used as probe cues is limited by the constraints of STM—traditionally described as 7 ± 2 units of information (Miller, 1956).

EXPERIMENTAL APPROACH

This research focuses on constraints imposed by the individual's LTM and by the writing task, topic familiarity, and audience type. Two experiments were designed to explore these constraints using a verbal protocol approach.[2] The first experiment focused on topic specification; the second experiment looked at the effects of intended audience. Both experiments included the variable of topic familiarity to test some of the constraining effects of LTM organization.

Writer's LTM

In generating and organizing ideas, the writer is limited (i.e., constrained) by his or her preexisting world knowledge and experience. Following Kintsch (1980) we can describe an individual's knowledge base, from which he will generate ideas, in terms of the density and organization (e.g., proximity) of the network of relevant propositions in LTM. As a constraint in the writing process, the proposed proposition network structure of LTM should affect idea generation in a very straightforward manner. The more familiar the subject matter, the greater the number of ideas one can generate, and the better the integration and organization between these ideas. Degree of familiarity, then, should affect the subjects' performance in the present experiments where they are asked to verbally generate ideas as a first step in producing a text on a prescribed topic. Analysis of the protocols should confirm the proposed organization effects as reflected in the following derived measures: (1) ideas per chunk, (2) number of chunks (or, following Flower & Hayes, 1981, "associated chains"), (3) number of levels in a hierarchical analysis of the idea units, and (4) number of clusters as determined by a lack of argument repetition, marking a discontinuation of a particular set of ideas. The greater the topic familiarity or expertise (knowledge space density), the higher the expected values for the above measures. (The operational definitions for these measures can be found in a subsequent section.)

An individual's knowledge base (LTM) can be viewed as a more-or-less fixed entity when it brings its resources to bear on any given writing task. For this reason, instead of observing topic familiarity in isolation, it is more interesting to view the effects of topic familiarity on idea generation as it interacts to enhance or diminish the constraining effects of the task environment.

---

[2] "A protocol is a description of the activities, ordered in time, which a subject engages in while performing an oral production task" (Flower & Hayes, 1979, p. 5).

Task Environment

This category of constraints on idea generation for writing includes topic specifications, intended audience, and purpose. To the extent that these constraints are external to the individual, they are flexible. Because of this flexibility they can differentially affect the actual search and retrieval processes of memory. The present research attempted to isolate some of the effects of the first two of these task constraints; the third, purpose, was held constant in these experiments. The effects of these constraints were, for the sake of discussion, divided into three major aspects: organization, interference, and temporal characteristics.

Organization.   What is assumed in this investigation is that in order to generate an idea, one must first develop a retrieval cue with which to probe LTM. This cue will determine the appropriate search set (propositions in LTM related to the probe) and ideas will be generated from this set. The size of the set depends on the specificity of the probe, as well as the density of the knowledge space as described earlier.

Experiment 1 was designed to investigate one way in which retrieval cues can be constrained by topic specificity. More general topics would be expected to generate more ideas, but they are likely to be only loosely organized. If the topic is more specific, then the search set will be smaller, hence fewer ideas. However, the relation between propositions may be more apparent, hence the resulting ideas better integrated and organized than they would be under less constrained circumstances.   .

Looking at the same organization measures as before, we might expect the following outcome: The more general topic should produce more ideas but less clustering of these ideas. This means fewer ideas per chunk (shorter associated chains), fewer chunks, and fewer clusters of ideas when compared to ideas generated to the more specific topic. However, number of levels (i.e., hierarchical organization) is something of an open question. If levels are determined by amount of information brought to bear from LTM, then the more general topic may produce more levels of ideas from the general-to-detail continuum. Yet viewed from a different standpoint, number of levels may be more influenced by some limited-output process (perhaps STM constraints) resulting in an equal number of levels for the general-topic and specific-topic conditions. In this case, a difference could still be anticipated between the two conditions in terms of where their levels fit on the general-to-detail continuum. The general-topic condition would yield more macro-level ideas while the specific-topic condition would cause more detail-level ideas to be produced.

In Experiment 2, a different pattern may emerge. With audience type providing the constraint we may find that, for both audiences, subjects generate the same number of ideas at the highest level of abstraction but differ when it comes to the more complex details. If a writer is indeed considering his audience, then he should take great care to avoid complexities for child audiences. The organization between these ideas may be more appropriate for an adult audience but lacking in some important way for child audiences as a function of how they are stored in the adult writer's LTM. In the initial idea-generation phase of writing this may show up as a relative lack of organization for the ideas produced for the child audience, as the writer abandons his organization schemes stored with the topic. This would not be a problem with the adult (peer group) audience situation.

Interference.   The actual search process can be viewed in a manner similar to the episodic memory-retrieval model of Raaijmakers and Shiffrin (1980). Instead of lists of paired associates, our search set consists of propositional nodes in semantic memory that are contacted by some retrieval cue. According to Raaijmakers & Shiffrin, larger search sets decrease the probability of sampling an item in the set and, conversely, smaller sets result in a higher probability of resampling the items in the set. Resampling increases the associative strength between sampled items and the retrieval cue, which in turn creates the phenomenon of output interference.

According to this model, the more constrained environment for idea generation (e.g., specific topic) would induce more output interference than the less constrained (general-topic) environment. This output interference prediction could be tested in the idea-generation verbal protocols by counting the number of repeated ideas.

In Experiment 1, which focused on topic specification, the actual search through memory according to the Raaijmakers & Shiffrin (1981) model was targeted as the source for output interference. The more constraining conditions were predicted to produce the most output interference. With audience type providing the constraints in Experiment 2, it is quite possible that the same results would be obtained, but for different reasons. Rather than the search set size influencing output interference, an editing process may ultimately be responsible.[3] Unfortunately, these two possible explanations cannot be distinguished by the idea-repetition measure of output interference used in Experiment 1. The editing explanation may be suspected, however, by looking additionally for differences in temporal patterns between Experiment 1 and Experiment 2.

Temporal characteristics—related to the notion of output interference—is the work done by Bousfield in the 1940s (Bousfield & Sedgwick, 1944).

---

[3] This editing process would be necessitated if we assume that knowledge of intended audience in LTM is not stored with any given topic information. In this case, considerations of topic determine the search set from which to generate ideas, while consideration of audience type has a potential effect only after an item is retrieved.

Basically, he gave subjects a category and asked them to generate all the appropriate exemplars (e.g., all quadruped mammals). Bousfield demonstrated that the temporal characteristics of the subjects' output could be represented by an equation which showed that the rate of production of associations is proportional to the total remaining available associations. In essence, as the set of possible associations is exhausted, subsequent associations become less frequent and eventually cease. Bousfield (1953) also found that related ideas were produced together in temporally distinguishable groups, but that not all temporally distinguishable groups consisted of obviously related items. In addition, the more common words, as measured by norms, were produced first. Using a list-learning paradigm Bousfield (1954) also showed that clustering of associated ideas in subjects' recall diminished over time, presumably due to an exhausted supply of items.

Using the verbal protocols generated by the proposed idea-generation task we can discover if Bousfield's findings with word lists transfer to the more complex task of language production. First we would expect that the rate of idea generation will decelerate over time, and that this deceleration would be greatest for the more constrained, small-search-set conditions. Second, we would expect that the more closely related ideas will occur in temporal proximity. Thus, we would expect pauses to temporally distinguish meaningful groups of ideas, i.e., pauses occur between connected (related) idea groups rather than in the middle of such a group. This pattern of results could possibly be influenced by the varying constraints. In general, conditions which foster greater organization and hence greater cohesiveness (small set, familiar topic) will likely produce higher values for pausally distinguishable idea groups when compared with conditions which produce less organization (large set, unfamiliar topic). Finally, we can expect that the number of idea chunks will diminish over time. This can easily be demonstrated by dividing the protocol into standard time units and then computing the average number of chunks per unit of time. This result should be more pronounced in conditions which foster a large search set.

In Experiment 1, we might expect that idea generation for the more constrained conditions of specific and unfamiliar topics would take less overall time than the less constrained conditions of general and familiar topics because the subject is generating ideas from a smaller pool of propositions. Conversely, we might expect an opposite outcome in Experiment 2 if we assume that search-set size (pool of propositions) is the same for both audience types, and the difference between them is in the amount of editing necessary to generate appropriate ideas. With audience type, we would expect more editing, and therefore more time, to generate ideas for the more constraining situation of a child audience.

Another potential source of difference in the temporal data concerns rate of idea generation. In Experiment 1 I anticipated a difference in the deceleration of the rate of ideas as a function of constraint. However, with audience type providing the constraint, the difference between conditions may be that, from the beginning, the rate of idea generation for the more constrained condition is slower than for the less constrained condition, due to increased editing demands. The rate of deceleration may be the same if both conditions are operating with the same search set.

Subjects

Sixteen subjects participated in Experiment 1, and another 16 served in Experiment 2. All subjects were recruited from an introductory psychology class at the University of Colorado.

Experiment Procedures

Subjects were given a 3 × 5 card specifying a topic they were to write about and the intended audience. Specifically, they were told that the text to be produced would appear in a pamphlet which presented all the facts on the topic. This pamphlet would be used by the legislature to design a new government program in education (or energy). Thus, an adult audience was implicitly identified.

To vary the intended audience, subjects were told one of two stories about the audience. The adult-audience version was the same as in Experiment 1. The children-audience version went as follows: Subjects were told that the text to be produced would appear in a pamphlet designed to present all the facts on the specific topic to children who were in the 5th grade. As a class project, they were to use this information to design the ideal educational (or energy) program for the country.

Subjects were told that I was interested in what they normally thought of when they began to write a paper. They were instructed to generate all the ideas that they felt should be included in such a text. They were then given a description of a verbal protocol. Subjects were advised that they should say not only what ideas came to them but also to verbalize every thought, no matter how trivial, that came into their head as they generated these ideas. They were also told not to be concerned about repeating themselves. The verbal report was selected over a writing protocol in order to measure idea repetition as well as temporal characteristics of the idea-generation process. It was assumed that subjects who verbalized would be relatively unaware of occurrences of repetition, whereas writing subjects would have an external reminder (the lists of ideas) and would therefore be less likely to repeat ideas.

Subjects spoke into a tape recorder. The 3 × 5 card was available for reference throughout the idea-generation process. Subjects were given one practice topic, followed by the experimental topics.

Table 1.

Topics

Practice
  Describe a trip to a supermarket
  Audience: Someone from another world

Familiar
  General Discuss/describe education systems and their function in our society. Consider all purposes.
  Specific Discuss/describe a technical-vocational training program and its function in our society.

Unfamiliar
  General Discuss our energy needs and energy sources—now and the future.
  Specific Discuss the role of nuclear energy in our energy needs—now and the future.

Audience
  Adult A pamphlet to be used by legislators to design an education (energy) program.
  Child A pamphlet to be used for a 5th-grade class project to design an education (energy) program.

Materials

One practice topic helped prepare subjects for two experimental topics. The practice topic was "a trip to a supermarket" to be written for someone from another world. This topic involves script-based information which simplified the task by requiring an event-based generic narrative. The choice of audience facilitated a script-type perspective, making the task more uniform.

Each subject responded to one experimental topic where the subject matter was familiar, and to another experimental topic with unfamiliar subject matter. The familiar topic concerned educational issues whereas the unfamiliar topic concerned energy issues, which were potentially more technical. Topics defined either a general or a specific realm of information concerning that subject. These experimental topics were more abstract in nature as compared to the practice topic, i.e., no script was suggested by the topics (see Table 1). Audience type was held constant in Experiment 1 by designating an adult group for all experimental conditions.

In Experiment 2, audience type was varied by designating either an adult or child audience. The topics in Experiment 2 did not differ according to specificity as they did in Experiment 1. The general form of the topics from Experiment 1 were used in all conditions. The familiar/unfamiliar topics used in Experiment 1 were used in Experiment 2 (providing an opportunity for a partial replication of results).

Design

There were two primary independent variables for each experiment. In Experiment 1, the first variable was within subjects and dealt with subject knowledge bases in the form of familiar and unfamiliar topics. The second, a between-subjects variable, dealt with constraining the topic of the writing task. Subjects generated ideas to write on prescribed topics; this process was recorded producing verbal protocols as data. Several dependent variables were analyzed according to a 2 × 2 mixed ANOVA with 8 subjects in each of the four cells; Familiar and General Topic, Familiar and Specific Topic, Unfamiliar and General Topic, Unfamiliar and Specific Topic, for a total of 16 subjects.

The dependent variables were: overall number of ideas, number of chunks, number of ideas per chunk (number of associated chains, length of associated chains), number of levels as determined by a hierarchical analysis, number of clusters (distinct groups of ideas produced by breaks in argument repetition), ideas per cluster, chunks per cluster, and finally, percentage of unassociated ideas. To assess the temporal characteristics and interference predictions of idea generation a third independent variable of time was added to the design. Protocols were divided into five sections, each representing an equal amount of time (20% of the total protocol duration), yielding a 2 × 2 × 5 design. This enabled the following measures: ideas per time unit, chunks per time unit, and ideas/chunk/time unit.

The prediction that closely related ideas are generated in temporally identifiable groups can be investigated by adding a different third variable to the original 2 × 2 design. This within-subject variable is meaningful versus nonmeaningful boundaries for pause occurrences.

Finally, protocols were scored for editorial comments. These were divided into two categories, once again providing a third variable. This within-subject variable was memory-search comments versus "what to write" comments.

In Experiment 2, the within-subjects variable was again topic familiarity. The between-subjects variable concerned intended audience: adults versus children. If subjects generated ideas to the same topic twice, once for adults and once for children, the second performance would be unaccountably influenced by the first idea-generation task.

Protocol Analyses

The verbal protocols of subjects were transcribed, preserving pauses and extraneous comments. Each transcript (64 total) was analyzed for idea units following a liberal definition of a proposition according to methods used by Kintsch—see Turner and Greene (1978). Idea units, like propositions, reflect basic information units which convey the gist of a text. These idea

Table 2. Comparison of Idea Unit Notation with Standard Propositional Notation

Idea Units
1. Describe what a good education does
2. (1) to our society
3. (2) and, how our current system works
4. (3) and, how people have gone about it
5. (4) or, the past education systems.

Propositions
1. (Do, Education, $)
2. (Qualify (1) good)
3. (For (2) society)
4. (Works, current system)
5. (Qualify (4) our)
6. ("go about it," people [4])
7. (Qualify: or, past education systems)
8. (Describe, $, and [3,5,6,7])

units were submitted to a structural analysis which produced a hierarchy of ideas indicating different levels of information. The units used in this research were given a different label because the notation used here is not as detailed as the standard propositional notation, but is sufficiently detailed for its present use. The less detailed notation was preferable over the usual propositional notation because it greatly simplified the analysis of the lengthy protocols, while still preserving the essential information. To assure uniformity in idea units across experimental conditions the average number of words per idea unit was computed for each group. The range was quite reasonable: 5.0 to 5.2 words per idea unit.

The Appendix provides an example of an idea-generation protocol and its analysis. Table 2 compares idea-unit notation with propositional notation for the first five ideas. From this example it becomes apparent that the idea-unit notation does not distinguish some of the qualifiers, but does preserve the basic units and their connections. It also represents the ideas in a chronological order, and as a result, sometimes does not make special note of the way in which something is expressed. For example, the fact that propositions 3, 5, 6, and 7 are connected by a conjunction is expressed in proposition 8. Connection is represented among idea units in a different manner. The idea unit begins with the number for the previous idea unit to which the present unit is connected. If the connection is the conjunctive type, then the number is followed by the appropriate conjunction, and finally, the present idea is represented. Ideas that are connected conjunctively are considered to be at the same level. Ideas that are connected by some other relationship (e.g., causation) show only the number of the unit to which they are connected. Ideas connected by these relationships are considered to be an expansion (detail) of the idea to which they are connected, and thus appear one level lower in a hierarchical analysis. If an idea unit does not begin with another number, then it is not explicitly related to the ideas which immediately preceded it.

The notation of "chunk" or "associated chains" is important in several of the measures used in these experiments. To ensure consistency of scoring, the definition of chunk was operationalized as follows: Information in a text can be assigned values indicating the relative importance of each idea with respect to each other. The resulting number of levels for any body of information is flexible and ranges from the most general or macro-level to the most detailed or subordinate level. If the macro-level idea is assigned to a value of one, then a chunk can be described by a level-one idea and all level-two ideas that are subordinated to it.

If one arranges the list of idea units graphically to show the hierarchical relationships among idea units, then the chunking becomes more apparent. For example, in the hierarchical analysis of the sample protocol idea-unit 1 is the superordinate idea in a chunk comprised of units 1 through 5. Ideas 2 through 5 are connected via conjunction and are therefore part of the same chunk initiated by the first idea. This chunk also corresponds to a cluster, an unusual, but possible, occurrence. Most clusters have multiple chunks. (See below for a definition of cluster.) Likewise, idea-units 6 and 7 are a chunk, idea-units 7 and 8 are a chunk, and so on. The string of chunks involving ideas 6 through 11 results from the successive elaboration to provide more detail; the latest idea qualifies in some way the idea that preceded it.

Thus, according to this procedure, chunk density (number of ideas) is assumed to be a reflection of elaboration breadth, while cluster density (number of chunks) is a reflection of elaboration depth.

Chunks that are connected through argument overlap are described here as forming clusters. A cluster of ideas is formed by the break in idea connection through argument overlap. In the example given, there is no argument overlap between idea-unit 5 and idea-unit 6. Thus, idea-unit 5 marks the end of the first cluster, and idea-unit 6 is the beginning of the second cluster of ideas. Clusters are, of course, related to one another (in varying degrees not determined here), but they are not explicitly connected via a common argument.

Unit of Analysis

The results of this research can only be interpreted within the context of the assumptions made about the unit of analysis. It is assumed here that a loose interpretation of propositions—the idea unit—was a meaningful unit in this production task. Idea units are very closely linked to the commonly

Table 3. Excerpt from a Sample Protocol and Analysis

Topic: Education System (Familiar, General, Adults)

First you would probably describe what good the education does to our society and how our current works, our current system works and how they um people have gone about it or the past education systems um one of the purposes right now that we're using for the education system is mostly an institution for the children so they um they first started our education system probably to get the children um doing something other than working after they passed the child labor laws . . .

Analysis of Idea Units

1. Describe what a good education does
2. (1) to our society
3. (2) & how our current system works
4. (3) & how people have gone about it
5. (4) or the past education systems
6. A current purpose of education systems
7. (6) an institution for kids
8. (7) so first started our educational system
9. (8) to get the kids doing something
10. (9) other than working
11. (10) after they passed the child labor laws.

Hierarchical Analysis

Levels:	1 2 3 4 5 6	Number of Chunks
Cluster:		
1	1—2	1
	⌐3	
	⌐4	
	⌐5	
2	6—7—8—9—10—11	5

---

used proposition units, for which a large body of research exists supporting their psychological validity in a variety of circumstances. Kintsch (1974) presents experimental evidence that the proposition maps on to the unit of information that subjects are actually using in comprehension tasks. For instance, it was discovered that reading rate could be described as a function of the number of propositions in a text whereas number of words was held constant. In recall tasks, subjects were likely to recall sentences in an all-or-none fashion if they are based on one proposition, but not if the sentences are based on two or more propositions. Furthermore, in a hierarchical analysis of propositions, the more superordinate propositions were more likely to be recalled than the subordinate propositions.

These examples demonstrate that propositions can be a useful tool of analysis in a variety of tasks involving discourse processes. Therefore, it seems reasonable to use this tool once more in the context of idea generation, especially because alternatives are not well defined. It is not claimed, however, that propositions/idea units are necessarily the only possible (or

Table 4. Groups Means for Measures Showing Organization Effects

	Topic		Audience	
	Familiar	Unfamiliar	Adult	Child
Total number of ideas	57.312	33.000		
Total number of chunks	28.875	15.250		
Number of levels	6.938	4.500	7.938	5.063
Number of clusters	9.563	7.438	10.938	18.562
Ideas/cluster	6.094	4.396	5.314	4.366
Chunks/cluster	3.064	1.958	1.694	2.347
Percentage repeated ideas	29.631	53.444	43.944	62.269
Percentage unassociated ideas	1.469	7.825	3.331	12.719
	General	Specific		
Percentage unassociated ideas	2.575	6.719		

best) unit of analysis. That is an issue that cannot be resolved by the current experiments.

RESULTS AND DISCUSSION

Writer's LTM Constraints

It appears that a writer's LTM can be a powerful constraint on idea generation and behaves roughly in a manner predicted by associative network models, at least insofar as the present variables are concerned. Not surprisingly, when subjects were generating ideas to familiar topics they produced more ideas than when the topic was unfamiliar (See Table 4[4]).

But more importantly, the conditions involving familiar topics persistantly displayed better organization than did unfamiliar topics, according to the organizational assessment used in the current experiments. For familiar topics, subjects produced significantly more chunks and clusters of ideas, suggesting greater elaboration of ideas. This is presumably a reflection of the increased relatedness of ideas (e.g., shared arguments) in LTM for familiar topics.

These shared arguments possibly allow more subsets of ideas to be activated when the superordinate node is activated by the retrieval cue. These results conform with the expectation that the organization of the ideas in the protocols reflect the notions of density and proximity in LTM organization. With a familiar topic, Kintsch (1980) suggested that the relatedness between propositions would be reflected in denser semantic neighborhoods

[4] For the variable Familiar/Unfamiliar topic, Experiment 2 replicated Experiment 1. Therefore, specific results reported for this variable come from Experiment 1 to avoid redundancy. All differences reported here were significant at $p \wedge \approx .01$.

where propositions share common arguments, and hence, better cohesion and organization. Further contributing to this conclusion were the measures chunks/cluster and ideas/cluster which were greater for familiar topics. The familiar topic protocols also reflected more depth; there were more levels represented in the ideas generated for familiar topics than for unfamiliar topics.

If LTM is organized as these results suggest, then what does this mean for the writing process? Taken together, these findings indicate that a writer's LTM can not only constraint the number of ideas that can be produced, but it can also inhibit the quality of the organization of these ideas in terms of breadth, depth, and cohesiveness.

We next turn to output interference in memory retrieval. According to the Raaijmakers and Shiffrin theory (1980, 1981), the probability of sampling an idea would increase as set size decreases, enhancing output interference. To the extent that an unfamiliar topic is more constraining (and hence triggers a smaller search set) than a familiar topic, it was expected that the unfamiliar condition would produce more output interference. Using percentage of repeated ideas across time, this interference effect was obtained; the ratio effect was enhanced by the more constrained conditions.

To obtain the effects of idea repetition each protocol was first divided into five temporally equal parts which were then used to derive several measures. The total number of ideas was divided by the number of repeated ideas generated for each time unit, resulting in the measure percentage of repeated ideas/time unit. As expected, the percentage of repeated ideas increased according to time unit. A Newman–Keuls comparison of means confirmed the trend that a greater percentage of ideas are repeated over time.

At the same time, using ideas/time unit as the dependent measure, there was no difference in the number of ideas generated from the beginning to the end of the protocols. Likewise, analysis of the number of chunks/time unit was also not significant. To ensure that this lack of difference was real and not due to a change in chunk density, an analysis was performed using ideas/chunk/time unit. This analysis was also not significant. These results are important in that they help to rule out the argument in both experiments that an increase in repeated ideas over time is an artifact of the number of ideas expressed per time unit.

It is still possible, however, that this finding is an artifact resulting from an increased pool of ideas over time. To clear up this point, the results were broken down into number of ideas repeated/time unit that first appeared in the same time unit, number of ideas repeated whose first occurrence was from an earlier time unit, and number of new ideas generated/time unit.

The significance of the numbers of repeated ideas across time becomes obvious if we compute the percentage of repetition that these numbers represent. For the unconstrained conditions (familiar topic and adult audience), rate of repetition from the same unit remains constant, as contrasted with the constrained conditions (unfamiliar topic and child audience) *where the percentage of repetition drops considerably by the end of the protocol.* For percentage of ideas repeated from earlier time units, both the unconstrained and constrained conditions show a decrease across time. This result is counter to the notion that repeating an idea is constant across time as predicted by a random process model. According to this random model one would expect a stable percentage of ideas repeated from earlier units. These results suggest, contrary to a random model, that some interference parameter does operate in memory.

Although it is apparent that these repetition effects are not due to random processes, it is far less clear that these effects are due to retrieval interference. An alternative explanation to interference effects for the idea-repetition results deals with an intuitive approach which postulates planning motives. According to this view, ideas are repeated as a method by which to further elaborate on a topic. If the generation of ideas in this research did indeed include this kind of planning then we could expect a tendency of repeated ideas to occur at the beginning of clusters which mark the beginning of an elaboration of an idea through a group of subordinate, explicitly interassociated, ideas. Analyses investigating this notion did not reveal any such tendency in any of the experimental conditions. In this experimental task, it appears that idea repetition results from some sort of interference in retrieval processes rather than from strategies to facilitate elaboration.

Predictions concerning the temporal characteristics of idea generation based on the work of Bousfield and his colleagues were essentially confirmed. Bousfield and Sedgewick (1944) reported that the rate of word-concept generation decelerated with time. In the present experiments, when all ideas were considered without regard to repeated ideas, it appeared that subjects generated an undiminished amount of ideas until they acknowledged they were finished. However, with a more fine-grained analysis a different picture emerged. If generation of new ideas is considered in isolation from any repeated ideas, then a deceleration in production begins to emerge. Like Bousfield's results, the data tend toward a negatively accelerated curve, but not nearly as pronounced as with the earlier work.

The pattern of responses in the present investigation appears to follow an exponential function similar to the Bousfield data which describes the production of ideas in relation to the maximum number of possible ideas relevant to the topic (see Figure 1). However, it is important to realize

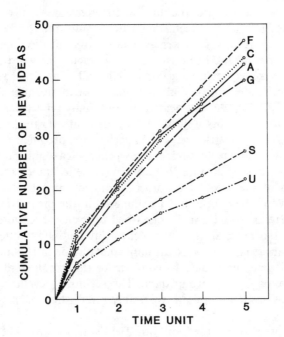

FIG. 1.   A cumulative graph of the mean number of new ideas produced per time unit for each of the independent variables for Experiment 1 and Experiment 2 (*F* = Familiar Topic, *U* = Unfamiliar Topic, *G* = General topic, *S* = Specific topic, *A* = Adult intended audience, *C* = Child intended audience).

that, as with Bousfield and Sedgewick (1944), this relationship fits the group average. A more critical perspective is whether or not this exponential function fits individual data. In order to determine this the log values for number of new ideas for each time were computed for each subject. In order for it to be possible for an exponential function to fit the data, the logarithmic values should decrease across time. This pattern can be observed simply by using the Sign test. The results of this test indicated that it was just as likely for the log values to increase as it was for them to decrease (Familiar Topic, 35/64; Unfamiliar Topic, 31/64; Adult Audience, 36/64; Child Audience, 30/64). Thus, in this case the group data does not describe the individual process. In fact, the individual timing data is suggestive of a cyclic process which emerged more clearly in the cluster data. However, speculations of this sort based on the timing data are tenuous at best since the points of comparison are based on arbitrary time units.

Looking back at the group data, the difference in the production-process rate of deceleration between Bousfield's results and the results reported here may be the result of greater associative organization among ideas in the present experiments. In Bousfield's experiments the word concepts that the subjects were expected to generate (e.g., all names that start with the letter *A*) were related in some manner that the experimenter dictated. The relationship specified did not necessarily optimally reflect the way the concepts were organized in subjects' LTM. In contrast, the present experiments were far less restrictive. The experimenter provided a topic, but it was up to each subject to decide appropriate ideas and interconnections among ideas. This task may therefore have relied more on the natural organization of ideas in LTM for each subject. If this is so, then idea generation would have been less encumbered in the present experiments.

This difference could also be described in terms of a finite versus limitless set of associated units. The effect of a potentially limitless search set in the present research may be an important factor in the inability of individual idea-generation data to conform to the exponential deceleration model suggested by the group data. The seemingly cyclic nature of the individual idea-generation data is possibly a reflection of memory organization.

Another prediction based on Bousfield's work was that meaningful groups of ideas could be temporally distinguished. This result was obtained, and was more pronounced, for the familiar topic condition. Hence, pauses were more likely to occur at meaningful boundaries for familiar topics than they were for the unfamiliar topic condition.

Effect of LTM Constraints on Writing

By integrating these findings on LTM effects, a picture of the idea-generation process begins to emerge. Individuals produce an idea and, depending on their knowledge base, elaborate on it, develop it in depth, forming a cluster of related ideas. Then they move on to another idea which begins a whole new cluster of closely related ideas. This process is engaged recursively until the subject decide they have exhausted the topic. (Subjects invariably followed their last idea with a declaration like "that's it!") However, it is quite likely that subjects have not expressed all they know on the topic. Instead, what they have "exhausted" is the contents of the search set which held all the idea nodes that were activated (i.e., brought into consciousness—STM) by the retrieval cue.

A model of writing that incorporates these notions concerning idea generation could offer some concrete suggestions for improving performance. For instance, due to the STM limitations suggested above, it may be more profitable (in terms of generating ideas) to distribute the writing task over several separate time periods rather than one massive effort. This could easily be tested by giving two groups of subjects the same amount of time to generate ideas (or even complete the entire writing task, depending on what you want to measure) but distribute the time for one group while giving one huge block of time to the other group. If we are measuring the ideas produced, the memory processes suggested here would predict a greater variety of ideas in the distributed condition.

Task Constraints

General vs. Specific Topic. This variable proved to have a weak effect at best on constraining the processes of idea generating. It was expected that a general topic would tap a much larger, less organized search set than would a specific topic. None of the effects of measures of organization were obtained. There was, however, a smaller percentage of unassociated ideas for the general topic, opposite of what would be expected if general topics are not as well organized as specific topics. This result should not be taken too seriously since no other measures corroborated this finding. Perhaps related to this finding is the data from percentage of ideas repeated. For specific topics, subjects generated fewer new ideas, repeating themselves to fill in the gap. This, then, may be the cause of more unassociated ideas in the specific topic conditions.

In an attempt to gain further insight into the results, the protocols were rated for idea relevance to the stated topic by an independent group of subjects.[5] These ratings were based on a subset of ideas from each experimental condition for both experiments, and represented approximately 5% of the total ideas generated. These ratings of idea relevance indicated that ideas were judged most relevant in the most constrained condition, unfamiliar, specific topics. If we assume that the unfamiliar specific topic triggers sparsely populated portions of LTM then the reason for these ratings is that subjects simply did not have the information to fill in at lower levels, details which would be judged less relevant.

It is possible, then, that topic specificity as used here offered so much constraint that subjects could not generate enough ideas to make organization an issue. The timing data further supports the constraining effect of specificity on idea generation. The rate of idea generation, ideas/minute, was lower for the specific topic condition. This means that in the specific condition, subjects took longer to generate their ideas.

It is rather counter-intuitive that specifying the topic should have such a paralyzing effect on idea generation when one considers the advice given

---

[5] Students from an introductory psychology class at the University of Colorado served as raters.

to writers: Narrow the topic, be specific. A possible explanation is that the constraining effects of topic specificity may follow a U-shaped function where the optimal topic specification in terms of idea organization and relevancy exists in the middle of the continuum. Of course, an alternative explanation is that in order to meet the demands of the task, the subjects "redefine" the general topic into one more specific, reducing any differences between these two conditions.

Adult vs. Child Audience. The findings suggested that the constraining effects of intended audience emanate from a different source than for topic specificity. If it is assumed that knowledge of intended audience is not stored in memory with any given topic, then it is necessary to posit the existence of an editing process to judge the suitability of ideas for a particular audience. These ideas would come from an already existing search set, based on topic and memory constraints.

When audience type was the source of constraint, the same number of ideas were produced in the constrained condition as in the unconstrained condition. This was reflected in the lack of differences between audience types for the measures, total number of ideas, number of chunks and ideas/chunk. However in the child-audience situation, there was less organization, less complexity, and reduced elaboration and depth, as indicated by fewer hierarchical levels, clusters, and ideas per cluster. In addition, the percentage of unassociated ideas was almost four times greater for the child-audience condition.

With respect to interference effects, it was predicted as before that the more constraining condition, child audience, would produce the most idea repetition. Indeed, significantly more ideas were repeated for child audiences as compared to adult audiences. The interaction of topic familiarity and audience type was also significant. A comparison of cell means revealed that the effect of increased ideas repeated for unfamiliar topics occurred only in the adult condition; percentage of repeated ideas was uniformly high for the child condition. If this high percentage of repeated ideas in the child-audience condition was due to a planning process for elaboration, then once again we would expect these repeated ideas to have a tendency to occur at the beginning of clusters of information. This tendency would reflect a plan to provide a starting point for further elaboration. However, the chi-square analysis of the pattern of repetition did not demonstrate any tendency for repeated ideas to occur more frequently at the beginning of clusters. Thus, the explanation of planning was not implicated as a motivation for idea repetition under these conditions.

One plausible explanation for the causes of idea repetition during retrieval processes when audience type provides the constraints involves allocation of more resources to increased editing demands. This explanation gains credibility in light of timing results. Normally we would expect that more constrained conditions would take less time to generate ideas due to a smaller number of relevant ideas in memory. For topic specificity this trend was apparent (although not significant, due probably to the general ineffectiveness of this factor in this research). In contrast, when the constraints were the result of intended audience, we might expect that the more constrained conditions require more time to generate ideas due to editing processes. In fact, it took nearly twice as long for subjects to generate ideas in the child-audience condition as compared to the adult-audience condition, in spite of the fact that both groups generated an equivalent number of ideas.

These editing processes unexpectedly proved to be more overt in nature, allowing for objective measurement. Subjects expressed at least some of their editing of ideas. They were generally concerned as to whether or not an idea they were currently thinking about was appropriate for children (e.g., too difficult, complex). Not only were there significantly more comments made for child audiences, but there was a significant interaction between audience type and type of editing comment. The number of memory-search comments was not affected by audience type. Conversely, what-to-write comments were far more frequent in the child-audience condition (see Figure 2). Overall, editorial comments increase in the more constrained conditions. From the protocols it is quite apparent that comments directed to the intended audience emerge only when the audience is children.

The timing results did produce some deceleration effects as predicted for both of the two task variables, replicating Experiment 1. Once again, degree of deceleration was much less than the deceleration found in Bousfield's work using words. As argued with the topic-familiarity data earlier, this difference could be the result of the greater organizational complexity of this idea-generation task.

The pause data used to assess temporally distinguishable groups of related ideas produced an interaction. There were more pauses at meaningful boundaries for adult audiences but not for child audiences (see Figure 3). This fits with the general picture emerging that writing for children places more constraints on the writer, interfering with the quality of the ideas generated.

Effect of Audience on Writing

When generating ideas for an intended audience of children, subjects attempted to say more, but the results were qualitatively inferior. Subjects repeated themselves more often, expressed less organized, disjointed ideas more often, did not elaborate as much on ideas or go into as much depth. From the analysis of meta-statements it appears that the source of the constraining effects were in deciding what ideas were appropriate (i.e.,

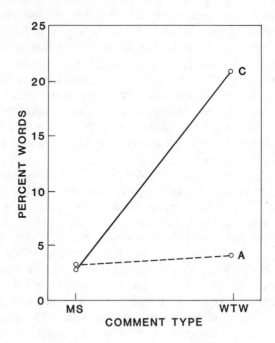

FIG. 2. The interaction of editorial comment type × intended audience for percentage of words devoted to comments (*MS* = Memory search comments, *WTW*
= What to write comments, *A* = Adult intended audience, *C* = Child intended
audience).

editing) once they were already selected from LTM and residing in some
Short-Term Store (STS). This is in contrast to the constraining effects of
topic familiarity which is believed to contain the number of ideas selected
from LTM.

These results suggests that attempting to account for intended audience
during the idea-generation phase is achieved only at the cost of the quality
of the ideas themselves because (not surprisingly) knowledge of intended
audience does not appear to be stored with subject matter. A model of
efficient writing, then, should probably recommend that when writing for
unfamiliar audiences one should first generate ideas with total disregard
for intended audience; later, recast the ideas to reflect the needs of the
intended audience.

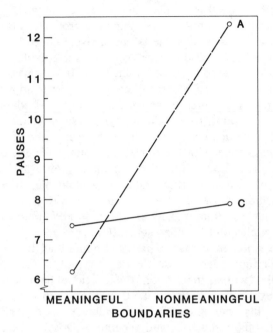

FIG. 3.   The interaction of boundary types × intended audience for mean number
of pauses (A = Adult intended audience, C = Child intended audience).

Directions for Future Research

In investigating the writing process the experiments reported here tackled
only a few of the very many unanswered questions that exist. For instance,
the writing-task analysis of Flower and Hayes (1979) designates several
processes other than idea generation. In the research reported in this chapter, psychological theories were applied to the idea-generation performance
data with reasonable success in helping to better understand the underlying
mechanism. Can we do the same for the processes of organization, translation, and editing? If so, will the same underlying principles hold when
these processes are allowed to interact naturally, compared to the results
of studying these processes in isolation, as in the present work? Idea generation can also be an integral part of the other processes of writing. For
example, arriving at the best organization of a text is tantamount to idea
generation. Are these different instances of idea generation the same process, subject to the same constraints?

Another avenue of further investigation concerns the phenomenon of
idea repetition. A problem-solving point of view would predict that at least

some instances of idea repetition (e.g., at the beginning of clusters of information) are a reflection of planning processes rather than interference in memory-retrieval systems. In describing the production process in terms of plans it is assumed that subjects can actively control the retrieval of information from LTM. While there appears some evidence for retrieval control in the Voss, Vasonder, and Spilich (1980) work when subjects generated fictitious innings to a baseball game, there was no evidence of this kind of control in the present experimental task. Although the current findings lend no support to a planning hypothesis, it seems much too premature to rule out such strategies. The present outcome of idea repetition is somewhat consistent with the more traditional interference explanation from a probabilistic model of memory search and retrieval. However, there do appear to be some important, albeit unexplainable, differences, when comparing memory retrieval during a recall task with that of a production task. As a result, the Raaijmakers and Shiffrin (1980) model is somewhat limited in its applicability to idea generation.

Another question concerns the present finding that the number of ideas generated over time does not decelerate as rapidly as has been observed with the recall of words. In addition, the individual data does not conform to the same exponential function as does the group data. What factors contribute to this phenomenon? This finding was quite resistant to the constraints of topic familiarity and generality. Does strength of interitem association have anything to do with rate of generation? How does it affect organization?

Yet another, related, issue, concerns the criterion for cessation of search that makes a subject "give up." Earlier it was argued that subjects cease generation when they have exhausted the contents of a limited-capacity working memory. Raaijmakers and Shiffrin (1981) prefer to attribute cessation on a component of LTM, but they base their model on data from the recall of words where rate of recall decelerates over time (e.g., Bousfield, Sedgewick, & Cohen, 1954). We know from the present data that this effect does not occur in idea generation in the same manner.

Another aspect of timing concerns pauses. Length of pauses was not assessed in the present research for practical reasons, but it is a potentially interesting measure. Gould and Boies (1978) found that two-thirds of the time taken to write a letter was spent on what they called planning pauses. Generating and reviewing comprised the other one-third. Looking at these pauses in more detail, Matsuhashi and Cooper (1978) found that pause times were shortest for reporting, intermediate for expressing and persuading, and longest for generalizing. In light of this, we can ask, what do the pauses mean during the idea-generation task of the present experiments? It has already been noted that they tend to occur at boundaries of meaningful groups of ideas, but what about the "nonmeaningful" pauses? Also, do the constraints imposed by the experiments here affect the length of these pauses?

The work of Matsuhashi and Cooper strongly implicate the constraint of purpose on pause duration. But, we can ask as well, how will purpose affect the organization and timing characteristics of idea generation? Purpose was a task constraint ignored in the present research but clearly an important factor. If we treat purpose as a dichotomous variable, for example, unusual versus typical purpose, then the constraint of purpose may behave as the task constraints outlined here. On the other hand, purpose may impact other processes of writing more than the process of idea generation. Purpose, in any case, is really a much more complex constraint than those considered in the present work, and would likely require a more elaborate framework than anything provided here, within which to interpret the results. By pursuing these questions and others, we may finally acquire the insight which is currently lacking to generate a useful, comprehensive model of the writing process.

SAMPLE PROTOCOL

Education System (Familiar, General, Adults)

First you would probably describe what good the education does to our society and how our current works, our current system works and how they um people have gone about it or the past education systems um one of the purposes right now that we're using for the education system is mostly an institution for the children so they um they first started our education system probably to get the children um doing something other than working after they passed the child labor laws and it also gives them a social environment in which they can learn to deal with other children their same age and also it gives them the knowledge of the world so that they can deal with it better and they wouldn't be totally ignorant and plus, how, the ways they go about teaching like uh like what they teach at what grades and what the purpose of what it is and what they must know first in order to learn something else and also they would teach them how to benefit society like in colleges and trade schools, they learn uh some things so they can go out and benefit society, provide something that would help other people or something that needs to be done and they would have the knowledge to do it and uh plus they have to look at all the problems that occur like when like children learning something or like children totally hating school and why they hate it and some things they'd have to make it entertaining for them or something, they have to want to learn and plus um ..oh. . . .um, you would have to first um..well, probably you would have to survey the children themselves and ask them what kind, you'd have to take like the idealistic view of children and the realistic view and kind of mold them together to provide a better one. You'd also have to ask the adults, but you wouldn't take the adults all too seriously because they probably wouldn't remember exactly all the they thought and believed when they were in in like the elementary school or going through school um..you'd also have to probably design books that so that children would learn about the same things, so there wouldn't be vastly different knowledge and they'd have to be provided with a wide scope of views of people and . . . I lost my thought I had . . . and they'd also, well, to prepare them for what they might have to deal with and probably you would have to have a lot of like deal with the children's minds, how they think and oh you would have a system where um they wouldn't exactly learn by age, but they would learn by their mental capacity so that others wouldn't be held back and bored with school and the children who were slow wouldn't be totally lost and just give up. Um, that's about it.

Analysis of Idea Units

1. Describe what a good education does
2. (1) to our society
3. (2) & how our current system works
4. (3) & how people have gone about it
5. (4) *or* the past education systems
6. (A) current purpose of education systems
7. (6) an instituition for kids
8. (7) so first started or education system
9. (8) to get the kids doing something
10. (9) other than working
11. (10) after they passed the child labor laws
12. It also gives a social environment
13. (12) they learn to deal with other kids
14. (13) their same age
15. It also gives them world knowledge
16. (15) so they can deal with world better
17. (16) & won't be totally ignorant
18. The ways they teach
19. (18) like what is taught at what grade
20. (19) & what's the purpose
21. (20) what they must know first
22. (21) in order to learn something else
23. Teach them how to benefit society
24. (23) like in college
25. (24) & trade schools
26. (25) they learn some things
27. (26) so they can benefit society
28. (27) & provide something to help others
29. (28) *or* something that needs to be done
30. (29) They would know how

31. Have to look at problems
32. (31) when kids learn &
33. (32) *or* when kids hate school
34. (33) why they hate it
35. How can it become entertaining
36. (35) They have to want to learn
37. Should survey the kids
38. (37) ask them what kind (of schooling)
39. (38) take their idealistic view
40. (39) & the realistic view
41. (40) mold the two together
42. (41) to provide a better one
43. Ask the adults too
44. (43) *but* don't take seriously
45. (44) because probably won't remember
46. (45) what they thought & believed
47. (46) in elementary school
48. Design books
49. (48) So kids would learn about same things
50. (48) so there wouldn't be vastly different knowledge
51. Should be provided with wide scope of views
52. (51) of people
53. (52) to prepare them
54. (53) for what they might have to deal with
55. Must consider kids minds
56. (55) & how they think
57. (56) have a system where they don't learn by age
58. (57) *but* they learn by mental capacity
59. (58) so others won't be held back
60. (59) & bored with school
61. (60) & slow kids wouldn't be lost
62. (61) then just give up.

Hierarchical Analysis

Levels: 1 2 3 4 5 6
Cluster:		Number of Chunks
1	1–2 3 4 5	1
2	6–7–8–9–10–11	5

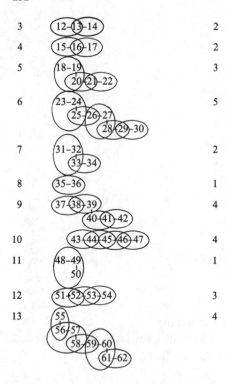

3	2
4	2
5	3
6	5
7	2
8	1
9	4
10	4
11	1
12	3
13	4

REFERENCES

Anderson, J.R. (1976). *Language, memory, and thought.* Hillsdale, NJ: Erlbaum.

Anderson, J.R., & Bower, G.H. (1973). *Human associative memory.* Washington, DC: Hemisphere Press.

Atkinson, R.C., & Shiffrin, R. (1968). Human memory: A proposed system and its control process. In K.W. Spence and J.T. Spence (Eds.), *The psychology of learning and motivation: Advances in research and theory* (Vol. 2). New York: Academic Press.

Atlas, M.A. (1979). Addressing an audience: A study of expert-novice differences in writing (Tech. Rep. No. 3, Document Design Project). Pittsburgh, PA: Carnegie-Mellon University.

Black, J. (1980). Psycholinguistic processes in writing. In S. Rosenberg (Ed.), *Handbook of applied psycholinguistics.* Hillsdale, NJ: Erlbaum.

Bousfield, W.A., & Sedgwick, C.H.W. (1944). An analysis of sequences of restricted associative responses. *Journal of General Psychology, 30,* 149–165.

Bousfield, W.A., Sedgwick, C.H.W., & Cohen, B.H. (1954). Certain temporal characteristics of the recall of verbal associates. *American Journal of Psychology, 67,* 111–118.

Collins, A.M., & Quillian, M.R. (1969). Retrievel from semantic memory. *Journal of Verbal Learning and Verbal Behavior, 8,* 240–247.

Flower, L.S., & Hayes, J.R. (1979). *A process model of composition* (Tech. Rep. No. 1, Document Design Project). Pittsburgh, PA: Carnegie-Mellon Institute.

Flower, L.S., & Hayes, J.R. (1981). A cognitive process theory of writing. *College Composition and Communication, 32,* 365.

Gould, J.D., & Boies, S.J. (1978). How authors think about their writing, dictating, and speaking. *Human Factors, 20,* 495–505 (a).

Humes, A. (1983). Research on the composing process. *Review of Educational Research, 53* (2), 201.

Kintsch, W. (1974). *The representation of meaning in memory.* Hillsdale, NJ: Erlbaum.

Kintsch, W. (1980). *Psychological processes in discourse production.* Paper for the Kassel Workshop "Psycholinguistic Models of Production."

Kintsch, W., & van Dijk, T.A. (1978). Toward a model of text comprehension and production. *Psychological Review, 85,* 363–394.

Meehan, J.R. (1976). *The metanovel: Writing stories by computer* (Research Rep. No. 74). New Haven, CT: Computer Science Department, Yale University.

Miller, G.A. (1956). The magical number seven, plus or minus two: Some limits on our capacity for processing information. *Psychological Review, 63,* 81–97.

Nisbett, R.E., & Wilson, T.D. (1977). Telling more than we can know: Verbal reports on mental processes. *Psychological Review, 84,* 231–259.

Raaijmakers, J.G.W. (1979). *Retrieval from long term store: a general theory and mathematical models.* Druk: Stichting Studentenpets Nijmegen.

Raaijmakers, J.G.W., & Shiffrin, R.M. (1980). Retrieval from long term store. Unpublished manuscript.

Raaijmakers, J.G.W., & Shiffrin, R.M. (1981). Search for associative memory. *Psychological Review, 88* (2), 93.

Shiffrin, R.M. (1970) Memory search. In D.A. Norman (Ed.), *Models of human memory.* New York: Academic Press.

Shiffrin, R.M. (1976). Capacity limitations in information processing, attention and memory. In W.K. Estes (Ed.), *Handbook of learning and cognitive processes, Vol. 4: Memory processes.* Hillsdale, NJ: Erlbaum.

Voss, J.F., Vesonder, G., & Spilich, G. (1980). Text generation and recall by high and low knowledge individuals. *Journal of Verbal Learning and Verbal Behavior, 19,* 651–667.

CHAPTER 10

Discourse Analysis of Children's Text Production

Carl H. Frederiksen
Janet Donin-Frederiksen
Robert J. Bracewell
McGill University

There are two separable ways to approach the study of writing: One can study the written product and one can study the writing activity. Recently, both approaches have made contributions to our knowledge of what skill in writing is and how it develops. Study of the written product has revealed textual and language structures in student writing (e.g., Loban, 1976), as well as more general characteristics such as communicative effectiveness and other traits suggested by rhetorical theories (e.g., Lloyd-Jones, 1977). Study of the writing activity has revealed aspects of writers' composing processes, particularly those which reflect their planning (e.g., Flower & Hayes, 1981).

Nonetheless, these separate efforts to build a descriptive theory of writing have left gaps in both theory and methodology. Consider two examples from research on planning. First, such research investigates composing processes (e.g., "what you want to say," "putting ideas into words") but fails to specify in any detail the cognitive and linguistic structures involved and the relationship of these structures to the processes. Consequently,we cannot link the written product with the processes that underlie its production. Second, research on planning employs methods that reveal reflective processes in writing. But the processes that generate text are not only reflective, they are also routine, allowing various constraints to be coordinated smoothly in writing. We require methods that will allow us to examine how writing processes operate in an unconscious, automatic, or routine manner, as well as how plans modify such routine processing.

One area of research on discourse communication that has been concerned with both of the above issues is that of discourse comprehension. The well-documented phenomenon that the understanding of discourse involves more than mere memory for a text's language structures has focused attention on relationships between a text's structure and the conceptual structures and inferential processes that epitomize competent readers' understanding (e.g., Carpenter & Just, 1977). Although comprehension processes generally operate in a routine manner, they can also operate in a conscious, reflective manner when problems of understanding a text are encountered (e.g., Brown, 1980). In investigating these issues, methods of discourse analysis have been developed that are closely related both to linguistic analyses of text structure and to cognitive theories of knowledge representation and conceptual structure developed within psychology and computer science (e.g., Frederiksen, 1985; Woods, 1980). These methods allow one to study the cognitive processes that underlie comprehension of text structure through analysis of readers' semantic structures and inferences. Consequently in this area there is a close relationship between conceptual and linguistic structures and the cognitive processes that operate on them.

Our research on text production attempts to address the gaps in writing research outlined above by employing methods of discourse analysis and theory derived from research on text comprehension (e.g., Frederiksen, 1985; Kintsch & van Dijk, 1978). Our principal objective is to build a model of text production that (a) explicitly links cognitive processes in composing to the conceptual and text structures that are produced or manipulated and (b) can account for routine production processes as well as for how writers' conscious strategies and plans modify these routine processes. In accomplishing this, we also seek to understand the relationships between the cognitive processes involved in producing text and those involved in comprehending text. Because basically the same conceptual and linguistic structures are involved in both, there ought to be strong similarities between the cognitive processes of a writer and those of a reader, and these should be reflected in the development of text production and comprehension skill.

In the present chapter we explore the applicability of cognitive discourse analysis procedures to the description of cognitive processes and structures in young children's text production. First, we review and compare cognitive processes and structures currently thought to be involved in text production and comprehension. Second, we discuss the applicability of cognitive discourse analysis methods to the comparative study of production and comprehension processes. Third, we present detailed analyses of texts produced by two (contrastive) subjects to illustrate the kinds of hypotheses about discourse processing that can be generated using cognitive discourse analysis methods. Finally, we summarize the account of discourse production our research suggests and discuss its relationship to descriptions of writing within rhetorical theory.

THEORETICAL APPROACH TO TEXT PRODUCTION
AND COMPREHENSION

Although their details may vary, theories of text comprehension agree on certain broad aspects of discourse structure and processing. With respect to discourse structure, all major theories regard texts in terms of (a) conceptual structures that represent the semantic content structure of a text (Frederiksen, 1975, 1985; Kintsch & van Dijk, 1978; Schank, 1973), and (b) textual structures that consist of a sequence of clause/sentence structures together with the various text-level linguistic devices they employ such as topic-comment structure and cohesion (Grimes, 1975; Halliday & Hasan, 1976). Conceptual structures are semantic cognitive entities that reflect types of semantic information represented in human memory. Consequently, they are not necessarily associated with particular language representations of those structures. In contrast, textual structures are governed by the syntax, lexicon, and textual devices of a particular language. Comprehension is viewed as a process by which a reader or listener constructs conceptual-meaning structure for a text. The information available to the comprehender consists of a textual structure and the reader's or listener's given or prior conceptual knowledge. (The latter may include knowledge derived from the extra-linguistic context of a textual message as well as the reader's/listener's general store of a world knowledge.)

To understand just how the comprehension process works, psychologists have constructed (a) models of conceptual and textual structures and (b) models of the cognitive processes by which one level or kind of structure is derived from another. Figure 1 represents schematically the major components of conceptual and textual structure and how they are related to one another. Two levels of conceptual structure (frames and propositions) and two levels of textual structure (clauses and texts) have been identified. In comprehending a text, a reader is seen as generating high-level conceptual structures, called frames, for a given text (Frederiksen, 1981). A text consists of a sequence of clauses, each of which encodes one or more propositions. Propositions represent the semantic content of clauses (i.e., the "sentence meanings"). They also represent chunks of semantic information from frame structures (Frederiksen, 1985). Thus, propositions are a kind of intermediary semantic structure that is used to chunk and specify frame information so that it may be encoded in language. To understand a text, a reader or listener must be able to:

1. generate propositions, "the local meaning structure," using syntactic and lexical information contained in sentence structures and sentence contexts; and
2. infer the conceptual frame structure(s) that are represented by these propositions, i.e., the "global meaning structure."

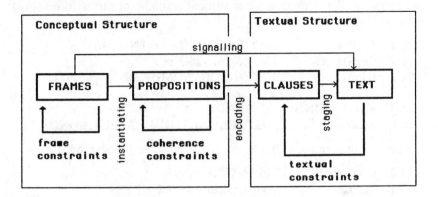

FIG. 1. Text structure viewed in processing terms (reproduced from Frederiksen, 1985)

The processes by which a comprehender can do this are controlled by the particular text-level linguistic devices the author has employed to establish an order of introduction of information, a topical focus, referential cohesion, and so forth.

To illustrate these ideas, consider the following sentence produced by one of our subjects:

> *He thought that he would be given something good if he saved them so he jumped into the water.*

We will analyze this sentence in terms of both its textual structure and its conceptual structure. As a textual structure, the above sentence consists of (using Winograd's (1972) system of clausal analysis) the following two clausal segments: a declarative major clause (DEC) containing an embedded secondary report clause (REPNG) and a bound adjunct (BAJT).

> (26) *He thought (DEC) [that he would be given something good (REPNG) [if he saved them (BAJT)]]*

and a secondary bound adjunct:

> (27) *so he jumped into the water* (BAJT)

(The numbers refer to clausal segments within this subject's text.) Textual devices in these segments include cohesive devices such as all pronouns (he, them) plus topicalization patterns within the sentence (e.g., compare (26) and *if he saved them, he would be given something good*). As a conceptual structure, encoded in (26) are the following five propositions (the propositional structure used in Frederiksen's (1975) model as recently simplified and formalized in terms of a propositional grammar of propositions (Frederiksen, 1985)):

26.0	THINK	PAT:HE,THM:26.1 = TNS:PAST;
26.1	COND.*IF*	[26.4], [26.2,26.3];
26.2	GIVE	REC:HE,OBJ:SOMETHING = ASPCT: COND;
26.3	SOMETHING	ATT:GOOD;
26.4	SAVE	AGT:HE,OBJ:THEM = ASPCT:COND;

Encoded in segment (27) are the following three propositions:

27.0	CAU:*SO*	[26.0],]27.1];
27.1	JUMP	AGT:HE,RSLT:27.2 = TNS:PAST;
27.2	HE	LOC.*INTO*WATER;

Here, propositions are numbered and consist of a predicate (which may be an action [e.g.,think], an object [e.g.,something]), or a relation which connects propositions (e.g., COND, the conditional relation); and a series of labelled arguments such as case relations (e.g., PAT, the patient of an action; AGT, the agent of an action; THM: the theme of a cognitive action; RSLT, the result of an action, etc.), identifying relations (e.g., LOC, the location of an object or action), tense (TNS), aspect (ASPCT), and modality (MOD). A propositional grammar specifies the possible propositional structures (Frederiksen, 1985). Propositions are generated for clauses such that each element of propositional structure is syntactically or lexically encoded in the clause.

As a first step in understanding this sentence, a reader or listener must be able to generate these propositions, that is, represent the semantic content for the relevant clause structures. At a higher conceptual level, these propositions represent chunks of higher level frame structures. For example, propositions (26.1) to (26.4) represent two procedures ("saving them" and "being given something good") and a conditional dependency between them ("he would be given something good if he saved them"). These segments are part of a text which elaborates the procedures for saving them and consequences of particular procedures. Such a conceptual structure is a type of frame, in this case a procedural frame.

Segment (27) refers to another type of frame. Here a second event is specified ("jumping into the water") that is a result of the event of proposition (26.0) ("thinking"). The conceptual frame involved here is a narrative frame in which events are related to one another causally and temporally. To understand (26) and (27), therefore, requires a reader or listener to construct both a narrative frame (involving a casual relation between the two events) and a procedural frame (involving dependent procedures). The propositions listed above represent one "instantiation" (or semantic realization) of these frames. Propositions provide a semantic linkage between high-level conceptual frames and language. In Figure 1, these relationships are labelled "instantiating" and "encoding." Understanding a text, then, involves "decoding" the propositional content that is encoded in clauses and inferring frame structure.

What, then, is the role of text devices such as topicalization and cohesion in comprehension? Topicalization controls the sequence and introduction of topics as old or new information, and cohesion entails memory search and inference procedures that connect text propositions. Thus, these devices function to regulate readers' or listeners' inferences as they construct a conceptual frame for a text. In the example, the highest level of topicalization (Clements, 1979; Grimes, 1975) reflects the narrative structure of the text. The two events in the narrative frame are also connected cohesively in the text by means of pronominal reference. At a lower level in the topicalization hierarchy is the procedural frame (lower because it is conveyed by means of an embedded secondary clause). For example, the child could have said:

If he saved them, he would be given something good. Thinking this made him jump into the water.

Here the procedures are the main topic of the discourse, and the narrative frame is subordinated. This example illustrates how textual devices reflect frame structure. They may be said (following Grimes' (1975) "staging" metaphor) to provide a "point of view" or perspective on the conceptual structures represented by a text, just as the directing and lighting in play manipulate the audience's perception of the events transpiring on the stage. Textual devices constitute a kind of signalling system for frames, just as clauses constitute encoding devices for propositions. Both this signalling system and a set of encoded propositions are available to a reader or listener as a basis for constructing a conceptual frame or frames for a text.

Although many of the details of these processes and structures are still unknown, all of these different aspects of textual and conceptual structure have been found to influence comprehension (Clements, 1979; Clark, 1977; Frederiksen, 1975; Kintsch & van Dijk, 1978; Marshall & Glock, 1978; Meyer, 1975). Interest is currently centering on such questions as: the nature of conceptual frames (or schemata) (Frederiksen, 1985; Kintsch & van Dijk, 1978; Rumelhart, 1975; Schank, 1973; van Dijk, 1977); how frame-based processes operate (Frederiksen, 1985; Mandler & Johnson, 1977; Stein & Glenn, 1978; Thorndyke, 1977; van Dijk, 1977); the nature and role of inferences at all levels of text processing (Bruce, 1980; Carpenter & Just, 1977; Clark, 1977; Frederiksen, 1981; Trabasso & Nicholas, 1978); how various types of textual constraints influence text processing (Bracewell, Frederiksen, & Frederiksen, 1982); and the use of prior knowledge in comprehension (Rumelhart & Ortony, 1977). Research on these questions involves analysis of texts at all of these levels, as well as analyses of subjects' text recalls in relation to text structure. Discourse and recall analysis (particularly of inferences), when used in conjunction with experimental variation of text structure and studies of individual and developmental differences in comprehension, enable inferences about specific comprehension processes.

Given this account of the principal component structures and processes in text comprehension, it is natural to ask how these processes might operate "in reverse" in discourse production. In outlining an account of discourse processing in writing and oral production consistent with this model of comprehension, it will be useful to distinguish between component processes and constraints on these processes. The major component processes in text production are:

1. constructing frames: generating one or more conceptual frames as an intended message or meaning structure to be communicated to a reader or listener;
2. instantiating frames as propositions: generating propositions that represent instances of frame information declaratively in terms of semantic structures expressible in language;
3. encoding propositions as clauses; and
4. staging the message: producing sequences of clauses that incorporate text-level linguistic devices of reference, conjunction, lexical cohesion, and topic-comment structure.

In terms of the example, the child telling this story produced text segments (26) and (27) as a part of a narrative frame in which procedures were embedded. The two events and their causal relation had to be represented in terms of propositions (one instance of a set of possibilities), the propositions had to be encoded as clauses, and the particular clause sequence and cohesive devices chosen to reflect the primary narrative frame structure. Thus, the general comprehension model leads to a natural account of the major component processes in text production in which processes are linked directly to products (aspects of discourse structure). Conversely discourse analysis of child-produced texts ought to reflect the processes that underlie their production. We are led, therefore to consider a text as a reflection of the specific processes that generated it.

Because these processes occur on-line during text production, at any point in the composing–translating process, the writer's or speaker's cognitive processes are subject to multiple influences. That is, the current product must have characteristics that satisfy multiple constraints (Frederiksen and Dominic, 1981). Figure 1 identifies the major types of constraints we are studying (each of which has its counterpart in influencing the process of text comprehension). The easiest way to think about these constraints is to consider how they influence the major component processes in text production.

Frame construction is subject to both constraints from the frame structure itself (e.g., a narrative frame requires the generation of connected events) and constraints from the text that has already been produced (e.g., prior frame information that has been encoded and signalled to the reader by text-level devices). Text constraints on frame production influence the order in which frame information is introduced in text.

The production of propositions is governed by two constraints. First, the propositions must instantiate chunks of frame information. And second, they are subject to local coherence constraints; that is, they must satisfy conditions of "relevance" requiring that propositions be topically and inferentially related to those that procede them in the text. This two-fold constraint on production constitutes a kind of "double bind" on the writer that may explain much of the subjective difficulty in writing. In writing, one must maintain the flow of an argument (through topically and inferentially related propositions) while at the same time communicating a discourse frame (often made explicit by a writer as an outline or other writing plan).

The encoding of propositions as clauses is also subject to two constraints. First, currently produced clauses must encode propositions, and second, choice among particular clause structures must reflect text-level structural choices (such as topicalization, referential ties, and conjunction).

Finally, staging processes that underlie the production of text-level linguistic structures are constrained by both the set of possible clausal structures for current propositions and the frame structure that is being signalled by means of textual devices.

To summarize, interactions among component processes in writing or oral language production (and the structures they output) reflect these different constraints or influences one level or kind of structure has on another. Thus, we characterize discourse production, like discourse comprehension, as an interactive constructive process. This theoretical approach motivates our discourse analyses of children's productions. An account of the details of these processes and their interactions is the major goal of our discourse-analysis procedures. These procedures and how they enable the study of component processes and their interactions are the subject of the next section.

METHODS FOR ANALYZING COGNITIVE STRUCTURES
AND PROCESSES IN DISCOURSE PRODUCTION

In order to view adequately the relationship between comprehension and production we found it necessary to analyze the different tasks that constitute discourse comprehension and production situations. An outline of the results of this analysis is found in Table 1. The analysis is described in greater detail in Bracewell et al. (1982). The different categories, features within the categories, and values that the features can take define the domain of discourse-processing tasks. This environment serves both conceptual purposes in thinking about language tasks and research purposes in designing studies to investigate discourse performance. The extent to which a task is regarded as a production or comprehension task depends on the specific constraints that are operating and affecting the comprehension and production processes of the language user. For research purposes, the task environment can be considered to provide an implicit design structure within which it is possible to explore systematically various kinds of relationships among composing and comprehension tasks.

The data presented here were collected as part of a larger design that examined children's text comprehension and production processes. On the production tasks, the study investigated children's ability to construct conceptual story frames for sequences of pictured events and to express these frames in language. Specifically, we were interested in comparing for grade-2 and -4 children the use of narrative and conversational frames in stories and in examining the way in which children used language to communicate these frames. The materials used for story production were picture sequences taken from *Les aventures de Globi* (1943), a series of language-free comic strips produced in Switzerland. The sequences were 18 to 20 pictures in length. Each child produced two stories. The children were directed first to look through the picture sequence and then to return to the beginning and, while viewing the pictures, to tell a story to accompany them. For one of the production tasks the child was directed to use a narrative frame ("tell a story to go with the pictures"). For the other production task the child was directed to use a conversational frame ("tell a story where the people talk like in a play or television program"). Each child viewed the same picture sequence for the two tasks. The order of the frame directions was counterbalanced across children. Further details on the experimental design may be found in Bracewell et al. (1982).

In the results that follow, we present detailed analyses of the texts produced by two children. These children were selected to be contrastive in age and the characteristics of the stories they produced. The children were in grades 2 and 4. The texts selected for analysis were produced under the dialogue-production conditions for the "Rescue" sequence of pictures.

Table 1.   Discourse Task Analysis Plan

I. Input Information

A. Modality: 1. text (written, oral)
              2. nontext (e.g., picture sequences, experienced events, scenes, etc.)
              3. mixed
B. Grain: 1. detailed closely spaced small units (e.g., specific events)
              2. coarse widely-spaced large units (e.g., superordinate events, "key" events in a sequence)
C. Relationship to frame(s):
              1. relatively direct representation of frame structure vs.
              2. highly specific "instantiation" of frame elements
D. Frame type: narrative, conversational, procedural, problem, etc.

II. Output Information

A. Modality. 1. text (written, oral discourse)
              2. nontext (e.g., execution of procedures)
B. Constraints on output provided by:
              1. input information
              2. additional output information:
                  a)   nontext information (e.g., pictures)
                  b)   new text information (questions, probes)
C. Frame type: narrative, conversational, procedural, problem, etc.

III. Communicative Task Conditions

A. Setting (e.g., participants, audience, physical setting)
B. Situation and functions
C. Characteristics and significance of output "code" (quality or type of output)
D. Relation of output to input (e.g., recall, summary, free production)

IV. Subject-Based Constraints on Discourse Processing

A. Prior knowledge
B. Familiarity with genre (type of text structure and functions)
C. General discourse processing skills (e.g., of lexical, syntactic, and textual structures)
D. Control processes (plans, communicative strategies, etc.)
E. Subject-generated output constraints

Discourse analyses of these texts reflect the aspects of text structure previously indicated in Figure 1: (a) segmentation of the story into clausal units, (b) analysis of propositional content, (c) analysis of frame structures, and (d) analysis of textual devices (cohesion and topic-comment structure).

Conclusions about framing and other component processes in story production can be made on the basis of differences observed across tasks and individuals in these different aspects of children's text productions. Thus, one child might produce texts that have highly elaborated frame structures, whereas another child might not. These children might differ with respect to frame structures produced, while at the same time producing similar clause and propositional structures. Individual differences, then, can establish the relative independence of different component processes and the structures they produce; and developmental patterns in different aspects of discourse structure provide evidence about the development of component processes in discourse production.

Process interactions can be studied by analyzing correspondences between different aspects of text structure in children's story productions. For example, textual devices of reference, conjunction, and topicalization might be studied in relation to conceptual frame structure. Such analyses reveal how textual features are constrained by frame structure. If a close correspondence is found in a child's text between textual features and frame structure, then we would conclude that the child has used frame constraints in producing textual devices that signal frame structure. This analysis consists of superimposing topicalization and cohesive tie structure on frame structure. If we also find children in our sample whose story productions do not show such correspondences, we would conclude that these children have not developed a facility in using frames to constrain the production of text-level linguistic devices—a process interaction. Thus, correspondences between different aspects of text structure constitute an independent feature of the data that reflects process interaction. The kind of evidence described would imply that writers/speakers must develop not only competency with respect to different component processes in text production, but also process interactions that enable them to integrate different aspects of textual and conceptual structure to communicate conceptual frames to an audience.

Finally, a child's text production can be viewed as an on-line process; that is, in terms of a sequence of "decisions" made as the child composed the text. Consequently, in on-line analysis of children's texts, the particular sequence of propositions in a child's text is examined to see how individual propositions jointly reflect frame and local coherence constraints. Individual propositions are analyzed in terms of inferential relations to prior propositions, and to frame structure, following the methods developed for the analysis of children's conversations by Frederiksen (1981). (In this earlier study, children's utterances in a task-oriented dialogue were found to be connected inferentially to the prior utterances of a teacher, to his own prior utterances, and to the frame structure of the task [a teacher-directed activity].) Inference analysis of children's texts reveals the child's ability to use local coherence and frame constraints in the production of propositions. Here, constrastive analyses are again informative. One child might produce propositions that strongly reflect (i.e., are inferentially related to) frame structure, whereas another might produce locally and sequentially connected (i.e., inferentially related) propositions that fail to reflect elaborated conceptual frames. A child with mature discourse-production skills would demonstrate both qualities, local coherence and frame constraints, in his or her inferences.

The discourse analyses which follow explore each of these kinds of questions: (a) component processes, (b) process interaction, and (c) on-line inferential processes in text production. The analyses employ a contrastive method. By examining closely how one writer or speaker differs from another, we hope to generate hypotheses about discourse processes and their interactions. We believe that the contrastive method of discourse analysis can, by establishing evidence for relative independence of discourse properties, be a productive tool for generating hypotheses about cognitive processes in written or oral discourse production. These hypotheses can then be tested in subsequent developmental and experimental studies.

DISCOURSE ANALYSIS OF CHILDREN'S STORY PRODUCTIONS

The texts to be analyzed in the present paper were obtained under the task condition in which children were asked to produce a dialogue for the "Rescue" picture sequence. The first text was produced by a grade-2 child:

F121PDRET

E: Let's go.
S: One day Anne and Paul decided to go butterfly catching.
E: And are the people saying anything to each other?
S: No
E: O.K.
S: Then they spotted a beautiful butterfly. Paul said Let's get it. # They weren't looking where [they,] they were going. They were just looking up in the air and the butterfly started flying over some water. # Anne and Paul fell in. Gus was still up on the land. # Gus looked down to see if he could see anything. He could just see the ripples in the water from Anne and Paul falling in. # He jumped in the water # and swam over to Albert's house. # He swam and swam # until he came to [Al-,] Albert's house. He came running in [in the,] barking wildly at Albert. # Albert jumped in his boat and started rowing towards the spot where Anne and Paul fell in. # Then Gus told Albert to stop. # [Albert, I mean] Gus jumped in and Albert rolled up his sleeves # and Albert reached in # picked up Anne and Paul by their clothes # bring them back to his house # bring them into his house # and give them something hot to drink. # Then they talked ((after)). #

The *E* indicates the experimenter's speech, *S* indicates the subject's speech, the # indicates that the child shifted to the next picture in the sequence, square brackets [] enclose false starts, and double parentheses (()) enclose information that was unclear and therefore uncertain in the transcript. The second text to be analyzed was produced by a grade-4 child under the same task conditions:

F144PDRET

S: OK. One day Anne and Paul [were, were going to catch some butterflies. Gus came along.
E: And what would the characters be saying to each other?
S: Um. ( ) Paul was saying [that they would ca-,] was saying [we'll,] we'll go and catch lots of butterflies today. Anne said I had a good idea and brought a bottle to put them in
E: Good. #
S: Then they went into some flowers and Paul said look Anne there's a butterfly. Anne said wow he's beautiful let's try and catch him.
E: Great. #
S: They were running and running. Even Gus tried to [catch,] catch the butterfly but he was too small. [Paul,] Paul said I wish I was [Armstro-,] um Stretch Armstrong 'cause I can't reach him.() # Then there was a little clift *sic* and the butterfly went [over,] over it. Gus started to bark. [Anne,] Anne told Gus to stop because he was scaring the butterfly away. Then # Anne and Paul both fell into the water. Over the clift *sic*. # Gus looked into the water he couldn't see them. He started to bark. # He thought that he would be given something good [so,] if he saved them so he jumped into the water. # When he was underwater he searched and searched but he couldn't find them. # So he came back up to the top of the water and saw Albert's house. So he [swam,] swam to shore. # Then when he got to Albert's house [he w-,] he was barking and making signs so Albert would know what to do. Then Albert said oh now I think I know what you mean. [Susan, uh I meant,] um Anne and Paul fell in the water and you can't find them eh? # So Albert got into his boat and started to paddle. Gus was in the front of the boat and looking around. # Then Gus started to bark and pointed to the water. Peter's hat, Paul's hat [was,] was floating on top of the water. # Albert told Gus to jump in the water and see if he could find them. Albert pulled up his sleeves # and searched in the water also. # Then he found them. Paul and Anne were coughing [and they,] but they were still happy that they got out of the water. # When they got to shore Albert put them in a sack and said that they'd be all right now. # When they got to the house Anne and Paul um were happy and they were nearly dry. Everyone was singing. # Then

[when,] when they were inside the house [Al-,] Albert asked them if they wanted some hot chocolate. They both said yes please! # Then Albert took out his pipe and started to smoke. They were all happy and Gus was happy too he's sleeping. #

Analysis of Clause Structure

Segmentation of these texts into clausal units revealed that subject 121 produced 27 segments, only 1 of which was direct dialogue. Subject 144 produced 68 segments, 12 of which were direct dialogue, and 3 indirect dialogue (see Appendices 1 and 2 for samples of the clausal analyses). Although the older child produced more than twice as many segments as the younger, there were no marked differences in the types of clause structures produced. This result implies that such syntactic analysis is not a sensitive measure of surface-structure differences in the texts produced by these children. (See Cohesion and Topic-Comment Structure, below.)

Propositional Analysis

Propositional analyses of these two subjects' texts are found in Appendices 3 and 4. The grade-2 subject produced 76 propositions and the grade-4 subject, 168 propositions. One index of the complexity of the proposition encoding process is *propositional density,* the average number of propositions per segment. For the present two subjects, these two measures were: subject 121:2.78 propositions per segment; subject 144:2.35 propositions per segment. By this measure, the grade-2 child, although producing fewer clauses and propositions, is encoding slightly more propositions per clausal segment than the grade-4 child. When types of propositions are examined, the picture is one of no great differences in the internal structure of the propositions these children produced. The distribution of major types of propositions (Frederiksen, 1975, 1977): events, states, algebraic relations, dependency relations, and identities, for both subjects is given in Table 2. (For a detailed discussion of these types of propositions see Frederiksen (1975, 1977, 1985).

The major difference in percent of segments of each type is in dependency relations (e.g., conditional and causal relations): subject 144 produced 5% dependency relations, whereas 122 produced only 1.3%. Another index of the internal structure of propositions is the number of propositions embedded in case slots within events. As may be seen in Table 2, subject 144 produced approximately the same percentage of embedded propositions (31.9% vs. 28.9% for 121). However, when these are counted separately for theme relations versus other case relations, subject 144 shows 20.6% embedded in theme slots, while 122 shows only 7.9%. This difference reflects the greater amount of dialogue produced by 144, because the

Table 2.   Distribution of Types of Propositions

Proposition Type	Subject 121		Subject 144	
	Number	%	Number	%
Propositions				
Events	46	60.5	95	59.4
States	21	27.6	38	23.8
Algebraic relations	8	10.5	18	11.3
Dependency relations	1	1.3	8	5.0
Identity relations	0	0.0	1	0.6
Total propositions	76		160	
Embedded propositions				
Theme	6	7.9	33	20.6
Other case relations	16	21.1	18	11.3
Total embedded propositions	22	28.9	51	31.9

theme relation is a component of cognitive events involving such verbs as *say, request,* or *know.*

In summary, other than a difference in propositional density, frequency of dependency relations, and frequency of propositions embedded in theme slots, these subjects are producing approximately the same types of clausal and propositional structures. Complexity of encoding (i.e., propositional density) is slightly greater for the grade-2 subject. The only pervasive difference between these two subjects is the amount of production. Therefore, any major differences that might explain this differential amount of production will have to be at the level of conceptual frames and related text-level linguistic devices. Guttman and Frederiksen (1985) found similar results in a study of the story and play discourse of preschool children.

Frame Analysis
Frame analysis involves the specification of a particular type of conceptual structure such as a narrative or procedure for a text. The analysis proceeds by first selecting the type of frame structure to be investigated for the text as, say, a narrative. The particular frame type is represented within Frederiksen's (1985) theory by a grammar which specifies: (1) the elements that are the "nodes" or building blocks of the frame, and (2) the various ways in which elements can combine to make a frame structure. For example, for a narrative frame, the frame elements are events, and the grammar allows events to be connected by relations of temporal order, causality, conditionality, similarity, or identity in location, or equivalence in time. The higher order structures thus generated include episodes (i.e., temporally ordered event sequences), causally or conditionally dependent events, scenes (events occurring at the same location), and coordinate events (occurring at the same time). A narrative frame consists of a set of connected

episodes, scenes, and coordinate events. To analyze a text, each event in the propositional structure is identified. Once an event is identified, it is linked to other events. The links may be explicit in the text, or marked linguistically but left to be inferred by the listener or reader.

The narrative frame analysis of subject 121 is presented in Figure 2. Each frame element (an event) is denoted by an E followed by a number. Propositions corresponding to events are marked in Appendix 3. Events in the frame are connected by arrows: A single arrow denotes a temporal order relation, a double arrow, equivalence in time. Locative relations are labelled LOC, short for "proximity in location"; causal or conditional relations are labelled CAU or COND, respectively. Subject 121 generated a narrative frame that consists of three episodes: Episode 1 contains 4 events (propositions 1.0–4.0), episode 2 contains 4 events, and episode 3, 17 events. Thus, this subject generated two short episodes, and one longer episode constituted the bulk of the frame. These episodes were connected by means of coordinated events, and there were locative relations between events (one within an episode and one between episodes).

The narrative frame for subject 144's story production appears in Figure 3 and propositions instantiating events are marked in Appendix 4. This frame consists of 10 episodes, varying in length from 2 to 8 events. The narrative frame constructed by this subject consisted of a large number of short episodes. Unlike the previous analyses, here the differences between the two subjects are striking: There are major differences in the extent and complexity of the narrative frame structures generated by the two subjects. The grade-2 child has successfully constructed an extensive, connected event chain to correspond to the pictures, whereas that constructed by the grade-4 child consists of a large number of short episodes. Furthermore, the grade-4 child's frame includes casual and conditional relations in addition to temporal order and equivalence. This indicates that the frame is based in part on more complex principles than that of the grade-2 child.

The second frame analysis explored this possibility that the story produced by subject 144 was based on more complex principles than that of subject 121. The aspect of story structure we explored is what would conventionally be described as plot structure. Here we used a second frame grammar developed by Frederiksen (in press) on the basis of the interactive plans analysis of Bruce (1980). The basic element of a problem frame is a procedure. A procedure is an action which, if executed, accomplishes a goal. A problem frame consists of one or more procedures which accomplishes one or more goals. The problem structure of a story corresponds to procedures which solve problems to achieve goals. The complexity of problem frames for stories comes from the fact that procedures are associated with the plans of particular characters in the story, and these plans can change and interact.

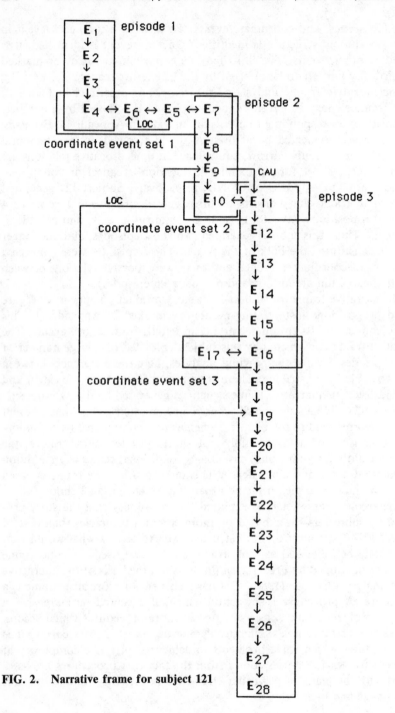

FIG. 2.   Narrative frame for subject 121

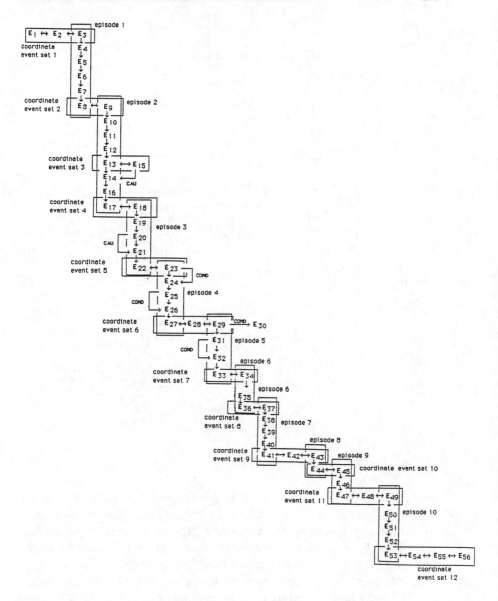

FIG. 3. Narrative frame for subject 144

Any procedure in a problem frame can be instantiated in more than one way: (1), it can be referred to as a plan (P); (2), it can be presented as an action that executes the plan (A); (3), it can be instantiated as a resolution (R) of the problem associated with the procedure (i.e., attainment of the

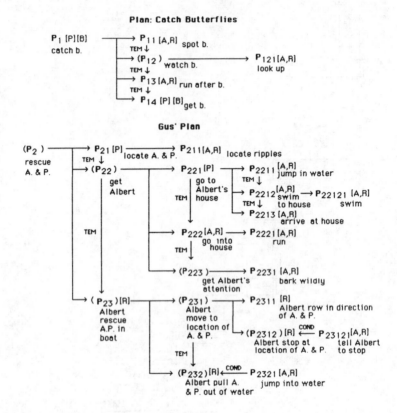

FIG. 4.   Problem frame for subject 121

goal of the procedure); (4), it can be represented by an event or state that blocks the resolution of the procedure (B); and (5), it can be instantiated by a neutral response to the procedure (RS) or a transition to another procedure (T). Procedures can be connected in problem frames by several relations: (1) subordination (one procedure is a component of another), (2) temporal order (the procedures occur in a given temporal order), and (3) conditionality (one procedure is conditional on another). These three types of relations form the basis for constructing procedural hierarchies and sequences. A problem frame is a set of such procedures, often that correspond to the plans of specific characters. As plans change during a story, new procedural hierarchies get added to the frame for the story.

To explore problem frames for our subjects, problem-frame analyses were made based on the frame grammar just described for the stories pro-

Albert's Plans

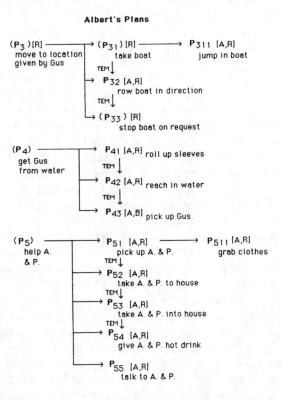

(continued)

duced by subjects 121 and 144. The frame analysis proceeded just as for the narrative-frame analysis: Procedures were identified (as instantiated in one of the ways specified above) and connected to other procedures by the relations allowed by the grammar. The resulting problem frame for subject 121 is presented in Figure 4. Notice that each procedure is represented by a short verbal label and accompanied by the proposition numbers of any propositions that instantiate it. A letter code indicates how the procedure was instantiated. If no proposition numbers occur, the procedure is inferred and was not explicitly referred to in the subject's text. Such procedures are included only to illustrate what procedures would be necessary to have a connected problem frame. In the problem frame for subject 121, the procedure "catching butterflies" was not really present as a connected frame structure. The procedure referred to as "Gus plan" (for rescuing Albert) consisted almost entirely of actions. There were two references to plans. Many elements of the plan were not explicit in the text (this frame reflects that which a reader could infer from the text). Plan components are generally referred to at a low level in the procedural hierarchy; that is, there are no references to high-level goals and procedures; and these by means of acts. Similarly, Albert's plans also are referred to as only low-level actions. Thus, there is little explicit information in this child's text to indicate the use of a problem frame during story production.

This absence of problem-frame structure may be contrasted with the problem frame for subject 144 which is presented in Figure 5. This elaborated problem frame consists of five procedures: (1) a procedure for catching butterflies, (2) Gus' plan for preventing Anne and Paul from falling, (3) Gus' plan for saving Anne and Paul, (4) Albert's plan for rescuing Anne and Paul, and (5) Albert's plan for making Anne and Paul happy. These procedures have a number of characteristics. First, there is reference to plan procedures at all levels of the hierarchies for each procedure. Second, there is use of the full range of types of instantiations of procedures— as plans, actions, resolutions, blocks, and responses. Third, the plans are very extensive and differentiated. Studying these results for this subject leaves little doubt that there was extensive construction of a problem frame in this subject's story production.

Thus, there is evidence for very substantial quantitative and qualitative differences between the two subjects in problem-frame use. The increased complexity in the narrative frame of subject 144 was presumably a reflection of the problem frame which underlies the long event chain. A purely linear structure may not have sufficiently differentiated components to be sustained without other principles of structuring. The frame analysis reveals that the conceptual structure constructed by subject 144 had two, not one, principles of structure. This subject thus had to coordinate the two, an advanced frame-based process. The existence of an elaborated problem structure also offers an explanation of the extensiveness of the production of this subject in comparison to subject 121. Furthermore, these frame-level differences were independent of clausal or intrapropositional structure, the two subjects were virtually identical in terms of the types of clauses and propositions they produced.

Cohesion and Topic-comment Structure
As discussed earlier, the surface structure of a text consists of a sequence of clauses. This sequence traces a single path through the conceptual frames of the text. Because the frames can be of different kinds and are nonlinear in character, one of the writer's major problems is that of using a linear surface structure to present the sometimes sequential but often contiguous and hierarchial structure of the frame relations. To present nonlinear frame structures in text, writers can make use of both lexical and syntactic options when producing text. Lexical options in text and the effects of choosing to repeat words, to use pronominal forms, to use conjunctions, and so forth, have been considered under the topic of cohesion (Halliday & Hasan,

Plan: Catch Butterflies

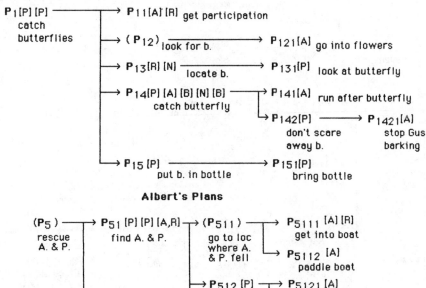

P_1 [P] [P]
catch
butterflies

→ P_{11} [A] [R] get participation

→ (P_{12}) look for b. → P_{121} [A] go into flowers

→ P_{13} [R] [N] locate b. → P_{131} [P] look at butterfly

→ P_{14} [P] [A] [B] [N] [B]
catch butterfly
→ P_{141} [A] run after butterfly
→ P_{142} [P] → P_{1421} [A]
don't scare   stop Gus
away b.   barking

→ P_{15} [P] → P_{151} [P]
put b. in bottle   bring bottle

Albert's Plans

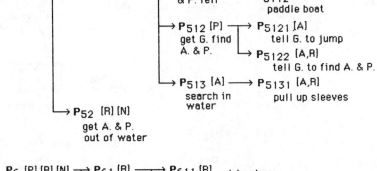

(P_5)
rescue
A. & P.

→ P_{51} [P] [P] [A,R]
find A. & P.

→ (P_{511})
go to loc
where A.
& P. fell
→ P_{5111} [A] [R]
get into boat
→ P_{5112} [A]
paddle boat

→ P_{512} [P]
get G. find
A. & P.
→ P_{5121} [A]
tell G. to jump
→ P_{5122} [A,R]
tell G. to find A. & P.

→ P_{513} [A]
search in
water
→ P_{5131} [A,R]
pull up sleeves

→ P_{52} [R] [N]
get A. & P.
out of water

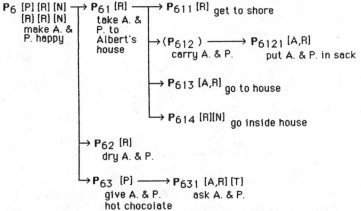

P_6 [P] [R] [N]
[R] [R] [N]
make A. &
P. happy

→ P_{61} [R]
take A. &
P. to
Albert's
house
→ P_{611} [R] get to shore

→ (P_{612})
carry A. & P.
→ P_{6121} [A,R]
put A. & P. in sack

→ P_{613} [A,R] go to house

→ P_{614} [R][N] go inside house

→ P_{62} [R]
dry A. & P.

→ P_{63} [P]
give A. & P.
hot chocolate
→ P_{631} [A,R] [T]
ask A. & P.

FIG. 5. Problem frame for subject 144

Gus' Plans

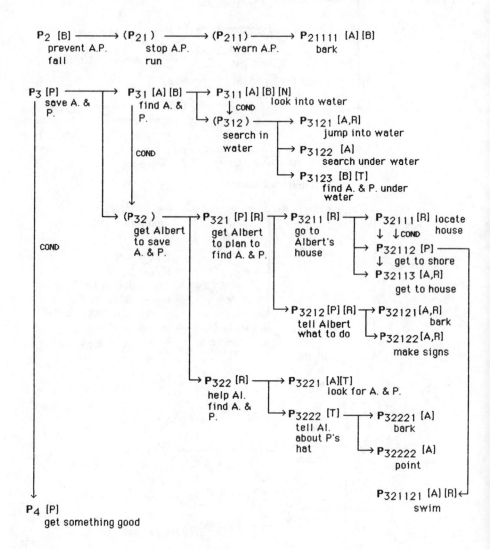

FIG. 5. *(continued)*

1976). Syntactic options in text and the effects of sequencing conceptual elements have been considered under the topic of topic-comment structure or staging (Grimes, 1975).

Cohesive devices in a text can be used to represent, explicitly, relations among conceptual elements (i.e., propositions and frame structures). Halliday and Hasan (1976) state that in a text there are "particular features which have in common the property of signalling that the interpretation of the passage depends on something else. If that 'something else' is verbally explicit, then there is cohesion" (p. 13). A procedure for coding cohesive features has been derived by Dillinger, Bracewell, and Fine (1983) from the analysis of Halliday and Hasan (1976). This procedure codes six major types of cohesive devices found in texts: reference, substitution, ellipsis, conjunction, lexicalization, and cataphora. Within these major types, subcategories of cohesive types are coded; for example, the reference category differentiates demonstrative, pronominal, and comparative types of cohesion. In addition, certain textually explicit types of collocation and types of exophora are coded.

Both protocols showed similar patterns of cohesive-tie use. However, two differences were found that were related to the differences in elaboration of the problem frame for the story and in coordination of the problem frame with the narrative frame. First, the average length of a cohesive tie was 3.4 for protocol 144 compared with 2.1 for protocol 121. (Tie length is indexed by the number of segment boundaries between a cohesive element and its referent. Thus, a pronoun that refers back to a noun in the previous segment is a cohesive tie with a length of 1). This greater length in the 144 protocol was produced primarily by long lexical ties consisting of character names or location nouns and provided a linkage in the text surface structure between different episodes in the narrative frame and between the problem and the narrative frame. Second, the proportion of complex conjunctions such as conditionals, contrastives, and temporals was greater for protocol 144 (0.35 per clausal segment vs. 0.15 per clausal segment). This difference is directly related to the elaboration of the problem frame in this protocol, in which the conjunctions present explicitly the relations among the levels of the problem frame.

The similarities and the differences in the use of cohesive devices in the two protocols, and the relationship of this use to the frame structure of the protocols can be illustrated by mapping chains of cohesive devices onto a diagram of a frame structure. Such a mapping is shown in Figures 6, 7, 8, and 9 for parts of the frame structures presented earlier in Figures 2 through 5.

Figures 6 and 7 present sections of the narrative frame for protocols 121 and 144, respectively. Events containing cohesive elements are designated by circles around the event label; the arrows point to the referent for the element (for all these elements the referent is an antecedent); the type of element is indicated by a label on the arrow (e.g., Rp denotes pronominal reference). For both subjects' narrative frames, the pattern of cohesive ties is similar. Ties are predominantly of lexical and pronominal

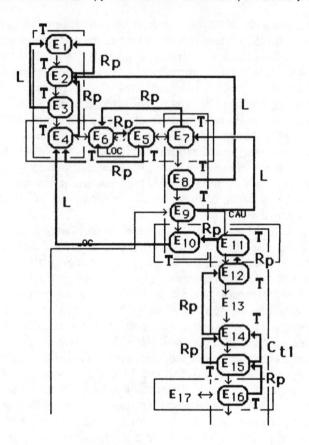

FIG. 6. Cohesive tie and topic-comment structure related to section of Narrative Frame for subject 121

reference; chains of pronominal reference tend to correspond to episode and scene structures of the narrative frame, particularly where a character is topicalized as the agent of a sequence of actions. The similarity is readily apparent for the episode in which the character Gus attempts to rescue Anne and Paul from the water, fails to find them, and then swims to Albert's house for help (events 11 to 16 in Figure 6 and events 17 to 28 in Figure 7). The principal difference in cohesive patterning also can be seen in this particular episode. In Figure 7, at event 22, the cohesive chain of propositional reference jumps from the narrative frame to problem frame and then returns to the narrative frame at event 23. Thus, the surface structure of the text, via the presence of cohesive ties, serves to integrate different conceptual structures, namely, the narrative and problem frames of the story.

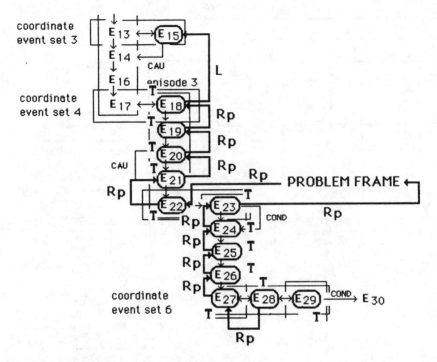

FIG. 7. Cohesive tie and topic-comment structure related to section of Narrative frame for subject 144

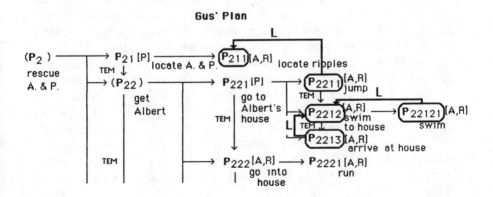

FIG. 8. Cohesive tie and topic-comment structure related to section of Problem Frame for subject 121

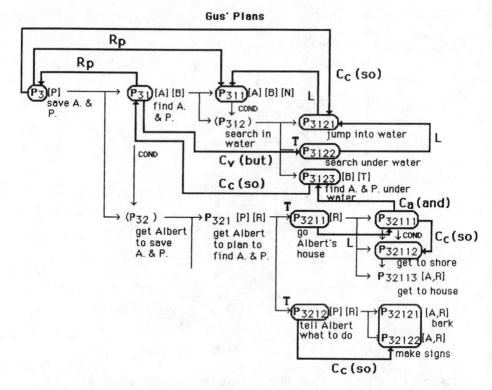

FIG. 9. Cohesive tie and topic-comment structure related to section of Problem Frame for subject 144

Figures 8 and 9 present sections of the problem frame for protocols 121 and 144, respectively. The pattern of cohesive ties for Gus's initial attempt to rescue Anne and Paul has been mapped for each subject's problem frame. As discussed above, the problem frame for protocol 121 is not elaborated, and this lack of elaboration is reflected in the cohesive ties, which are lexical and fragmented. In contrast, the pattern of cohesive ties for the elaborated problem frame of protocol 144 is complex and integrated. Ties are a number of different types and serve to link together and to make explicit the relationships between procedures and, hence, between different levels of the problem frame. In particular, extensive use has been made of causative conjunctions (denoted by the label Cc in Figure 9) which make explicit a number of the procedure–subprocedure relations in the frame.

The cohesive devices discussed above are a means of signalling nonlinear frame relations between conceptual elements in the text surface structure. As discussed earlier, another means of signalling frame structure is via topicalization structure in the clause sequence. Within-text, within-paragraph, and within-clause decisions must be made on what information to present first and what to present subsequently. Such choices establish a topical hierarchy for a text that present a "point of view," or saliency pattern for the text propositions. In Grimes' (1975) metaphor, such decisions about information sequence establish a 'staging' for the information. In our discourse-analysis procedures we are using Clements' (1979) adaptation of Grimes' (1975) staging analysis to code topic-comment structures. Clements' adaptation allows one to code both the topic-comment structure of a text, and, through the coding of whether information is new to the text or has been previously introduced, to establish topicalization levels for the text.

In applying the staging analysis to the protocols, we have found the coding of topic-comment structure and its relationship to frame type to be the most informative. The information that is presented as a topical constituent in the text surface structure is denoted by a 'T' in Figures 6 to 9. Comparison of the topicalization patterns for the narrative frames in Figures 6 and 7 reveals similar patterns; for both protocols the agents of actions are topicalized. In contrast, topicalization patterns of the problem frames in Figures 8 and 9 differ markedly. No information in the rather rudimentary problem frame for protocol 121 is topicalized, whereas information in the problem frame for protocol 144 is topicalized.

In summary, patterns of both cohesive ties and topic-comment structure differ between protocols 121 and 144. In both protocols cohesive patterning corresponds to frame use, and the topicalization pattern serves to make the frames salient. It is only in protocol 144 that the problem frame is made explicit through the use in particular of cohesive conjunctions and is made salient through topicalization of information instantiated in the frame. Thus, the contribution of each frame type is more balanced for the latter protocol, and some coordination of the frame types is achieved through the use of cohesive ties.

Analysis of On-line Inferences

The sequence of propositions in a text serves to invite inferences that can be made between propositions. Such inferences create coherence in the text. Depending on the distance over which the inference is made, it may establish either local coherence among adjacent or near propositions or more global coherence across distant propositions that reflects the frame structure of a text. An analysis of such inferences reveals the "decisions" made by the writer in sequencing propositional information so as to relate current propositions to previous propositions in a coherent manner.

Inferential relations in the initial propositional sequence for subjects 121 and 144 are presented in Figures 10 and 11, respectively. In these figures

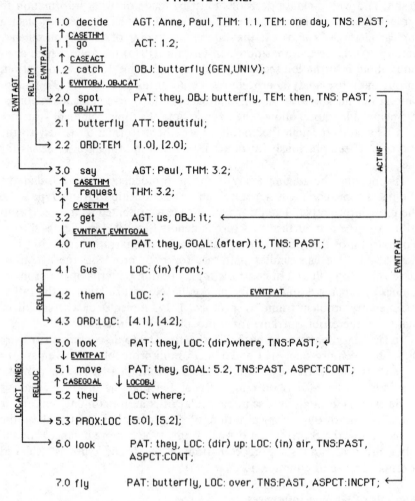

FIG. 10.   Inferential relations in initial proposition sequence for subject 121

inferential relations between propositions are indicated by arrows. Labels on the arrows denote the type of inference that is invited (Frederiksen, 1981).

Examination of Figure 10 reveals that most inferential relations for protocol 121 are local in nature, linking adjacent or nearby propositions. In contrast, Figure 11 reveals both local inferential relations and relations that span a greater propositional distance. These longer relations link both events and procedures and thus serve to establish coherence in the narrative

File: F144PDREP

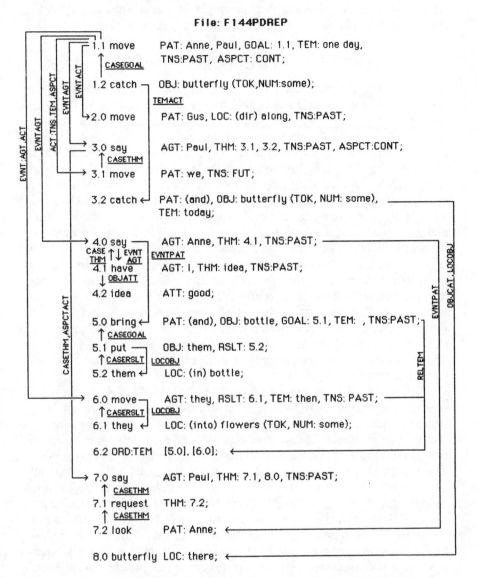

FIG. 11.   Inferential relations in initial proposition sequence for subject 144

and problem frames (e.g., the EVNT(AGT,ACT) inference between propositions 1.0 and 6.0, and the CASETHM inference between propositions 3.2 and 7.0, respectively). Consequently, for protocol 144 as compared with protocol 121, one can see that the constraints determining which proposition to include next in text production are more than local, reflecting both immediate propositional and more global frame constraints. In this sense, protocol 144 shows more coherence than protocol 121.

DISCUSSION

The theoretical perspective we have adopted in our analysis of discourse production is a procedural one in which we emphasize the cognitive processes writers or speakers use in building textual and conceptual structures. This viewpoint coincides with current "interactive constructivist" theories of text comprehension that emphasize structure-building processes in text understanding. Text structure in such a theory is a reflection of a series of component structure-building operations that function interactively as they satisfy multiple constraints on their products (Frederiksen & Dominic, 1981). Earlier, we identified major component processes in text production and constraints on these processes (Figure 1). Each component process, as it operates in real time, results in a product that is reflected in some aspect of text structure. Discourse analysis reveals specific processes by making their respective products opaque. Thus, frame analysis is a method for investigating frame-construction processes, propositional analysis is a technique for making proposition-generating procedures explicit, and so forth. Furthermore, the manner in which these processes operate interactively as their products constrain one another may be uncovered by analysis of relations among discourse structures at different levels of textual and conceptual structure.

The results we have presented illustrate how discourse structures revealed by discourse analysis reflect structure-building processes in story composition. In our model (Figure 1), text production is "frame-driven," that is, propositional, clause, and text structures reflect frame structure through instantiating, encoding, staging and frame-signalling relationships. The results of our discourse analyses are consistent with this viewpoint. The two subjects were very similar in the types of clauses and propositions they produced. What differences were found appeared to reflect differences in frame and text-level linguistic structure. Thus, propositions and clause structures appear to have an intermediary role in discourse production, connecting frames (high-level conceptual structures) to texts (high-level linguistic structures). Differences in amount of production (at propositional and clausal levels) are hard to explain without reference to higher levels of conceptual or linguistic structure.

In contrast, analysis of frame structures produced by these two subjects revealed striking differences in the narrative and problem frames they were able to construct in response to the same series of pictures. Differences in the extent of their narrative structures appeared to reflect differences in their problem frames. There appears to be some limit on the extent to which purely narrative structures can be produced in the absence of underlying problem-oriented plans that provide further principles for structuring the narrative.

Text cohesion and topic-comment structures also differentiated these subjects. Although both types of text-level linguistic structure are realized in clause structure, clause-structure differences cannot account for the observed differences which were more extensive. However, when cohesive-tie structures and topics were mapped onto frame structures, differences in these text-level devices became explicable. Both reflect a process of linearizing nonlinear frame structure and signalling frame information as salient (or nonsalient).

Finally, although frame constraints appeared to be of central importance in the structure-building processes of these subjects, local coherence constraints reflected in inferential relations among propositions also differentiated the two subjects. The older child produced propositions having more "distal" inferential relations that reflect frame relations as well as local text coherence. It appears as if the older child was able to make local coherence, as well as cohesion and topic-comment structure, reflect frame structure, and thus serve to signal frame-related inferences to the listener.

The procedural or process-oriented view we adopt as cognitive psychologists is compatible with the point of view within rhetoric expressed so well by Lloyd-Jones (1981) who described the rhetorical perspective on writing as concerned with a writer's choice among discourse alternatives. He expands this seemingly simple statement by reviewing some of the discourse alternatives to be considered by a writer, some of the bases, principles, or policies governing choice, and the role of audience and voice in these decisions. From such a rhetorical point of view, our efforts may be regarded as attempts to specify some of the processes writers use to make choices at a rather basic or elementary level. In this sense, we are attempting to provide a "basic theory" of text production that will have to be extended to account for how these basic structure-building processes operate to achieve different communicative purposes in varied situations, social settings, and for different real or imagined audiences. To achieve such an "extended theory" of discourse production, we will have to understand how writers plan in complex, realistic writing environments and how these plans modify or interact with basic structure-building processes in text production.

In view of this complementarity between rhetorical and psychological perspectives on writing, research on the cognitive processes of writers seems most likely to contribute by making more explicit the processes that underlie different aspects of rhetorical choice and their relationships to discourse structure. As our account of these processes and structures becomes more precise, so too should our ability to assess and teach them.

Appendix 1.   Section of Segmented Text for Subject F121PDRE
Segment

(E: Let's go.)

(1) One day Anne and Paul decided to go butterfly catching.
CLAUSES: DEC(TONG(IAJT))   PROPOSITIONS: 1.0,1.1,1.2
(E: And are the people saying anything to each other? S: No E: O.K.)

(2) Then they spotted a beautiful butterfly.
CLAUSES: DEC   PROPOSITIONS: 2.0,2.1,2.2
(3) Paul said Let's get it.
CLAUSES: DEC(REPNG = IMP)   PROPOSITIONS: 3.0,3.1,3.2
(4) They ran after it with Gus in front of them.
CLAUSES : DEC   PROPOSITIONS: 4.0–4.3
(5) They weren't looking where [they-,] they were going.
CLAUSES : DEC(WHNG)   PROPOSITIONS: 5.0–5.2
(6) They were just looking up in the air
CLAUSES : DEC   PROPOSITIONS: 6.0
(7) and the butterfly started flying over some water.
CLAUSES : DEC(INGNG)   PROPOSITIONS: 7.0–7.2
(8) Anne and Paul fell in.
CLAUSES : DEC   PROPOSITIONS: 8.0–8.1
(9) Gus was still up on the land.
CLAUSES : DEC   PROPOSITIONS: 9.0
(10) Gus looked down to see if he could see anything.
CLAUSES : DEC(TAJT(WHNG))   PROPOSITIONS: 10.0–10.2
(11) He could just see the ripples in the water from Anne and Paul falling in.
CLAUSES : DEC(INGNG)   PROPOSITIONS: 11.0–11.4
(12) He jumped in the water
CLAUSES : DEC   PROPOSITIONS: 12.0–12.1

Appendix 2.   Section of Segmented Text for Subject F144PDRE
Segment

(S: [OK.])
(1) One day Anne and Paul [were-,] were going to catch some butterflies.
CLAUSES: DEC(TAJT)   PROPOSITIONS: 1.0–1.1
(2) Gus came along.
CLAUSES: DEC   PROPOSITIONS: 2.0
(E: And what would the characters be saying to each other? S: [Um.])

(3) Paul [was saying that they would ca-,] was saying [we'll-,] we'll go and catch lots of butterflies today.
CLAUSES: DEC(REPNG = DEC-SF) PROPOSITIONS: 3.0–3.2
(4) Anne said I had a good idea
CLAUSES: DEC(REPNG = DEC)   PROPOSITIONS: 4.0–4.2
(5) and brought a bottle to put them in.
CLAUSES: SF = DEC(TORSQ)   PROPOSITIONS: 5.0–5.2
(E: Good.)

(6) Then they went into some flowers

	CLAUSES: DEC	PROPOSITIONS: 6.0–6.2
(7)	and Paul said look Anne	
	CLAUSES: DEC(REPNG = IMP)	PROPOSITIONS: 7.0–7.2
(8)	there's a butterfly.	
	CLAUSES: DEC	PROPOSITIONS: 8.0
(9)	Anne said wow he's beautiful	
	CLAUSES: DEC(REPNG = DEC)	PROPOSITIONS: 9.0–9.1
(10)	let's try	
	CLAUSES: IMP	PROPOSITIONS: 10.0–10.1
(11)	and catch him.	
	CLAUSES: SF = IMP	PROPOSITIONS: 11.0

Appendix 3. Section of Propositional Analysis for Text Produced by Subject F121PDRE

		Events	Procedures
1.0 DECIDE	AGT:ANNE,PAUL,THM:1.1 = TEM:ONE DAY,TNS:PAST;	E1	P1
1.1 GO	ACT:1.2;		
1.2 CATCH	OBJ:BUTTERFLY(GEN,UNIV);		
2.0 SPOT	PAT:THEY,OBJ: BUTTERFLY = TEM:THEN,TNS:PAST;	E2	P11
2.1 BUTTERFLY	ATT:BEAUTIFUL;		
2.2 ORD:TEM	[1.0],[2.2];		
3.0 SAY	AGT:PAUL,THM:3.1 = TNS:PAST;	E3	
3.1 REQUEST	THM:3.2;		
3.2 GET	AGT:US,OBJ:IT;		P14
4.0 RUN	PAT:THEY,GOAL:(AFTER)IT = TNS:PAST;	E4	P13
4.1 GUS	LOC:(IN)FRONT;		
4.2 THEM	LOC:;		
4.3 ORD:LOC	[4.2],[4.2];		
5.0 LOOK	PAT:THEY = LOC:(DIR)WHERE, TNS:PAST,ASPCT:CONT,NEG;	E5,E6	
5.1 MOVE(GO)	PAT:THEY,GOAL:5.2 = TNS:PAST,ASPCT: CONT;		
5.2 THEY	LOC:WHERE;		
5.3 PROX:LOC	[5.0],[5.2];		
6.0 LOOK	PAT:THEY = LOC:(DIR)UP:LOC:(IN)AIR, TNS:PAST,ASPCT:CONT;	E7	P121
7.0 FLY	PAT:BUTTERFLY = LOC:OVER,TNS:PAST, ASPCT:INCPT(START);	E8	P1,P14
7.1 WATER (TOK:SOME)	LOC:;		
7.2 ORD:LOC	[7.0],[7.1];		
8.0 FALL	AGT:ANNE,PAUL,RSLT:8.1 = TNS:PAST;	E9	
8.1 ANNE,PAUL	LOC:IN;		
9.0 GUS	LOC:UP:LOC:(ON)LAND,TNS:PAST;		

Appendix 4.   Section of Propositional Analysis for Text Produced by Subject F144PDRE

		Events	Procedures
1.0 MOVE(GO)	PAT:ANNE,PAUL,GOAL:1.1=TEM:ONE DAY,TNS:PAST,ASPCT:CONT;	E1	P1
1.1 CATCH	OBJ:BUTTERFLIES(TOK,NUM:SOME)=;		
2.0 MOVE(COME)	PAT:GUS=LOC:(DIR)ALONG,TNS:PST;	E2	
3.0 SAY	AGT:PAUL,THM:3.1,3.2= TNS:PAST,ASPCT:CONT;	E3	P1,P11
3.1 MOVE(GO)	PAT:WE=TNS:FUT;		
3.2 CATCH	PAT:(AND),OBJ:BUTTERFLIES(TOK,NUM: LOTS)=TEM:TODAY;		
4.0 SAY	AGT:ANNE,THM:4.1=TNS:PAST;	E4	P11
4.1 HAVE	AGT:I,THM:IDEA=TNS:PAST;		
4.2 IDEA	ATT:GOOD;		
5.0 BRING	PAT:(AND),OBJ:BOTTLE,GOALS: 5.1=TEM:,TNS:PAST;	E5	P151
5.1 PUT	OBJ:THEM,RSLT:5.2=;		P15
5.2 THEM	LOC:(IN)BOTTLE;		
6.0 MOVE(GO)	AGT:THEY,RSLT:6.1=TEM:THEN, TNS:PAST;	E6	P121
6.1 THEY	LOC:(INTO)FLOWERS(TOK,NUM:SOME);		
6.2 ORD:TEM	[5.0],[6.0];		
7.0 SAY	AGT:PAUL,THM:7.1,8.0=TNS:PAST;	E7	P131
7.1 REQUEST	THM:7.2;		
7.2 LOOK	PAT:ANNE;		
8.0 BUTTERFLY	LOC:THERE;		P13
9.0 SAY	AGT:ANNE,THM:9.1=TNS:PAST;	E8	P13
9.1 HE	ATT:BEAUTIFUL;		
10.0 REQUEST	THM:10.1,11.0=;		P14
10.1 TRY	PAT:US=;		
11.0 CATCH	PAT:(AND),OBJ:HIM=;		

REFERENCES

Les aventures de Globi. (1943). Zurich: Globi Publishing Co.

Bracewell, R.J., Frederiksen, C.H., & Frederiksen, J.D. (1982). Cognitive processes in composing and comprehending discourse. *Educational Psychologist, 17,* 146–164.

Brown, A.L. (1980). Metacognitive development and reading. In R.J. Spiro, B.C. Bruce, & W.F. Brewer (Eds.), *Theoretical issues in reading comprehension.* Hillsdale, NJ: Erlbaum.

Bruce, B. (1980). Plans and social actions. In R.J. Spiro, B.C. Bruce, & W.F. Brewer (Eds.), *Theoretical issues in reading comprehension.* Hillsdale, NJ: Erlbaum.

Carpenter, P.A., & Just, M.A. (1977). Reading comprehension as eyes see it. In M.A. Just & P.A. Carpenter (Eds.), *Cognitive processes in comprehension.* Hillsdale, NJ: Erlbaum.

Clark, H.H. (1977). Inferences in comprehension. In D.LaBerge & S.J. Samuels (Eds.), *Basic processes in reading: Perception and comprehension.* Hillsdale, NJ: Erlbaum.

Clements,P. (1979). The effects of staging on recall from prose. In R. Freedle (Ed.), *Advances in discourse* (Vol. 2). Norwood, NJ: Ablex.

Dillinger, M., Bracewell, R.J., & Fine, J. (1983). *Cohesion as a guide to discourse processes: Codebook*. Montreal: McGill University, Laboratory of Applied Cognitive Science.

Flower, L.S., & Hayes, J.R. (1981). Plans that guide the composing process. In C.H. Frederiksen & J.F. Dominic (Eds.), *Writing: Process, development, and communication*. Hillsdale, NJ: Erlbaum.

Frederiksen, C.H. (1975). Representing logical and semantic structure of knowledge acquired from discourse. *Cognitive Psychology, 7,* 371–485.

Frederiksen, C.H. (1977). Structure and process in discourse production and comprehension. In M. Just & P. Carpenter (Eds.), *Cognitive Processes in Comprehension* (pp. 313–322). Hillsdale, NJ: Erlbaum.

Frederiksen, C.H. (1981). Inferences in preschool children's conversations: A cognitive perspective. In J. Green & C. Wallat (Eds.), *Language and ethnography in educational settings*. Norwood, NJ: Ablex.

Frederiksen, C.H. (1985). Cognitive models and discourse analysis. In C.R. Cooper & S. Greenbaum (Eds.), *Written communication annual. Vol. 1: Studying writing: Linguistic approaches*. Beverly Hills, CA: Sage.

Frederiksen, C.H. (in press). *Knowledge and inference in discourse communication*. Norwood, NJ: Ablex.

Frederiksen, C.H. & Dominic, J.F. (1981). Perspectives on the activity of writing. In C.H. Frederiksen & J.F. Dominic (Eds.), *Writing: Process, development, and communication*. Hillsdale, NJ: Erlbaum.

Grimes, J. (1975). *The thread of discourse*. The Hague: Mouton.

Guttman, M. & Frederiksen, C.H. (1985). Preschool children's narratives: Linking story comprehension, production, and play discourse. In L. Golda & A. Pellegrini (Eds.), *Play, language, and story: The development of children's literate behavior*. Norwood, NJ: Ablex.

Halliday, M.A.K., & Hasan, R. (1976). *Cohesion in English*. London: Longman.

Kintsch, W., & van Dijk, T.A. (1978). Toward a model of text comprehension and production. *Psychological Review, 85,* 363–394.

Lloyd-Jones, R. (1977). Primary trait scoring. In C.R. Cooper & L. Odell (Eds.), *Evaluating writing: Describing, measuring, judging*. Urbana, IL: National Council of Teachers of English.

Lloyd-Jones, R. (1981). Rhetorical choices in writing. In C.H. Frederiksen & J.F. Dominic (Eds.), *Writing: Process, development, and communication*. Hillsdale, NJ: Erlbaum.

Loban, W. (1976). *Language development: Kindergarten through grade twelve* (Research Rep. No. 18). Urbana, IL.: National Council of Teachers of English.

Mandler, J.M., & Johnson, N.S. (1977). Remembrance of things parsed: Story structure and recall. *Cognitive Psychology, 9,* 111–151.

Marshall, N., & Glock, M.D. (1978). Comprehension of connected discourse: A study into the relationships between structure of text and information recalled. *Reading Research Quarterly, 14,* 10–56.

Meyer, B.J.F. (1975). *The organization of prose and its effect on recall*. Amsterdam: North Holland.

Rumelhart, D.E. (1975). Notes on a schema for stories. In D.G. Bobrow & A. Collins (Eds.), *Representation and understanding: Studies in cognitive science*. New York: Academic Press.

Rumelhart, D. & Ortony, A. (1977). The representation of knowledge in memory. In R.C. Anderson, R. Spiro, & W.E. Montague (Eds.), *Schooling and the acquisition of knowledge*. Hillsdale, NJ: Erlbaum.

Schank, R. (1973). Identification of conceptualizations underlying natural language. In R.Schank & K. Colby (Eds.), *Computer models of thought and language.* San Francisco, CA: Freeman.

Stein, N.L., & Glenn, C.G. (1978). An analysis of story comprehension in elementary school children. In R. Freedle (Ed.), *Advances in discourse* (Vol. 2). Norwood, NJ: Ablex.

Thorndyke, P.W. (1977). Cognitive structures in comprehension and memory of narrative discourse. *Cognitive Psychology, 9,* 77–110.

Trabasso, T., & Nicholas, D.W. (1978). Memory and inferences in comprehending narratives. In J. Becker & F. Wilkins (Eds.), *Information integration by children.* Hillsdale, NJ: Erlbaum.

van Dijk, T.A. (1977). Macro-structures and cognition. In M.A. Just & P.A. Carpenter (Eds.), *Cognitive processes in comprehension.* Hillsdale, NJ: Erlbaum.

Winograd, T. (1972). Understanding natural language. *Cognitive Psychology, 3,* 1–191.

Woods, W.A. (1980). Multiple theory formation in speech and reading. In R.J. Spiro, B.C. Bruce, & W.F. Brewer (Eds.), *Theoretical issues in reading comprehension.* Hillsdale, NJ: Erlbaum.

Author Index

Italics indicate bibliographic citations.

U
Ungeheuer, G., 21, *33*

V
Vachek, J., 8, *33*
van Bruggen, J.A., 114, 127, *132*
van Dijk, T.A., 200, 205, *222*, 225, *253*,
   255, 256, 259, *289, 290*
Venezky, R., 7, *33*
Vesonder, G., 248, *253*
Voss, J.F., 248, *253*
Vygotsky, L., 61, *80*

W
Waldrop, M.M., 125, *132*
Walker, C., 61, *80*
Wallat, C., 136, *159*
Walmsley, S., 6, *31*
Wardhaugh, R., 37, *57*
Wason, P.C., 7, *33*

Widerspiel, M., 7, *31*
Wilbur, R.B., 164, 168, 169, 176, 189, *196*
Williams, F., 116, *132*
Wilson, T., 125, *131, 253*
Winograd, T., 257, *290*
Witte, S., 9, *28,* 60, *80*
Weinheimer, S., 12, *30*
Wiener, M., 8, *31*
Wolfe, T., 83, *107*
Wood, B.S., 116, *132*
Woods, W.A., 255, *290*
Woodward, V.A., 140, *159*

Y
Yawkey, T., 6, *32*

Z
Zambrano, R., 165, *196*
Zamel, V., 34, 35, *57*
Zolkovskij, A., 21, *31*

Subject Index

A

Abstraction, 40, 48, 69
 abstract symbol system, 110
Acoustic language system, 166
Articulation rate, 111–112, 126–127
Attention, xiv, 162, 166, 173, 183, 199, 206
Audience, xv, 229–234, 244–247

C

Case study, 82, 207
Chunk, 229, 234, 236, 256, 258
Cognitive processes, x, xiv, xvi, 25, 61–62,
 110, 118, 179, 183, 198, 202, 205,
 224–226, 254–255, 284
Cognitive science, 224
Cohesion, 259–260, 263, 284
Competence, 172
Composing process, see Writing process
Computers, 81–82
Conceptual structure, 256–259
Conceptual connectivity, 206, 213, 215–218
Conferences, viii, ix, xi, 59–60
 as dialogue, 62
 teacher-student interaction, 59–61
 self-evaluative response, 61
Context, 2, 4, 14, 84
 classroom, 63
 context cues, 227
 context for research, ix
 context-sensitive, 63
 discourse context, 215

D

Deaf writers, ix, xiii, 161–163
 writing sample, 163
Dialect, 7, 134
 non-standard dialect, 162
Dictation, xiii, 139–144
Discourse analysis, ix, 5, 110
 of children's text comprehension, 255
 of children's text production, 255, 262–265
 clause structure, 267
 cohesion and topic-comment structure,
  274–281
 frame analysis, 268–274
 on-line inferences, 281–284
 propositional analysis, 267–268

Discourse analysis (cont.)
 of classroom conversations, 63–64
  Initiation-Response-Evaluation, 68
 of conference conversations, xi, 62–64
  backchannel cues, 69
  topic shift, 72
  turn allocation, 66
  turn order, 66
 of conversational turn-taking, 63–64
 of deaf writers' prose, 164–165
 of verbal protocols, 234–238
  idea units, 234–238

E

Editing, 82–83, 87, 96–100, 103, 110, 230,
 244
 repair, 199
Educational process, viii, 9, 25, 35, 59–60,
 110, 162
 classroom discourse, 78
 classroom interaction, 78
 computer-assisted instruction, 81–82
 development, 61
 for deaf writers, 166–169, 174, 186–192
 language experience, 143
 procedural facilitation, 61
 scaffolding, 61
 substantive facilitation, 61
Emergent literacy, xiii, 135
 emergent reading, 135
 emergent writing, 135
Experimental design, ix, 84, 111
 method, ix, 122
 methodological problems, xii, 114, 117,
  118, 225
Expert/novice writers, viii, 42, 218
 experienced writers, 81, 85, 198
 inexperienced writers, xiv, 166, 173, 174,
  198
 unskilled writers, see inexperienced writers

F

Frame structure, xvi, 256, 259–261,
 263–264, 284

G

Gist, 40, 46, 234